The
Akron Genesis
of
Alcoholics
Anonymous

By the same author

DR. BOB'S LIBRARY
ANNE SMITH'S SPIRITUAL WORKBOOK
THE OXFORD GROUP & ALCOHOLICS ANONYMOUS

The Akron Genesis of Alcoholics Anonymous

An A.A.—*Good Book Connection*

Dick B.

Seattle, Washington

9-7-95

Published by Glen Abbey Books, Inc.

© 1992 by Anonymous

Cover Design: Sean L.

Library of Congress Catalog Card Number: 92-97026

ISBN: 0-934125-31-7

The publication of this volume does not imply affiliation with nor approval or endorsement from Alcoholics Anonymous World Services, Inc.

"For it hath been declared unto me of you, my brethren, by them *which are of the house* of Chloe that there are contentions among you.
Now this I say, that every one of you saith, I am of Paul; and I of Apollos; and I of Cephas; and I of Christ.
Is Christ divided? was Paul crucified for you? or were ye baptized in the name of Paul?"

1 Corinthians 1:11-13

"For while one saith, I am of Paul; and another, I am of Apollos; are ye not carnal? Who then is Paul, and who is Apollos, but ministers by whom ye believed, even as the Lord gave to every man?
I have planted, Apollos watered; but God gave the increase.
So then neither is he that planteth any thing, neither he that watereth; but God that giveth the increase.
Now he that planteth and he that watereth are one; and every man shall receive his own reward according to his own labor.
For we are labourers together with God; ye are God's husbandry, ye are God's building."

1 Corinthians 3:4-9

Contents

Where and When Did Alcoholics Anonymous
Begin? (2);
The Unique Status of Akron (5);
What This Book Will Cover (8);
Why This Particular Book? (10)

Part 1   The Beginnings

Jim Newton Comes to Akron (17);
Newton's Background (19);
Miss Eleanor Napier Forde (22);
Newton's Part in the Larger A.A. Picture (27);
Newton, Dr. Walter Tunks, and the Firestones (29);

Part 4 The Akron Taproot

List of Appendices

Foreword

For anyone seeking to understand in depth the inspiration and insights that brought into being the Alcoholics Anonymous way of living, this book will be a treasure house.

First, it is a masterful job of scholarship, digging out and carefully documenting the facts about A.A.'s spiritual roots and objectively fitting them together. For this achievement alone, the world owes Dick B. an immense debt of gratitude. He has given us "just the facts," but the facts themselves are gripping, especially when presented in the author's lucid and orderly style.

But there is more in this book. The author, like the millions of other people, both alcoholics and non-alcoholics, whose lives have been revived and redirected through their participation in A.A. or related programs, has obviously not ceased to search for greater spiritual understanding. His book, as he says, is not so much concerned with where and when A.A. was founded but how it happened. Dick B. quite clearly was excited and uplifted in his work of discovery. His readers will be too.

My mother, Henrietta Buckler Seiberling, who was at the core of the events described in this book, took me, then a teenager, with her to the Oxford Group meetings in Akron, starting with the first ones in January, 1933. My two sisters and I all shared with her the effort to live in accordance with the spirit of First Century Christianity, as embodied in the Oxford Group discipline. Truly, it did change our lives.

Eventually, of course, A.A. evolved its own steps and traditions, with the remarkable results we know today. We know also that the same spiritual principles that are uplifting for members of A.A. work for many others. By faithfully leading us back to A.A.'s origins, Dick B.'s book will surely bring renewed inspiration to all who read it, as indeed it did for me.

JOHN F. SEIBERLING
Former United States Congressman

Akron, Ohio
November, 1992

Preface

This is the fourth in a series of books the author has undertaken to discern the basic ideas which A.A. obtained from the Bible. As the research has broadened, so has the scope of the intended books.

The first, *Dr. Bob's Library*, was a study of the immense number of spiritual books that A.A.'s Co-Founder, Dr. Bob, read and recommended to those he helped. Foremost among those books was the Bible, from which he said A.A. had obtained its basic ideas.

The second book, *Anne Smith's Spiritual Workbook*, examined the spiritual ideas that Dr. Bob's wife, Anne, had gleaned from the Bible, the Christian literature she read, and the Oxford Group ideas to which she had been exposed while she and Dr. Bob were attending their meetings in A.A.'s formative years. Anne read the contents of her book—contents containing many of the ideas that now can be found in the Big Book—to the alcoholics and their families who came to the Smith home for what Dr. Bob and Anne called "spiritual pablum."

The third book, *The Oxford Group & Alcoholics Anonymous*, examined in depth the origins of the Oxford Group, the ideas it developed, the biblical principles it espoused, and the influence its ideas had on A.A. For it was to the Oxford Group and one of its chief American spokesmen, Reverend Sam Shoemaker, that Bill Wilson attributed most of A.A.'s recovery ideas.

This present book is a study of the birthplace of Alcoholics Anonymous in Akron, Ohio, on June 10, 1935. It looks at the way the Oxford Group came to Akron with a splash in January of 1933, the effect that event had on the founders-to-be of A.A., and the early meetings there. Then it examines the backgrounds and principal contributions of the progenitors of Akron A.A.—T. Henry Williams, Clarace Williams, Henrietta Seiberling, Dr. Bob, Dr. Bob's wife, Anne, and Bill Wilson.

The development of the A.A. program is the next subject—how it began with Dr. Bob and Bill, what occurred at the early meetings at T. Henry's, what AAs did at Dr. Bob's home, at T. Henry's, at hospitals, and in their own homes. It examines what they read—in the Bible and in other literature, how they surrendered, how they prayed, how they meditated, and how they shared their homes. Akron's contributions to the Big Book are reviewed.

The final portion looks at Akron's unique focus on the Bible, the particular parts of the Bible—the Sermon on the Mount, 1 Corinthians 13, and the Book of James—and just what might have come to A.A. from those Bible sources. There is an examination of Akron's special focus on the Four Absolutes of the Oxford Group and what they meant.

Our book closes with a review of the importance today of having an accurate historical account of A.A.'s spiritual roots. The importance is underlined by the concern of some Christians that A.A. had no Christian origins and detracts from the Christian message, the statements of other Christians that A.A. is Christian but needs some Christian dressing in its Steps, the questions of others as to just how Christian it is or was, and the criticisms of those in the "secular" recovery movements who think A.A. is neither Christian, nor sound, nor successful. All these views deserve examination in the light of the rather substantial history in Akron which shows exactly what A.A. was at that time, at least as the Akron AAs, including Bill Wilson from New York, were developing and practicing its principles.

The biblical quotations from 1 Corinthians in the epigraph were favorites of Henrietta Seiberling, one of the major participants in A.A.'s founding days in Akron, Ohio. She referred to these verses by notes in her Bible. She made it clear in those notes that she felt it is not the work of this or that co-founder of Alcoholics Anonymous that should receive the real credit for what A.A. has accomplished. It is God!

Acknowledgements

Our previous books listed our immense gratitude to those who have helped make the research and the writing possible. And the list has grown a great deal.

Special recognition goes to my son, Ken, who again has worked into the wee hours of the night for long periods of time, providing patience, computer wisdom, editorial assistance, rhetorical know-how, and gentle admonitions as to the need for accuracy, detail, and scholarly critique.

Those who made the work possible fall into many categories.

There are the growing number of A.A. historians, who have shared their wisdom, their manuscripts, and their research, in their books and personally: Mel B., Charlie B., Dennis C., Mary Darrah, Earl H., Mitch K., Frank M., Tim M., Merton M., Charlie P., Bill P., and Dr. Ernest Kurtz.

There are the A.A. archivists, Ray G. at Dr. Bob's Home, Gail L. at Akron, Paul L. at Stepping Stones, and Frank M. at A.A. General Services, and the highly knowledgeable Nell Wing (A.A.'s first archivist). The doors have been open, and the rewards have been great. Then there are the archives themselves to which the author owes a debt: A.A. Archives in New York, Ray G.'s archives at Dr. Bob's home, Dennis C.'s in Connecticut, Gail L.'s Founders Day Archives, Stepping Stones Archives, Hartford Seminary Archives, and the archives at New York University. There are also the libraries at Akron University,

Golden Gate Baptist Seminary in Tiburon, Graduate Theological Union in Berkeley, and San Francisco Theological Seminary in San Anselmo.

There are people who were members of or connected with the Oxford Group or Calvary Church, who have been extremely helpful: Morgan Firestone, Julia Harris, Jim Houck, Willard Hunter, Garth Lean, Jim and Eleanor Newton, Dick Ruffin, and George Vondermuhll, Jr. They are my own Oxford Group mentors

No acknowledgement would be meaningful without mentioning the continuing help, encouragement, and support that has been received from the families of A.A.'s founders—Dr. Bob's family (Bob and Betty S. and Sue Smith Windows), Henrietta Seiberling's family (Mary Seiberling Huhn, Dorothy Seiberling, and John F. Seiberling), and T. Henry Williams's daughter, Dorothy Culver.

Much information keeps flowing my way from A.A. Oldtimers whose memories, manuscripts, tapes, and enthusiasm for A.A.'s early achievements seem to know no bounds. Now and then, AAs who read my books or share my passion for A.A. history will send me religious, Oxford Group, Shoemaker, and A.A. books. Then there are the A.A. "newtimers," with whom I associate: my sponsor, Henry B., and the men I sponsor who have been most patient with my frequent and extended travels and absorption with writing and computer. Thanks to Yannick W., who helped me research the Akron news articles; to Sean L., for the cover design; and to Craig G., who helped me check the footnotes. There are my Bible fellowship buddies, Mike and Robin, Craig, and Mark, who share my enthusiasm for a quest into A.A.'s Good Book Connection. Ken's wife, Cindy, has been supportive of her husband's sacrifices for this work; and my son, Don, his wife, and daughters, are still great supporters though they see far less of me due to these projects. Thanks to the staff of the Aston Kamaole Sands for immeasurable help in Maui. And to Dr. Norman Vincent Peale for inspiration and support.

Introduction

There is a quip that has made the rounds of A.A. rooms in recent years. It goes like this: Akron is like Bethlehem. Something good happened there a long time ago; and nothing much has happened there since.

Is Akron, Ohio, just to be noted as the heart of the U.S. rubber tire industry, but merely the insignificant and remote birthplace of the fellowship known as Alcoholics Anonymous? Or, perhaps as with the tire industry, did something of great importance begin, develop, and grow there that produced a product of worldwide and continuing importance? We can't say this book will answer that question, but we hope it will provide the material for further thought.

On June 10, 1992, A.A. was said to be 57 years old. Its General Service Office estimated the total membership at 2,120,130 and stated further that "there is no way to count members who no longer have a home group."[1] Thus, at any given point in time today, there are in excess of two million people moving in and out of the doors of the A.A. Fellowship. This from a humble beginning of about 100 men and women at the time its

---

[1] See *Box 459* (June/July 1992 issue, News and Notes From the General Service Office of A.A.).

official text—the Big Book—was published in 1939.[2] Our book is about A.A.'s birthplace and the part it played in the founding of Alcoholics Anonymous.

Where and When Did Alcoholics Anonymous Begin?

If one asks where and when A.A. began, there is an answer that is generally accepted in the Fellowship of Alcoholics Anonymous today. Alcoholics Anonymous was "founded" at 855 Ardmore Avenue in Akron, Ohio, on June 10, 1935. June 10th was the day A.A.'s Co-founder, Dr. Robert Holbrook Smith, had his last drink and began successfully and in earnest helping other alcoholics to recover, working in tandem with A.A.'s other Co-founder, William Griffith Wilson, whom Dr. Bob had met three weeks before on Mother's Day, May 11, 1935. The founding event took place at the Ardmore Avenue home of Dr. Bob and Anne Smith, with whom Bill Wilson was then staying.

---

[2] See *Alcoholics Anonymous* (New York: Works Publishing Company, 1939). Throughout our book, this volume, and the subsequent editions of it that were published by Alcoholics Anonymous World Services, Inc., will be referred to as the "Big Book"—the affectionate term AAs bestowed on their basic textbook. For the number in the original A.A. fellowship, we adopted the Big Book's mention of "more than" 100 men and women, exemplified by Bill Wilson's original "One Hundred Men" corporation prospectus. Ray G., archivist at Dr. Bob's Home in Akron, wrote the author on July 14, 1992, and stated, "the correct figure is 79." Apparently, A.A.'s first archivist, Nell Wing, stated that the number was "79;" and this may have been the number at some point during the writing of the Big Book. But we have used the 100 figure because of its use by the Big Book, *Alcoholics Anonymous*, 3d ed. (New York: Alcoholics Anonymous World Services, Inc., 1976), at page xiii; by Bill in his 1939 promotional brochure, and by his wife, Lois Wilson, in the March 1, 1939, entry in her book, *Lois Remembers* (New York: Al-Anon Family Group Headquarters, Inc., 1987), at page 198.

A number of A.A.'s "Conference Approved" books specify the Akron date and place as that of the founding.[3] But over time, there have been divergent views on this matter as evidenced by the following statement in *DR. BOB and the Good Oldtimers*:

> Although arguments have been made and will be made for other significant occasions in A.A. history, it is generally agreed that Alcoholics Anonymous began there, in Akron, on that date: June 10, 1935.[4]

The "arguments" in favor of other founding dates and places have come from those who chose to emphasize the date that Bill Wilson's longtime friend and "sponsor," Ebby Thatcher, carried to Bill at his home at 182 Clinton Street in Brooklyn, New York, the message of Ebby's recovery from alcoholism in the Oxford Group. That date was in late November of 1934.[5] Then there was the date at Towns Hospital, 293 Central Park West, in New York City, sometime after December 11, 1934, and before December 18, 1934, when Bill had his religious experience—called by Bill his "hot flash"—after which Bill never drank again.[6] In June of 1985, Lois Wilson wrote to a Brooklyn A.A. newsletter and said,

---

[3] *Alcoholics Anonymous Comes of Age* (New York: Alcoholics Anonymous World Services, Inc., 1957), pp. vii, 71; *DR. BOB And The Good Oldtimers* (New York: Alcoholics Anonymous World Services, Inc., 1980), p. 75; *Pass It On* (New York: Alcoholics Anonymous World Services, Inc., 1984), p. 149; *Alcoholics Anonymous*, 3d ed., p. xv; *The Language of the Heart* (New York: The A.A. Grapevine, Inc., 1988), p. 199.

[4] *DR. BOB*, p. 75.

[5] *The Language of the Heart*, pp. 196-197; *Alcoholics Anonymous Comes of Age*, pp. vii, 58; Big Book, pp. 8-12; Ernest Kurtz, *Not-God: A History of Alcoholics Anonymous*. Expanded ed. (Minnesota: Hazelden, 1991), p. 33. For an indication that Ebby regarded himself, rather than Dr. Bob, as the co-founder of Alcoholics Anonymous, see Nell Wing, *Grateful To Have Been There* (Illinois: Parkside Publishing Corporation, 1992), p. 9.

[6] *Alcoholics Anonymous Comes of Age*, p. vii; *Pass It On*, p. 104; Big Book, pp. 13-14; Kurtz, *Not-God*, pp. 33, 311, n. 39; Mel B., *New Wine: The Spiritual Roots of the Twelve Step Miracle* (Minnesota: Hazelden, 1991), pp. 77-88.

"As far as I am concerned, A.A. began in 1934 in my father's old house on Brooklyn Heights where Bill and I were living. When Bill came home to 182 Clinton St. from Towns' Hospital in New York after his spiritual awakening, he began immediately bringing drunks to the house."[7] Some wistfully point to the day when Akron Oxford Group members got on their knees with Dr. Bob at the T. Henry and Clarace Williams home at 676 Palisades Drive, in Akron, to pray for Dr. Bob's recovery.[8] And that date was shortly before the Mother's Day, 1935, meeting of Dr. Bob and Bill. Then there is the focus on the date when alcoholics began using the name "Alcoholics Anonymous" for their fellowship. This view would hold that A.A. began shortly after Dr. Bob's sponsee, Clarence S., declared at the T. Henry Williams home on May 10, 1939, that meetings would be held in Cleveland for *alcoholics*. Clarence S. said "This would be a meeting of 'Alcoholics Anonymous.'"[9] Both Clarence and an A.A. account said Clarence borrowed the meeting name from the just-published Big

---

[7] See the Brooklyn, New York A.A. newsletter, *the Junction*, for June, 1985, copy of which was provided to the author by A.A. archivist Dennis C., and which is in the author's possession.

[8] Willard Hunter, Oxford Group leader and non-alcoholic friend of A.A., interviewed T. Henry Williams in Akron, Ohio, and later passed on the following details to the author in a personal interview at Claremont, California. In the presence of Willard Hunter, Williams pointed to the spot on the floor of his home where "Bob Smith got on his knees." Henrietta Seiberling, who was conducting an Oxford Group meeting at the Williams' home in early 1935, had suggested that all share something costly in an endeavor to get Dr. Bob to confess his alcoholism. When they had done this, Dr. Bob shared with those present that he was a "secret drinker." Henrietta asked him if he wanted to surrender. And all present, including Dr. Bob, knelt and prayed. T. Henry declared to Willard Hunter: "It all started right there." Compare the account in Mel B., *New Wine*, p. 70 (footnote). And see *Pass It On*, p. 145. James D. Newton, the Oxford Group member of whom we shall write at a later point, was a good friend of T. Henry Williams from the 1930's on; and Newton informed the author in an interview at Fort Myers Beach, Florida, in July, 1992, that T. Henry had made the same statement and pointed to his carpet many years ago, just as he had done in the Willard Hunter interview many years later.

[9] Kurtz, *Not-God*, p. 78.

Book—*Alcoholics Anonymous.*[10] And this did prompt Clarence to call himself the "founder" of Alcoholics Anonymous in its present form.[11] But that is certainly not the view expressed in A.A.'s "Conference Approved" literature. Officially, the genesis of Alcoholics Anonymous was in Akron, Ohio, at Dr. Bob's home at 855 Ardmore Avenue, on June 10, 1935.

The Unique Status of Akron

Our work is not much concerned with where and when A.A. was founded in Akron, but how. For we will be dealing, not with the time and place of A.A.'s founding, but rather with its *foundations* and the unique Akron role.

Certainly one accepted foundation involved the sequence of events that began with Dr. Carl G. Jung in Switzerland in 1931 (when Jung told Rowland Hazard that it might be possible for him to recover from alcoholism by aligning himself with a religious organization and achieving a religious or conversion experience). These events concluded in New York, in November, 1934, when Bill's "sponsor" and friend, Ebby Thatcher, surrendered his life to God at the Calvary Episcopal Church Rescue Mission in New York. Ebby had been rescued from institutionalization for alcoholism through the help of Oxford Group members Rowland Hazard, F. Shepard Cornell, and Cebra Graves. And it was at that time that Ebby carried to Bill the message of Ebby's own recovery, stating to Bill that God had done for him (Ebby) what he

---

[10] *Pass It On*, p. 203. Clarence also is on record, in one of his own talks to members of A.A., as stating that the name "Alcoholics Anonymous," that was used by the Cleveland fellowship, came from the name of the Big Book.

[11] Mitch K., one of Clarence's sponsees, so informed the author in an interview at Charleston, West Virginia, in August, 1992. And A.A. historian, Dr. Ernest Kurtz, told the author that an Orlando, Florida, obituary described Clarence as a "Co-Founder of A.A."

could not do for himself.[12] However that historical focus was primarily on the *solution* and *program of action* A.A. obtained from religion—that recovery from alcoholism could be achieved through a conversion experience arising out of the application of Oxford Group principles and practices.

Another foundation involved Bill's own deliverance from alcoholism after he had heard the recovery message from Ebby Thatcher. At that time, Bill applied Oxford Group principles and had his own religious experience at Towns Hospital, in New York, in late December of 1934. Perhaps that historical focus would be on the *problem*—defined in terms of the medical facts about the deadly and seemingly hopeless disease of alcoholism—that Bill had learned from Dr. William D. Silkworth at Towns Hospital. These devastating facts had turned Bill to his Maker and had given him occasion to surrender to God, as Ebby had, and experience Ebby's religious solution.

But the technique of *successfully sharing* a *recovery message* with another alcoholic was not yet in place. Bill's first six months of Oxford Group evangelism after he left Towns Hospital failed utterly. Though "burning with confidence and enthusiasm" and though he relentlessly "pursued alcoholics morning, noon, and night," he failed to help one single alcoholic achieve recovery.[13] And this, he was informed by Dr. William D. Silkworth, was because he was "preaching to the drunks" instead of hitting them first with the deadliness of their disease.[14]

We believe the record is clear that what we shall call the four parts of A.A.'s practical and successful program of action—(1) the admission of defeat and lack of power at the hands of alcohol, (2) the necessity for finding God to achieve power, (3) the undertaking of a spiritual program for wiping the slate clean of spiritual blocks to God, and (4) the attainment of a conversion experience and then

---

[12] Big Book, pp. 26-28; *Pass It On*, pp. 111-115, 381-386; Mel B., *New Wine*, pp. 9-26.

[13] *Pass It On*, pp. 131-133.

[14] *Pass It On*, pp. 127-133.

carrying the recovery message with love and service to others—received their crucial and effective trial in Akron.

Akron was the laboratory where the recovery message was developed through experience and was, with substantial success, shared with other alcoholics who did recover. Only after the successes that occurred primarily in Akron was Co-founder Bill Wilson able to say with conviction that A.A.'s "flying blind period" was over and its basics were in place. As Bill put it, "God had shown alcoholics how it [the message] might be passed from hand to hand."[15] Medicine had revealed the problem. And there is no doubt about the Towns Hospital, New York, genesis of that aspect. Religion had revealed the solution—primarily through events focused at Dr. Samuel Moor Shoemaker, Jr.'s Calvary Episcopal Church, Calvary House, and Calvary Rescue Mission in New York. And practical experience—developed and brought to full fruit in Akron—had proved that the solution could be applied to the problem and that, through the Oxford Group's practical program of action, suffering alcoholics could be relieved by God of their seemingly hopeless alcoholism when one alcoholic conveyed the message of hope to another. In other words, it was in Akron that the message-carrying—the service aspect—was developed and turned into an effective program of action.[16] This meant more than the fact that Bill and Dr. Bob had learned in Akron *how* to carry the message. It meant they had studied the

---

[15] See *DR BOB*, p. 96; *RHS*, The A.A. Grapevine (New York: A.A. Grapevine, Inc., January, 1951 memorial issue on Dr. Bob's death), p. 8; Nell Wing, *Grateful To Have Been There*, p. 80.

[16] See *The Co-Founders of Alcoholics Anonymous* (New York: Alcoholics Anonymous World Services, Inc., 1972), p. 8, where Dr. Bob is quoted as follows, "But the one thing that they [the Oxford Group people] hadn't told me was the one thing that Bill did that Sunday [in Akron]—attempt to be helpful to somebody else." Bill D., "A.A. Number Three," said much the same thing in his Big Book story. Bill D. said, "Bill [Wilson] was very, very grateful that he had been released from this terrible thing and he had given God the credit for having done it, and he's so grateful about it he wants to tell other people about it. That sentence, 'The Lord has been so wonderful to me, curing me of this terrible disease, that I just wanted to keep telling people about it,' has been a sort of golden text for the A.A. program and for me" (Big Book, p. 191).

Bible and other spiritual resources there and then *articulated the message* and program of action that they began suggesting for recovery.

What This Book Will Cover

We will explore the Akron beginnings from: (1) the day Oxford Group member Jim Newton came to Akron, Ohio, and made a decision to help his alcoholic friend, Russell Firestone, to (2) the day in December of 1939 when the Big Book had been published and the "alcoholic squad of the Oxford Group" in Akron had taken its leave of the T. Henry Williams meetings and become the King School Group—A.A.'s first group.[17]

Our study commences with details about James D. Newton and Russell ("Bud") Firestone. Newton was a young man whose life had been changed through the Oxford Group. He was steeped in Oxford Group principles and practices. He later married Eleanor Napier Forde, who, herself, had an influence on both Anne Smith and Lois Wilson, the wives of A.A.'s co-founders. And he came to Akron and conveyed to Harvey Firestone, Sr.'s alcoholic son, Bud Firestone, the message that there was hope through Jesus Christ. Bud was transformed through a religious experience brought about by the good offices of Newton and Newton's friend, Reverend Samuel Moor Shoemaker, Jr., of the Oxford Group. This occurred on a train ride back from Denver, Colorado, in late 1931. Bud's father then brought Oxford Group founder, Dr. Frank

---

[17] In *The Language of the Heart*, at page 353, Bill Wilson described this group as "our first group, Akron Number One" and said that Dr. Bob's wife, Anne Smith, was "quite literally, the mother" of the group. For other sources establishing that Anne Ripley Smith was called the "Mother of A.A." by Bill Wilson and others, see Bob Smith and Sue Windows, *Children of the Healer: The Story of Dr. Bob's Kids* (Illinois: Parkside Publishing Corporation, 1992), pp. 29, 43, 132; Dick B., *Anne Smith's Spiritual Workbook* (Corte Madera, CA: Good Book Publishing Company, 1992), pp. ix, 7.

N. D. Buchman, and an Oxford Group team, to a much-publicized series of meetings in Akron, Ohio, in January of 1933, to witness to the changed lives that all the participants had achieved through giving their lives to God. Bud and the speakers all boldly shared their experiences and gave details to the press on Oxford Group principles that were soon to find their way into A.A.'s Fellowship, Big Book, and Twelve Steps. In attendance were people who had some very desperate needs in their lives, who learned much at those meetings, and who were inspired to study and pass on in a very substantial way to Bill W. and Dr. Bob the biblical and Oxford Group principles they initially heard so dynamically presented at the 1933 evangelistic Oxford Group meetings.

We will give details about these people: About T. Henry and Clarace Williams, the devoted, spiritual couple, who opened their home in Akron for Oxford Group meetings and welcomed alcoholics. About Henrietta Seiberling, who was deeply filled with faith in God, intensely studying the Bible and Oxford Group ideas, and trying to use them to help others at the meetings she had helped organize for the alcoholics. About Dr. Bob's wife, Anne Ripley Smith, who was busy attending these meetings, studying the Bible and religious literature, and recording very specifically in writing most of the biblical and Oxford Group principles that were to influence A.A.'s program. About Dr. Bob and his intense reading of the Bible, Christian literature, and Oxford Group books that prepped him for his later studies and discussions with Bill Wilson. And finally about the medical information, spiritual experience, Oxford Group spiritual program, and concepts of working with other alcoholics to maintain sobriety that Bill Wilson injected into the Akron, Oxford Group scene.

Then we'll cover the summer of 1935, when Bill, Dr. Bob, and Anne lived together; when A.A.'s basic ideas were studied and began to gel; and when success occurred on the date Bill D., A.A. Number Three, achieved sobriety. We will follow this with a review of the meetings of the "alcoholic squad of the Oxford Group" at T. Henry's home, meetings which shifted briefly to Dr. Bob's home and then moved to King School in Akron where the

King School Group began and continues to this day at another location. We will see at these meetings the Quiet Times, Bible study, prayer; discussions of spiritual principles; the making of surrenders; the sharing of experience; and the attainment and maintenance of sobriety during A.A.'s "flying blind" period. We'll look at the hospitalizations of alcoholics and the reading and meditation they did outside of meetings. We'll examine Akron's part in the writing of the Big Book as the A.A. Fellowship recorded a recovery program peopled in great majority by the alcoholics who got sober in the Akron area and who contributed their personal stories to the Big Book. And we will conclude with an analysis of Akron's unique contributions to A.A.'s founding—contributions from the Bible, Christian literature, and the Oxford Group.

Basically, then, we will try to shed very specific light on the rich A.A. history in Akron that gave A.A. a very substantial part of its successful roots.

Why This Particular Book?

Bill Wilson put it this way:

> A.A. should always give full credit to its several well-springs of inspiration . . . should always consider these people among the founders of our Society.[18]

---

[18] Kurtz, *Not-God*, p. 323, n. 33; Nell Wing, *Grateful To Have Been There*, p. 25. Bill was speaking of the Oxford Group; but he was equally specific in crediting all who were part of A.A.'s founding events. As to Anne Smith, Dr. Bob's wife, see *The Language of the Heart*, p. 353. As to Ebby Thatcher, Bill's sponsor, see *The Language of the Heart*, p. 368. As to Dr. Samuel Moor Shoemaker, Jr., rector of Calvary Church in New York, see *The Language of the Heart*, p. 380. As to Professor William James, whose book validated Bill's conversion experience, see *Pass It On*, p. 124. As to Dr. Carl G. Jung, who provided A.A. with the information that recovery had been achieved through conversion experiences, see *Pass It On*, p. 383. As to Dr. Frank N. D.

(continued...)

Speaking on A.A.'s spiritual roots, A.A.'s current archivist, Frank M., often quotes this bit from Carl Sandburg:

Whenever a society or civilization fails, there is always one condition present. They forgot where they came from!

There is an adage in A.A. which is most usually attributed to A.A.'s Co-Founder, Dr. Bob. The adage is, "Keep it simple."[19] And A.A.'s twelve recovery suggestions *are* simple in form. In fact, as the Twelve Steps were being developed from the Bible and from Oxford Group principles, Dr. Bob commented that they were not yet *in* "terse and tangible form."[20] But just as the popping of a pill for escape from polio does not cause people to ignore the history of Jonas Salk and the development of a polio vaccine, even more should the "Keep it simple" slogan not be the thing that sways people from a study of the divine help received in Akron and elsewhere.

Neither Bill nor Dr. Bob was a theologian, a member of the cloth, nor a specialist in religious matters. Yet each continued throughout his life to build spiritual conceptions arising out of the religious foundations of early A.A. Dr. Bob never shirked his study of the Bible and Christian literature; and Bill relied heavily on spiritual help from his Roman Catholic spiritual advisor, Father Ed Dowling.[21] To be sure, Bill wrote, after Dr. Bob's death, that while Dr. Bob and he each held certain religious convictions,

---

[18] (...continued)
Buchman, founder of the Oxford Group, see *Pass It On*, pp. 127, 247, 387. As to Henrietta Seiberling, who introduced and helped Bill and Dr. Bob, see Kurtz, *Not-God*, p. 40. As to T. Henry and Clarace Williams, who taught the AAs Oxford Group principles and provided their home for the early meetings, see *Pass It On*, p. 146.

[19] See, for example, *Alcoholics Anonymous Comes of Age*, p. 9; *DR. BOB*, pp. 227, 338; *Pass It On*, p. 339; Kurtz, *Not-God*, pp. 42, 321 n.17.

[20] *DR. BOB*, pp. 96-97.

[21] As to Bill's reliance on Father Ed Dowling as his "spiritual sponsor" and his interest in Roman Catholicism, see Nell Wing, *Grateful To Have Been There*, p. 48; *Pass It On*, pp. 241-243; *Alcoholics Anonymous Comes of Age*, pp. 253-254; Kurtz, *Not-God*, p. 52.

nothing could be so unfortunate for A.A.'s future as an attempt to incorporate personal theological views into A.A. teaching, practice, or tradition.[22] Yet in his tribute to the clergy, he wrote in later years:

> Though still rather gun-shy about clergymen and their theology I finally went back to them—the place where A.A. came from. If they had been able to teach me the principles on which I could recover, then perhaps they might now be able to tell me more about growth in understanding, and in belief.[23]

A strong implication that the Big Book itself was based on this assumption can be found in the following language at page 87:

> Be quick to see where religious people are right. Make use of what they offer.

Our book, then, is not intended as a manual for the newcomer in A.A. today. Nor as a statement as to what AAs do or do not believe today. Nor as to what its Twelve Traditions suggest for A.A. unity. It is intended, in part, to show how Akron AAs proceeded to make use of what the Bible, Christian literature, the Oxford Group, and the clergy offered to them as they were developing their spiritual program of action. This bit of early history may help some readers to remember where A.A. came from as its early progenitors in Akron sought help for recovery from a disease which seemed to offer deliverance only through "divine help."[24] Bill Wilson said to T. Henry and Clarace Williams:

---

[22] See *Alcoholics Anonymous Comes of Age*, p. 232.

[23] See *The Language of the Heart*, p. 179.

[24] See Big Book, p. 43.

God knows we've been simple enough and gluttonous enough to get this way, but once we got this way [became alcoholics], it was a form of lunacy which only God Almighty could cure.[25]

This particular book should show a good part of the picture in Akron as to how early AAs sought and received His help.

---

[25] From the transcript at A.A. Archives in New York of Bill Wilson's December 12, 1954 interview of T. Henry and Clarace Williams in their Akron, Ohio, home.

Part 1

The Beginnings

1

The Roles of James D. Newton
and Russell ("Bud") Firestone

Jim Newton Comes to Akron

In one very real sense, the Akron Genesis study must begin with
James Draper Newton. Some of the story has been told in detail
elsewhere.[1] But there is a great deal more to add—historical facts
pertinent not only to A.A.'s Akron roots, but also to the entire
history of early A.A.[2]

---

[1] See James D. Newton, *Uncommon Friends: Life with Thomas Edison, Henry Ford,
Harvey Firestone, Alexis Carrel, & Charles Lindbergh* (New York: Harcourt Brace
Jovanovich, Publishers, 1987), pp. 26-92; Mel B., *New Wine* (Minnesota: Hazelden,
1991), pp. 63-66; T. Willard Hunter, *Uncommon Friends' Uncommon Friend: a tribute
to James Draper Newton on the occasion of his eighty-fifth birthday* (Pamphlet, March
30, 1990, prepared by Newton's life-long friend, Willard Hunter, a copy of which is in
the author's possession).

[2] Some of these facts can be found in Newton, *Uncommon Friends*, and in Eleanor
Napier Forde, *The Guidance of God* (Oxford: Printed in Great Britain at the University
Press by John Johnson, Printer to the University, 1930). Most were obtained by the
author in an intensive, two-day, personal interview with James D. Newton and his wife,
Eleanor Napier Forde Newton, at their home in Fort Myers Beach, Florida, and also at
their offices at Newton Place in Fort Myers Beach, on August 5 and 6, 1992. Materials
there obtained included some early Oxford Group books, letters, and memoranda, and
a great many notices of, and invitations to, Oxford Group houseparties during the period

(continued...)

In 1924, the Florida real estate boom was at its height; and James D. Newton, an enterprising young luggage salesman, who was working for Belber Bag and Trunk Company, arrived in Fort Myers, Florida, from Philadelphia, at age 20. With the help of his father, Newton acquired fifty-five acres of raw land in Fort Myers. The tract was adjacent to the homes of the famous inventor, Thomas Alva Edison, and the auto manufacturer, Henry Ford. At the time, Edison and his wife, Mina, had been wintering in Fort Myers over a period of 40 years. On April 7, 1926, Jim Newton officially opened the residential real estate development known as Edison Park. In the interim, between his arrival in Florida and the opening of the park, Newton had become well acquainted with Thomas Edison, becoming almost a second son to Mr. and Mrs. Edison. Edison, in turn, had two younger friends—well-known in American business. One was Edison's neighbor, Henry Ford, and the other was Edison's frequent visitor from the Miami winter scene, Harvey Firestone, Sr. During the last decade of Edison's life, the press began making something of the inventor's birthday, February 11th. By that time, Edison had become extremely deaf. And with many well-wishers coming to town for the event, Mrs. Edison asked Jim Newton if he would take charge of the Edison birthdays. Newton became the greeter, introduced guests to each other, and arranged accommodations at the Royal Palm Hotel. A good many of the rich and famous, including President Herbert Hoover, Henry Ford, and Harvey Firestone, Sr., were there. Following one of these occasions in 1928, Newton was approached and befriended by an admiring Firestone. Firestone asked Newton to leave Florida and come to Akron as "Secretary to the President" of Firestone Tire and Rubber Company. Newton accepted, moved to Akron, was lodged at the Portage Country Club, and shortly

---

[2] (...continued)

from 1928 to 1934, copies of which are in the author's possession. Without exception, the notices referred to "A First Century Christian Fellowship," the name by which the American Oxford Group adherents chose to continue calling themselves in the early 1930s.

was placed in charge of the real estate department at Firestone, becoming President of Firestone Realty. Later, Firestone moved Newton into the sales field. And Newton was told he was being groomed for the presidency of Firestone.[3]

Newton's Background

We must digress and see who this Jim Newton was, and what he was to do that was very much intertwined with early A.A. history. To date, historical accounts about Newton and A.A. have centered on what he did for Russell Firestone prior to 1933. But there are many additional facts that need telling and that make the Jim Newton story a good deal more meaningful to A.A. than perhaps has been thought. The facts concern Newton and his Oxford Group friends, Dr. Frank N. D. Buchman, Reverend Samuel Moor Shoemaker, Jr., Eleanor Napier Forde (Newton's wife-to-be), and a host of Oxford Group people who were to have a part in A.A. history. These included T. Henry Williams of Akron; Hanford Twitchell, Victor Kitchen, Charles Clapp, Jr., Rowland Hazard, F. Shepard Cornell, A. S. Loudon Hamilton, Professor Philip Marshall Brown from the New York area, and some other people who were members of the New York business community in the 1920's and 30's. Newton's friends also included the Calvary Church Staff, who were so very much involved in the Oxford Group in the 1930's—people such as Reverend J. Herbert Smith; Reverend John Cuyler, Jr.; Reverend W. Irving Harris; Harris's wife, Mrs. Julia Harris; Miss Olive Jones; and *their* Oxford Group associates, Reverend Sherwood Day, Reverend Cleveland Hicks, Reverend Ray Purdy, and Reverend Garrett Stearly. Finally, there

---

[3] In his August, 1992 personal interview with the author, Newton said that J. W. Thomas, Executive Vice President of Firestone, had made it clear that Newton was slated for the top position, but Newton decided to leave Firestone in 1937 and work for the Oxford Group.

was Newton's relationship with Dr. Walter F. Tunks, pastor of St Paul's Episcopal Church in Akron. Newton's friendship with the foregoing people, his lifelong work with and commitment to the Oxford Group, his devotion to St. Paul's Episcopal Church in Akron and Calvary Episcopal Church in New York, and his close association with an Oxford Group businessmen's "team" on the East Coast have provided this author with a good many answers to his questions about A.A.'s spiritual roots—questions that have been simmering for some time as to where Bill Wilson might have obtained the many Oxford Group-Shoemaker ideas that are quite evidently present in A.A. customs and literature.[4]

We will touch on some of the Newton story in this digression and detail more of it as our book continues.

James Draper Newton was born in Philadelphia on March 30, 1905. He was hired as a salesman by the Belber luggage firm in 1923. Newton that year wandered into a winter sports hotel in Winchendon, Massachusetts. He was looking for a dance and some young people. And he found the young people, at least, in the Toy Town Tavern in Winchendon. He heard them telling stories of how their lives had changed. He learned they were part of Dr. Frank Buchman's "A First Century Christian Fellowship"—later to be called the Oxford Group, and still later, Moral Re-Armament. He heard a man in the group say, "Let's be quiet for a minute." He asked the young man how he found a sense of *direction*.[5] The man replied that he found it by *experiment*. He told Newton how

---

[4] See Appendix Nine, where we have included a number of the words and expressions in the Oxford Group-Shoemaker writings that should be familiar to AAs.

[5] When Oxford Group people spoke of "direction," they were speaking of the guidance of the Holy Spirit. See The Layman with a Notebook, *What Is The Oxford Group?* (London: Oxford University Press, 1933), where the author says, at page 67, "Divine guidance to a life changed from Sin to God is the Holy Spirit taking a normal intelligence and directing it in the fullest harmony with His will for the good of the individual and his neighbors." Oxford Group founder, Dr. Frank Buchman, said, for example, "The Holy Spirit is the most intelligent source of information in the world today. He has the answer to every problem. Everywhere when men will let Him, He is teaching them how to live." See Frank N. D. Buchman, *Remaking The World* (London: Blandford Press, 1961), p. 12.

he had used Jesus Christ's Sermon on the Mount as a guide for his actions and motives. He said the guide had been reduced to four absolute standards—honesty, purity, unselfishness, and love. Then the man told Newton how his own life had not measured up to these standards. Asking about "purity," Newton was in turn asked how he would feel if his thoughts were flashed on a screen. Newton understood the significance of the question, admired the man's honesty, and could relate to the man's shortcomings.

Newton asked how he himself could conduct the life-changing experiment; and the young man suggested "that I turn over as much of my will as I understood to as much of God as I comprehended."[6] Later Newton got down on his knees with another young man and said this: "I have my ideals, but I can't live up to them. I don't have what it takes. If you're there and can call the shots, here's my will and my life. You run it. You fly it." His companion suggested to Newton that, the next morning, he should listen and see what thoughts came into his mind. This he did; and two thoughts came: (1) I had to go and give back the money I'd gotten "mixed up with mine" when I was operating a cash register in high school. (2) I should go to my customers and tell them I hadn't been entirely honest. Newton asked his friend if the thoughts were direction or guidance from God. The friend said the answers could be found in the experiment. Newton proceeded onward. He started each day by being quiet, praying, reading the Bible, and giving God a chance to show him through his thoughts how God wanted him to live. He began to experience a sense of direction he had never experienced before. Newton said, "I had moved from *believing* to *knowing*."

Many years later, Newton explained the experiment to his friend, Charles Lindbergh. He said one must make a commitment to "relinquish as much of your will as you understand to your

---

[6] This idea of surrendering all one knows of self to all one knows of God was a very common idea in the Oxford Group. See Stephen Foot, *Life Began Yesterday* (New York: Harper & Brothers, 1935), p. 175; Samuel M. Shoemaker, Jr., *Children of the Second Birth* (New York: Fleming H. Revell, 1927), p. 25; Dick B., *Anne Smith's Spiritual Workbook* (Corte Madera, CA: Good Book Publishing Company, 1992), p. 28.

Creator—to the degree you know him or believe in him or recognize him or trust him." Then "ask God—if there is a God—to make clear what you should do." And Newton said God had done exactly that for him. He said "An inner voice tells you not only what you may have done wrong, but an intuition about what you need to do, a direction in which to go, a feeling or illumination." Newton explained, "I consciously try to let God's presence soak in. It's all in the New Testament. Be willing and obedient, and you will experience a new power and a new sense of direction in your daily life."[7]

Miss Eleanor Napier Forde

Newton had learned something of the life-changing experiment conducted by adherents to "A First Century Christian Fellowship" (the name by which the Oxford Group was known in the 1920's and early 1930's). His initial education came from his own experiment in Massachusetts in the early 1920's. But there was more to come. He soon met a striking young lady in the Oxford Group, and her name was Eleanor Napier Forde. Miss Forde was to become Newton's wife in 1943. But their friendship in the 1920's began to bear fruit quite soon. And the influence of Miss Forde on A.A. history is much more than that of being Newton's wife.[8] Here is her story.

---

[7] The reader should find it interesting to compare Newton's language with that on pages 62 and 63 of the Big Book, which states as to A.A.'s Third or "Surrender" Step: "Next, we decided that hereafter in this drama of life, God was going to be our Director. . . . When we sincerely took such a position, all sorts of remarkable things followed. . . . As we felt new power flow in, as we enjoyed peace of mind, as we discovered we could face life successfully, as we became conscious of His presence, we began to lose our fear of today, tomorrow or the hereafter."

[8] The author's book, *Anne Smith's Spiritual Workbook*, can be consulted for details about the notebook Dr. Bob's wife, Anne, kept of her Bible studies, reading, and Oxford

(continued...)

Eleanor Forde was born in Montreal in 1897. On October 11, 1920, she had gone to the Old Baptist Temple in Brooklyn. The minister had preached Christ as Savior. He asked if anyone wished to give the reign of his or her life to Jesus Christ—a living person. And this she did. She made a decision for Christ. But there remained the question as to what she was to *do* with her life. Should she become a missionary? What? How could she serve her Lord, Jesus?

During Easter week in 1922, Eleanor went to Grace Church in New York; and a young minister, Samuel Moor Shoemaker, Jr., was there preaching. Eleanor said she gave God an "ultimatum." She wanted to know what to do with her life *now*! That was April 6, 1922. She asked Shoemaker how to get an answer; and he replied, "I can't tell you when; but if you are willing, God will find a way to tell you."

By 1925, Shoemaker had become rector of Calvary Episcopal Church in New York. On September 26, 1925, he asked Miss Forde to come to Calvary Church to work with young women who were looking for a new start in their lives. She worked there for

---

[8] (...continued)

Group thoughts during the 1930's. And Anne's Smith's book is discussed in some detail in Chapter 5 of this book. But the author has not previously written about the portions of Anne Smith's notes that refer to the teachings by "Elinor (sic) Forde." However, Anne discussed the teachings of Eleanor Forde at pages 26 through 30 of her 64 page workbook. Topics included spiritual poise, surrender, willingness, a maximum experience of Jesus Christ, helping people, guidance of the Holy Spirit, the plan of salvation, the four standards, God's plan, honesty, being in touch with God, the Cross, spiritual children, faith, getting a Christ that can rid you of your sins, prayer, restitution, responsibility, team work, checking, a group, God's guidance of a group, witness, conversion, William James's definition of conversion, and denial. Much of Anne's workbook is devoted to discussing Oxford Group ideas, but the portion pertaining to Eleanor Forde indicates the amount of Oxford Group material that Dr. Bob's wife learned by studying Miss Forde's ideas. Interestingly, the author learned on his most recent visit to the archives at Bill Wilson's home at Stepping Stones, Bedford Hills, New York, that Bill's wife, Lois Wilson, also had an "Oxford Group workbook" of sorts. We will have more to say of this at a later point. Lois Wilson not only discusses many of the same Oxford Group principles (in less detail) that Anne discussed, but she also mentions the presence of Miss Forde and a number of other Oxford Group personages at the Oxford Group houseparties that Lois and Bill attended between 1934-1937.

two years and frequently saw Jim Newton, who was becoming more and more involved in Oxford Group activities.

In 1925, Shoemaker introduced Miss Forde to Dr. Frank Buchman at a dinner welcoming Buchman back to the United States. In 1927, Buchman wrote Miss Forde from Great Britain and asked her to come to Oxford to help him with life-changing work abroad. From that year on, Eleanor Napier Forde spent her full time working with the Oxford Group. For the next several years, she went with teams to Edinburgh, Holland, South Africa, and Canada. To the date of this writing, at age 93, she still maintains Moral Re-Armament (the Oxford Group successor) as a major life activity. In October of 1930, Miss Forde wrote an Oxford Group pamphlet, *The Guidance of God*, which is still in circulation and still being reprinted.

In the opening pages of her pamphlet, she wrote:

Within the Bible, running through the dark perplexing panorama of time, is a crystal stream of communication with the unseen world of the Spirit. Men talked with God. More important, God talked with men. Conversations took place and were recorded because they knew God to be a personal Spirit, and not always because they were better men than some whose noble lives challenge us out of pagan history. They were the chosen who knew Him intimately. The mass of people lived by the progressive revelation given through these men. . . . Casuistry often masquerades in the guise of religion, so when we speak of guidance, let it be remembered that we speak of *that process of communication at whose other end is the Living God*. Nor is it a God who conforms to our prejudices and superstitions, but the Eternal Spirit as we begin to know Him through His self-revelation in Jesus Christ.[9]

---

[9] Forde, *The Guidance of God*, pp. 1-2.

Elsewhere in her pamphlet, Miss Forde wrote:

It is faith in the power and presence of the Living Christ to which the world has been—and is still—bearing witness (p. 7).

A short time ago, some one said, "Psychology helped me enormously. It emptied me, but it didn't fill me with anything new. It took Jesus Christ to do that." A noted psychologist recently gave several hours of sound psychological schooling as it bore on the great mission of winning people to Christ. Closing, he said, "The person with an experience of God and a poor technique will make fewer mistakes in the end than the person with a high technique and no God." One sees in this statement of a trained psychologist whose power is avowedly of God, the experiential knowledge that the Holy Spirit is the great Teacher and Christ the Cure (p. 8).

No power, no victory. . . . There are notorious slums of those Christians who lack power: Compromise and Inertia. And there are slums of Resentment, Self-Righteousness, and Criticism which are difficult to clean up because their tenants have such intense pride of ownership. Independence, Prejudice and Pride of Reputation seem to be handsome blocks, but many families and friends are sacrificed to pay the mortgage on them. . . . Jealousy has a high picket fence where love and friendship are often impaled and die bleeding. The night cries of Fear disturb all the peace of these parts. . . . Selfishness hangs like a choking fog over everything (pp. 13-14).

I saw in myself three great sins—pride, selfishness, wilful independence of God. I was restless; then unhappy, throwing myself with abandon into anything that chanced along in an effort to forget. But I grew to hate myself, and correspondingly, I began to love Jesus Christ. . . . The purpose of the Cross in His mind. . . . "I am the only One who can meet this evil in its full strength and conquer. . . ." Can you do it yourself? I could not. . . . The Spirit of God seeks to release one's whole personality and to co-ordinate them to the mind of God and training one's imagination and sympathies to carry out His redemptive will for the individual and the world (pp. 16-17).

The question arises: How are we to find the particular will of God? There must be absolute readiness to obey, coupled with a faith resolute enough to carry conviction into action. . . . Knowledge comes with willingness: power with obedience (p. 18).[10]

The God-directed life has its signposts. The first is the Bible. . . . It is a magnificent and complete story of man's developing relationship to God. . . . The second signpost is this: "Look for the coincidences." . . . The third signpost is a question: "Where is the Cross?" . . . the selfish inclination and desire; the discipline of the look, the thought, the tongue. . . . The fourth signpost is an intuitive conviction that a course of action is inherently right, the certainty that, hard as it may be, there can be no other way. . . . The fifth signpost, "What say others to whom God speaks?" is the unwritten law of fellowship (pp. 19-22).

Realize the presence of God—"the ineffable something that holds the mind." . . . you can let God so order your day that everything in His will for that day will be done. . . . I had been trying to "pilot" them myself. . . . Prayer . . . became a tapping of the power-house of God. . . . Guidance comes in action. . . . Be still and listen to Him who knows better than you. . . . If you do not feel reasonably sure that a thought is from God, wait. See whether it conforms to Christ's rounded teaching and, if you can, use the test, "What say others to whom God speaks?" (pp. 23-27).

Of Eleanor Forde, Dr. Frank Buchman had said: (1) You have a remarkable concept of the Gospel message. (2) It is a privilege in these days of loose thinking to find one who has so thoroughly

---

[10] Frank Buchman was well known and much quoted for his expression: "When man listens, God speaks. When man obeys, God acts." See Frank N. D. Buchman, *Remaking The World* (London: Blandford Press, 1961), pp. 35, 29.

gripped the truths of Christ. (3) I certainly want you [Eleanor Forde] to hold me to God's best. (4) I haven't forgotten that you want a full hour to tell me where I have fallen short.[11] This Eleanor Forde was the lady with whom Newton was exchanging spiritual ideas in the 1920's and 30's.

There are several more points about Jim Newton's spiritual growth as he was becoming involved with the Firestone Tire and Rubber Company, the Firestone family, and A.A.'s formative period in Akron.

Newton's Part in the Larger A.A. Picture

Jim Newton was having a good many personal difficulties and concerns in 1927. At that time, he was in New York on the occasion of the Dempsey-Tunney prize fight. Lacking a place to stay, he contacted his friend, Dr. Frank Buchman. He told Buchman that he was about to do what AAs today call "doing a geographic." He proposed to leave the United States to escape his problems. Buchman suggested that he would be taking *himself* with him, and that he would be better advised to have a talk with Reverend Sam Shoemaker. Newton met with Shoemaker and was completely honest about his life. He then sought God's guidance as to what he should do with his life. He received a strong leading thought that his father needed him in Florida. This turned out to be true, and once again Newton found that "when man listens, God speaks." Newton soon became a very good friend of Dr. Shoemaker's. Newton's friendship with both Frank Buchman and Sam Shoemaker seemed to set the stage for Newton's deep involvement in many, many Oxford Group houseparties in the eastern United States, as well as in the activities of what he called

---

[11] See Garth Lean, *On The Tail of a Comet* (Colorado Springs: Helmers & Howard, 1988), p. 166.

an Oxford Group "business team," of which Bill Wilson himself may briefly have been a member.

Newton's Oxford Group business team associates came primarily from the Calvary Church in New York, where most were quite active. In the late 1920's and early 1930's, Newton was meeting regularly with a group of men from the Oxford Group whose names included Hanford Twitchell,[12] Victor Kitchen,[13] F. Shepard Cornell,[14] Rowland Hazard,[15] Charles Clapp, Jr.,[16] and Professor Philip Marshall Brown, a Princeton professor, Oxford Group speaker, and author.[17] Newton informed the author that the Oxford Group businessmen's team, occasionally included T. Henry Williams of Akron, A. S. Loudon Hamilton, and Russell Firestone. These team members met on Fridays and Saturdays. Their purpose was to inventory their shortcomings, apply Christian principles in their lives, obtain God's guidance in business

---

[12] About Bill Wilson's close friendship and work with Hanford Twitchell, see Nell Wing, *Grateful To Have Been There* (Illinois: Parkside Publishing, 1992), p. 68.

[13] See V. C. Kitchen, *I Was A Pagan* (New York: Harper and Bros., 1934), in which Kitchen not only recounts how he recovered from alcoholism through his experiences in the Oxford Group, but actually describes at page 123 of his book the businessman's group of which Jim Newton spoke at length in the author's interview with him in August of 1992.

[14] See *Lois Remembers*, in which Lois Wilson states that she, her husband, Bill Wilson, Shep Cornell, and Ebby Thatcher "constantly went to Oxford Group meetings at Calvary Episcopal Church," and states that "Shep" was a fellow Oxford Group member and worked on Wall Street (p. 91).

[15] It was to Rowland Hazard that Bill attributed A.A.'s discovery of the spiritual solution which Rowland had obtained from Dr. Carl Jung; and it was with Rowland Hazard that Bill and Ebby frequently met at Stewart's Cafeteria after Oxford Group meetings in Bill's early sobriety. See *Lois Remembers*, p. 94; *Pass It On* (New York: Alcoholics Anonymous World Services, Inc., 1984), p. 132; Robert Thomsen, *Bill W.* (New York: Harper & Row, 1975), pp. 229-230.

[16] See Charles Clapp, Jr., *The Big Bender* (New York: Harper & Row, 1938). In this book, Clapp recounts how he recovered from alcoholism with the assistance of Shep Cornell and Dr. Samuel Shoemaker.

[17] See Philip M. Brown, *The Venture of Belief* (New York: Fleming H. Revell, 1935). We shall have more to say of Professor Brown in Chapter 7.

situations, and achieve an "abundant life."[18] Through the efforts of Dr. Frank Buchman, the team utilized the services of a Miss Mary Angevine, a Bible teacher, whom Buchman had procured for the team to teach them a greater knowledge of Scripture.

Jim Newton provided the author with a large number of printed announcements promulgated in the period 1928-1934, by The Oxford Group (which then called itself "A First Century Christian Fellowship"). Several more of these announcements were found by the author during a visit in August of 1992 to the archives of Hartford Seminary, where Frank Buchman lectured in his earlier years. The announcements were of houseparties in New York at the Plaza Hotel, the Waldorf Astoria, and Briarcliff Lodge; in Massachusetts at the Hotel Northhampton, The Hotel Hawthorne, and the Dedham Country and Polo Club; in Asheville, North Carolina at The Battery Park Hotel; in Philadelphia at the Belleview Stratford Hotel; and in Detroit at The Book-Cadillac Hotel. Newton and many of the Oxford Group business team members regularly attended the foregoing houseparties; and Miss Mary Angevine also taught Scripture at these events.

Newton, Dr. Walter Tunks, and the Firestones

The foregoing accounts of Jim Newton's experiences with the First Century Christian Fellowship, Eleanor Forde, Frank Buchman, Sam Shoemaker, the Oxford Group business team, and Oxford Group houseparties provide the spiritual backdrop in James D. Newton's life when Harvey Firestone, Sr., made him the offer to come to Akron and join Firestone's rubber company.

According to Newton, Harvey Firestone "was a regular churchgoer and I knew he had a firm belief in God that he tried to apply in his own life." Firestone's pastor was Dr. Walter F. Tunks, rector of St. Paul's Episcopal Church in Akron. And Tunks

---

[18] See John 10:10.

keeps appearing and re-appearing in Akron—A.A. history.[19] Tunks was interested in the Oxford Group. When Newton came to Akron, he became a member of St. Paul's Episcopal Church, of which Tunks was pastor. In 1946, Newton headed up a building campaign for Tunks's new church. It was Tunks who, acting on behalf of the Akron Ministerial Association, welcomed Dr. Frank Buchman to Akron in 1933 and introduced most of the public meetings that Buchman held there at that time. It was in Reverend Tunks's church that Dr. Frank Buchman shared from the pulpit during the 1933 Oxford Group campaign. It was Tunks whom Bill Wilson was led to call from the lobby of the Mayflower Hotel on May 10, 1935, when Bill was searching for another alcoholic to help. Though the routing was circuitous, it was Tunks who put Bill in touch with Henrietta Seiberling, who said Bill's phone call to her was "manna from heaven;" for it was that call which enabled her to bring Bill W. and Dr. Bob together for their important Mother's Day meeting on May 11, 1935 at Henrietta's Gatehouse home at "Stan Hywet Hall" (the name for the Seiberling Estate in Akron). It was Dr. Tunks's Episcopalian Church that Dr. Bob and his family joined when another Akron minister had apparently let the Smith family know they were not welcome in his congregation.[20] And it was Tunks who delivered the oration at Dr. Bob's funeral.

Harvey Firestone, Sr., was married to Idabelle Smith of Jackson, Michigan; and the couple had six children, five sons and a daughter. Newton became good friends with the two eldest sons, Harvey, Jr., and Russell, who was known as Bud. Newton said, "the son I knew best was Bud. He was about my age and we worked together, necessarily spending a lot of time in each other's company. We also went through a lot together over the years and

---

[19] See a similar observation that was made in Bob Smith and Sue Windows, *Children of the Healer* (Illinois: Parkside Publishing Corporation, 1992), p. 5.

[20] Bob Smith and Sue Smith Windows, *Children of the Healer*, p. 127.

became the closest of friends." That friendship continued to the end of Bud's life.[21]

Bud Firestone had a serious drinking problem. About it, Newton wrote:

> Bud and his wife, Dorothy, and I were good friends from the time I first started at Firestone. We were all of the same age, and as I was unmarried, I often would go over to their house, which was very near where I lived át the Portage Country Club. I found out about Bud's problem from Bud himself. He was a hard drinker. One day he told me that he had been in and out of institutions to "dry out." His father had sent him in great hopes, but by the time I came into the picture I think Firestone had about given up on Bud's alcoholism. It was tearing him up, but he just didn't know what to do.[22]

Here the author is reminded of the following in the Big Book's Chapter "More About Alcoholism":

> One of these men [doctors and psychiatrists], staff member of a world-renowned hospital, recently made this statement to some of us: "What you say about the general hopelessness of the average alcoholic's plight is, in my opinion, correct. As to two of you men, whose stories I have heard, there is no doubt in my mind that you were 100% hopeless, apart from divine help. Had you offered yourselves as patients at this hospital, I would not have taken you, if I had been able to avoid it."[23]

The author is also reminded of two of the "abc's" in the Big Book, page 60:

---

[21] Russell's son, Morgan Firestone, informed the author in a telephone interview in January of 1992, that his father was born in 1900 and died in 1950 after nine months of suffering from cancer of the esophagus, an illness possibly stemming from Russell's alcoholism.

[22] The foregoing materials, and this quote, were taken from Newton, *Uncommon Friends*, pp. 83-84.

[23] Big Book, p. 43.

   a. That we were alcoholic and could not manage our own lives.
   b. That probably no human power could have relieved our alcoholism.

Newton wrote more about his concern for Bud Firestone. He said:

> Bud and I talked often about his problem. When he decided to go into yet another institution and try another cure, I went to his father and asked permission to join Bud, to share the experience with him. In spite of the tremendous business pressures, Firestone was grateful and made arrangements for me to leave work.[24]

Newton joined his friend, Russell Firestone, in sharing the ordeal of one more human effort to stem Firestone's progressive slide toward alcoholic defeat. Would the hospitalization work? Predictably, the answer was "no." But Newton was to carry a different message to Bud Firestone, one honed from Newton's own faith and life-change experience in the Oxford Group.

The Bud Firestone Miracle on the Train from Denver

Jim Newton's own words, in his book, *Uncommon Friends*, best express the message of love and service that he carried to his despondent friend, Bud Firestone.[25] Of Bud's trip to the hospital, one more time, Newton said:

> The institution on the Hudson River I attended with Bud was run like the army. I'd been sitting at a desk for a few years by then and was not prepared to be awakened at dawn and made to run all

---

[24] Newton, *Uncommon Friends*, pp. 83-84.

[25] See Newton, *Uncommon Friends*, pp. 83-85.

over the countryside. They were intent on drying these guys out and drying me out right along with them. [Newton was *not* an alcoholic.] I got more exercise than I'd had for a long, long time. The place did help Bud, and our talking helped. I shared with him the times I had found myself unable to handle things and told him that in my experience there was always an answer. The God who made us would have an answer for us if we only gave him the chance. Bud was somewhat receptive, but he didn't really believe anything could change—not for him anyway.

Newton then made a proposition to Bud:

> Several weeks after we'd returned to Akron, I invited Bud to go with me to a conference in Denver where he would meet people I knew who were involved in what was then called the Oxford Group. It was an informal association of men and women, started by an American, Frank Buchman, who were committed to creating sound homes, teamwork in industry, and unity within and between nations, based on moral and spiritual change.

Bud agreed to go to Denver with Newton. At the time, Bud had been drinking a fifth of whiskey or more each day. He agreed to let Newton carry his liquor flask for him. And that was supposed to deter Bud's drinking on the way. However, as Newton put it, "it slowed down the consumption some, but it wasn't enough."

The Denver occasion was a Conference of Episcopal Bishops to which Shoemaker—himself an Episcopal priest—and Newton had been invited along with other Oxford Group people. At Denver, Newton managed to get Bud Firestone together with Newton's friend, Dr. Samuel Moor Shoemaker, Jr., rector of Calvary Episcopal Church in New York City. Shoemaker was Frank Buchman's close associate in the Oxford Group. In Denver, Shoemaker spent a good deal of time with Bud Firestone; and Shoemaker joined Firestone and Newton on the return train trip from Denver. Shoemaker and Firestone went into a private train compartment together.

According to the account given by A.A. historian, Mel B., Firestone said that, in Shoemaker's presence in the train compartment, "I gave my life to Jesus Christ." Firestone later added, "I let God guide my life now."[26] This "decision" by Firestone to surrender and to live by God's Guidance was, of course, part of the Oxford Group's life-changing process. In a telephone interview with the author in March of 1992, Newton elaborated on what Bud had done thereafter with the Oxford Group. Bud had not merely made a "decision" to surrender; he had followed through with the Oxford Group's life-changing program that later found its way into A.A.'s Twelve Steps. Thus Firestone made restitution. He studied the Bible and observed Quiet Times with Newton for many years. He witnessed to others. He shared his experience. In fact, the author learned from Newton that Bud Firestone had met with the Oxford Group "business team," of which Newton was a member, and that Bud attended several of the houseparties the team members attended on the East Coast and which we have mentioned. Newton told the author: Bud was a Christian who found freedom, became a constructive person, and witnessed. And though he later returned to drinking, he continued to observe Oxford Group practices and did substantially less drinking than he had done prior to his Denver experience.

The fact that he later had an occasional lapse has caused some to discount the importance of the Firestone "miracle" in A.A.'s Akron genesis. But the fact remains that Bud Firestone did undergo a dramatic change. Newton wrote:

> Bud's decision to put his life into the hands of a Higher Power, to trust and obey him, had an extraordinary effect. His whole life changed. It was visible right away; his face relaxed, some of the lines were gone. He had come to terms not just with the drinking, but with the underlying cause that was making him drink.

---

[26] Mel B., *New Wine*, p. 67.

[Speaking of Harvey Firestone, Sr.'s visit with Bud after Bud's experience on the train, Newton wrote] I will never forget the look of wonder that came over Firestone's face. The father could scarcely believe what he saw—a son come back to life. He had come to believe that the situation with Bud was hopeless, something he couldn't control.

Bud went home and started taking his responsibilities to the company seriously. He became a real husband to Dorothy [Bud's wife] and a real father to his two sons. Dorothy had been trying as hard as she could, but the alcoholism had put a terrible strain on their marriage. There were times when she had thought she would have to leave him. All of that soon changed. The family doctor called the transformation a medical miracle. He had thought withdrawal would take much longer.

After that weekend, I saw a deepening of the relationship between Bud and his father. Firestone spent more time with Bud; he relied on him much more, and Bud became a real part of the business. Firestone's involvement with the community also took on a new dimension. In fact, Bud's change and his father's response to his son surprised Akron.[27]

It is not our purpose to minimize or write some kind of justification for Firestone's later return to drinking. But we do point to the Big Book's own report on its early "success rate":

Of alcoholics who came to A.A. and really tried, 50% got sober at once and remained that way; 25% sobered up after some relapses, and among the remainder, those who stayed on with A.A. showed improvement.[28]

A.A.'s Co-founder, Dr. Bob, relapsed after his first three weeks of working with Bill and only then recovered and maintained his

---

[27] For the foregoing quotes, see Newton, *Uncommon Friends*. pp. 85-88.

[28] Big Book, p. xx.

sobriety for the rest of his days. Bill W.'s friend and "sponsor," Ebby Thatcher, returned to drinking not long after he had witnessed to Bill. Ebby spent many of his later days in hospitals. So A.A. itself could do no more than promise, through God's grace, a restoration of sanity as far as the drinking obsession was concerned.[29] But its Big Book carefully pointed out:

> It is easy to let up on the spiritual program of action and rest on our laurels. We are headed for trouble if we do, for alcohol is a subtle foe. We are not cured of alcoholism. What we really have is a daily reprieve contingent on the maintenance of our spiritual condition.[30]

Part of that maintenance is the practice of A.A.'s Twelfth Step—which suggests working with others—and about which the Big Book says:

> Practical experience shows that nothing will so much insure immunity from drinking as intensive work with other alcoholics. It works when other activities fail. This is our *twelfth suggestion*: Carry this message to other alcoholics![31]

This, of course, was a concept to which Bud Firestone had not been introduced in any significant way. Nor by another alcoholic. Dr. Bob and Bill found it necessary to follow the twelfth suggestion for the rest of their lives.

Whatever alcoholic fate ultimately befell Russell Firestone, the fact is that his recovery amazed and touched Akron in 1933!

---

[29] Big Book, p. 57.

[30] Big Book, p. 85.

[31] Big Book, p. 89.

2

A Grateful Harvey Firestone, Sr., and the 1933 Oxford Group Events

The Newspaper Coverage

The two principal newspapers in the Akron area tell this part of the story about as well as it can be told. And the author combed the pages of these two papers for the details. Initially, it should be said that Bud Firestone had a religious experience to share and, as Oxford Group people were doing as part of their witnessing technique, he wanted to attest to his experience of Christ, to his deliverance from alcoholism, and to his life-change. His father, though proclaiming he was not a part of the Oxford Group, was nonetheless a believer, deeply grateful, and desirous of carrying to Akron the message of what God had done for his son. Hence Harvey Firestone, Sr., invited Dr. Frank N. D. Buchman, founder of the Oxford Group, to bring a "team" to Akron. And that is what happened in January of 1933. Because of the social status of the Firestone family and the wide scope of the intended witnessing, the events made headlines and commanded press attention before, during, and after the arrival of the Oxford Group people. Here is how the events were covered in Akron's local newspapers:

Heralding the coming, *The Akron Times-Press* for Monday, January 16, 1933, announced on its front page:

> Business and professional men, women's groups and college students will have an opportunity to meet with disciples of the "Oxford group" coming here Thursday under the sponsorship of Russell [Bud] Firestone at small individual meetings, it was indicated today.
>
> While Dr. Frank N. D. Buchman, leader of the group, and his 30 disciples are definitely scheduled for four public meetings here, they may be able to arrange many smaller group sessions. . . .
>
> Dr. Buchman and his group of 30 brokers, bankers, business and professional men will arrive here Thursday for the series of evangelistic appearances in their movement, described by Mr. Firestone as "a revival of old-time religion."
>
> The first meeting will be held in the Mayflower [hotel] ballroom at 8:15 p.m. Thursday. Similar meetings will be held at the same hour Friday and Saturday at the Mayflower. Sunday, members of the group are scheduled for a series of appearances at Akron churches. . . .
>
> [In] the group of 30 converts coming here to expound the cult will be James Watts of Edinburgh, former Communist who led the Fifeshire general strike in 1926, Sir Walter Windham of London, and Baroness Lillian Van Keekeren Van Kell of Holland.
>
> Though Mr. Firestone, a son of Harvey S. Firestone, Sr., was "converted" more than a year ago, and has traveled through the country attending and speaking at meetings of the group, the Akron sessions will introduce the Oxford Group teaching to Ohio for the first time.
>
> Mrs. Russell Firestone, Mr. and Mrs. Harvey Firestone, Sr., Miss Katherine Reed, Mrs. Lisle Buckingham, and Rev. Walter

F. Tunks of St. Paul's Episcopal church are interested in the Akron appearance of the group.

Harvey Firestone, Sr., is not a member of the Oxford Group, Russell Firestone explained today, nor has he attended any of its meetings, "but he is interested in it as he is interested in all good things."

On the next day, Tuesday, the same paper told of the religious activities that were planned. It said:

More than a score of Akron pulpits will be thrown open to Dr. Frank N. D. Buchman, leader of the Oxford group, and his disciples Sunday as a climax of the new type of evangelistic campaign that opens here Thursday night.

Rev. Walter F. Tunks, rector of St. Paul's Episcopal church, who will welcome the "Group" to Akron, said today that many Akron pastors had asked that members of the visiting evangelistic party speak at their churches Sunday. . . .

In addition to Mr. Firestone [Bud] and his wife, Miss Katherine Reed of Akron university, Mrs. Lisle Buckingham, James D. Newton and Harvey S. Firestone, Sr. are sponsoring appearance of the Oxford Group here.

Thursday's *Times-Press* was filled with details of the arrival of the team. On the front page, Bud Firestone's wife was shown greeting Dr. Buchman at Akron's Union Train Station. There was an article on the front page in which Harvey Firestone, Sr., was quoted as saying "Need 'Rebirth.'" It said, "Rubber Magnate Declares World Must Learn To Serve Others." It said the senior Firestone was "pleading for the restoration of the Golden Rule as the guiding influence of humanity." And then an entire section of the paper was devoted to a discussion of "Buchmanism: 'A Life Hid With Christ.'" It said in headlines: "Russell Firestone Calls It 'Getting Down To Fundamentals.'" Details were given about the Oxford Group principles. Headings were as follows:

1. *Life, Not A Sect* was the subhead for a portion on the nature of the Oxford Group.

2. *Revival of Religion* was the next subhead. That portion said:

   "The Group" has no tenets. It contents itself with reaffirming truths of the New Testament. Among the truths it reaffirms and has for its foundation are those which it terms: God-Guidance, Fearless Dealing With Sin, Sharing, The Necessity for Adequate Expressional Activity, Stewardship, Team-work and Loyalty.[1]

   God-guidance is interpreted by the group to mean communion with God. "Thinking God's thoughts after him," "Two-way prayer" and "listening to God" are some of the terms by which it is known.

   "Quiet Times are regular with the group. . . ."

   "Mrs. Firestone and I start each day by reading the Bible. That in itself would be something if we did nothing more. Then we welcome God's guidance."

   There isn't any such thing as God telling you every step to take during the day but you do get a general idea of how the day's work should be conducted. . . .

---

[1] These seven principles were properly attributed by the Akron newspaper to Reverend Sherwood Day. The principles were those which Day had expounded in a popular Oxford Group pamphlet: Sherwood Sunderland Day, *The Principles of the Group* (Oxford: Printed in Great Britain at the University Press, by John Johnson, Printer to the University, n.d.). A slightly modified version of the principles, plus an explanation of how the principles were formulated by Reverend Day at the request of Dr. Samuel Moor Shoemaker, Jr., will be found in Irving Harris, *The Breeze of the Spirit* (New York: The Seabury Press, 1978), pp. 18-21.

Fearless Dealing with Sin requires "getting the facts and facing them" spiritually. . . .

Anything that separates a person from God or from another person is sin.

3. *Share Experiences* was another subhead. The text added:

Under Sharing comes the "confessions" that have distinguished the group movement.

. . . The admonition of St. James—"Confess your faults one to another" is deep-rooted in the groups. . . .[2]

An experience that is not shared dies or becomes twisted and abnormal, the group believes. For this reason there must be expressional activity in sharing—a communication of the good things of life and the belief to others. . . .

4. *Loyalty To Truth* was the concluding subhead. The text said:

Firm adherence to the Loyalty "truth" is what makes the movement what it is. . . .

These, then, are the principles on which the Oxford movement is based. Akron and Ohio will get a chance to see how they work and what possibilities lie in them when Dr. Buchman brings his "soul surgery" and his group here tonight.[3]

---

[2] See James 5:16.

[3] The term "soul surgery" was used in connection with Buchman's "art" of life-changing. It described the method used to bring about and maintain a "conversion." Buchman himself was called the "Soul Surgeon;" and his technique involved the "5 C's"—Confidence, Confession, Conviction, Conversion, and Continuance. See Dick B., *The Oxford Group & Alcoholics Anonymous* (Seattle: Glen Abbey Books, 1992), pp. 141-

(continued...)

The *Akron Beacon Journal* for Thursday evening, January 19, 1933, featured a front page picture of Rev. Walter Tunks and Mrs. Russell Firestone greeting Dr. Frank Buchman at the train station. The headline said "Oxford Party Is Welcomed By Akronites." It said Oxford Group members would be remain for four days, giving public lectures and audiences at the Mayflower hotel each evening except Sunday. It quoted the elder Firestone as follows:

> While I am not a member of the Oxford Group, . . . [I] am a firm believer that churches and church organizations—no matter of what denomination—are the channels through which we can best serve God and our fellowmen; however, the people today need an awakening. And in watching my son's and his wife's activities in the group, I believe that the Oxford group has a vital contribution to make to the religious and social life of today. Mrs. Firestone and I are very happy to join with our son, Russell, and his wife in welcoming the Oxford group to Akron.

The Friday papers carried headlines on the success of the Group's first night of meetings. The *Akron Beacon Journal* for January 20th announced, "Many Hear Dr. Buchman On Religion." Further, "Business, Industrial, Social Leaders Attend; Overflow Meeting Necessary." It said that Russell "Bud" Firestone faced an audience of at least 1,200 persons in the Mayflower's ballroom and "talked about religion." Arrangements were made hastily to open the Polsky store tea room across the street for an overflow meeting of about 400. The society page reported that 130 out-of-town guests and persons prominent in Akron society circles attended the dinner given by the Firestones at the Mayflower Hotel and which preceded the Oxford Group meeting. Pictures of the elite—decked out in tuxedos and evening gowns—were featured.

---

[3] (...continued)
145; H. A. Walter, *Soul-Surgery*. 6th ed. (Oxford: Printed at the University Press by John Johnson, Printer to the University, 1940); Samuel M. Shoemaker, *Realizing Religion* (New York: Association Press, 1921), pp. 79-80; Harold Begbie, *Life Changers* (London: Mills & Boon, Ltd., 1932), pp. 24-41.

The *Beacon Journal* reported that Reverend Walter F. Tunks had welcomed the visitors to the Oxford Group meeting in the name of the ministerial association, spoken briefly, and then introduced Bud Firestone. Bud was reported to have said to a hushed auditorium:

Dorothy and I . . . discovered this group 16 months ago at a time when our mode of life and companionship was colored with discontent—Dorothy found the way out first, and I found it through her. . . . Christ to many people is an ideal. He was to me and it's only through this new conception that I've come to accept Him in a personal way, to see that there can be a personal religion that will fit in any person's life. I'm not an idealist; I'm practical, but I can see how the principles of this group can fit in every day life. Christ can give a sense of well being, can lend meaning to your life and provide a true sense of values.

Russell was followed by Dr. Buchman, who said:

Life changing on a colossal basis is the only hope left in the world today.

Buchman was followed by Sir Walter Windham, Reginald Holme, Marie Clarkson, and Malcom Ross of Oxford; then by Frau von Cramon of Germany; then by Dr. Frank Bladen, chief surgeon at the Henry Ford hospital in Detroit; then by Jimmie Watt, a former communist leader; then by George Wood of Aberdeen, Scotland; then by Ruth Buchanan of a well-known Virginia family; then by Miss Olive Jones, author of two Oxford Group books and former president of the National Educational Association; and then by Hanford Twitchell, a gentleman active in Sam Shoemaker's Calvary Church in New York.[4] All witnessed

---

[4] In Chapter 7, we will see that this same Hanford Twitchell possibly had a part in passing on to Bill Wilson some of the Oxford Group ideas he would have shared at the Akron meetings in 1933. Interestingly, a newspaper account of late 1934 shows that Dr. Shoemaker, Hanford Twitchell, and Rowland Hazard—who was to be a factor in Bill Wilson's story—all were in Cincinnati as part of an Oxford Group team and shared in local church pulpits in 1934 just as the 1933 team had done in Akron.

briefly. The news account continued, naming prominent Akron personages such as the Litchfields, Seiberlings, and Firestones, the family names of the famous rubber magnates, who were in the audience.

The *Akron Times-Press* for Friday, January 20, carried front page pictures of Russell Firestone, Dr. Buchman, Sir Walter, A. F. Holme, and Rev. Tunks taken just before what was termed "Akron's 'Dinner Jacket Revival.'" The story of the throngs that attended the first meeting said that guests listened to exhortations "to get right with God" from people in dinner jackets and evening gowns. It said they heard "witnesses" tell what the Oxford Group movement had done for them. Another article featured the "Akron Society" that had turned out for the Oxford Group meeting. It ran pictures of the socialites.

Both the *Akron Times-Press* and the *Akron Beacon Journal* for Friday contained detailed announcements of just which Oxford Group team members had been assigned to fill pulpits on Sunday in the Churches of Akron. The churches included Bethel and Wooster Avenue Reformed; Wooster, Trinity, Woodland, First, Firestone Park, and High Street M. E.; Goodyear, Second, and Arlington Street Baptist; North Hill United Brethren; Riverside Church of Christ; Oak Hill, Margaret Park and North Hill U.P.; Hudson, St. Andrew, and St. Paul Episcopal; Christ and Keninore Methodist; First Congregational; and Universalist. Speakers included those mentioned above as well as Kenaston Twitchell, Dr. Shoemaker's brother-in-law; Jim Newton, and Reverend Cleveland Hicks, who often led Bible studies at Oxford Group functions.

Another of the Friday articles, this one in the *Times-Press*, contained a few critiques by Akron clergymen. Rev. G. Taylor Wright, president of Akron Ministerial Association, said "no comment." Reverend Charles E. Liebegott of St. Paul's Lutheran Church said he could see nothing new in the preaching, that it "is a drawing room interpretation of religion and it doesn't seem to put enough emphasis on the works of Christ." He added, "The claims that it will save civilization are not in conformity with Scripture. The Bible says that the readjustment will not be made

until the second coming of Christ." Rev. O. A. Keach, pastor of First United Presbyterian Church, said, "I was very much impressed by last night's meeting. It is not a theological religion but an experimental one and it has fine possibilities." Rev. Walter F. Tunks, rector of Firestone's own church, St. Paul's Episcopal, said, "I was very much pleased with the response of the city.
. . . I have always been a great believer in the power of the Christian church, which has been working for centuries, and I am always willing to welcome any new influences. I am sure that most of the brethren in the city feel the same way."

Saturday's *Akron Beacon Journal* said on its front page, "Testimony Given By Firestones," adding "Oxford Group Crowds Grow As Members Tell Of 'Changed' Lives." It reported that by Friday, fully 1,800 people were accommodated in three meetings Friday night with even more anticipated for Saturday. Mrs. Russell Firestone was quoted as follows:

> I had grown weary of the task of running my own life and I was willing to let God run it. "He who loves me is he who keeps my commandments."

A host of other testimonials were briefly quoted, mentioning, for example, "God has given me power to help other people;" "things that don't follow the teachings of Jesus must go and of all these, perhaps the worst is selfishness, self-centeredness;" and "impotent Christians [are] people who are unwilling to take the message to others." The *Journal* contained comments on the meetings by a very large number of the members of Akron Protestant Clergy. The comments were mixed. Some simply said they had no opinion, didn't know a thing about it, or that the Oxford Group was probably as effective as 101 other religious denominations. Many others were "impressed" and thought the meetings a "helpful sign." There were more "society" pictures and a picture with Frank Buchman and a physician, Dr. Irene Gates, stating, "Religion is Fun."

By Monday, January 23, 1933, the *Akron Beacon Journal* was reporting that the majority of the Oxford Group members were departing, but that Dr. Buchman was leaving six team members in Akron. The paper also contained brief quotes as to Bud Firestone's talk at the Sunday church service he addressed in which Russell explained that "The Oxford group follows a simple Christian religion in which Christ becomes personal to the individual."

The Saturday *Times-Press* contained a very detailed account of Mrs. Russell Firestone's witness. She said:

> The power of God was an empty phrase to me. I believed in God as an abstract force and I did not have a personal God to whom I could turn until I came to know the Groups. The abstract God seemed to shut you off, but the personal God opens a person up. I was disillusioned with life. I faced the same problems that many people of my age, between 25 and 30, must face. I was coming up against the real realities of life and had begun to find that some of the ideals that I had brought from college were not practical. There was a restlessness inside me. I was struck by the complete faith of the Oxford Group. I came to realize what the power of God stood for. I wanted God to take my life and I asked God to take my life. I began to read the Bible. I had a course in college concerning the Bible and knew all the historical connections but I didn't understand it. Now I read it like a novel before I go to bed and grasp what it means. "He who loves me is he who keeps my commandments," the Bible says. That was one of the things I found. . . . I found that my self-centeredness was my biggest fault. . . . My conversion to the Group has meant a completely new relation with my husband. . . . And now wherever I go I am going to go where God wants me to go.

The *Times-Press* for Saturday reported that Mr. and Mrs. F. A. Seiberling, "Stan Hywet Hall," would be entertaining Dr. Frank Buchman and other Oxford Group team members at their home on Sunday evening. The Sunday edition quoted Russell Firestone as stating, "Christ has got to be in business or we might as well say 'school's out.'" He said he faced spiritual bankruptcy until 16 months before and added about business that "we must get it on an honest, Christian basis." There was an article featuring a picture of young Communist leader, Jimmy Watt, who had turned to the Oxford Group, been converted, and become a devoted worker for the group. Another article said:

> The sins which members of the Group said they had seen eliminated included many prevalent in Akron. One man had been disagreeable to his wife, another had not given her her share of the family income, one woman had enjoyed breaking hearts, a young man had been addicted to drink and swearing, and many had been selfish.

The concluding *Times-Press* article on Monday said that six Oxford Group members were holding a meeting on Monday night to give instructions on how attendees should go about becoming "life-changers." It said a "house-party," one of the features of the Group's operations, probably would be held in the Akron vicinity soon. Harvey Firestone, Sr., was quoted as saying of the Group:

> It has brought religion in a very vivid way. It is through the Groups that I have been brought a very great happiness. It has brought my family closer to God.

Thus ended a veritable blitzkrieg of news on the Oxford Group party, covering everything from testimonials at the large meetings, sharing in the pulpits, small meetings, articles on Oxford Group principles, quotes from Oxford Group leaders and from Akronites, commentaries by the Akron clergy, tidbits on the society dinners and teas that accompanied the event, feature articles on particular Oxford Group members, and personal comments from several members of the Firestone family.

The Significance of the Events

And what was the relevance of all this to A.A.'s Akron genesis?

People had been recovering from alcoholism for centuries as the result of spiritual or religious experiences. That is what Dr. Carl Jung wrote to Bill Wilson a good many years after A.A. had begun.[5] In fact, by the year 1900, many doctors and specialists in alcoholism were convinced that religious conversion was the most effective of all cures for alcoholism.[6] As one of the people whom Bill Wilson called a founder of A.A. apparently put it, the only cure for "dipsomania" was "religiomania."[7] So it probably did not jump-start either the Akron medical fraternity or the Akron clergy to hear that Russell Firestone and other Oxford Group witnesses were attesting deliverance from alcoholism as the result of Christian conversion experiences.

The events were nonetheless a special part of A.A.'s roots. Critically important elements of what were to become part of A.A.'s program were being broadcast in a special way. They were addressed to the very community where A.A.'s founders were to meet some two-and-a-half years later and find themselves individually involved in Oxford Group fellowships and mutually interested in the Oxford Group program for conversion experiences. The meetings of 1933 were attractive to those people in Akron who were, by the grace of God, to play key roles in the subsequent founding of A.A. Let's look at some of the attraction elements.

First, though it seemed to have been little spoken of in the press, many in Akron were apparently aware of Bud Firestone's

---

[5] See *Pass It On* (New York: Alcoholics Anonymous World Services, Inc., 1984), pp. 381-385; Big Book, pp. 26-28.

[6] See Bill Pittman, *AA The Way It Began* (Seattle: Glen Abbey Books, 1988), pp. 72-79; G. B. Cutten, *The Psychology of Alcoholism* (New York: Scribner's & Sons, 1907). pp. 277-317.

[7] Professor William James was so quoted in Pittman, *AA The Way It Began*, p. 72. See also, Cutten, *The Psychology of Alcoholism*, p. 280.

drinking problems. Second, it was very clear to these people and to those attending the meetings that Bud Firestone was sober and had changed. Third, the sincerity of the Firestone family's testimonials and the extent of this powerful family's gratitude was manifest. Fourth, the presence of Dr. Buchman himself and of such a large contingent of Oxford Group members from the East and from Europe was news and was no doubt impressive to all of Akron. Fifth, the meetings and the newspaper articles gave explicit details on the nature of the Oxford Group program. The details were there for all to see; so Akron got a very real exposure to the nature of Frank Buchman's "life-changing" program. Sixth, some very key people in the founding of A.A. were in attendance at the meetings. And those people had needs that were addressed by the testimonials: Henrietta Seiberling was downtrodden with family problems, and the Oxford Group members held out hope. The Firestones attested to family problems that they had overcome through religious experiences. Anne Smith was desperately seeking help for herself, her family, and Dr. Robert H. Smith, because of Dr. Bob's seemingly hopeless alcoholism. And the story of Russell Firestone himself held out hope for her in the Oxford Group fellowship. Clarace Williams and Delphine Weber, friends of Henrietta and of Anne, were present and were also attracted to the Akron Oxford Group. They were to be instrumental in providing meeting places where the "alcoholic squad of the Oxford Group" would later hold their meetings. Most importantly, the "key man" strategy of the Oxford Group unquestionably produced an impact in Akron. The presence of so many important witnesses, the support of so many prominent Akronites, and the acceptance of Oxford Group people in most church pulpits provided integrity to the Oxford Group's mission. All these elements attracted the *Akron* "founders" of A.A. to the Oxford Group program which was to become the principal part of A.A.'s own spiritual program of action as that was developed in the Akron crucible.

Of equal importance, perhaps, were the number of Oxford Group expressions that were emblazoned in the newspapers and in the testimonials. These phrases were to become very familiar to alcoholics.[8] One way or another, the Oxford Group expressions found their way into A.A.'s literature and recovery program. Thus the papers mentioned the "power of God" with frequency.[9] "Selfishness" and "self-centeredness" were proclaimed to be the root of man's spiritual malady.[10] Confession of faults and the familiar, relevant verse from James 5:16 were mentioned.[11] Sharing was given prominence.[12] Much was written on Quiet Time and Prayer.[13] Giving one's life to God was a frequently-quoted phrase.[14] Honesty was a keynote.[15] Guidance was also important.[16] Service and helpfulness to others was stressed.[17] That God was a "personal God" was frequently mentioned.[18] And speakers were quoted as mentioning "willingness"—a word which

---

[8] In December of 1954, Bill Wilson taped an interview he had with Wally and Annabelle G., two Akron A.A. pioneers, who had had great success in helping alcoholics to recovery. Bill introduced the interview by saying of the two: "They were the pioneers in the A.A. work here in Akron since the very early days, and it was in their house that so many people were rehabilitated after having been taken from the hospital here in Akron. Under the tutelage and inspiration of these folks, probably more people have recovered than in any A.A. home in the world. They were the first to make it a success." Wally G. said in the interview, "I had read in the newspapers a great deal about the meetings of the Oxford Group here at the Mayflower. . . . I was interested in the mechanics of the thing because I knew I had to make it work. We pretty much acted as though these things were so and finally they became so—we tried it as an experiment and you knew it had to work."

[9] Compare Big Book, pp. 52, 46, 68.

[10] Compare Big Book, pp. 62, 61, 64, 67, 14.

[11] See James 5:16: "Confess your faults one to another, and pray for one another, that ye may be healed. The effectual fervent prayer of a righteous man availeth much." Compare *Pass It On*, p. 128; Big Book, p. xvi.

[12] Compare Big Book, p. xxii.

[13] Compare *DR. BOB and the Good Oldtimers* (New York: Alcoholics Anonymous World Services, Inc., 1980), p. 86, 71; Big Book, pp. 85-88.

[14] Compare Big Book, pp. 59, 60.

[15] Compare Big Book, p. 58.

[16] Compare Big Book, pp. 85-87.

[17] Compare Big Book, pp. 14, 20.

[18] Compare Big Book, p. 10.

was later to become a key part of A.A. language.[19] Finally, there was recognition by the speakers of the importance of God's power and presence in one's life.[20]

These, then, were some of the important foundation stones for A.A.'s program that were laid by the presence of an evangelistic Oxford Group team in Akron, Ohio, in January of 1933:

1. Witness to religious experiences that produced victory over alcohol and spiritual problems rooted in self-centeredness.

2. Integrity lent to the witnessing by the presence and support of influential members of the business community, society, and clergy.

3. Familiarity with basic Oxford Group life-changing terms and procedures gained by the Akron community through the widespread publicity.

4. The presence at the Akron events of several people who were to play key roles in A.A.'s birthing process, based on their own conviction that the Oxford Group message spoke to their needs—T. Henry and Clarace Williams, Henrietta Seiberling, Anne Ripley Smith, and even Reverend Walter F. Tunks.

5. The stimulus the events gave to Akron's A.A. progenitors, T. Henry and Clarace, Henrietta, Anne, and Dr. Bob, to bone up on the Bible, the spiritual literature of the day, and Oxford Group practices that were all to play a major role in shaping A.A.'s Big Book, Twelve Steps, and Fellowship.

---

[19] Compare Big Book, pp. 47, 76, 570.

[20] Compare Big Book, pp. 51, 55-56, 14.

Part 2

A.A.'s Akron Progenitors and Their Major Contributions

3

An Overview

The author and many another real, recovered alcoholic can attest from vivid personal experience to the confused, frightened, forgetful mind that exists in the early days of acute withdrawal and even in later days of delayed withdrawal from alcohol. Such a mind is hardly capable, by itself, of assimilating or producing complex new ideas of a medical, religious, or even experiential nature; and it seems likely that the minds of Bill W. and Dr. Bob, in early sobriety, were no exception. Yet each of the two men was possessed of a fine mind, a good education, and substantial professional training—Bill in the law, and Dr. Bob in medicine. And each man developed substantial intellectual resources as he moved deeper into alcoholism. The two founders of A.A. were blessed with major assistance from sober people as they wound their way toward the recovery path they developed.

Their Qualifications

In New York, Bill had received much help not only from Dr. William D. Silkworth at Towns Hospital, but also from Reverend Samuel Moor Shoemaker, Jr., Shoemaker's dedicated staff, members of the Calvary vestry, and Bill's other Oxford Group business team friends. In Akron, Dr. Bob *and* Bill were fed spiritual knowledge by the clear, sober-thinking minds of T. Henry Williams, a non-alcoholic business executive and inventor; Clarace Williams, an Ottowa University graduate who had also trained for missionary work; Henrietta Seiberling, a Vassar College graduate, who had come from a well-educated family and had studied psychology; and Anne Ripley Smith (Dr. Bob's wife), whose family had been highly successful in business and who had, herself, graduated from Wellesley and been a teacher. In addition, Bill and Dr. Bob had become vested, directly or indirectly, with some of the ideas of Professor William James, Dr. Carl G. Jung, the writings of leading Christian spokesmen, the literature of Oxford Group adherents, and certainly with many basic ideas in the Bible itself.

The Oxford Group Literature

There was a formidable array of Oxford Group literature, by Sam Shoemaker, and by other Oxford Group writers, that was available to and used by all of Akron's progenitors—T. Henry, Clarace, Henrietta, Anne, Dr. Bob, and Bill—as they assembled together in Akron to help alcoholics and their families. In our book, *The Oxford Group & Alcoholics Anonymous*, we list and discuss in some detail the Oxford Group literature which was made available in America through the Oxford Group bookstore in the basement of Sam Shoemaker's Calvary House in New York.[1] We here set forth Calvary House's Oxford Group Literature list for the spring of 1939 (without prices), which we discuss in more detail in Appendix One. The list is just as it was published in the March, 1939 issue of *The Calvary Evangel*:

---

[1] Dick B., *The Oxford Group & Alcoholics Anonymous* (Seattle: Glen Abbey Books, 1992), pp. 81-84.

Oxford Group Literature

BOOKS EVERYONE SHOULD READ

Inspired Youth . . . . Olive Jones
For Sinners Only . . . . A. J. Russell
I Was A Pagan . . . . V. C. Kitchen
Life Began Yesterday . . . . Stephen Foot
The Church Can Save the World . . . S. M. Shoemaker

INFORMATION ON THE SPREAD OF
CHRISTIAN REVOLUTION

The God Who Speaks . . . . B. H. Streeter
Children of the Second Birth . . . . S. M. Shoemaker
Twice-Born Ministers . . . . S. M. Shoemaker
If I Be Lifted Up . . . . S. M. Shoemaker
Confident Faith . . . . S. M. Shoemaker
The Gospel According to You . . S. M. Shoemaker
He that Cometh . . . . Geoffrey Allen
Inspired Children . . . . Olive Jones
What Is the Oxford Group . . . . A Layman with a
                                     Notebook
Religion that Works . . . . S. M. Shoemaker
The Conversion of the Church . . . S. M. Shoemaker
National Awakening . . . . S. M. Shoemaker
Venture of Belief . . . . Philip M. Brown
Realizing Religion . . . . S. M. Shoemaker
Church in Action . . . . Jack C. Winslow
Why I Believe in the Oxford Group . Jack C. Winslow
Soul Surgery . . . . Howard Walter
When Man Listens . . . . Cecil Rose
Guidance of God . . . . Eleanor Forde
New Leadership . . . . Lean & Martin
New Enlistment . . . . Wilfrid Holmes-
                                     Walker

Twenty-Eight Oxford Group Principles That Influenced Alcoholics Anonymous

There were in place in Akron and thoroughly discussed, in the Oxford Group writings of the 1920's and 1930's, some twenty-eight Oxford Group concepts we believe influenced Alcoholics Anonymous.[2] We have set them out in some detail in Appendix Two, with appropriate references, because they bear on the principles Akron's progenitors were studying, discussing, and contributing. We list them below in outline form. The author found from his research that the language and concepts in the 28 principles can be found in the language of the day that was used in Akron. The twenty-eight concepts, grouped for easier understanding, are:

In the beginning, God

1.   *God*—Biblical descriptions of Him, such as Creator, Maker, Almighty God, Lord, Father, Love, Spirit, Living God.

2.   *God Has a Plan*—His will for man—and provides definite, accurate information for the individual who wants the plan fulfilled.

---

[2] See discussion in Dick B., *The Oxford Group & Alcoholics Anonymous*, pp. 111-295.

3. *Man's Chief End*—To do God's Will, thereby receiving the blessings God promises to those who align their lives with His will.

4. *Belief*—We must start with the belief that God IS.

Sin—Estrangement from God—The Barrier of Self

5. *Sin is a reality*—The selfishness and self-centeredness that blocks man from God and from others.

Finding or Rediscovering God

6. *Surrender*—The turning point which makes it possible for man to have a relationship with God by surrendering his will, ego, and sins to God.

7. *Soul-Surgery*—The "art" or way which enables man through Confidence, Confession, Conviction, Conversion, and Conservation (the 5 C's) to have the sin or spiritual disease cured.

8. *Life-change*—The result in which man, through a spiritual experience, becomes God-centered instead of self-centered, and focuses on helping others.

The Path They Followed To Establish a Relationship With God

9. *Decision*—The action by which man verbalizes his surrender and gives in to God, saying, essentially, "Thy will be done."

10. *Self-examination*—A "moral" inventory in which man takes stock of his sins and their consequences.

11.   *Confession*—Sharing with God and another the inventory results.

12.   *Conviction*—Readiness to change resulting from man's conviction that he has sinned and that Christ miraculously can cure.

13.   *Conversion*—The New Birth—Change, namely, that which occurs when man gives himself to God, is regenerated, has part of God's nature imparted to him, and finds the barrier of sin gone.

14.   *Restitution*—Righting the wrong and enabling man to cut the cord of sin that binds him to the past.

Jesus Christ

15.   *Jesus Christ*—The source of power as the Divine Redeemer and Way-Shower by whose transforming power man can be changed.

Spiritual Growth-Continuance

16.   *Conservation*—Continuance as an idea, by which man maintains and grows in his life of grace.

17.   *Daily surrender*—A process in which man engages in daily self-examination and surrender to get rid of newly accumulated sin and selfishness.

18.   *Guidance*—The walk by faith in which the Holy Spirit gives Divine Guidance to a life that is changed from sin to God.

19.   *The Four Absolutes*—Christ's standards, the standards of absolute honesty, purity, unselfishness, and love by

which man's life can be tested for harmony with God's will.

20. *Quiet Time*—A period in which man can receive Divine Guidance and be sensitive to the sway of the Spirit.

21. *Bible Study*—Meditation which enables man daily to feed his soul on God's revelation of His Will in the written Word.

22. *Prayer*—Talking to God.

23. *Listening to God for Leading Thoughts and Writing Down Guidance Received*—The means of receiving revelation of God's particular will.

24. *Checking*—Testing thoughts to be sure they represent God's Guidance and not just self-deception.

The Spiritual Experience or Awakening

25. *Knowledge of God's will*—Attaining, with the Guidance of the Holy Spirit, a knowledge of God's Universal Will as revealed in the Bible, and receiving knowledge of His particular Will through obedience to His Universal Will.

26. *God-consciousness*—The total change resulting from the experience of God when His will is known, lived, and witnessed.

Fellowship with God and Believers,
and Witness by Life and Word

27. *Fellowship*—The fellowship of the Holy Spirit in which believers maintain fellowship with God and mutually sacrifice to win others to the fellowship of the love of God revealed by Jesus Christ.

28. *Witness by Life and Word*—Sharing with others by personal evangelism the fruits of the life changed and the proof of God's forgiveness and power.

Dr. Bob and His Wife, Anne

Dr. Bob studied and recommended to the alcoholics with whom he worked, an immense amount of literature, including the Bible, Oxford Group writings, and other Christian literature. In our book, *Dr. Bob's Library*, we discussed in detail the books Dr. Bob read.[3] In Appendix Three of this book, we have listed, with appropriate references, not only the books that are discussed in *Dr. Bob's Library*, but also a number of additional books we have since, through further research, found to have been a part of Dr. Bob's reading.

Finally, there was a large amount of work done by Dr. Bob's wife, Anne Ripley Smith, as she read the Bible, Oxford Group books, and other Christian literature between 1933 and 1939. She prepared and kept a workbook in which she recorded the names of the books she had read and was recommending, the Bible verses she stressed, the Oxford Group principles she had learned, and her own ideas as to how these resources should be utilized.[4] Research

---

[3] Dick B., *Dr. Bob's Library* (West Virginia: The Bishop of Books, 1992).

[4] Dick B., *Anne Smith's Spiritual Workbook* (Corte Madera, CA: Good Book Publishing Company, 1992).

done by the author since the writing of *Anne Smith's Spiritual Workbook* has now established that Anne Smith read the contents of her workbook to many of the alcoholics she helped in Akron.[5]

Lois Wilson's Oxford Group Notes

Also, as we've discussed elsewhere, Lois Wilson kept a tiny "Oxford Group Notebook" of sorts. The author recently found this notebook with the help of Paul L., archivist at Stepping Stones, during the author's visit to Bill and Lois Wilson's Stepping Stones home at in Bedford Hills, New York. Lois's notebook, along with entries in Lois's diary for 1937, illustrates the Oxford Group practices and principles that were being studied and/or utilized in the Wilson household during the 1934-1939 period.

Lois stated, in *Lois Remembers*, in her memorandum of the period 1935-1941:

> After throwing my shoe, recognizing my need for the Oxford Group, I became quite pious for a period. When later Bill and I travel to spark new A.A. groups, I speak at many gatherings of wives and tell of my spiritual need. Annie S. and other wives of early AAs do the same.[6]

---

[5] Dennis C., an A.A. historian, informed the author during an interview in New Britain, Connecticut, in August, 1992, that John R., an Akron A.A. oldtimer, had told him that Anne Smith read from her spiritual workbook to the people she helped. See also, Mary C. Darrah, *Sister Ignatia* (Chicago: Loyola University Press, 1992), pp. 115-116; Bob Smith and Sue Smith Windows, *Children of the Healer* (Illinois: Parkside Publishing Company, 1992), p. 29.

[6] *Lois Remembers* (New York: Al-Anon Family Group Headquarters, Inc. 1987), p. 197.

Bill's Synopsis of What He Found

Bill Wilson put the Akron situation in context with these words
which we have taken from a taped interview he made with T.
Henry and Clarace Williams:

> I learned a great deal from you people [T. Henry and Clarace
> Williams], from the Smiths themselves, and from Henrietta
> [Seiberling]. I hadn't looked in the Bible, up to this time, at all.
> You see, I had the [conversion] experience first and then this
> rushing around to help drunks and nothing happened.[7]

With this background material, let us now take a very close
look at Akron's six progenitors in a way we do not believe has
been previously done. Here we will endeavor to set forth the
spiritual resources these people possessed and pooled together in
the formative years of A.A. at Akron.

---

[7] From the transcript of Bill Wilson's taped interview with T. Henry and Clarace
Williams on December 12, 1954, which transcript is on file in A.A. Archives in New
York.

4

T. Henry and Clarace Williams

A Brief Biography of T. Henry

T. Henry Williams was born in South Woodstock, Connecticut, on August 29, 1886. He often proudly said he was a descendent of the American colonist, Roger Williams. At the age of nine, T. Henry moved to Putnam, Connecticut and there attended grade school and high school. He worked at some truck farms and began a lifelong interest in photography. It was in this community that he learned his trade of pattern maker, took a drafting course at the YMCA, and began to work at a foundry in connection with the manufacture of rubber machinery. One morning in his high school years, he felt prompted to go to a Baptist church. He joined its Sunday school class, and later joined the church itself. He used to go to a city mission as part of his church work and did this for two or three years before he graduated from high school. He also began studying the Bible at Woodstock, a little town nearby, where he was taught by a famous Bible teacher, L. Ammidown. He maintained his interest in the Bible and church work for the rest of his life. T. Henry never drank, but at an early age, he became concerned over the plight of those he had observed to have drinking problems.[1]

T. Henry married his first wife, Bertha, in Connecticut; and the couple had one child, their daughter, Dorothy. T. Henry, Bertha, and Dorothy came to Akron in 1915 where they lived for five or six years until Bertha died of the flu and pneumonia in early 1920. Williams took a position with the drafting department of the Goodyear Tire and Rubber Company. He became a deacon of a large downtown Baptist church in Akron. He taught a young man's class in the church. When the church needed a "young folks worker who would take charge of religious education," Williams voted for a young girl (Clarace) who was to become his wife.

Williams later worked at the Adamson Machine Company where he met his future partners; and these men formed the Akron Rubber Mold Company. T. Henry designed the famous "watchcase" mold for manufacturing tires. In his own words, he "did a great deal in the development of machinery in the rubber industry."

In late 1921, Clarace and T. Henry were married. He briefly joined a small branch Baptist church in Akron, but then was invited, by the pastor of a Methodist Church that was near to his home, to join that church. And he did so. He remained a member of the Methodist church, taught Sunday School there, and regularly attended church there with Clarace for the rest of his life.

In 1930, he designed the family home at 676 Palisades Drive in Akron; and this home later became the first meeting place for

---

[1] The material in this chapter was obtained from several sources, including: 1) A taped interview of T. Henry and Clarace Williams done by Bill Wilson on December 12, 1954—a transcript of the tape being on file in A.A. archives in New York; 2) A taped interview of T. Henry's daughter that was made by T. Willard Hunter, Oxford Group leader and writer. A transcript of that interview is part of the files of Gail L., Akron A.A. archivist, who made the records available to the author during Founders Day events in June, 1992; 3) The author's personal interview with Mr. and Mrs. James Newton at Fort Myers Beach, Florida, in August, 1992; 4) The author's personal correspondence and interviews with Dorothy Culver, particularly his telephone interview with her at her home in El Dorado Hills, California, on September 25, 1992; 5) Several letters written by Dorothy Culver to A.A. historians.

A.A. Group Number One when it was still part of the Oxford Group. A member of T. Henry's church built the home; and it was finally left to T. Henry's church for a parsonage.

About 1932, the Depression caught up with the Williams family. T. Henry's salary was cut in half, and he couldn't pay his bills. He had the feeling that if he died, the insurance company would pay off his mortgage; but he hadn't stopped to think of what would happen to his wife, Clarace, and his daughter, Dorothy, if that were to occur. Meanwhile, Clarace Williams had met the Oxford Group when they first came to Akron in 1932. However T. Henry was not yet ready. As he put it, "I, being a good church member, didn't think I needed anything like that because I was saved already." A year later, however, he came to the conclusion that he did need something. And when the Oxford Group team came to Akron in January of 1933 for the much touted Firestone events, T. Henry commenced to become active in their meetings. It was very common in those days for Oxford Group people to "swap" Oxford Group literature; and T. Henry said he had read some of it. He said one of the stories showed him just like he looked in the glass. It told of a particular man who had surrendered his problems to God. And it was then that T. Henry realized he had a real problem in the house on Palisades Drive.

At that point, T. Henry said, "God, I'm giving this house to you. It's your house. You can do with it what you want. If you want me to sign the mortgage back to the insurance company and give them the house, that's okay. If you want me to stay in it, you'll have to show me how, because I don't see any hopes of it. It's all I have. It's yours. I'm going to cease worrying. I'm going to depend on you and whatever else there is in my life that's wrong, I want you to help me straighten that out."

He said that, after this decision, he commenced to find a new reality in religion and a new reality in loving. He said he had taken his church as a fire insurance policy that only paid off after death. Instead, he found out through the Oxford Group that he didn't have to wait until death—that he could get a real forgiveness of the thing that was wrong with his life. He said that the thing was selfishness and pride. He said he commenced to let God have a chance to work in his life, and that this came about through other people.

The Oxford Group in Akron were having regular meetings at the Mayflower Hotel, and there was just one group. Doc, Anne, Henrietta, T. Henry, and Clarace went and listened to the stories of other people as to what happened in their lives. People would have a victory over something in their life and tell about it. Williams said it was these stories that hit him. He said when something happens in somebody else's life, it gives you an idea that it can also happen in your life. He began to see himself as in a glass, how selfish he was. And he said that, little by little, he commenced to find an answer to the selfishness in his life.

Just after Bill Wilson came to Akron in 1935, Clarace Williams had felt it was right for her to go to Oxford for a houseparty. The Oxford Group people had a meeting at the Akron YMCA; and practically all of the active, Oxford Group people were there to see Clarace off. T. Henry began to feel sorry for himself because there were not the finances for both T. Henry and Clarace to go.

Then the thought came to him, "Why be sorry for yourself? You don't have to go to Europe to get an inspiration. God can speak to you just as well here alone in this house if you're willing to let him." He said he quit feeling sorry for himself and, within a few days, began thinking of what he could do for Ernie G., an alcoholic. He said he was having a morning quiet time, and there came a voice, just as if somebody were standing behind him, saying, "Why don't you do something for Ernie?" The thought came three mornings in a row. After the third morning, T. Henry went to see Ernie G.'s family; and because of the follow-through, Ernie came into the Oxford Group fellowship. T. Henry began working with other alcoholics, and was present when Bill D. (A.A. Number Three) made his surrender at the hospital.

T. Henry's version of the beginning of the Oxford Group meetings at his home seems to differ from that of Henrietta Seiberling. T. Henry said meetings eventually ceased to meet at the Mayflower. He thought it was partially because of the fact that the cost of the room was high, and members decided they wouldn't meet there any longer. He said many who knew the Williams couple said, "Why can't we come over to your house?" And, he said, "They've been coming there ever since."

T. Henry died suddenly on June 17, 1967. The Akron Area Inter-Group News (of Alcoholics Anonymous) wrote this at the time of his death:

> He had no alcoholic problem himself, but he left a rich heritage of service to his fellow man, devotion to duty, love of God and neighbor, and loyalty to high principles which time cannot touch nor age crumble.

In a talk he made to many groups, T. Henry had these things to say:

> Our conception of God makes all the difference in the world as to our attitude toward others. Either we accept the fact that there is a God and put Him on the throne in our lives and community or we deny His existence and climb up and usurp the throne for ourself. . . .
>
> I like to think of good will as a bridge built between people. It must have foundations or it will fall just at the time it is most needed. There are four fundamental principles which I have found we must use if the bridge is to be stable. First—uncompromising truth, honor, honesty, in dealing with myself, family and the world. Next comes purity in thought, motive and action. The third, and perhaps the hardest for me, or at least the one I have fought hardest to attain is unselfishness. It just sticks out all over me and as soon as I get it licked in one area, it shows up somewhere else. The fourth is love. I came from a family where each looked after self. They got what they could and never said thank you for anything. There was no music, no little courtesies, and very little social life, and no

church activities. I have had to learn to love people and to care for them and their needs.[2]

Clarace

And now we turn to Clarace Williams's story. She began it, in her interview with Bill Wilson, by stating that she went to Kansas City and got a job with Montgomery Ward, her first job. She went to church there and, through her church, was sent to a Baptist missionary school in Chicago to do definite work in a Christian field. She had been thinking of doing church work and specialized in the field of religious education. While in Chicago, she had a chance to finish going through college. And she did this at Ottowa University, a Christian school in Ottowa, Kansas. Upon graduation, she wrote the president of the Baptist missionary training school and asked if there were any church positions open. The president informed her that there was one in Akron and gave Clarace the name of the church. She wrote and sent her picture and was hired to work with young people in the church and to do secretarial work there as well.

Clarace was several years older than T. Henry. About a year and a half after the death of T. Henry's first wife, Bertha, he and Clarace were married. And Clarace went to work in the church as a volunteer. One day, she came into the church office and said, "You know, it seems to me my life is so superficial. I'm not doing the thing I feel God wants me to do." She said that though she had had special training as to receiving guidance, she did not get an answer as to what to do with her life. But then she spoke with a lady in the church who was the widow of a minister and said, "If there were some way that two or three people in this church and in every church could get together and think through and get

---

[2] Copy of speech sent to the author by Dorothy Culver on September 22, 1992.

guidance as to what God really wants us to do, we could have a force that was interested in a thing that would really count."

It was then that Clarace heard that Oxford Group Founder Frank Buchman was coming to Akron with 300 overseas people. She went down to hear what they had to say. She heard a woman speak who was in a position similar to hers in one of the big churches in London. Clarace said she wasn't able to do what she wanted to do and felt God wanted her to do because she was afraid to try to talk to people about Christ. She said she was afraid they would laugh at her or argue with her. She had been unable to get over that fear complex, thinking that if they laughed at her or argued with her, she'd be through forever. But the lady in the Oxford Group team said, "Never argue with anybody. You tell them what God has meant to you, and they can't laugh about that, nor can they argue about that." Convinced of that, Clarace said she got absolutely released from her fear.

In 1935, Clarace went to Oxford and learned better how to carry on witnessing work. She said that when she and T. Henry built their home, the first thing they did was to dedicate it to God. She said that every time they wanted to make a change in the home, they asked themselves if it was going to help carry on their work. And, she said, it was on that basis that they tried to carry on in their home. She said requests came for them to open their home for Oxford Group meetings; that for a time between the Mayflower Hotel meetings and coming to the Williams home, Oxford Group adherents met in homes throughout the city; and that they finally gravitated to the Williams home.

Clarace said that Bob and Anne and Henrietta Seiberling were among the people who came to the Mayflower Hotel meetings and that they continued to attend. She said that when the Group first commenced to realize what Dr. Bob's problem was, he had advanced from the place where he was drunk every night to the place where maybe it was two weeks or three weeks or many weeks between drunks. He had slowed down, but hadn't quite found the answer until Bill Wilson came. Clarace remarked to Bill, "You helped clinch the deal."

The Home They Offered in Service

T. Henry and Clarace had these things to say about Oxford Group meetings and practices and the use of their home:

1. On Mondays, they would hold what they called a "set-up" meeting. They got together those who felt they had a part and felt responsibility for it. They would think through who was going to come and how they might be affected. In other words, there were certain people just out of the hospital, and they would know these people would be coming. They would try to plan who would be the best one to lead the meeting. They would sit down and have some guidance and direction as to what to put together for the meeting. Sometimes it would be the people who were present who were selected to lead, and sometimes somebody else. If necessary, they would call people and ask them to prepare to take a certain part and be willing to give, keeping the new person in mind.

2. As to the regular Wednesday meetings, Clarace said, "Well, the person who was going to lead the meeting, he took something. He used a little book for quiet time every morning. It was *The Upper Room* at that time.[3] He used something at the meeting from that or something else that appealed to him as a basis for the meeting. As a theme. Sometimes we used *My Utmost For His Highest* for the people who were a little further along.[4] Another thing we used a lot was 'As a Man Thinketh in his heart, so is he.'[5] Then we'd stop and

---

[3] See Appendix Four for an excerpt from this daily Bible devotional.

[4] See Appendix Five for an excerpt from this daily Bible devotional.

[5] It is probable that Clarace here referred to the pamphlet by James Allen, *As A Man Thinketh* (New York: Peter Pauper Press, n.d.). The theme of the pamphlet is taken from
(continued...)

have a quiet time, and then different people would tell something out of their own experience."

3. T. Henry added, "There was one other thing. It usually happened that after the meeting was over, or sometimes before, we would take the new man upstairs. A group of men would ask him to surrender his life to God and start in to really live up to the four standards and go out and help the other man who needed help. The standards were absolute honesty, courage [sic], unselfishness, and love. Very often the surrender followed the meeting. Then they went up and several of the boys would pray together, and the newcomer would make up his own prayer, asking God to take the alcohol out of his life. When he was through, he would say, 'Thank you for taking it out of my life.'"

4. Clarace said that they emphasized the quiet time every morning. She pointed out that some of the surrenders were done in the hospital. She said they always planned for having something on Saturday night—the night that people needed it. She said they had a party, sometimes at their place or someplace else, with plenty of food and lots of coffee.

T. Henry's daughter, Dorothy, said that the Oxford Group had a profound influence on his life. She said that through the Oxford Group meetings and the people he met, he became more sure of himself. His closest friends were in the Group. Of particular importance to the early meetings was the size of the Williams home. Meetings were often held in a basement recreation room.

---

[5] (...continued)
the verse in Proverbs 23:7, "For as he thinketh in his heart, so is he." The pamphlet was strongly recommended by Dr. Bob for reading by the alcoholics with whom he worked. See Dick B., *Dr. Bob's Library* (West Virginia: The Bishop of Books, 1992), p. 56.

Next to that room was a large furnace room where boxes of Oxford Group books and pamphlets were spread out on tables. Oxford Group people, including the alcoholics and their wives, would move from the recreation room meetings to the furnace room book tables and pick up books and literature to be read. Sometimes meetings were held in the large living room upstairs; and surrenders were often conducted, for privacy purposes, upstairs in a room which contained T. Henry's office and regular library. Over and over, those who knew Mr. and Mrs. Williams said they were struck by the compassion and love showered on the people who came to their home. It was common for others to remark that everyone who met the couple felt enriched and blessed.[6]

Summary of Their Contributions

Very little has been written about the precise contributions made by Mr. and Mrs. Williams to the early AAs. But certain general points are clear:

1. T. Henry and Clarace were participants in the Oxford Group meetings that took place in Akron after the events of 1933. T. Henry participated in Oxford Group houseparties and in the Oxford Group business team with Jim Newton. In fact,

---

[6] Remarks of this nature can be found frequently in A.A.'s own literature. See *Alcoholics Anonymous Comes of Age* (New York: Alcoholics Anonymous World Services, Inc., 1957), p. 141; *DR. BOB and the Good Oldtimers* (New York: Alcoholics Anonymous World Services, 1980), pp. 78, 141, 161, 217; *Pass It On* (New York: Alcoholics Anonymous World Services, Inc., 1984), p. 145; *The Language of the Heart* (New York: The A.A. Grapevine, Inc., 1988), p. 357. See also the recollections by Dr. Bob's son, "Smitty," in Bob Smith and Sue Smith Windows, *Children of the Healer* (Illinois: Parkside Publishing Corporation, 1992), p. 123. Jim Newton and his wife, Eleanor Newton made similar comments about the fine qualities of the Williams couple during the author's extensive interview with the Newtons in Florida in August, 1992. Both of the Newtons knew T. Henry and Clarace very well.

T. Henry remained very active with the Group throughout his life.[7]

2. It was Mr. and Mrs. Williams who made their home available to Henrietta Seiberling so that something could be done to have an Oxford Group meeting for Dr. Bob.

3. When the Group started meeting on Wednesdays at the Williams home, T. Henry was one of the leaders. His daughter, Dorothy, recalls cooking a dinner for Dr. Bob, Anne, Bill, Lois, T. Henry and two of Lois's friends from New York who had brought her to Akron in the summer of 1935. Clarace was at Oxford at the time.

4. Later, T. Henry and Dr. Bob "teamed" the meetings.

5. The leaders, including T. Henry, would hold set-up meetings on Mondays to determine whose stories would best help the alcoholic newcomers and who could best lead the meetings.

6. These leaders sought guidance from God as to how the meeting on Wednesday should be conducted.

7. On meeting night, T. Henry often took care of the prayers with which the meeting was opened and closed.

8. He was one of those who would take a newcomer upstairs after a meeting and ask him to surrender his life to God, to start in living up to the four absolutes, and to begin helping other new men who needed it.

9. Then Mr. and Mrs. Williams would make their home available on Wednesdays for at least an hour-and-a-half for the social part of the evening.

---

[7] Interview of Jim Newton by the author, Fort Myers Beach, Florida, August, 1992.

10. And the Williams couple were very much a part of planning parties at their home and elsewhere for Saturday nights with plenty of food and lots of coffee—"the night people needed it."

11. Mr. and Mrs. Williams may have borne the brunt of those in the Oxford Group who apparently objected to time being spent on alcoholics.

Whatever additional, needed historical research may unearth about T. Henry and Clarace Williams and their contribution to the founding of Alcoholics Anonymous, they certainly provided the physical quarters for meetings that taught the program. They contributed their warmth and loving personalities to people with low self-esteem. They were knowledgeable about the Bible, the Oxford Group, and Christian literature. As we discussed in our chapter on Jim Newton, T. Henry participated in the work of the Oxford Group business team. Its members included men who were traveling and working closely with Dr. Frank Buchman and Reverend Sam Shoemaker. And they frequently "swapped" Oxford Group books and pamphlets as they read them and as new literature came out.[8]

Isadore K., a very dear friend of T. Henry and Clarace, wrote T. Henry's daughter, Dorothy, the following:

What outsiders noticed about him was that he was true to his guidance. T. Henry did not move without seeking guidance first. Both T. Henry and Clarace would begin the morning hours with pens in their hands and a note book and, closing eyes, would indulge in what they called "quiet time" period. When through, they would write down their random thoughts—whatever they might be. Shared them by reading them aloud. That became a personal custom within themselves and what followed, at group meetings in their large home on Palisades. They didn't consider

---

[8] Interview of Jim Newton by the author in August, 1992.

that to be their home only. They thought of it to be "God's Home." And so did most of their visitors.

In another letter, Isadore wrote Dorothy the following:

This brings me to the subject I most want to write to you about. It is about Dr. Bob's book. . . . Throughout my reading it I saw your Dad, T. Henry, whenever Dr. Bob was described. Especially, when Dr. Bob was persistent in sticking to what he learned from T. Henry—"Self Surrender"! Dr. Bob seemed to remember that he was powerless to conquer that hold on him—the urge for that alcoholic drink—until he learned to surrender that "urge" to God. With God's help Dr. Bob found that extra help he needed to set him free. . . .

I call your father *The Saintly T. Henry.* . . . They [T. Henry and Clarace] immortalized themselves by being instruments for God. I can remember the time, seeing him wearing a somewhat shabby overcoat, humbly thinking that someone he knew needed one more than he did. At one time in a private conversation between the two of us he let himself say that he already had given, to an organization that was close to their hearts, very substantial sums; and I am sure, before he passed away, he must have doubled that amount. Humility was his middle name. I am sure he would not appreciate my candidness in revealing him to the public. May I be forgiven. I am motivated in doing this to remind us that there are still some saints living in our midst. . . . Incidentally, their cars were never traded. They were given away to someone they knew who needed one, and couldn't afford it. I never heard them discuss their contributions. It was not their style.

With their Bible, church, and Oxford Group backgrounds, with Clarace's missionary training, with T. Henry's Bible teaching experience, and with the compassion for others—particularly alcoholics—that seemed their stock-in-trade, the Williams couple were certainly able to bring to the early fellowship some important evangelistic, pastoral, and teaching capabilities. They did far more than host meetings and social events. They were fully qualified to help give meaning to God, Jesus Christ, surrenders, quiet times, prayer, Bible study, Guidance, the Four Absolutes, the 5 C's, fellowship, life-changing, restitution, witness, love, kindness, and service. And this they did.[9]

---

[9] The author found, in his interviews and research, a common impression that there had been no Oxford Group activity in Akron prior to the Firestone events in 1933. Hence John Seiberling asked if the text was correct in quoting Clarace Williams as saying she had become involved in the Oxford Group prior to January of 1933 (and thus before Henrietta Seiberling and Anne Smith started attending). In a telephone interview with the author on November 9, 1992, Jim Newton said there had been a great deal of Oxford Group activity in Akron prior to the 1933 testimonials. Both Russell and Dorothy Firestone were active with the Group in Akron after Bud's 1931 Denver train ride conversion. Dr. Walter Tunks was active, and Newton was familiar with many Oxford Group people who were in and out of Akron prior to January, 1933. Several of them, including Jim Newton, Dr. Walter Tunks, and the Firestones, were busy prior to 1933 preparing for the visit of Dr. Frank Buchman and his team members who arrived in January.

5

Henrietta Seiberling's Spiritual Infusion

We pointed out that Henrietta Seiberling was one of those who attended the 1933 Oxford Group events in Akron; that she was there with Anne Smith, Delphine Weber, and Clarace Williams; and that she was endeavoring to help Dr. Bob with his drinking problem. But there is a good deal more to Henrietta's contributions to Alcoholics Anonymous, particularly those she made in the early days in Akron.

Henrietta's Interaction With Bill and Dr. Bob

Bill Wilson gave very few details as to what Henrietta Seiberling did in the early Akron days. Yet Bill's comments indicate the substantiality of Henrietta's role. Wilson said:

> Right here I want to set on record the timeless gratitude that A.A.'s will always have for Henrietta Seiberling, who had first brought Dr. Bob and me together. Of the ten people to whom I had been directed by Clergyman Walter Tunks, Henrietta was the only one who had understood enough and cared enough. And this had been only the beginning of her mission. During that first summer at Akron she affectionately counseled many an

alcoholic's family, just as Anne [Dr. Bob's wife] was doing. Despite the fact that she had no direct experience of alcoholism, Henrietta had a rare capacity for identification with us. Therefore she was eagerly sought out for her great spiritual insight and the help she could give. What Alcoholics Anonymous owes to her will always be beyond anybody's reckoning. And Dr. Bob's debt and mine are the greatest of all.[1]

A few older Clevelanders remembered how some of them had gone to the Akron meetings, then held in the home of Oxford Groupers T. Henry and Clarace Williams. There they had met Dr. Bob and Anne and had looked with wonder upon alcoholics who had stayed sober one and two and three years. They had met and listened to Henrietta Seiberling, the nonalcoholic who had brought Dr. Bob and me together in her house three years previously—one who had understood deeply and cared enough and who was already seen as one of the strongest links in the chain of events that Providence was unfolding.[2]

[After Bill and Dr. Bob's work with their first newcomer prospect had failed, Bill said] Then came a lull on the Twelfth Step front. In this time, Anne and Henrietta infused much needed spirituality into Bob and me.[3]

Bill said Henrietta provided a "spiritual infusion" to Akron.[4] The question is, what did Henrietta infuse?

There is little record at all of what Dr. Bob might have thought. In his last major talk, Dr. Bob spoke of "our good friend

---

[1] *Alcoholics Anonymous Comes of Age* (New York: Alcoholics Anonymous World Services, Inc., 1957), p. 73.

[2] *Alcoholics Anonymous Comes of Age*, p. 19.

[3] *The Language of the Heart* (New York: The A.A. Grapevine, Inc., 1988), p. 357.

[4] See also a brief discussion of Bill's use of this term. Ernest Kurtz, *Not-God: A History of Alcoholics Anonymous*. Expanded ed. (Minnesota: Hazelden, 1991), pp. 40, 320 n. 11.

Henrietta."[5] He said, as to Henrietta's efforts to get him and Bill W. together, "Henry [Dr. Bob often called her "Henry" or "Hen"] is very persistent, a very determined individual."[6] And Dr. Bob even shared that he "used to get a little peeved at our Heavenly Father, because He had been a little slow on the trigger in my own case. I thought I would have been ready to receive the message quite a while before He got around to presenting it." Dr. Bob presented his plight to Henrietta in this way:

"Henry, do you think I want to stop drinking liquor?" She, being a very charitable soul, would say, "Yes, Bob, I'm sure you want to stop." I would say, "Well I can't conceive of any living human who really wanted to do something as badly as I think I do, who could be such a total failure. Henry, I think I'm just one of those *want*-to-want-to guys." And she'd say, "No, Bob, I think you want to. You just haven't found a way to work it yet."[7]

Dr. Bob's daughter, Sue Smith Windows, provided the author with the following statement about Henrietta:

Henrietta was a sweet, Southern Lady. She and mother were very friendly and would talk on the phone for hours. We used to kid Mom about Henry calling at supper time. She spent a lot of time with Dad too.[8]

DR. BOB and the Good Oldtimers said these things about Henrietta's interaction with Dr. Bob and Bill:

---

[5] *The Co-Founders of Alcoholics Anonymous: Biographical sketches; Their last major talks* (New York: Alcoholics Anonymous World Services, Inc. 1972, 1975), p. 6.

[6] *Co-Founders*, p. 6.

[7] *Co-Founders*, pp. 10-11.

[8] *Henrietta and early Oxford Group Friends* (Typed statement by Sue Smith Windows given to the author in Akron, Ohio, on June 6, 1991).

[Bill said] She was to become a vital link to those fantastic events which were presently to gather around the birth and development of our A.A. Society.[9]

[In April of 1936, Bill wrote his wife] "Bob and Anne and Henrietta [Seiberling] have been working so hard with those men and with really wonderful success. There were very joyous get-togethers at Bob's, Henrietta's, and the Williams' by turns."[10]

One of Dr. Bob's strongest characteristics was loyalty—not only to Bill, but to Henrietta Seiberling and T. Henry and Clarace Williams. These three had done so much to help him before he stopped drinking, and then—in the face of criticism from members of their own Oxford Group—had given so much support to him and the early members in the crucial years that followed.[11]

We need not document further the fact that Henrietta Seiberling made very clear, substantial, continuing, and personal contributions to the Akron founding and founders. But what *were* her contributions? Existing A.A. histories simply have not told us. Without such evidence, the Akron genesis history is incomplete.

[9] *DR. BOB*, p. 64.

[10] *DR. BOB*, p. 108.

[11] *DR. BOB*, p. 161.

A Brief Biography of Henrietta Seiberling[12]

Henrietta Buckler Seiberling was born in Lawrenceburg, Kentucky, the only child of Judge Julius A. and Mary Maddox Buckler. The date was March 18, 1888. Henrietta's childhood was spent in Texas where her father was Judge of the Common Pleas Court in El Paso. She attended and received an A.B. degree from Vassar College, where she majored in music and had a minor in psychology. She met J. Frederick Seiberling, her husband-to-be, while he was serving as a lieutenant in the Ohio National Guard on duty in Texas. Seiberling was the son of Akron's rubber industry leader, Frank A. Seiberling. And Henrietta was married in Akron on October 12, 1917. The marriage took place at the senior Seiberling's estate, known as "Stan Hywet Hall." Three children, one later to become a U.S. Congressman from Ohio, were born to J. Frederick and Henrietta Seiberling.[13]

Henrietta was a Presbyterian from childhood, but not an avid churchgoer. She was, however, an avid student of the Bible. Distressed over family and financial problems, and living separate from her husband, she was attracted to the January, 1933, Oxford Group meetings that were held in Akron at the instance of Harvey Firestone, Sr. Henrietta then set about reading most of the Oxford Group books of the 1930's, together with spiritual works by many Protestant leaders of the day. She began attending the Thursday West Hill Oxford Group meetings. And she was probably the organizer of the Wednesday meetings at the home of T. Henry and Clarace Williams where the "alcoholic squad of the Oxford Group" met from 1935 to 1939. Henrietta led many of these meetings. After she became involved in the Oxford Group, she

---

[12] The following portion on biographical material was assembled by the author primarily through correspondence with, phone calls to, and an extensive personal interview with former Congressman John F. Seiberling in Akron, Ohio, during the Founders Day Convention in Akron, Ohio, in June of 1992.

[13] The children, all of whom were involved in early Oxford Group meetings in Akron, are John F. Seiberling, Mary Seiberling Huhn, and Dorothy Seiberling.

joined the Presbyterian Church in Akron on West Market Street. Its minister, J. C. Wright, was also in the Oxford Group. She brought her children into that church where they were baptized in their teens. For a few years, they all often went to church; all went to Oxford Group meetings; and the family learned to have their own "quiet times."

It was Henrietta who put Bill Wilson in touch with Dr. Bob on Mother's Day, May 11, 1935, at a meeting in her home at the Gatehouse on the Seiberling Estate. For the next three months, Henrietta, Bill W., Dr. Bob and Dr. Bob's wife, Anne, studied the Bible and Oxford Group literature, prayed, and had "quiet times" together; discussed spiritual principles extensively; sought out alcoholics to help; and attended Oxford Group meetings at the Williams home. Henrietta worked closely with Dr. Bob and his wife, Anne, helping many alcoholics to recovery. She continued for many years as friend, counselor, and supporter of both Dr. Bob and Bill W. When the Ohio contingent of A.A. broke with the Oxford Group in 1939, Henrietta also left the Oxford Group fold.

Henrietta Seiberling died in New York City on December 5, 1979. She is buried at Lawrenceburg, Kentucky. On her gravestone is an inscription familiar both to Oxford Group people and to the fellowship of Alcoholics Anonymous: "Let go and let God."

The Spiritual Books That Henrietta Read

The first portion of the evidence concerning what Henrietta might have contributed to A.A. has to do with her reading. We are of the belief that the books a person admires, studies, mentions, and quotes—particularly in the religious realm—tell much about that person's convictions and values. The Seiberling children have provided the author with a great deal of information about Henrietta Seiberling's reading.

On August 14, 1991, John F. Seiberling wrote the author, stating:

Of the books listed in your letter to Sue [Dr. Bob's daughter], I can recall my mother owning and discussing the following:

1. *Life Changers* by Harold Begbie.[14]
2. Several books by E. Stanley Jones.[15]
3. *If I Be Lifted Up* by Sam Shoemaker.[16]
4. *For Sinners Only* by A. J. Russell.[17]
5. *Soul-Surgery* by H. A. Walter."[18]

Previously, on July 5, 1991, John Seiberling had written the following concerning his mother's reading:

My mother, I am sure, read *all* the Oxford Group books of the 1930's. *For Sinners Only*, by A. J. Russell, she quoted quite often and urged others to read it. She also read his [A. J.

---

[14] Harold Begbie, *Life Changers* (London: Mills & Boon, Ltd., 1932). This is a book about Oxford Group founder, Dr. Frank N. D. Buchman, and his life-changing program. Buchman often gave copies of this book to world leaders and others he met.

[15] Dr. Bob and Anne Smith also read many of the books by E. Stanley Jones, a Methodist. Specific details about these books are set forth in Appendix Three. We believe Henrietta probably read most of the E. Stanley Jones books.

[16] Samuel M. Shoemaker, *If I Be Lifted Up* (New York: Fleming H. Revell, 1931). Shoemaker wrote, "This book is about the Cross"(p. 7). Anne Smith highly recommended the book.

[17] A. J. Russell, *For Sinners Only* (London: Hodder And Stoughton, Ltd., 1932). This book, containing many stories about Oxford Group members, sets forth most of the Oxford Group principles and was part of Dr. Bob's "required reading list." See Bill Pittman, *AA The Way It Began* (Seattle: Glen Abbey Books, 1988), p. 197.

[18] H. A. Walter, *Soul-Surgery*. 6th ed. (Oxford: Printed at the University Press by John Johnson, Printer to the University, 1940). Oxford Group Founder, Dr. Frank Buchman, was often called the "soul surgeon." And Oxford Group life-changing procedures were sometimes described in terms of "soul surgery." This book was about Buchman's "art" of life-changing through personal evangelism and emphasized Buchman's five C's—Confidence, Confession, Conviction, Conversion, and Conservation.

Russell's] book, *One Thing I Know*.[19] Another book that she often quoted was *The Soul's Sincere Desire* by Glenn Clark. . . . My mother thought highly of his writings.[20] Also high on her list were the writings of Dr. Samuel Moor Shoemaker. She also was very fond of a collection of daily readings, entitled *My Utmost For His Highest*.[21]

Note that John Seiberling said he was *sure* his mother read *all* the Oxford Group books of the 1930's. In our book, *The Oxford Group & Alcoholics Anonymous*, and at the beginning of Part 2 of this book, and in Appendix One, we list and discuss in some detail the Oxford Group literature which was made available through the Oxford Group bookstore at Calvary House in New York.[22] Since Henrietta read *all* the Oxford Group books of the 1930's, and Dr. Bob said he had done an *immense* amount of reading that Oxford Group members recommended, we believe it likely that both Henrietta and Dr. Bob, and perhaps even Bill, read most or all of the books available at the Oxford Group's American Headquarters at Calvary House.

Henrietta's daughter, Dorothy Seiberling, wrote the author on July 5, 1991, the following about her mother's reading:

---

[19] See A. J. Russell, *One Thing I Know* (New York: Harper & Brothers, 1933). This was the book Russell wrote to confirm his belief in the Atonement. The author found that Anne Smith, Dr. Bob's wife, also owned and read this book.

[20] See Glenn Clark, *The Soul's Sincere Desire* (Boston: Little, Brown, 1925). This book was a favorite of Dr. Bob's as were all the Glenn Clark books. See Dick B., *Dr. Bob's Library* (Wheeling, WV: The Bishop of Books, 1992), pp. 35, 45, 58-62.

[21] See Oswald Chambers, *My Utmost For His Highest* (London: Simpkin Marshall, Ltd., 1927). This was a daily devotional that was widely used in the Oxford Group, by Dr. Bob and Anne Smith, and by Bill and Lois Wilson. See Dick B., *Dr. Bob's Library*, pp. 32-33; Pittman, *AA The Way It Began*, p. 183.

[22] See Dick B., *The Oxford Group & Alcoholics Anonymous* (Seattle: Glen Abbey Books, 1992), pp. 81-84.

Mother did indeed read *The Upper Room*.[23] And I'm sure she must have read Sam Shoemaker—some of the titles sound so familiar, e.g. *'Children of the Second Birth,'*[24] and, of course, *'If I Be Lifted Up.'* Mother definitely owned *'For Sinners Only.'* . . . She owned *Practicing The Presence of God* (by Brother Lawrence),[25] and I have a small pamphlet of Brother Lawrence, also mother's. I believe she read *In His Steps* (by C. M. Sheldon);[26] I know she read *'The Soul's Sincere Desire'* (by Glenn Clark). I have her copy, and *The Meaning of Prayer* (by Raymond Fosdick)."[27]

On July 19, 1991, Dorothy Seiberling wrote the author, adding the following:

I also have her edition of the Bible with the Moffatt translation (Actually it's the New Testament). This was her bedside reading, and it's full of marginalia, underlinings, clippings. In addition I have: *The Soul's Sincere Desire* by Glenn Clark; *Inspired*

---

[23] See *The Upper Room: Daily Devotions for Family and Individual Use*. This was a quarterly issued by the General Committee On Evangelism Through The Department of Home Missions, Evangelism, Hospitals, Board of Missions, Methodist Episcopal Church, South. The first issue for April, May, and June was published in 1935. This Bible meditation book was widely used in and out of the early A.A. meetings. The quarterly was distributed to AAs by Lucy Galbraith. It was used by Dr. Bob and Anne quite frequently in their Quiet Times in the morning. See Dick B., *Dr. Bob's Library*, pp. 30, 33-34.

[24] See Samuel M. Shoemaker, *Children of the Second Birth* (New York: Fleming H. Revell, 1927).

[25] See Brother Lawrence, *The Practice of the Presence of God* (Pennsylvania: Whitaker House, 1982). This is one of several Christian Classics owned and read by Dr. Bob. See Dick B., *Dr. Bob's Library*, pp. 28-29.

[26] See Charles M. Sheldon, *In His Steps* (Nashville: Broadman Press, 1935). Owned and read by Dr. Bob. See Dick B., *Dr. Bob's Library*, p. 71.

[27] We believe Dorothy Seiberling intended to refer to Harry Emerson Fosdick, *The Meaning of Prayer* (New York: Association Press, 1915), one of the many Fosdick books read also by Dr. Bob. See Dick B., *Dr. Bob's Library*, p. 64.

Children by Olive Jones;[28] *I Will Lift Up Mine Eyes* by Glenn Clark;[29] *My Utmost For His Highest* by Oswald Chambers—all well read!

Finally, in March of 1992, Dorothy Seiberling wrote the author that she had begun digging up her mother's books and found Kagawa. She said her mother did read him. Dorothy had noted in the author's book, *Anne Smith's Spiritual Workbook*, that Toyohiko Kagawa was the author whose book on Love was the volume most discussed by Anne in her spiritual workbook.[30]

On February 4, 1992, Henrietta's other daughter, Mary Seiberling Huhn, wrote as to her mother's reading:

> I should like to add, in case I didn't tell you over the phone, that Bill Wilson gave mother a copy of Jung's *Modern Man In Search of a Soul* which he evidently found to be very enlightening.[31] I read it and was fascinated, but I don't think mother read it, because she wasn't much interested in the psychotherapist approach. I have that book, someplace in the house, also her

---

[28] See Olive Jones, *Inspired Children* (New York: Harper & Brothers, 1933). Olive Jones was a former president of the National Educational Association, one of the Oxford Group team that visited Akron in 1933, a frequent participant in Oxford Group houseparties, some of which were attended by Bill and Lois Wilson, and a major assistant to Dr. Samuel Moor Shoemaker, Jr., in his Oxford Group work at his Calvary Episcopal Church in New York. Miss Jones authored two books recommended and used by the Oxford Group. See Dick B., *The Oxford Group & Alcoholics Anonymous* (Seattle: Glen Abbey Books, 1992), pp. 64, 82, 137, 156.

[29] See Glenn Clark, *I Will Lift Up Mine Eyes* (New York: Harper & Brothers, 1937). This was a book read and recommended by Dr. Bob. See Dick B., *Dr. Bob's Library*, pp. 58-60. Nell Wing, Bill Wilson's secretary, indicated the book was widely read by early AA's. See Pittman, *AA The Way It Began*, p. 192.

[30] See Toyohiko Kagawa, *Love: The Law of Life* (Philadelphia: The John C. Winston Company, 1929). See also Dick B., *Anne Smith's Spiritual Workbook* (Corte Madera, CA: Good Book Publishing Company, 1992), pp. 11, 14-17.

[31] See C. G. Jung, *Modern Man in Search of a Soul* (New York: Harcourt Brace Jovanovich, Publishers, 1933). Dr. Bob owned and read this book. See Dick B., *Dr. Bob's Library*, pp. 54-55.

copy of *For Sinners Only*. . . . She also had several of Fosdick's books. I came across one called *On Being Fit To Live With*.[32]

The author also ran across two additional books that Henrietta owned. They were by Dr. Leslie D. Weatherhead, who—though not a "member" of the Oxford Group—wrote extensively and admiringly on its principles.[33] At the present time, there is a copy of Weatherhead's *Discipleship*, with Henrietta Seiberling's name inscribed in it, at Bill W.'s home at Stepping Stones in Bedford Hills, New York.[34] Bill gave his secretary, Nell Wing, a copy of Weatherhead's *Psychology And Life*; and this copy also has Henrietta Seiberling's name inscribed in it.[35]

From the foregoing list of Henrietta's books and from what we shall have to say in a moment about Henrietta and her Bible, we can see many of her substantial spiritual resources. Shortly, we will see that the books she read were read as well by Dr. Bob and by Anne and, in some cases, by Bill. These included Oxford Group books, Sam Shoemaker books, the Bible devotionals that AAs used in the early Akron days, and books by prominent Christian writers such as Glenn Clark, E. Stanley Jones, Oswald Chambers, Harry Emerson Fosdick, Charles M. Sheldon, and Leslie Weatherhead, as well as the classics, such as Brother Lawrence.

In terms of what she *read*, then, Henrietta had *much* spiritually to infuse. And since Dr. Bob's intense reading period was resumed

---

[32] As to Dr. Bob's extensive reading of Fosdick's books, see Dick B., *Dr. Bob's Library*, pp. 63-66. The Fosdick books were also read and recommended by Dr. Bob's wife, Anne. See Dick B., *Anne Smith's Spiritual Workbook*, p. 14.

[33] See Dick B., *The Oxford Group & Alcoholics Anonymous*, pp. 9, 128, 134; *Dr. Bob's Library*, pp. 79-80. In an interview with Mitch K., at New Britain, Connecticut, in August of 1992, the author learned that Clarence S., who was one of the men Dr. Bob sponsored, and who was himself Mitch K.'s sponsor, had Weatherhead books in his collection.

[34] See Leslie D. Weatherhead, *Discipleship* (New York: The Abingdon Press, 1934).

[35] See Leslie D. Weatherhead, *Psychology And Life* (New York: The Abingdon Press, 1935).

largely after his 1933 contact with the Oxford Group, it seems quite possible that Henrietta's own reading list was recommended to or shared with Dr. Bob and Anne, and possibly with Bill. Henrietta, Dr. Bob, and Anne, seemed to have had many of the same reading interests when it came to the Oxford Group, Shoemaker, and the other Christian writers.

Henrietta And Her Bible

Each of Henrietta's children provided insight on Henrietta's study and use of the Bible.

Her daughter, Mary Seiberling Huhn, provided very substantial details. In a letter to the author of February 4, 1992, Mrs Huhn said:

> I spent a great deal of time yesterday going through the four Gospels to pick out those passages which I remember mother having stressed during our growing up and while AAs were getting underway. Of course mother's knowledge of the Bible began in her youth because my grandmother Buckler was a devout Christian and quoted the Bible frequently. But it wasn't until the advent of the Oxford Group to Akron and her subsequent involvement with the smaller group and then A.A. that mother became intensely interested in the teachings and story of Jesus. She turned to it for help with her own problems and then was able to use the insights gained as she nurtured the developing A.A. I remember at one point she associated the passage in Luke 12:32ff "Fear not, little flock . . ." with "the group."[36]

---

[36] Luke 12:32 and following reads, "Fear not, little flock; for it is your Father's good pleasure to give you the kingdom. Sell that you have, and give alms; provide yourselves bags which wax not old, a treasure in the heavens that faileth not, where no thief approacheth, neither moth corrupteth. For where your treasure is, there will your heart be also." This is a version in Luke of the same material found in the Sermon on the Mount, Matthew, Chapter 6.

But before I get at the passages, I would like to say a couple of things about mother's influence on the early A.A. that were not mentioned in your [the author's] letter. Rather than the expression "calling the shots"—which has a rather imperious tone to it—a tone which mother would have thought to be running counter to what Jesus taught—I would have said that she wanted to steer them away from the mistakes (avoiding the pitfalls) which she felt had kept the Oxford Group from having the impact it could have had.[37] She clung to the inspiring version of First Century Christianity as it paralleled Christ's own methods—in other words, it seemed she would favor the "bubble-up" rather than the "trickle-down" theory with regard to matters spiritual. In line with this idea, she advised Bill against seeking Big Money contributions from foundations, etc. because she felt—and I remember her saying it—that if it was *right* and *meant to be*, God would see that the necessary funding would be forthcoming. This of course is completely in the spirit of the Sermon on the Mount, the part about not being anxious about what clothing to be put on, etc. because God, who clothes the lilies of the fields and etc. will take care of his children.[38] Then too, when Bill was

---

[37] Note: In his letter to Mrs. Huhn, the author had included a statement from *DR. BOB and the Good Oldtimers* in which Akron oldtimer, Bob E., was quoted at page 157 as saying, "But we were limited. We couldn't question the guidance. We used to sit around in a circle when we first started there because there were so few of us. T. Henry and Clarace, Florence Main, and Hen Seiberling called the shots. They were the leaders. They had us in silence, listening for guidance, half the time. It made the drunks very restless. We couldn't stand that. We got the jitters. As we increased in numbers the silence was almost cut out."

[38] Mrs. Huhn is referring to Matthew 6:25-34 of the Sermon on the Mount in which Jesus states, "Therefore I say unto you, Take no thought [be not anxious] for your life, what ye shall eat, or what ye shall drink; nor yet for your body what ye shall put on. Is not the life more than meat, and the body than raiment? Behold the fowls of the air; for they sow not, neither do they reap, nor gather into barns; yet your heavenly Father feedeth them. Are ye not much better than they? Which of you by taking thought [being anxious] can add one cubit unto his stature? And why take ye thought for raiment? Consider the lilies of the field, how they grow; they toil not, neither do they spin: And yet I say unto you, That even Solomon in all his glory was not arrayed like one of these. Wherefore, if God so clothe the grass of the field, which today is, and to morrow is cast into the oven, shall He not much more clothe you, O ye of little faith? Therefore take
(continued...)

considering putting his name as author on the book about A.A.'s beginnings, it was mother who counseled him strongly—and I believe it was on the basis of guidance—that everyone must be anonymous. She recognized that anonymity was not only for the sake of protecting reputations—in fact I don't think *that* was her idea at all; it was to keep the *ego* out of it. And what a wise insight this was! "Blessed are the poor in spirit for their's is the kingdom of heaven."[39]

As I told you over the phone, mother was always quoting from the Bible to teach us how to get along better. When we were quarreling or angry and said spiteful things, she would say, "If you don't love your brother whom you have seen, how can you love God whom you haven't seen." I can't seem to find that particular passage,[40] but one which she seemed to say to us quite often—whenever one of us complained "John—or Babe (Dorothy)—or Mare [Mary]—gets to do it, or have it, or doesn't have to do it, so why not me?" was from John 21:21, "What is that to thee, follow thou me." Also the part about forgiving 70 x 7. I remember calculating how many times that would be.[41] This was a marvelous way to help us think of ourselves as individuals so that we weren't always focusing on the seemingly better lot of the other fellow. Also, we had to think—if my

---

[38] (...continued)

no thought [be not anxious], saying, "What shall we eat?" or, "What shall we drink?" or "Wherewithal shall we be clothed?" For after all these things do the Gentiles seek; for your heavenly Father knoweth that ye have need of all these things. But seek ye first the kingdom of God, and His righteousness; and all these things shall be added unto you. Take therefore no thought [be not anxious] for the morrow: for the morrow shall take thought for the things of itself. Sufficient unto the day is the evil thereof."

[39] Again, Mrs. Huhn refers to the Sermon on the Mount, this time to Matthew 5:3.

[40] The verse to which Mrs. Huhn and her mother, Henrietta, referred is 1 John 4:20, "If a man say, 'I love God,' and hateth his brother, he is a liar: for he that loveth not his brother whom he hath seen, how can he love God Whom he hath not seen?"

[41] Mrs. Huhn refers to Matthew 18:21-22, "Then Peter came to Him [Jesus] and said, 'Lord, how oft shall my brother sin against me, and I forgive him? till seven times?' Jesus saith unto him, 'I say not unto thee, until seven times; but Until seventy times seven.'"

course is a good one, I shouldn't worry about what others are doing.

Of course she loved the Sermon on the Mount and impressed on me what Jesus said about how one should treat one's fellow man. (We didn't bother about sexist language in those days because we understood what was meant). And I especially remember her telling us about the difference between the way the Pharisees, and hypocrites in general, prayed and the way prayer should be. Matthew 6:8: ". . . for your Father knows what you need before you ask him."

Much of what she taught us reflected the original OG [Oxford Group] ideas about returning to the roots and not getting hung up on institutional baggage. The teachings about what does and does not defile a man (Matthew 15:11)[42] . . . that God is not God of the dead but of the living (Matthew 22:32 and Luke 24:5)[43]—all those ideas that must have seemed appallingly radical to the Establishment at the time in which Jesus pronounced them.

Then I especially remember one of the passages which she read as guidance that she had been seeking with respect to something going on in the Group (unfortunately I can't remember what) was that marvelous passage from John 14:15-17 about the Spirit of Truth (also John 16:12-13).[44] The message that I kept getting

---

[42] In Matthew 15:11, Jesus said: "Not that which goeth into the mouth defileth a man; but that which cometh out of the mouth this defileth a man."

[43] Jesus stated in Matthew 22:31-32, "But as touching the resurrection of the dead, have ye not read that which was spoken unto you by God, saying, I am the God of Abraham, and the God of Isaac, and the God of Jacob? God is not the God of the dead, but of the living."

[44] Jesus said in John 14:15-17, "If ye love Me, keep My commandments. And I will pray the Father, and He shall give you another Comforter, that He may abide with you for ever; Even the Spirit of Truth; Whom the world cannot receive, because it seeth Him not, neither knoweth Him: but ye know Him; for He dwelleth with you, and shall be in you." And in John 16:12-13, "I have yet many things to say unto you, but ye cannot bear them now. Howbeit when He, the Spirit of truth, is come, He will guide you into all truth; for He shall not speak of Himself; but whatsoever He shall hear, that shall He speak; and He will shew you things to come."

was that what is real, authentic, from-the-depths of one's being—that is what is important, and if that is whole and vital, then the rest will take care of itself. And of course love was the vital element. I heard mother say many times, "Perfect love casteth out fear." before I found it in the Bible.[45]

The passage in Luke (21:33) "Heaven and Earth may pass away but my words will not pass away" reminds me of a conversation I had with mother when she was very old. She and I did not always agree on the theological basis for Christianity—I being inclined toward the Quaker belief and the Unitarian liberal religious orientation, but I have always valued the teachings and example of Jesus, even taught a course in Jesus' life and teachings for several years at our UU Sunday school. I had come to the belief that if humankind does not evolve in the direction of Jesus' teachings—as well as the similar teachings of all the great religious figures, we are doomed to destroy ourselves and the planet. On this particular occasion, mother said to me, "You know, Mary, I've been thinking that it doesn't matter whether the *name* of *Jesus* or *Christ* endures, because what will endure is what he taught because what he taught has to become the way people live and treat one another." That was the gist—maybe not her *exact* words—of what she said anyway. And I told her "You know, that's amazing, because I had come to the same conclusion myself." Mother and I were always seeking to agree in spirit if not in particulars. She once asked me, also when she was very old, what I felt was the most important thing she ever taught me, and I could easily answer her without searching my mind: That as long as things are right on the inside, it doesn't matter about the outside, the outside will take care of itself. She then said, "Good. Because that is what I most wanted to get across to you children."

Her other daughter, Dorothy Seiberling, in a letter to the author dated August 14, 1991, added these points:

---

[45] See 1 John 4:18: "There is no fear in love; but perfect love casteth out fear: because fear hath torment. He that feareth is not made perfect in love."

Mother did read Corinthians a great deal, but she read a lot, just picking up the Bible wherever it opened & going on from there. And she quoted from Corinthians, & from John. (She also quoted her mother's Bible "quotes"!). P.S. Mother's mother (Mary Maddox Buckler) taught mother to say, "Thou, God seest me." I think that had a major impact on mother as a little girl though she was far from goody-goody; maybe that was why grandmother inculcated that verse to curb mother's mischievousness.[46]

There is no question that mother was concerned about the spiritual core of A.A. She always feared its secularization into a kind of how-to-do-it. Of course, she believed in God & Christ, & looked to the Bible for guidance—but she was not hidebound or a literalist & she didn't feel that there was only one way to God, one approved belief. In short, she was not orthodox. But she did feel that what helped A.A.s was not just the fellowship alone, but "The power beyond oneself"—The putting of oneself into the realm of transcendence—"not my will, but Thy will"—she would say.[47]

Henrietta's son, John, in a letter to the author dated July 5, 1991, had the following to say about his mother's study of the Bible:

The Bible passages she mentioned most often were Christ's talks to his disciples, as set forth in the gospel of St. John, and the writings of St. Paul, especially I Corinthians, Ch. 13.

Her Bible readings and her daily "quiet time" were an effort to let God guide her life; her attitude was, "Speak, Lord, for thy

---

[46] Dorothy Seiberling cited no verse; but perhaps her grandmother referred to Jeremiah 12:3, "But Thou, O Lord, knowest me; Thou hast seen me, and tried mine heart toward Thee."

[47] See Luke 22:42 where Jesus said, "nevertheless not My will, but Thine, be done."

servant heareth."[48] That was how she got the guidance that Bob shouldn't take even one drink of alcohol.

The Book of John was most important.

Now what do Henrietta's Bible resources tell us? First, of course, she was highly knowledgeable of the Bible's contents. She studied it, quoted it, and tried to apply it and gain guidance from it. From her daughter, Mary, comes information as to Henrietta's emphasis on the Sermon on the Mount. Henrietta was also very much interested in 1 Corinthians 13—Paul's famous chapter on "Love." A.A. Oldtimers considered this chapter essential to their program.[49] Henrietta certainly picked up on verses from the book of John and from 1 Samuel 3:9 that stressed the importance of guidance by God. We shall have more to say of that in a moment; but the concept of guidance was vital in the Oxford Group and very much survives in A.A. today.[50] Henrietta also emphasized the phrase, "Thy will be done," from the Lord's Prayer, and there was great emphasis in the Oxford Group on this phrase. And there is great emphasis in A.A. today on doing God's will—Thy Will be done.[51]

---

[48] See 1 Samuel 3:9. This verse was very much quoted and relied upon in the Oxford Group and its writings to convey the idea that man should listen for God to reveal *His will* instead of asking God to do *man's* will. See Dick B., *The Oxford Group & Alcoholics Anonymous*, pp. 244-45.

[49] See *DR. BOB*, pp. 96, 151, 310-311.

[50] See Dick B., *The Oxford Group & Alcoholics Anonymous*, pp. 207-18, 242-57, 307, 315.

[51] See Robert Thomsen, *Bill W.* (New York: Harper & Row, 1975), p. 229; Dick B., *The Oxford Group & Alcoholics Anonymous*, pp. 34, 48-50, 111-14, 120-26, 307-08, 315; Big Book, pp. 63, 67, 88.

Henrietta and the Oxford Group Ideas
That Influenced A.A.

As we've previously stated, we have detailed and analyzed some twenty-eight Oxford Group concepts that we believe influenced Alcoholics Anonymous.[52] The significant thing with respect to Henrietta and these concepts is that when we reviewed them with her son, John F. Seiberling, in an interview in June of 1992, John said he would "have had to be deaf not to hear" his mother talking frequently about every one of these concepts. He confirmed the frequency with which each was mentioned and was involved in the life practices of Henrietta. Thus, whether T. Henry, Clarace, Henrietta, Bill W., Dr. Bob, or Anne—or all of the above—taught or learned these twenty-eight concepts, individually or together, these basic ideas were a part of what Henrietta Seiberling was conveying to and discussing with all of the Founders of Alcoholics Anonymous.

Henrietta's Beliefs and Remarks

In her own recollections to her son, John, Henrietta spoke much about God, faith, and guidance. For example, she felt she got "guidance" when she received the thought from God, "Bob [Dr. Bob] must not touch one drop of alcohol." She felt that Bill Wilson's call to her for help from the Mayflower Hotel on May 10, 1935 was the result of "guidance." She said, "that is the way that God helps us if we let God direct our lives." She said a Hollywood actor had been looking all over the country but found something in the [Akron A.A.] King School Group that wasn't in any other group. "I think it was our great stress and reliance on guidance and quiet times," she said. Of her work with AAs,

---

[52] See Dick B., *The Oxford Group & Alcoholics Anonymous*, pp. 111-295.

Henrietta said, "And I tried to give to the people something of my experience and faith. What I was most concerned with is that we always go back to faith."

When Dr. Bob and Bill suggested to Henrietta that they should not talk too much about religion or God, Henrietta said:

> Well, we're not out to please the alcoholics. They have been pleasing themselves all these years. We are out to please God. And if you don't talk about what God does, and your faith, and your guidance, then you might as well be the Rotary Club or something like that. Because God is your only source of power.

She said Bill and Dr. Bob agreed with her on that point.

In her later years, Henrietta attended an A.A. dinner with over 3000 people and was very disappointed about it. She heard two speakers and said, "You would have thought they were giving you a description of psychiatrists work on them. Their progress was always on the level of psychology." And she bared her objections to Bill Wilson, commenting that there was no "realization [by the speakers] that they have lost their source of power." In the last public record of her remarks before she died, she is quoted as saying:

> And then there is one other thing I'd always like to stress, and that is the real fact of God's guidance. People can always count on guidance, although it seems elusive at times.[53]

Speaking of her leadership at Oxford Group meetings in Akron at the T. Henry Williams home, she said, "Every Wednesday night, I would speak on some new experience or spiritual idea I had read."[54] In a letter to the author, Dorothy Seiberling recalled these things about her mother's spiritual ideas:

---

[53] The foregoing three paragraphs contain quotes from an article by John F. Seiberling, entitled *Origins of Alcoholics Anonymous* (Employee Assistance Quarterly, 1985) (1); pp. 8-9, 12.

[54] Seiberling, *Origins of Alcoholics Anonymous*, p. 9.

1. She was a seeker and it took the form of Christian belief.
2. She had aspirations toward spiritual and moral improvement.

In a letter to the author, John Seiberling added:

1. Henrietta made a constant effort to lead a life of Christian Spirituality and to help others to do the same.

2. She was insistent on following the OG [Oxford Group] "Four Standards" of Absolute Honesty, Purity, Unselfishness and Love.

3. Also important to her were the OG practices of daily surrender to God, "Quiet Times," witnessing (i.e. sharing your shortcomings and what God had done to change your life), and making restitution to those you may have hurt.

4. She was also very firm that when one witnessed, he or she should talk "news, not views," i.e. tell what had *happened* in one's life, not what one *thought* about things.

5. Humility and the belief that "people are more important than things" were also uppermost in her messages.

6. The importance of being right on the *inside*, not just the *appearance* of being right.

7. Her Bible reading and her daily Quiet Times were an effort to let God guide her life.

DR. BOB and the Good Oldtimers makes clear that Henrietta prayed for others (p. 58), believed strongly in guidance (p. 59), encouraged Dr. Bob and Bill as to church attendance (p. 60), worked hard with Dr. Bob and Anne, helping Akron AAs "with really great success" (p. 108), and stressed reliance on God and faith (p. 159).

Dorothy Seiberling allowed the author to copy the following notes and marginalia which the author found in Henrietta's Bible:

What does it matter if external circumstances are hard? If we give way to self pity and indulge in the luxury of misery, we banish God's riches from our lives and hinder others from entering in His provision. No sin is worse than self-pity—it obliterates God and puts self interest on the throne.

Be stamped with God's nature & His blessings will come through you all the time. Let not your heart be troubled—and hurting Jesus by allowing it to be troubled. Realize the Lord is here now.

We have to share each others lives. Man is lonely—we erect barriers between ourselves & God. . . . God as a father—Behold thy son—God wants us first to perform our responsibilities.

Eye hath not seen nor ear heard, neither have entered into the heart of man the things God has prepared for them that love him. But God hath revealed them unto us by the Spirit for the spirit searcheth all things yea the deep things of God. For what man serveth the things of man save the spirit of man which is in him. Even so, the things of God knoweth no man but the Spirit of God. We have received the Spirit which is of God that we might know the things that are freely given us of God.

Speak of surrender. Speak of guidance. . . . Keep it simple means quiet time for guidance and the next step.

To say something of the beginnings of this work . . . but quote Paul . . . would like all our people to be able to see the hand of God doing this work . . . 2 years . . . Firestone . . . 1st Century . . . Bread cast on waters . . . couldn't stay away . . . Why I surrendered.

Cross helps us recognize sin. X revealed sin—that which hurts God which crucifies Christ. Haven't you found yourself part of these—1st step in conquering sin—cost of sin borne by Him. Gratitude for a new chance & new thoughts. Prison within ourselves. . . . Sin conquered by forgiveness of God.

Sin is what separates us from God. Bible is story of man's reconciliation with God. Man made for companionship of God. Man says I want my own way—estranged from God—didn't succeed. New Testament—God coming down to man—only way men are reconciled.

My judgment is just because I seek not mine own will. He that commiteth sin is the servant of sin & he abideth not in this house forever. Romans XIV.

The Father's will—that of all He giveth me, I shall lose nothing.

Rise to the occasion—Do the thing—It does not matter how it hurts as long as it gives God the chance to manifest Himself in your mortal flesh. He allows difficulties to come in order to see if you can vault over them properly. "By God, I have leapt over a wall." All the Almighty God is ours in the Lord Jesus & He will . . . bless us if we obey Him.

The reason why rivers and seas are able to be lords over a hundred mountain streams is that they know how to keep below them. I have 3 precious things which I hold fast & prize. The first is gentleness. The 2nd—frugality & the 3rd is humility which keeps me from putting myself before others. Be gentle & you can be bold. Be frugal & you can be liberal. Avoid putting yourself before others & you can become a leader among men.

In an interview with the author in New York on October 4, 1991, Dorothy Seiberling made these points regarding her mother's principal beliefs and actions:

1. *Humility*—Mother was a very strong and powerful person who had a lot of self-esteem and confidence. If she had not encountered the Oxford Group, she might have met the circumstances of her life in a less constructive way. By observing and trying to live by the standards of the Oxford Group, she achieved greater humility and surrendered her ego and fears to God. She tried to meet the problems that

beset her by letting go of her own ego and fears and let some power beyond her show her the way to cope with her problems. This enabled her to overcome a lot of adversity. It opened her to another kind of life in relationship to other human beings. She became an instrument.

2. *Her "spiritual infusion" to Bob and Bill in 1935*—I think mother had dedicated herself to living a different kind of life—the 1st century Christianity principles. Since this was uppermost in her mind and life—living a God-oriented life—she had to carry it through. It was her primary concern. They (Henrietta, Bob and Bill) were bound together to share experiences and to help each other in the journey of living a God directed life.

3. *God, the Bible & Jesus*—I think it easier for her to talk in terms of Jesus. Despite contradictions and discrepancies in the Bible, she believed Jesus did indeed exist and his message was from beyond the earth. Jesus was not just a prophet or a being of charisma or insight. He was sent by God.

4. *First Century Christianity*—trying to follow the teachings of Christ without an overload of dogma, doctrine, or church traditions.

5. *God's Will*—In her Quiet Times she felt if she was getting something that would not have come to her from natural response or out of the blue, like: (a) Message from God; (b) Answer to how to face a difficulty.

A Brief Sketch of Henrietta's Role in A.A.'s Early Days

The author believes the following represent the major aspects of Henrietta's part in the birthing of A.A.[55]

1. Henrietta Seiberling attended the 1933 Oxford Group team events that Harvey Firestone hosted. And she decided, "This is for me. I'm going to live this way."

2. Oxford Groups sort of formed themselves, and Henrietta aligned herself with the West Hill Group and, for the next two-and-a-half years, attended it with her family members, T. Henry and Clarace Williams, Delphine Weber, Mabel Dudley, and Dr. Bob and Anne Smith.[56]

3. Delphine Weber drew Henrietta's attention to Dr. Bob's drinking problem; and Henrietta got the guided thought that a meeting should be held to help Dr. Bob.[57]

4. Shortly before Mother's Day in 1935, Henrietta asked T. Henry and Clarace Williams to make their home available for a meeting at which all would share something costly and induce Dr. Bob to acknowledge his drinking problem.[58]

5. At the meeting, Dr. Bob confessed that he was a "secret drinker;" all present joined him on his knees in prayer for a solution to the problem.

6. This was the beginning of the Wednesday meetings that continued at the Williams home from May, 1935, to the fall

---

[55] The points are largely taken from the author's interviews of and letters from Henrietta's children.

[56] *DR. BOB*, p. 56.

[57] *DR. BOB*, pp. 56-58.

[58] *DR. BOB*, pp. 56-58.

of 1939. And those meetings were usually led by T. Henry, Clarace, Florence Main, and Henrietta.[59]

7. By what the Oxford Group members considered an answer to their prayers, Bill was guided to place a phone call to Dr. Tunks at the Mayflower hotel on May 10, 1935; and Tunks put him in touch with Henrietta.

8. The next day—May 11, 1935—Henrietta arranged for Dr. Bob and Bill to spend six hours together at Henrietta's home at the Gatehouse on the Seiberling Estate. Bob and Bill then began developing a program of recovery.

9. Henrietta arranged for Bill to be housed at the Portage Country Club until he went to live with Bob and Anne Smith.

10. Depending on whose account is accurate, Henrietta phoned the Smith home almost daily in the summer of 1935 or visited with its founders almost daily. But it is quite clear that she spent a good deal of time with Dr. Bob and Bill and Anne.

11. The Smiths and Bill and, briefly Lois when she visited Akron, all attended Oxford Group meetings on Wednesdays at the Williams home; and Henrietta was there as one of the leaders.

12. Henrietta often hosted get-togethers at her home for the "alcoholic squad of the Oxford Group."

13. She and the Smiths worked together a great deal in the ensuing four years helping alcoholics to their recovery and endeavoring to pass on to them the principles from the Bible and the Oxford Group that were to be the foundation for their recovery program.

---

[59] *DR. BOB*, p. 157.

14. Henrietta remained the counselor and friend of the Smiths and of Bill Wilson for many years thereafter and continued close contact with Bill Wilson after she moved from Akron to New York.

15. We covered in much detail the specific books that Henrietta read, the portions of the Bible that she stressed, the Oxford Group principles that she espoused, the beliefs she held, and some of the remarks she made. And we have underlined Bill Wilson's remarks about Henrietta's spiritual infusion. Though Bill never described the infusion, we believe it reasonable to assume that the foregoing aspects of her life and beliefs provide a record of what she contributed to Bill and Dr. Bob.

6

Anne Smith, Her Love, and Her Spiritual Workbook

To report adequately the contributions that Dr. Bob's wife, Anne Ripley Smith, made to Alcoholics Anonymous requires far more writing than will be undertaken in this book. Such a work, with appropriate research, is long overdue; and the author hopes to undertake it in the future. But this book is about A.A.'s Akron Genesis, and Anne Smith's contributions were, from a geographical standpoint, made *almost exclusively in Akron*. Thus it is important here at least to outline the immense scope of Anne's role. Immense, yet humble and quiet.

Anne Smith-Mother of A.A.

For one thing, Dr. Bob's wife was frequently called the "Mother of A.A."—by those who knew her contributions,[1] by people who

---

[1] In a letter to Bill W., dated December 15, 1949, Margaret and Ted wrote "in memory of our late friend, Anne Smith," that "Anne was, by her unfathomable love, an inspiration, and truly the Mother of all A.A.'s." [A copy of the letter was supplied to the author by Dr. Bob's son and daughter-in-law.] Years later, in an unsolicited phone
(continued...)

were known to her children, Bob and Sue,[2] and, in writing, by
A.A.'s Co-Founder, Bill Wilson. Bill called her "one of the
founders of Alcoholics Anonymous" and "quite literally, the
mother of our first group, Akron Number One."[3] She was one
who opened the Smith home to alcoholics and their families and
literally shared with drop-ins the bread and milk meals that the
Smiths were often eating during the difficult years of the great
Depression.[4] She was well remembered as the lady who sat near
the rear of the room at almost every early meeting of A.A.'s King
School group, paid special attention to newcomers, and endeavored
quickly to call people by their first names and make them feel
welcome.[5] She was acknowledged to have been particularly
successful in understanding and helping the wives of early AAs.
The author is in possession of copies of a large number of letters
about Anne Smith that were provided by her son, Bob, and which
speak of her loving, unselfish, kind, thoughtful qualities.

An eight page memorandum by Florence B., of Akron, dated
January 29, 1950, describes Anne's contributions in detail, telling
of friends moving in and out of her house at will, of her helping
new AAs to find a job, and of her being "evangelist, nurse,

---

[1] (...continued)
call to the author, Eddie S., an oldtimer from Colorado, phoned to ask for more
information on Anne and stated she had heard Bill Wilson speak of Anne as the "Mother
of A.A." One obituary also referred to Anne as "Mother" of A.A.

[2] See Bob Smith and Sue Smith Windows, *Children of the Healer* (Illinois: Parkside
Publishing Corporation, 1992), pp. 29, 43, 132.

[3] *The Language of the Heart* (New York: The A.A. Grapevine, Inc., 1988), pp. 353-
54.

[4] This statement is made by Dorothy of Cleveland in a four page letter she wrote Bill
Wilson after Anne's death, a copy of which letter is in the author's possession.

[5] Letter to Bill Wilson from Gabe B., written on the occasion of Anne's death;
memorandum of interview by the author of Sue Smith Windows during Founders' Day
at Akron, Ohio, in June, 1991; 8 page memorandum, entitled, "This was Anne Smith,"
by F. D. B., Akron, dated January 20, 1950; transcript of taped interview of Dorothy
S. M., former wife of Clarence S., by Bill Wilson on August 30, 1954. Copies of all the
foregoing are in the author's possession.

salesman, employment bureau, all in one." As to Anne's religious convictions, this same memorandum said:

> Anne's personal religion was simple and workable. She never sought to rewrite the Bible nor to explain it. She just accepted it.

Anne's Spiritual Workbook

This comment brings us to the spiritual workbook which Anne compiled during the years 1933 to 1939, which her daughter partially typed up for her, and which she used to record and teach to others the spiritual ideas she was deriving from her study of the Bible, her wide reading of Christian books, and her involvement in the Oxford Group. That workbook seems to be the only written record written in A.A.'s formative years in which an A.A. founder described precisely some of the spiritual ideas that were then being developed, that influenced the literature early AAs read, and that was itself used to guide newcomers.

In our book, *Anne Smith's Spiritual Workbook*, we have covered many of the items in Anne's 64 pages of notes.[6] We do not intend to repeat the workbook material here at much length. But we will give a sketch of it because we believe that Anne's workbook fully reflects the type of biblical, Christian, Oxford Group, and other spiritual material that Akron AAs were hearing, discussing, and practicing in their program of the 1930's.

When the author wrote *Anne Smith's Spiritual Workbook*, he had found, in Mary C. Darrah's book, *Sister Ignatia*, the suggestion that Anne had shared from her workbook with the newly sober people she helped. Since that date, the author has obtained from Dennis C., an A.A. historian in Connecticut, Dennis's own recollections of written and oral material given him

---

[6] See Dick B., *Anne Smith's Spiritual Workbook* (Corte Madera, Ca: Good Book Publishing Company, 1992).

as to Anne's workbook by John R., an Akron oldtimer who died in 1989. At the time of his death, John R. was said to be the A.A. member with the longest period of continuous sobriety—just short of 50 years.[7] When asked by Dennis C. whether A.A. was what it used to be, John R. replied that A.A. used to *require* a number of things and that Akron AAs often congregated in Dr. Bob's home to establish and maintain a strong spiritual life. John said:

> Before one of these meetings [in Dr. Bob's home], Anne used to pull out a little book [her spiritual workbook] and quote from it. We would discuss it. Then we would see what Anne would suggest from it for our discussion.[8]

We believe this statement that Anne's spiritual workbook was shared with early AAs, and presumably Bill Wilson, in Dr. Bob's home, gives the document special importance as an historical record of early A.A. in Akron. Anne's daughter, Sue, told the author in a phone interview in September, 1992, that AAs used to call their visits to the Smith's home, visits to get their "spiritual pablum." The material that Anne read them becomes all the more important historically when one compares it with language found in the subsequent Big Book and Twelve Steps.

And now for a brief review of the contents.

---

[7] Both Sue Smith Windows and Robert R. Smith, Dr. Bob's children, have confirmed their close friendship with John R. In fact, it was Sue who introduced Dennis C. to John R. and made the interview possible that provided the information about Anne's workbook. In a telephone interview with the author on September 5, 1992, Dr. Bob's son, "Smitty," told the author that John R., and his wife, Elgie, lived quite close to Dr. Bob's daughter, Sue. He said John R. got sober on March 1, 1939 and died in January, 1989, just short of his 50th sobriety "birthday."

[8] This statement by John R. was provided to the author in a telephone interview by the author with Dennis C. on September 5, 1992.

The Bible and Other Books Anne Recommended

One of the major topics that Anne Smith covered in her workbook concerned the books that she read and recommended to those to whom her remarks were addressed.

First and foremost of her recommendations was the Bible. She wrote:

> Of course the Bible ought to be the main Source Book of all. No day ought to pass without reading it. Read until some passage comes that "hits" you. Then pause and meditate over its meaning for your life. Begin reading the Bible with the Book of Acts and follow up with the Gospels and then the Epistles of St. Paul. Let "Revelation" alone for a while. The Psalms ought to be read and the prophets.[9]

Anne held the Oxford Group view that God could, would, and should guide reading. She wrote:

> LET ALL YOUR READING BE GUIDED. What does God want me to read? A newly surrendered person is like a convalescent after an operation. He needs a carefully balanced diet of nourishing and easily assimilated food. Reading is an essential part of the Christian's diet. It is important that he read that which can be assimilated and will be nourishing. If you do not know what books to read see someone who is surrendered and who is mature in the Groups.[10]

Anne suggested biographies or stories of changed lives by Oxford Group writers. She listed Begbie's *Life Changers* and *Twice-Born Men*; Shoemaker's *Children of the Second Birth* and *Twice-Born Ministers*; Russell's *For Sinners Only*; and Reynold's

---

[9] Dick B., *Anne Smith's Spiritual Workbook*, pp. 12-13.

[10] Dick B., *Anne Smith's Spiritual Workbook*, p. 12.

New Lives For Old.[11] She recommended specific books by some of the leading Christian writers of the day—Geoffrey Allen, Samuel M. Shoemaker, Jr., E. Stanley Jones, Harry Emerson Fosdick, and Toyohiko Kagawa.[12] In fact, Anne thought so much of Kagawa's book on love that she devoted four pages of her sixty-four page workbook to discussing it. Anne urged her audience to read at least one book a year on the life of Christ, saying that more would be better. And she recommended well-known books on Jesus Christ by Stalker, Barton, Glover, and Speer.[13]

Anne's Interpretations of the Twenty-Eight Oxford Group Principles

Anne's spiritual workbook comments were certainly not limited to remarks about the Oxford Group and its ideas. Some have called her workbook an *Oxford Group* handbook, workbook, notebook,

---

[11] See Harold Begbie, *Life Changers* (London: Mills & Boon, Ltd., 1932); *Twice-Born Men* (New York: Fleming H. Revell, 1909); Samuel M. Shoemaker, Jr., *Children of the Second Birth* (New York: Fleming H. Revell, 1927); *Twice-Born Ministers* (New York: Fleming H. Revell, 1929); A. J. Russell, *For Sinners Only* (London: Hodder & Stoughton, 1932); Amelia S. Reynolds, *New Lives For Old* (New York: Fleming H. Revell, 1929).

[12] Anne cited Geoffrey Allen's *He That Cometh* (New York: The Macmillan Company, 1933); Samuel M. Shoemaker's *The Conversion of the Church* (New York: Fleming H. Revell, 1932); *If I Be Lifted Up* (New York: Fleming H. Revell, 1931); and *One Boy's Influence* (New York: Association Press, 1925); *all* of the E. Stanley Jones books (See those we listed in *Anne Smith's Spiritual Workbook*, p. 13, 17-18); Harry Emerson Fosdick's *The Meaning of Prayer* (New York: Association Press, 1915) and *The Manhood of the Master* (London: Student Christian Movement, 1924); and Toyohiko Kagawa's *Love: The Law of Life* (Philadelphia: The John C. Winston Company, 1929).

[13] See Rev. James Stalker, *The Life of Jesus Christ* (New York: Fleming H. Revell, 1891); George A. Barton, *Jesus of Nazareth: A Biography* (New York: The Macmillan Company, 1922); T. R. Glover, *The Jesus of History* (New York: Association Press, 1919); Robert E. Speer, *Studies of the Man Christ Jesus* (New York: Fleming H. Revell, 1896).

or journal.[14] Its contents are not so circumscribed! However, as we did point out and analyze in our book, *Anne Smith's Spiritual Workbook*, Anne discussed every single one of the twenty-eight Oxford Group principles we mentioned at the beginning of this part of our book and which we have detailed in Appendix Two. As Anne discussed these Oxford Group principles, there emerged words and phrases that have become words of art in Alcoholics Anonymous, whether they came from her workbook, the Oxford Group, or elsewhere. The following, with footnote references to page numbers assigned to a copy of Anne's workbook by A.A. Archives in New York, are some significant words and phrases—many of which were used by the Oxford Group:

1. God as God, Spirit, the living God, Father;[15]
2. Sin as:
   a. Anything that blocks God,[16] and

---

[14] When the trustees' Archives Committee transmitted a copy of the document to the author and to Sue Windows from the General Service Board of Alcoholics Anonymous, A.A.'s Archivist, Frank M., called it Anne's "Oxford Group Handbook." In his book, *Not-God*, Dr. Ernest Kurtz refers to "Anne Smith's OG 'workbook' in A.A. archives." See Ernest Kurtz, *Not-God*. Expanded ed. (Minnesota: Hazelden, 1991), p. 331, note 32. In Mary C. Darrah, *Sister Ignatia* (Chicago: Loyola University Press, 1992), at pages 115 and 116, Darrah states: "In addition to reading passages from Holy Scripture to the newly sober men, she [Anne Smith] read from her own Oxford Group notebook, disclosing the personally meaningful ideas and spiritual guidance she had gathered over the years. . . . Many present-day A.A. practices, slogans and ideals leap out of Anne Smith's Oxford Group journal."

[15] Anne mentions God with a capital "G" on almost every page. The Big Book contains similar usages 132 times in its first 164 pages and appendices. Anne mentions with great frequency Holy Spirit and Spirit, with the Big Book using the word "Spirit" (See Big Book, pp. 46, 66, 84-85, 164). On page 42, she refers to "the living God," as do the Bible and the Oxford Group and the Big Book—the latter, when it refers on page 28 to "a living Creator." The author inspected an earlier draft of the Big Book at Stepping Stones. Chapter # 1, which at that point, was entitled "There is a Solution," referred at page 12 to "the living God." On pages 8 and 11 of her workbook, Anne refers to God as "Father," as does the Big Book in several places (See Big Book, pp. 14, 62, 181, 260).

[16] Anne uses this expression on page 38; and the Big Book several times speaks of the things in ourselves that block us from God (See Big Book, pp. 64, 71, 72).

      b. Independence toward God—living without Him;[17]

3. Surrender of self-will, anger, resentment, pride, fear, dishonesty, sins, and wills;[18]

4. The 5 C's—Confidence, Confession, Conviction, Conversion, and Continuance;[19]

5. "Decision" as a concept connected with surrender;[20]

6. The "moral test" in connection with self-examination;[21]

7. Confession;[22]

8. Power greater than ourselves;[23]

9. *Removal* of sins;[24]

10. Daily surrender;[25]

---

[17] On page 4, Anne uses the expression, "living without God," while the Big Book speaks on pages 28 and 29 of discovering and establishing a relationship with God. The Big Book multilith version of the language on page 29 speaks of finding or rediscovering God.

[18] She speaks of these on pages 17-18, 25, 37, 43, 61-62; and the Big Book speaks of getting rid of or turning these over to God on pages 14, 59-60, 62, 64, 67-68, 70, 84, 86.

[19] Anne devoted all of page 4 of her workbook to the 5 C's. And see Dick B., *The Oxford Group & Alcoholics Anonymous* (Seattle: Glen Abbey Books, 1992), pp. 144-145 and elsewhere, for a discussion of these Oxford Group concepts and their corresponding ideas in the Big Book.

[20] Anne discussed the "decision" idea at pages 4, 37, and 42; and the "decision" idea is the heart of A.A.'s Step Three.

[21] Anne twice spoke of making the "moral test" in connection with self-examination (pp. 4, 14); and the idea finds its A.A. counterpart in the taking of a "moral inventory" in Step Four.

[22] Anne devoted substantial portions of her workbook to discussing sharing and confession; and this concept finds its counterpart in Step Five.

[23] Anne spoke at page 37 of: (1) "lack of power" (Compare Big Book, p. 45), and (2) the need for "a stronger power" which God provided through Christ (Compare Big Book, pages 45-46, which says "We had to find . . . a Power greater than ourselves." It calls the "Power": "that Power, which is God").

[24] Anne speaks at page 36 of Christ removing them, and the Big Book speaks in Steps 6 and 7 of God's removing these "defects of character" and "shortcomings"—which were called "sins" in earlier versions of the Steps.

[25] See Dick B., *Anne Smith's Spiritual Workbook*, pp. 37-43, 75.

11. Daily quiet time;[26]
12. Guidance;[27]
13. Fellowship;[28]
14. Trust in God;[29]
15. Restitution;[30]
16. Prayer;[31]
17. Listening and checking;[32]
18. The Four Absolutes;[33]
19. Witness;[34]
20. Knowing God's Will;[35]
21. Putting things in God's hands;[36]
22. Grace of God;[37]

---

[26] See Dick B., *Anne Smith's Spiritual Workbook*, pp. 44-47; and compare Steps Ten and Eleven.

[27] Anne wrote frequently of her belief in the Guidance of God (pp. 2, 8-10, 15-16, 27, 31); and the Big Book frequently speaks of asking God for direction (pp. 68-69, 80, 86-87, 100, 164).

[28] Anne wrote much on the Oxford Group and biblical idea of Fellowship, quoting 1 John 1:3 (pp. 11, 16, 26, 49-51); and A.A. often speaks of a Fellowship (Big Book, pp. xv, 45, 90, 164).

[29] Anne wrote, "Trust God fully for results" (p. 9); and the Big Book specifically emphasizes trust in God (Big Book, pp. 68, 98).

[30] Anne wrote much on the amends concept—"restitution" (pp. 18, 26, 43, 44, 51); and the pre-Big Book language used in A.A. for amends was "restitution." See *Alcoholics Anonymous Comes of Age* (New York: Alcoholics Anonymous World Services, Inc., 1957), p. 160; Big Book, p. 292.

[31] See Dick B., *Anne Smith's Spiritual Workbook*, pp. 47-49; Big Book, p. 85.

[32] See Dick B., *Anne Smith's Spiritual Workbook*, pp. 52-54.

[33] See Dick B., *Anne Smith's Spiritual Workbook*, pp. 56-58.

[34] See Dick B., *Anne Smith's Spiritual Workbook*, pp. 60-61. Anne wrote on page 2 of her workbook a phrase that is familiar to AAs "We can't give away what we haven't got."

[35] See Dick B., *Anne Smith's Spiritual Workbook*, pp. 61-63; Step Eleven.

[36] On pages 24 and 39 she used this figure of speech as did the Big Book at pp. 100, 120, and 124.

[37] See Luke 2:40; Acts 11:23; Romans 5:15; 2 Corinthians 1:12; Anne's Workbook, at page 57; and Big Book, page 25.

23. The intuitive thought;[38]
24. Abandoning yourself to God;[39]
25. Willingness;[40]
26. Faith in God;[41]
27. Seek ye first the Kingdom of God;[42]
28. God-consciousness.[43, 44]

---

[38] Anne wrote at page 8, "Guidance comes through direct intuitive thought." The Big Book says, in its discussion of the Eleventh Step at page 86, "Here we ask God for inspiration, an intuitive thought or a decision."

[39] Anne wrote at page 42, "Surrender is a complete handing over of our wills to God, a reckless abandon of ourselves." The Big Book states at page 59, "We asked His protection and care with complete abandon," and at page 164, "Abandon yourself to God as you understand God."

[40] See Anne's remarks at page 42 and those of the Big Book at pages 46-47, 570.

[41] See Anne Smith's discussion at pages 2 and 30 and the Big Book at page 55, "We finally saw that faith in some kind of God was a part of our make-up . . . ."

[42] Anne wrote of this verse from Matthew 6:33 in the Sermon on the Mount, a verse often used in the Oxford Group, "We must put all that we have under God's direction-'Seek ye first the Kingdom of God.' He will show us how to handle these things" (p. 39). In his interview of Mitch K., Clarence S.'s sponsee, the author learned in August, 1992, at Charleston, West Virginia, that Clarence S., who was a man sponsored by Dr. Bob, said that Dr. Bob said the A.A. Slogan—First Things First—was taken from Matthew 6:33. See also *DR. BOB and the Good Oldtimers* (New York: Alcoholics Anonymous World Services, Inc., 1980), p. 192.

[43] Anne spoke of "God-consciousness" at pages 13 and 19.

[44] The Big Book speaks of "God-consciousness" at pages 13, 85, 569, and 570.

Biblical Principles She Discussed

Anne wrote at length on biblical principles—principles that certainly were not the exclusive province of the Oxford Group.[45] There is a more complete discussion of these Bible verses and ideas at pages 67 to 71 of our book, *Anne Smith's Spiritual Workbook*; and we refer to them in various portions of this book. In any event, Anne placed great stress on the Bible as *the* most important reading item. She read it herself each day. She read it to Bill Wilson and Dr. Bob each morning while Bill was staying at the Smith home in the summer of 1935. She read and quoted from it to the people she helped in her home. Her workbook is surfeited with Bible references and quotations.

Some were to such concepts as:

1. love;
2. forgiveness of sins;
3. confession;
4. speaking the truth in love;
5. sharing as a Gospel concept;
6. witness;

---

[45] Not too realistically, the Oxford Group felt it offered a program acceptable to and within all denominations. In The Layman with a Notebook, *What Is The Oxford Group?* (London: Oxford University Press, 1933), the author said on page 3: "The Oxford Group works within churches of all denominations, planning to bring those outside back into their folds and to re-awaken those within to their responsibilities as Christians." Contrast Darrah, *Sister Ignatia*, at page 30: "Literature about A.A. had not yet been written, so there was no sure way to convince incoming alcoholics that the Oxford Group was not a religion or a Protestant sect. This posed a critical problem for the alcoholic pioneers who still easily confused religion with the nonsectarian spirituality that only later characterized Alcoholics Anonymous. Left unresolved, the situation held serious religious consequences for Catholics who needed the sobriety support available from the Oxford Group but whose faith did not permit active participation in religious denominations outside the Catholic tradition." And, while we will not detail the facts here, the Oxford Group was not all that well received in many Protestant denominations, including Dr. Frank Buchman's own, the Lutheran Church. In any event, Anne's own focus in her writing was on the Bible first, and also on writers such as Toyohiko Kagawa, E. Stanley Jones, and many others who had nothing to do with the Oxford Group or its ideas.

7. regeneration through the power of Christ;
8. the power and direction of the Holy Spirit;
9. rebirth;
10. the beatitudes in the Sermon on the Mount;
11. salvation through obedience;
12. God's will that believers should prosper and be in health;
13. patience, tolerance, and humility; and
14. courage, faith, peace, power, and joy.

She certainly mentioned living "one day at a time." At page 9 of her workbook, she suggested: "Be willing to live a day at a time, an hour at a time." That idea is, of course, a foundational approach in Alcoholics Anonymous. Dr. Bob once commented that the A.A. motto "Easy does it" means you take it a day at a time.[46] And he informed his sponsee, Clarence S., that the concept of "one day at a time" came from Matthew 6:34 in the Sermon on the Mount: "Take therefore no thought [do not be anxious] for the morrow: for the morrow shall take thought for the things of itself. Sufficient unto the day is the evil thereof."[47]

Traces of Anne's Concepts in the Twelve Steps

There are a good many items in Anne's workbook that may have influenced or found their way directly into the Twelve Steps. Consider these things that Anne wrote:

1. *As to an unmanageable life*—"Oh God, manage me because I cannot manage myself;"[48]

---

[46] See *DR. BOB*, p. 282.

[47] Mitch K., Clarence's sponsee, gave this information to the author in an interview in Charleston, West Virginia, in August, 1992.

[48] Anne wrote a prayer of this nature on three different pages of her workbook (pp. 42, 51, 26). Compare Step One: "We admitted we were powerless over alcohol—that our lives had become unmanageable."

2. *As to coming to believe*—A "stronger power than his [Paul's] was needed;" a "relationship with God;"[49]
3. *About surrender*—A "decision to give my life to Christ;"[50]
4. *About inventory*—Making the "moral test;"[51]
5. *About confession*—"Being honest to God, self, and other people;"[52]
6. *About conviction*—"Christ can only remove them [sins];"[53]
7. *About conversion*—"Surrender is a complete handing over of our wills to God, a reckless abandon of ourselves, all that we

---

[49] Anne used these two phrases on page 37 of her workbook. Compare Step Two: "Came to believe that a Power greater than ourselves could restore us to sanity." See Big Book, p. 46: "that Power, which is God;" p. 29: "Each individual, in the personal stories, describes . . . the way he established his relationship with God."

[50] Anne used the decision language on page 42. Compare Step Three: "Made a decision to turn our will and our lives over to the care of God *as we understood Him.*"

[51] Anne wrote in page 14: "Make the moral test." She added: "4 standards." And this was the Oxford Group method of "making written moral inventory." The life-change prospect would make a written inventory, measuring his moral life against the four "yardsticks" (as Dr. Bob called them)—Absolute honesty, absolute purity, absolute unselfishness, and absolute love. As to "making the moral test," see H. A. Walter, *Soul-Surgery.* 6th ed. (Oxford: Printed at the University Press by John Johnson, Printer to the University, 1940), pp. 41-48. As to taking a written "business inventory" with pencil and paper and notes, See Clarence I. Benson, *The Eight Points of the Oxford Group* (London: Humphrey Milford, Oxford University Press, 1936), pp. 44, 162, 7; Cecil Rose, *When Man Listens* (New York: Oxford University Press, 1937), pp. 17-19. As to conducting the self-examination process by writing down sins that failure to measure up to the Four Absolutes revealed, see Samuel M. Shoemaker, Jr., *How To Become a Christian* (New York: Harper & Brothers, 1953), pp. 56-57; *Twice-Born Ministers* (New York: Fleming H. Revell, 1929); Rose, *When Man Listens*, pp. 18-19; A. J. Russell, *For Sinners Only* (London: Hodder & Stoughton, 1932), pp. 20, 36; Olive Jones, *Inspired Children* (New York: Harper & Brothers, 1933), pp. 47-68; *Inspired Youth* (New York: Harper & Brothers, 1938), p. 41; Hallen Viney, *How Do I Begin?* (The Oxford Group, 1937), pp. 2-4. Compare Step Four: "Made a searching and fearless moral inventory of ourselves."

[52] Anne wrote this phrase at page 34. Compare Step Five: "Admitted to God, to ourselves, and to another human being the exact nature of our wrongs."

[53] Anne wrote this language at page 36. Compare Step Six: "Were entirely ready to have God remove all these defects of character."

have, all that we think, that we are, everything we hold dear, to God to do what he likes with;"[54]

8. *About listing harms*—Making "a list;"[55]
9. *About amends*—"Restitution";[56]
10. *About maintenance of the spiritual condition*—"Daily surrender" and "continuance;"[57]
11. *About prayer and meditation*—"A genuine contact with God;"[58] and
12. *About service*—"People are more important than things. . . . We must put ALL THAT WE HAVE under God's direction."[59]

Anne Ripley Smith wrote her workbook well before the Big Book was published. She read its contents to AAs in her home in Akron. And

---

[54] Anne wrote the surrender language at page 42. Compare the "Seventh Step Prayer" on page 76 of the Big Book: "My Creator, I am now willing that you should have all of me, good and bad. I pray that you now remove from me every single defect of character which stands in the way of my usefulness to you and my fellows. Grant me strength, as I go out from here, to do your bidding. Amen."

[55] See Dick B., *Anne Smith's Spiritual Workbook*, p. 75. Compare Step Eight: "Made a list of all persons we had harmed, and became willing to make amends to them all."

[56] The Oxford Group and early AAs did not use the word "amends," but rather spoke of "restitution," "apology," and setting things right. Anne wrote in several places on "restitution" and spelled out several aspects of setting things right. Compare Step Nine: "Made direct amends to such people wherever possible, except when to do so would injure them or others."

[57] Anne did not use the phrase "continued to take personal inventory," but she did write about daily surrender and continuance at pages 4, 14, 31, 33-35, 45-49. Compare Step Ten: "Continued to take personal inventory and when we were wrong promptly admitted it." Discussing Step Ten, the Big Book says at page 85: "It is easy to let up on the spiritual program of action and rest on our laurels. . . . What we really have is a daily reprieve contingent on the maintenance of our spiritual condition. Every day is a day when we must carry the vision of God's will into all our activities. 'How can I best serve Thee—Thy will (not mine) be done.'"

[58] Anne used this phrase at page 2. Compare Step Eleven: "Sought through prayer and meditation to improve our conscious contact with God *as we understood Him*, praying only for knowledge of His will for us and the power to carry that out."

[59] See Dick B., *Anne Smith's Spiritual Workbook*, p. 76. Compare Step Twelve: "Having had a spiritual awakening as the result of these steps, we tried to carry this message to alcoholics, and to practice these principles in all our affairs."

the listeners would seem, almost inevitably, to have included Bill Wilson. She read to them while AAs were developing their principles and program through study of the Bible and Oxford Group principles and achieving recovery in Akron as the "alcoholic squad of the Oxford Group." The contents of her workbook therefore are highly significant when we are speaking of the resources that A.A.'s progenitors contributed to the recovery program in the early days.

Love and Service

We close as to Dr. Bob's wife by pointing to the two Bible verses most quoted in connection with her words and life:

He that loveth not knoweth not God; for *God is love* (1 John 4:8). [emphasis added]

For as the body without the spirit is dead, so *faith without works is dead* also (James 2:26). [emphasis added]

God is love, and faith without works is dead.

Anne was well remembered for opening her Bible and reading "God is love."[60] Her "favorite verse" was said to be "Faith without works is dead."[61] The latter verse from the Book of James is mentioned with frequency in the Big Book itself.[62] And it seems very possible that it spilled over into:

---

[60] Transcript of the taped interview of Akron oldtimer, Bob E., by Bill Wilson on June 18, 1954, page 7. A copy of this transcript was provided to the author by Ray G., archivist at Dr. Bob's home in Akron. See also *DR. BOB and the Good Oldtimers* (New York: Alcoholics Anonymous World Services, Inc., 1980), p. 117; Ernest Kurtz, *Not-God*. Expanded ed. (Minnesota: Hazelden, 1991), p. 55.

[61] See *DR. BOB*, p. 71; *Pass It On* (New York: Alcoholics Anonymous World Services, Inc., 1984), p. 147.

[62] Big Book, pp. 14, 76, 88.

1. "Works Publishing Company"—the Big Book's first publisher;
2. "Keep coming back. It works"—the group exclamation that ends almost every A.A. meeting; and
3. "It works"—the shortest paragraph in the Big Book.[63]

In any event, the two verses (from 1 John 4:8 and James 2:26)—which are directly attributable to Anne and possibly to Anne alone—simmer down to *love* and *service*.

In his last address to A.A., Dr. Bob had this to say about love and service:

> Our Twelve Steps, when simmered down to the last, resolve themselves into the words *love* and *service*. We understand what love is, and we understand what service is. So let's bear those two things in mind.[64]

Bill Wilson gave Anne Smith this loving tribute at the time of her death:

> Anne was the wife of Dr. Bob, co-founder of Alcoholics Anonymous. She was, quite literally, the mother of our first group, Akron Number One. Her wise and beautiful counsel to all, her insistence that the spiritual come before anything else, her unwavering support of Dr. Bob in all his works; all these were virtues which watered the uncertain seed that was to become A.A. Who but God could assess such a contribution? We can only say

---

[63] See that observation in Nell Wing, *Grateful To Have Been There* (Illinois: Parkside Publishing Corporation, 1992) pages 70-71. Compare also Big Book, page 88: "It works—it really does. We alcoholics are undisciplined. So we let God discipline us in the simple way we have just outlined. But that is not all. There is action and more action. 'Faith without works is dead.' The next chapter is entirely devoted to *Step Twelve*."

[64] *DR.BOB*, p. 338.

that it was priceless and magnificent. In the full sense of the word, she was one of the founders of Alcoholics Anonymous.[65]

Yes, Anne Smith was truly and often called the "Mother of A.A."[66] To nurture the fledgling society, this lady "founder" brought a deep knowledge of and trust in the Bible; a wealth of material from spiritual books of the day; a very specific and detailed written study of Oxford Group principles; a good many phrases that were to become lodged in A.A.; and strong, oft-quoted biblical convictions about its two most important concepts—love and service. Moreover, she shared unstintingly with and for others these resources, as well as her own home, her food, her time, her prayers, her guidance, her compassion, her friendship, and her love.

---

[65] *The Language of the Heart* (New York: The A.A. Grapevine, Inc., 1988), pp. 353-54.

[66] See Bob Smith and Sue Windows, *Children of the Healer: The Story of Dr. Bob's Kids* (Illinois: Parkside Publishing Corporation, 1992), pp. 29, 43, 132; Dick B., *Anne Smith's Spiritual Workbook*, pp. ix, 7; *The Language of the Heart*, p. 353, and the previous references to oldtimers who heard Anne so described.

7

Dr. Bob, His Library, and His Spiritual Studies

Here, as in the case of Dr. Bob's wife, Anne Smith, we have written a book—*Dr. Bob's Library*—that covers in much detail the contribution that Dr. Bob brought to A.A. through his love and study of the Bible, Oxford Group books, and a good many other religious writings—both classical and contemporary.[1] We will not repeat that study, but we will summarize it because much of the *breadth* of A.A.'s spiritual background can be understood from a brief review of Dr. Bob's spiritual quest as revealed by his reading.

Dr. Bob's Spiritual Research

Dr. Bob himself pointed out that, long before he met Bill, he had been intensely studying the Good Book and much other religious literature. He said:

---

[1] See Dick B., *Dr. Bob's Library* (West Virginia: The Bishop of Books, 1992).

Now the interesting part of all this is not the sordid details but the situation that we two fellows were in. We had been associated with the Oxford Group, Bill in New York for five months, and I in Akron, for two and a half years. Bill had acquired their idea of service. I had not, but I had done an immense amount of reading they had recommended. I had refreshed my memory of the Good Book, and I had had excellent training in that as a youngster.[2]

RHS, the memorial article written at the time of Dr. Bob's death, says of the 1933-1935 period of Bob's attendance at the Oxford Group:

Anne became deeply interested in the group and her interest sustained Dr. Bob's. He delved into religious philosophy, he read the Scriptures, he studied spiritual interpretations of the lives of the Saints. Like a sponge he soaked up the spiritual philosophies of the ages.[3]

Another version added:

For the next two and a half years, Bob attended Oxford Group meetings regularly and gave much time and study to its philosophy. . . . "I read everything I could find, and talked to everyone who I thought knew anything about it," Dr. Bob said. He read the Scriptures, studied the lives of the saints, and did what he could to soak up the spiritual and religious philosophies of the ages.[4]

---

[2] *The Co-Founders of Alcoholics Anonymous* (New York: Alcoholics Anonymous World Services, Inc., 1972), p. 7.

[3] *RHS*, Grapevine Memorial Issue for January, 1951 (New York: The A.A. Grapevine, Inc.), p. 21.

[4] *DR. BOB and the Good Oldtimers* (New York: Alcoholics Anonymous World Services, 1980), p. 56.

Dr. Bob and the Good Book

Dr. Bob was very specific about the contribution of the Bible to the Twelve Steps and even more specific about the parts he considered most essential. He said:

> I didn't write the Twelve Steps. I had nothing to do with the writing of them. But I think I probably had something to do with them indirectly. . . . . There was hardly a night [during the three months of Bill Wilson's stay at the Smith home in the summer of 1935] that we didn't sit up until two or three o'clock talking. It would be hard for me to say that, during these nightly discussions around our kitchen table, nothing was said that influenced the writing of the Twelve Steps. We already had the basic ideas, though not in terse and tangible form. We got them . . . as a result of our study of the Good Book.[5]

> They [the early AAs] were convinced that the answer to their problems was in the Good Book. To some of us older ones, the parts we found absolutely essential were the Sermon on the Mount, the 13th chapter of First Corinthians, and the Book of James.[6]

As we previously mentioned, he "cited the Sermon on the Mount as containing the underlying spiritual philosophy of A.A."[7] And he indicated his adherence to and reliance upon the "four absolutes" as the yardsticks that were used before the Twelve Steps.[8] These came from the teachings of Jesus in the Sermon on the Mount and from other New Testament verses.[9]

---

[5] *DR. BOB*, pp. 96-97.

[6] *DR. BOB*, p. 96.

[7] *DR. BOB*, p. 228.

[8] *Co-Founders*, pp. 12-13.

[9] See Dick B., *Dr. Bob's Library*, p. 10; *The Oxford Group & Alcoholics Anonymous* (Seattle: Glen Abbey Books, 1992), pp. 220-22.

Dr. Bob was said to have had a "required reading list."[10] And this is how the list was described:

The Holy Bible, King James Version
    The Sermon on the Mount
    The Lord's Prayer
    The Book of James
    The 13th Chapter of First Corinthians
The Upper Room (Methodist periodical)
The Greatest Thing in the World, by Henry Drummond
The Varieties of Religious Experience, by William James.
For Sinners Only, by A. J. Russell.

When the author interviewed Dr. Bob's daughter, Sue Smith Windows, Mrs. Windows doubted that Dr. Bob had a "required" list. Further, as our research has continued, we have become convinced that, while all of the foregoing books—and certainly the Bible—were strongly recommended by Dr. Bob, other people that were close to him or that he helped would add other Dr. Bob "favorites" to the list. These would include the Glenn Clark books, the E. Stanley Jones books, Emmet Fox's *The Sermon on the Mount*, and James Allen's *As A Man Thinketh*.[11] What is clear, however, is that Dr. Bob's special interest in the portions of the Bible having to do with the Sermon on the Mount, the Corinthians chapter on love, and the Book of James was, to some extent, matched by the books most mentioned as his favorites.

---

[10] See Bill Pittman, *AA The Way It Began* (Seattle: Glen Abbey Books, 1988), p. 197.

[11] Thus Sue Smith Windows specifically informed the author in a personal interview in June, 1991, at Akron that all of Glenn Clark's books were favorites of Dr. Bob; and there are many Glenn Clark books in his library. There are also many references by Anne Smith, Henrietta Seiberling, and Dr. Bob to the E. Stanley Jones books. The transcribed tape of Dorothy S. M., former wife of his sponsee, Clarence S., makes it clear that Dr. Bob thought highly of Emmet Fox's *The Sermon on the Mount*. The transcript of the tape by Bill W. of Bob E., together with the information supplied to the author by Mitch K., Clarence S.'s sponsee, makes it clear that Dr. Bob stressed James Allen's *As a Man Thinketh*. See also Dick B., *Dr. Bob's Library*, pp. 55-56.

Dr. Bob's Other Books

We researched and chose to look from a special viewpoint at the vast number of spiritual books that Dr. Bob read, recommended, and loaned out. Our question was: On what areas did his spiritual quest seem to be focussed. We believe his reading significantly traversed the following categories; and we presented most of them in *Dr. Bob's Library*. More details can be found in Appendix Three:[12]

1. ***The Bible***. Both Dr. Bob and his wife, Anne, stressed that reading the Bible was most important—*the* most important reading item. Each of them read it daily, in Quiet Times, and when they were attending meetings.

2. ***Books on the life of Jesus Christ***. We have already discussed these in connection with Anne Smith's recommended reading. In Appendix Three, we have added additional books Dr. Bob read on this topic. We recently discovered them in further interviews of Dr. Bob's family.

3. ***Christian classics***. These include *The Confessions of St. Augustine*, *The Imitation of Christ* by Thomas A Kempis, and *The Practice of the Presence of God* by Brother Lawrence.

4. ***Daily Bible devotionals***. These include *Daily Strength For Daily Needs*; *My Utmost For His Highest*, *The Runner's Bible*, and *The Upper Room*, as well as other books falling in that category such as Fosdick's *The Meaning of Prayer*, E. Stanley Jones's *Victorious Living* and *Abundant Living*, Glenn Clark's *I Will Lift Up Mine Eyes*, and Lewis Dunnington's *Handles of Power*. Dr. Bob owned, read, and used them all.

---

[12] In Appendix Three, we have set out in full the authors, titles, and publishing data on Dr. Bob's books as we found them as of the date of this writing.

5. ***Books on prayer***. Dr. Bob read Glenn Clark's *The Soul's Sincere Desire, I Will Lift Up Mine Eyes,* and *How To Find Health Through Prayer*; Starr Daily's *Recovery*; Lewis L. Dunnington's *Handles of Power*; Mary Baker Eddy's *Science and Health With Key To The Scriptures*; Charles and Cora Filmore's *Teach Us To Pray*; Harry Emerson Fosdick's *The Meaning of Prayer*; Emmet Fox's *Getting Results By Prayer* and *The Sermon on the Mount*; Gerald Heard's *A Preface To Prayer*; E. Stanley Jones's *Victorious Living*; Frank Laubach's *Prayer (Mightiest Force in the World)*; and William R. Parker's *Prayer Can Change Your Life*. In Appendix Three, we have added some new books on the subject of prayer that additional research on our part has established were a part of Dr. Bob's reading.

6. ***Books on the Sermon on the Mount***. Dr. Bob read Oswald Chambers' *Studies In The Sermon on the Mount*; E. Stanley Jones's *The Christ of the Mount*; Emmet Fox's *The Sermon on the Mount*; and Glenn Clark's *The Soul's Sincere Desire* and *I Will Lift Up Mine Eyes*.

7. ***Books on Christian love***. See Toyohiko Kagawa's *Love: The Law of Life*; Henry Drummond's *The Greatest Thing In The World*—a study of 1 Corinthians 13; and Glenn Clark's *The Soul's Sincere Desire*.

8. Probably **all of the Oxford Group books that were disseminated by Dr. Samuel Moor Shoemaker's Oxford Group bookstore at Calvary House**, the American headquarters of the Oxford Group. We have listed these books in Appendix One and made some comments about them in the portions of this book having to do with Akron's progenitors.

9. ***The Sam Shoemaker books*** included in the *Calvary Evangel* list, together with some additional pieces of Shoemaker literature we have established as being a part of "Dr. Bob's Library."

10. ***Books by A.A.'s "Founders,"*** Professor William James and Dr. Carl Jung.

11. ***Books by leading Christian writers popular in the 1930's***, who were of special interest to Dr. Bob. These include James Allen, Oswald Chambers, Glenn Clark, Henry Drummond, Charles Filmore, Harry Emerson Fosdick, Emmet Fox, E. Stanley Jones, Fulton Oursler, Norman Vincent Peale, Vincent Sheean, Fulton J. Sheen, and Charles M. Sheldon.

12. ***Books on Christianity and the Mind.***

13. ***Books about the Bible, the Church Fathers, and Healing.***

14. ***Books by modern Roman Catholic authors.***

15. ***Books about Quiet Time.***

16. ***A wide variety of other religious books*** on Confucius, Gandhi, the occult, and the saints.

We believe it important here to note the tremendous study resources available to early A.A. in its founding moments. The resources included not only the Bible, but also the beautiful expositions of Henry Drummond, the Oxford Group writings, and the rich prose of Reverend Sam Shoemaker in New York. And they included books by those contemporary masters of Christian writing of the day such as Chambers, Clark, Eddy, Filmore, Fosdick, Jones, Kagawa, Sheldon, Sheean, Sheen, *and* such popular "new thought" writers as James Allen, Emmet Fox, and Ralph Waldo Trine.

As we believe will be established in a later book analyzing the foregoing writings, A.A.'s thoughts, phrases, and concepts from the Good Book that are found in the Big Book did *not* merely come from Oxford Group writings or those of Emmet Fox.[13] They were grounded in specific concepts of the other writers mentioned in connection with Dr. Bob and with T. Henry and Clarace Williams, Anne Smith, and Henrietta Seiberling. When Bill Wilson spoke of A.A.'s concepts as being borrowed mainly from the fields of "religion" and medicine,[14] and as being the "common property of mankind,"[15] we think he intended to open the door to, and incorporate a broader base than actually existed at A.A.'s beginnings. Yet those expressions apply as well to the very broad biblical and Christian base to which Bill himself had attested, as did Dr. Bob, Anne, and Henrietta.

Consider, for example, this statement by Dr. Ernest Kurtz in *Not-God*:

> Bill Wilson found himself in awe of Dr. Bob's "spiritual knowledge" and cherished the guidance of Anne Smith as each morning her pleasant voice read and interpreted the Christian Scriptures and the Oxford Group devotional books (p. 32).[16]

We now have some grasp of the material to which Bill referred. It is highly unlikely that Anne spoke only of the Bible and of

---

[13] See Igor Sikorsky, Jr., *A.A.'s Godparents* (Minneapolis: CompCare Publishers, 1990). Without providing specific citations to A.A. literature, Sikorsky makes this statement about Emmet Fox at page 23: "A.A. used much of his simply stated profundities to create a philosophy that now transforms the lives of millions of recovering alcoholics." To date, we have found nothing in the reported statements of Bill Wilson, Dr. Bob, Anne Smith, T. Henry Williams, Clarace Williams, or Henrietta Seiberling that would support this statement. We *have* found much talk of the importance of the Bible, the Oxford Group and Shoemaker literature, and the *many* Christian books, including *some* by Fox, that were widely read in early A.A.

[14] *Twelve Steps And Twelve Traditions* (New York: Alcoholics Anonymous World Services, Inc., 1952), p. 16.

[15] See *Alcoholics Anonymous Comes of Age* (New York: Alcoholics Anonymous World Services, Inc., 1957), p. 39.

[16] See Dr. Bob's statements about the Bible and the Sermon on the Mount. *DR. BOB*, pp. 96-97, 228; compare pages 151, 111. As to Anne's statement on the Bible, see Dick B., *Anne Smith's Spiritual Workbook*, p. 12. As to Henrietta's focus on the Bible, see Chapter Two of this book.

Oxford Group "devotionals." For we now know the full scope of Dr. Bob's reading and the full scope of Anne Smith's workbook. We know also that if Anne was giving "interpretations" of the Bible and of devotional books, the "interpretations" in part consisted of what she was reading *from her workbook* to people, probably including Bill, who were there in the Smith home for "spiritual pablum." The reading done by Anne and Dr. Bob provided a rich spiritual mix for the early meetings, the visits to the Smith home, and the personal contacts Anne and Dr. Bob had with newcomers.

8

Bill Wilson and the Akron Genesis

It is easy to get a fixation about Akron's being different from the rest of A.A., or being at variance with mainstream A.A. ideas, or being a part of tensions between New York and Akron, Cleveland and Akron, or New York and Cleveland AAs.[1] But such a focus here—perhaps based on *the post-Big Book-publication era*—would materially detract from our learning the very real and substantial part that Bill Wilson played in the Akron laboratory work during A.A.'s infancy there.

Bill Wilson was the moving factor at A.A.'s Akron beginnings in Henrietta Seiberling's Gatehouse. He was *in Akron every moment of* the summer of 1935. He *continued in close contact* with Dr. Bob through phone, travel, and mail.[2] Bill was *well acquainted with the Akron personalities*, both the non-alcoholics in the Oxford Group and the AAs in the "alcoholic squad" of the Oxford Group. His relationships with and *loyalties to Dr. Bob*

---

[1] For a thorough discussion of conflicting patterns and ideas, see Ernest Kurtz, *Not-God*. Expanded ed. (Minnesota: Hazelden, 1991), pp. 231-249.

[2] See, for example, Nell Wing, *Grateful To Have Been There* (Illinois: Parkside Publishing Corporation, 1992), pp. 82-83. Also, in a visit to the archives at Bill's home at Stepping Stones, the author personally inspected copies of a steady stream of correspondence between Bill and Dr. Bob—all written before the 1939 publication of the Big Book.

were close, continuous, loving, and free of acrimony.[3] In fact, many observers commented on how well the two founders balanced each other. And Bill's submission of Big Book drafts to Dr. Bob, apparently with no adverse feedback from Dr. Bob, reflected the mutuality of their thinking and confidence.

Bill and the Akron Resources He Found There

William Griffith Wilson was a major figure in the Akron genesis. He brought substantial wisdom and resources to the Akron scene between 1935 and 1939. His ideas at that time seemed very much in harmony with the biblical, Christian, and Oxford Group concepts that were hammered out in Akron and seeded the A.A. program. Not only did Bill Wilson almost always mention Dr. Bob when he mentioned Oxford Group and Shoemaker sources; he simply had to be referring, in part, to the very resources we have just been discussing. And Bill Wilson fully contributed to and participated in the draw on those resources.

In fact, if one unique contribution in Akron was its emphasis on the Bible, we need to repeat here Bill's statement to T. Henry and Clarace Williams:

I learned a great deal from you people [T. Henry and Clarace Williams], from the Smiths themselves, and from Henrietta [Seiberling]. I hadn't looked in the Bible, up to this time at all.[4]

And Bill, in all his later zeal to credit Sam Shoemaker, still could not, and usually did not, ignore the fact that much of his

---

[3] See, for example, Wing, *Grateful To Have Been There*, pp. 77-83; *Lois Remembers* (New York: Al-Anon Family Group Headquarters, 1987) pp. 96, 108.

[4] From the transcript of Bill Wilson's taped interview with T. Henry and Clarace Williams on December 12, 1954, which transcript is on file in A.A. Archives in New York.

Oxford Group exposure was in Akron as well as in New York. Let's consider some remarks about the resources of the Oxford Group, of which *both* Bill Wilson and Dr. Bob were enthusiastic members until at least early 1937. Bill said:

> So far as I am concerned, and Dr. Smith too, the O.G. [Oxford Group] seeded A.A. It was our spiritual wellspring at the beginning.[5]

Bill wrote Sam Shoemaker the following:

> It is also entirely true that the substance of A.A.'s Twelve Steps was derived from the O.G.'s emphasis on the essentials and your unforgettable presentation of this material time after time. Certainly there were other indispensable contributions without which we should probably have got no place. But none of these were so large or so critical as your own. Though I wish the "cofounder" tag had never been hitched to any of us, I have no hesitancy in adding your name to the list![6]

However, Shoemaker had cautioned Bill on this point, saying:

> It sounds as if I had been the sole determining factor. There's not a word about Young [Jung] or James or Dr. Silkworth. I pick up from time to time the idea that I was almost responsible for the Twelve Steps. This bothers me, Bill, because I am sure that while a little of the spiritual inspiration for the thing came through us at 61 Gramercy Park [the American headquarters of the Oxford Group at Shoemaker's Calvary House in New York City], there

---

[5] Letter from William G. Wilson to Samuel M. Shoemaker, 14 July 1949, a copy of which the author inspected in the archives at Bill's Stepping Stones home at Bedford Hills, New York.

[6] Letter from William G. Wilson to Samuel M. Shoemaker, 23 April 1963, a copy of which the author inspected at the archives at Stepping Stones.

were many other factors, and it is highly important that this be generally known.[7]

A.A.'s own publication, *Pass It On*, said this:

Criticism and rejection notwithstanding, Lois and Bill did not become immediately disillusioned with the Oxford Group or with its principles, *from which Bill borrowed freely.*[8]

Bill was about to write the famous fifth chapter [of the Big Book], "How It Works." The basic material for the chapter was the word-of-mouth program that Bill had been talking ever since his own recovery. It was *heavy with Oxford Group principles*, and had in addition some of the ideas Bill had gleaned from William James and Dr. Silkworth. Moreover, *Bill had worked with Dr. Bob and other alcoholics in testing and sifting the workability and effectiveness of the early program.* While he would be the nominal author of the fifth chapter, he was in fact serving as spokesman for all the others (pp. 196-197, emphasis added).

In addition to being a talker and a listener, Bill was also a writer and a planner, and neither activity interested Dr. Bob. Dr. Bob, however, furnished ideas and sound judgment that found their way into Bill's writings (p. 157).

[Bill said] "I am always glad to say privately that some of the Oxford Group presentation and emphasis upon the Christian message saved my life" (p. 171).

The bottom line to be derived from these quotations is that Bill Wilson had a very real part in the assimilation of biblical, Christian, Oxford Group ideas, whether he heard them in Akron or in New York or in both places. He worked with Dr. Bob in

---

[7] Letter from Samuel M. Shoemaker to William G. Wilson, 10 April 1963, a copy of which the author inspected at Stepping Stones.

[8] *Pass It On* (New York: Alcoholics Anonymous World Services, Inc., 1984), p. 169 (emphasis added).

Akron to develop a program from them. And he borrowed heavily from those principles in his A.A. writings.

What Bill Wilson Brought with Him
to Akron in 1935

But what did Bill Wilson himself bring to the Akron scene between 1935 and 1939? What spiritual resources of *his* were infused into the Akron crucible? Let us outline some of the facts about Bill Wilson that figured in his Akron genesis role. These are not by way of some apology and effort to compromise A.A. divisions. We believe the facts are emerging from the plethora of historical research now taking place as to A.A.'s spiritual roots—roots that were often obscured by generalities, by desires not to offend, and by a concerted effort to open wider doors to various belief systems entering A.A. at a later point. There is little doubt that, after A.A.'s 1935 beginnings, Bill made concessions to the "atheists and agnostics."[9] There is also little doubt that efforts were made to enable Roman Catholics to feel more comfortable in what was, at first, a Protestant, Oxford Group atmosphere.[10] According to Bill's wife, Lois Wilson, the tone of the Big Book itself was altered in the interest of "a universal spiritual program." She said:

> Finally it was agreed that the book [the Big Book] should present a universal spiritual program, not a specific religious one, since all drunks were not Christian.[11]

---

[9] See, for example, the discussions about Bill's "battles" and "compromises" with his partner, Hank P., and with the atheist, Jim B., recorded in part in *Pass It On*, p. 199.

[10] See, for example, the discussion in Mary C. Darrah, *Sister Ignatia* (Chicago: Loyola University Press, 1992), pp. 30-31.

[11] *Lois Remembers* (New York: Al-Anon Family Group Headquarters, Inc., 1987), p. 113.

Whether there was such an "agreement," at least at the Akron end, is, in the author's opinion, questionable. For the author has not found any stories or written documents that would support Lois's statement. But Bill's ultimate draft of the Big Book's basic text omitted all specific mention of the Bible, reduced references to Jesus Christ to one sentence—somewhat derogatory in nature,[12] and used Bible language and quotations sans attribution or reference to the Bible. Dr. Ernest Kurtz summarized what he felt was part of the transition that occurred:

> Yet A.A.'s total omission of "Jesus," its toning down of even "God" to "a Higher Power" which could be the group itself, and its changing of the *verbal* first message into hopeless helplessness rather than salvation: these ideas and practices, adopted to avoid any "religious" association, were profound changes [from the

---

[12] In Bill's Story, the Big Book states, at page 11, of Bill's musings: "To Christ I conceded the certainty of a great man, not too closely followed by those who claimed Him. His moral teaching—most excellent. For myself, I had adopted those parts which seemed convenient and not too difficult; the rest I disregarded." As the author's research disclosed, Bill's early Big Book manuscripts and his own views reflected a good deal more interest in Christ and Christianity than he had had earlier when he was arguing with Ebby while still in his cups. Bill's later associations with Reverend Sam Shoemaker and Father Ed Dowling and his taking of instruction in the Roman Catholic Faith with Monsignor Fulton J. Sheen are only part of the picture. In *Not-God*, Ernest Kurtz wrote at page 323 concerning an interview Kurtz had with John C. Ford, S.J.: "Ford himself is a significant figure in the history of A.A.: America's leading Roman Catholic moral theologian in the 1950's and a frequent writer on the moral problems of alcoholism and alcoholics, Ford met Wilson at Yale in 1943 and mailed A.A.'s co-founder a copy of his paper, 'Depth Psychology, Morality, and Alcoholism,' in 1951. Wilson apparently was 'impressed with Ford as a writer, for he sought the Jesuit's editorial assistance for both 12 & 12 [*Twelve Steps and Twelve Traditions*, an A.A. Conference Approved book] and AACA [*Alcoholics Anonymous Comes of Age*, also Conference Approved].' Ford offered extensive editorial and some theological comments on both texts; his main concern—'too explicit MRA attitudes.'" Wilson's own interest in Christianity, possibly arising after his experiences in Akron, his connections with the Oxford Group, and his close personal association with Father Dowling, Father Ford, Reverend Sam Shoemaker, and a good many Christian businessmen on the East Coast, is substantially documented in writings which have seldom, if ever, been examined from an historical standpoint.

Oxford Group's "conscious attempt to return to primitive fundamental Christianity"].[13]

Now for an outline of the resources and ideas Bill brought with him to Akron in the summer of 1935 and during the early years before the Big Book was published.

The Oxford Group People Who Helped Bill in New York

Bill Wilson was in very close touch with some strong and knowledgeable Oxford Group personalities in the New York area, both before and after he started working with Dr. Bob, Anne, Henrietta, T. Henry, and Clarace in Akron.

Rowland Hazard

One was Rowland Hazard, a member of the vestry at Shoemaker's Calvary Church.[14] Rowland had been informed of a spiritual solution to his alcoholism by Dr. Carl G. Jung in Switzerland and had helped rescue Bill's sponsor, Ebby Thatcher, from alcoholic oblivion in August of 1934, just before Ebby carried his Oxford Group message to Bill. Rowland had had a thorough indoctrination in Oxford Group teachings and passed many of these on to

---

[13] See Ernest Kurtz, *Not-God*, p. 50.

[14] See Charles T. Knippel, *Samuel M. Shoemaker's Theological Influence on William G. Wilson's Twelve Step Spiritual Program of Recovery*. Ph D. diss. (St. Louis University, 1987), p. 72. See our earlier note on Hazard's travels with Dr. Sam Shoemaker and Hanford Twitchell, also a Calvary Church vestryman, when the three went to Cincinnati with an Oxford Group team in 1934 and, among other events, shared in Cincinnati church pulpits, just as Buchman and his Oxford Group team had done during the Firestone events in Akron in 1933.

Ebby.[15] In fact, he apparently passed some on directly to Bill Wilson. It was with a handful of Oxford Group ex-drunks, from Oxford Group meetings, whose names included Rowland Hazard and Ebby Thatcher, that Bill himself began meeting in New York. Their meetings were held at Stewart's Cafeteria in New York City after the regular Oxford Group meetings that Bill and these men were attending. Bill started meeting with them right after his spiritual experience at and release from Towns Hospital at the end of 1934.[16] Interestingly, Bill was never quite sure whether it was Rowland Hazard or Ebby Thatcher who had given him the copy of William James's *The Varieties of Religious Experience*, which he had read just following his "hot flash" experience at Towns.[17] In any event, the Oxford Group teachings that Rowland was espousing included ridding oneself of thoughts of the material world, finding God's plan for one's life, and following whatever guidance came from God. Rowland was also emphasizing the Four Absolutes—particularly absolute honesty.[18]

Bill's own statements about the Oxford Group, which are summarized in *Pass It On*, make it appear that Rowland had passed on to Ebby and, through Ebby, to Bill the Oxford Group concepts of confession, restitution, morality, spirituality, God-centeredness versus self-centeredness, personal housecleaning through sharing, Bible study, prayer, listening for guidance, writing down leading thoughts, quiet time, checking, conversion, and personal evangelism.[19]

There is an interesting aside as to Rowland's Oxford Group background and what he might have passed on to Bill directly or indirectly. In 1954, Bill Wilson interviewed and taped Cebra Graves, who was one of the trio that included Rowland Hazard

---

[15] *Pass It On*, p. 114. See also Part 1, Chapter 2, of our book for the discussion of Rowland's participation in Oxford Group houseparties and in its business team.

[16] Robert Thomsen, *Bill W.* (New York: Harper & Row, 1975), pp. 229-230.

[17] Thomsen, *Bill W.*, p. 230.

[18] See *Pass It On*, p. 114.

[19] See *Pass It On*, pp. 127-130.

and F. Shepard Cornell and that rescued Ebby Thatcher from institutionalization for alcoholism and induced him to come into the Oxford Group. During Bill's interview, Cebra Graves several times mentioned Rowland Hazard's friend, Philip Marshall Brown, and the conversations that Rowland and Cebra had with Brown. Brown was an Oxford Group scholar, a professor of international relations at Princeton, a frequent Oxford Group speaker, and the author of *The Venture of Belief*—a book highly recommended in the Oxford Group.[20] Brown's book contains what we believe to be some of the most fundamental words and ideas found in A.A.'s Second and Third Steps. Brown's analysis had to do with "willingness," "decision," "surrender," and "religious experiences." Brown also expounded on conceptions of God that can be seen in the language of A.A.'s Big Book.[21]

Brown had participated in a number of houseparties of "A First Century Christian Fellowship" and in business team meetings Rowland attended.[22] According to Cebra Graves, Professor Brown, Rowland, and Cebra had discussed together Rowland's visits with Dr. Carl G. Jung in Switzerland during which Rowland

---

[20] Philip M. Brown, *The Venture of Belief* (New York: Fleming H. Revell, 1935). The book was on the Oxford Group Literature list of the *Calvary Evangel* (See Appendix One). In the foreword to Brown's book, Reverend Sam Shoemaker wrote, "The author, whom I have known for upwards of twenty years, has been, both by taste and by principle, a believer in the things of the mind. . . . This writer emphasizes a very necessary truth, that "one cannot *know* the religious experience unless he is willing to *have* the religious experience." . . . This author has found a faith which gives coherence to life, and I think that this book is going to help others to find the same faith. . . . I cannot but hope that this book will be widely used, especially among those who need just such a convincing proof that modern intellectuals need God, and can find Him."

[21] See discussions in Dick B., *The Oxford Group & Alcoholics Anonymous* (Seattle: Glen Abbey Books, 1992), pp. 115-16, 127-28, 137, 311-12, 304-05.

[22] This was established by the author in his interview of Jim Newton at Fort Myers Beach in August, 1992. Newton knew Rowland, Brown, and the business team members quite well and was very active with them in team activity. Dr. Brown's name appeared on a number of the Oxford Group houseparty programs and invitations that Newton made available to the author, and also on other houseparty programs and invitations the author located in the archives at Hartford Seminary, Hartford, Connecticut, where many of Frank Buchman's early papers and letters are lodged.

discovered the spiritual solution to alcoholism—a conversion experience. The author believes it is entirely possible that Bill Wilson learned some of Professor Brown's ideas from Rowland Hazard, or from hearing Brown at Oxford Group houseparties Bill and Lois attended, or possibly even from reading Brown's book—which Shoemaker and the *Evangel* recommended.

F. Shepard Cornell

F. Shepard Cornell was a member of the vestry at Shoemaker's Calvary Church.[23] Shep had helped Rowland Hazard and Cebra Graves save Ebby Thatcher from institutionalization.[24] He had also met with Bill and Ebby before Bill got sober; and both Ebby and Shep imparted to Bill the serenity of their new life, the power of prayer, the rewards of meditation, and their interest in a new kind of loving—a complete giving of oneself that had no price tag on it.[25] Shep had recovered from a drinking problem of his own. And he had spent a substantial amount of time helping alcoholics. One was Ebby Thatcher, and one was Charles Clapp, Jr., who wrote the book, *The Big Bender*, to tell the story of how Clapp had overcome drinking by working with the Oxford Group, Sam Shoemaker, and Shep Cornell.[26] Of Shep Cornell and Bill's early contacts with him, Lois Wilson wrote:

> It was an ecstatic time for us both [Bill and Lois]. With Ebby and another alcoholic, Shep C., as our companions, we constantly went to Oxford Group meetings at Calvary Episcopal Church on Fourth Avenue (now renamed Park Avenue South) at 21st Street

---

[23] Knippel, p. 72.

[24] *Pass It On*, p. 113.

[25] See *Pass It On*, p. 116; Thomsen, *Bill W.*, pp. 211-12.

[26] See Charles Clapp, Jr., *The Big Bender* (New York: Harper & Row, 1938); Thomsen, *Bill W.*, pp. 211-12; *Pass It On*, pp. 116, 122, 169.

in New York. Shep not only was a fellow grouper but also worked on Wall Street and summered in Manchester.[27]

Like Rowland Hazard, Shepard Cornell was a member of the Oxford Group business team—of which even Bill Wilson might possibly have been a member.[28] Shep also attended a number of the Oxford Group houseparties that the business team attended. His name appears on several different houseparty invitations and programs of which the author has copies. The author located Shep Cornell's name and address in an address book of Bill's that is currently lodged in the archives at Bill's Stepping Stones home.

Pass It On adds two other vignettes about Bill and Shep:

> Shep remembered the meeting [his first] with Bill. He said that he and Ebby had attended church, so that they had had a "quiet time" together, an Oxford Group practice. In the quiet time, it came to Ebby that they ought to visit Bill. The only one of the three men who had a job, Shep took Ebby, Lois, and Bill to dinner in Manhattan. (p. 122, n.3).

> In the fall of 1935, Bill and Lois began to hold weekly meetings on Tuesday nights in their home on Clinton Street. . . . Shep C., their friend from Vermont, also attended a few times (p. 162).

---

[27] *Lois Remembers*, p. 91.

[28] Lois Wilson stated in *Lois Remembers* at page 93: "Bill belonged to a team for a while, but I didn't." Jim Newton informed the author that the Oxford Group business team was heavy with stockbrokers, advertising executives, and Wall Street people that Bill knew; and the author is of the opinion that research is needed to see if Lois's reference to Bill's team membership might not have had reference to Bill's participation in the business team, its Bible study, and the Oxford Group work they were doing. Certainly the business team members that Bill knew, such as Rowland Hazard, Hanford Twitchell, and Shepard Cornell were "in Bill's league" and also in the New York area. See references in *Pass It On* to Shep Cornell, to Oxford Group houseparties the business team members attended, and to John Ryder (pp. 162, 168-69, 173-74). See similar references in Nell Wing, *Grateful To Have Been There*, pp. 68-69, and Irving Harris, *The Breeze of the Spirit* (New York: The Seabury Press, 1978), pp. 31, 38-39, 40-41.

Hanford Twitchell

Still another important Oxford Group contact for Bill was Hanford M. Twitchell. Twitchell was the brother of Kenaston Twitchell, Sam Shoemaker's brother-in-law. Several members of the Twitchell family, including Hanford, Hanford's wife, Kenaston, Kenaston's wife, Marian, and Shoemaker's wife, Helen (who is the sister of Kenaston's wife), were extremely active in the Oxford Group.[29] Hanford was a vestryman at Sam Shoemaker's Calvary Church.[30] As our 1933 Akron newspaper accounts showed, Hanford Twitchell was part of the Oxford Group team that joined Dr. Buchman at the Firestone events of 1933. He shared in one of the Akron church pulpits that January. Bill's secretary, Nell Wing, reports this of Bill's close contact with Hanford:

> Mr. Hanford Twitchell, a nonalcoholic and well-known professional man in New York, knew Bill well in those Oxford Group days of 1935-1936. He often accompanied Bill to Towns Hospital and to Calvary Mission where Bill talked to alcoholics. Reminiscing about Bill, he remembered that at first Bill was alone, and didn't seem especially a part of the Oxford Group meetings, but that soon changed because people would follow him. He was always more interested in talking to drunks during

---

[29] See, for example, Garth Lean, *On The Tail of a Comet* (Colorado Springs: Helmers & Howard, 1988), pp. 132, 146, 184, 223n, 225, 249n, 252, 349, 350, 387, 388, 473, 494; Kenaston Twitchell, *Regeneration in the Ruhr* (Princeton: Princeton University Press, 1981); Helen Smith Shoemaker, *I Stand By The Door* (New York: Harper & Row, 1967), pp. 61-68; Samuel Moor Shoemaker, *Calvary Church Yesterday And Today* (New York: Fleming H. Revell, 1936), pp. 249, 250-51, 272. Hanford's active participation in the Oxford Group can be determined also by the fact that his name appeared in the Akron newspapers when the Oxford Group team came there in January of 1933, in the Cincinatti newspapers when the Oxford Group team came there in 1934, and in almost every Oxford Group houseparty invitation and program pertaining to the United States that the author has thus far seen.

[30] John Potter Cuyler, Jr., *Calvary Church in Action* (New York: Fleming H. Revell, 1934), p. 13; Samuel Moor Shoemaker, Jr., *Calvary Church Yesterday And Today* (New York: Fleming H. Revell, 1936), p. 272.

and after the Oxford Group meetings than in carrying their message to a team member.[31]

Of Hanford M. Twitchell, Sam Shoemaker recorded that Twitchell made his decision for Christ on October 24, 1926. Shoemaker then said:

> No other layman has come into the church in recent years who has given to it more generously of himself and of his labor than he. He it was who sold the 22nd Street property in 1927 which helped to finance Calvary House. He was made a Vestryman in 1927, associate treasurer in 1930, and treasurer of the church upon Mr. Parish's resignation in 1935. His spiritual contribution is most clearly seen in the hours which he gives to planning with us the policy of the parish, and to numberless men whom he has helped and trained.[32]

Jim Newton informed the author that Twitchell was the center of the Oxford Group men's business team. Newton also provided the author with copies of programs and invitations to the Oxford Group's "A First Century Christian Fellowship" houseparties in the east that were attended by Buchman, Shoemaker, Hazard, Cornell, Professor Philip Brown, Jim Newton, and even T. Henry Williams and Bud Firestone on occasion. Hanford Twitchell's name almost invariably appeared on these programs and invitations.[33] The record is clear that Bill Wilson attended a number of these houseparties, sometimes with Lois. On one occasion they met Oxford Group founder, Frank Buchman.[34]

---

[31] Nell Wing, *Grateful To Have Been There*, p. 68. And see our earlier comments about Shoemaker, Rowland Hazard, and Twitchell.

[32] Shoemaker, *Calvary Church Yesterday And Today*, p. 251.

[33] The foregoing information was obtained by the author in his interviews with Jim Newton at Fort Myers Beach, Florida on August 4th and 5th, 1992; and copies of the First Century Christian Fellowship programs and invitations are in the author's possession.

[34] See *Pass It On*, pp. 168-70, and *Lois Remembers*, p. 103.

James W. Houck

The author is of the belief that Bill Wilson had a number of friends in the Oxford Group whose names have not previously surfaced in A.A. histories or in biographies of Bill. One such person is James W. Houck, who presently lives in Timonium, Maryland. Houck was and is a member of the Oxford Group (now M.R.A.). He was a friend of Bill Wilson's. He was a friend of Sam Shoemaker's. And Shoemaker frequently came to his home in Frederick, Maryland, between 1936 and 1937, when Shoemaker visited his nephew, Toby Johnson, an Episcopal Minister in that area. During this period, Shoemaker would also visit the Oxford Group team in Maryland, of which Houck was a member. Houck attended a number of Oxford Group meetings at Calvary House in New York. He is not an alcoholic and has not been associated with the A.A. Fellowship. The author has corresponded with and had telephone interviews with Mr. Houck.

According to Houck, Bill Wilson had friends near Leesburg, Virginia, close to Washington, D.C. On Saturdays, Bill made the short drive over to Frederick, Maryland for the Saturday night meetings of the Oxford Group in the Francis Scott Key Hotel. Houck said Bill came almost every two weeks. Houck said Bill was "obsessed" with the idea of carrying the message to drunks. He said Bill's first question on arriving at the Maryland Oxford Group meetings was, "Are there any drunks here tonight?" Houck said his conversations with Bill seemed always to center around alcohol. Bill once remarked to Houck that for his first six months of sobriety, he had worked with some 50 alcoholics and that not one was different. Bill said his wife, Lois, said to him: "Bill you must remember that during this time of responsibility for these men, you, yourself, did not want to drink." Bill said he had replied to Lois, "You're right."

Houck said that when Wilson came to Maryland, he often spoke of Sam Shoemaker. Houck was quite well acquainted with T. Henry and Clarace Williams. He said he knew that the Williams couple had and read the "three basic Oxford Group books"—*For*

Sinner's Only, *I Was A Pagan*, and *Life Began Yesterday*, as well as many of its pamphlets.[35] Houck was well acquainted with Hanford and Kenaston Twitchell and Eleanor Forde. He was on the National Board of Moral Re-Armament in later years.

The conclusion the author drew from his contacts with Jim Houck was that Bill Wilson had a widespread group of friends in the Oxford Group between 1935 and 1937, that Wilson's Oxford Group participation was certainly not confined to Calvary House or Shoemaker, and that Wilson was observably dedicated to working with alcoholics during his Oxford Group years. These facts may or may not be new; but they tend to show the amount of Oxford Group knowledge and zeal that Bill Wilson brought with him to Akron in May of 1935.

Other Oxford Group Members

Pass It On indicates Bill had important New York Oxford Group member contacts in addition to those just mentioned. It says:

Bill had friends in the Oxford Group who understood his view of the situation. One of them was John Ryder, a New York advertising executive who knew Bill in the days of the Calvary Mission.[36] Ryder made these comments about Bill's separation from the Oxford Group: "I was, or felt, quite close to Bill Wilson in the early days before A.A. was started. Herb Wallace, a close teammate of mine, spent much time with Bill, causing him to take a public speaking course at the Downtown Athletic Club; but I think the 'group' proper disowned Bill when he proceeded on his guidance to create a special group for A.A.'s. At that time, if you were associated with the 'group,' your guidance seemed to be of questionable worth unless okayed by Sam Shoemaker or Frankie

---

[35] At Stepping Stones Archives, the author located a letter from Clarace Williams to Bill and Mrs. Wilson, dated September, 1935, stating as to T. Henry's brother, "I gave him Stephen Foot's new book, *Life Began Yesterday*."

[36] See also Nell Wing, *Grateful To Have Been There*, p. 69.

Buchman or one of their accredited representatives" (pp. 173-174).[37]

Lois Wilson's Oxford Group Notebook

In the author's most recent visit to the archives at Bill and Lois Wilson's home at Bedford Hills, New York, Paul L., the archivist at Stepping Stones, made available a small notebook that was kept by Lois Wilson during the years of her Oxford Group involvement between December, 1934 and August of 1937. The notebook in no way resembles Anne Smith's workbook. It commences with the notation that it is for the period 1935-1936. It contains, in Lois's own words, "Oxford Group Notes," and was kept by "Lois B. Wilson, 182 Clinton Street, Brooklyn." It records Oxford Group ideas that attracted Lois and may well have been heard by her at houseparties. It lists Oxford Group houseparties she and Bill attended. It mentions a number of well-known Oxford Group leaders that she and Bill heard, or met, or both, with notations as to their backgrounds.

Lois made the following notations about her Oxford Group thoughts:

1. "A supernatural network over live wires. Why not the voice of God in every parliament, every business? Every last man

---

[37] On reading this quote in the author's manuscript, Jim Houck was prompted to write: "You refer to Buchman as 'Frankie.' In all my life I have never heard him referred to as 'Frankie.' I do not know where this came from, but if it came from Ryder, he is definitely wrong. I knew and was closely associated with Buchman for 23 years, and no one ever called or referred to him as 'Frankie.' In fact he was very often referred to as Dr. Buchman. . . . If "Guidance" had to be approved by either Shoemaker or Buchman, that may be somewhat of an overstatement. In the O.G. context, it was and still is a practice to "check" guidance with someone else who is living on this basis, to see if they feel the thoughts are inspired or self induced."

in every last place. Definite adequate, accurate information from God" (p. 3).[38]

2. "Repentance is sorry enough to quit" (p. 4).

3. "Sat. A.M. Chas. Haines—Bible . . . Home Quiet Time" (p. 7).

4. "I realized that I had not really put my reliance in God but have been trying under guidance as I thought to do it all myself" (p. 8).

5. "Read July 22—*Utmost For My Highest*—I really saw myself" (p. 9).[39]

6. "List of sins: Feeling of being special, self conscious, feeling of inferiority, self indulgence in small things, dependency on human law" (p. 10).

7. "Sin blinds, binds, multiplies, deadens" (p. 11).[40]

---

[38] See this expression, frequently used by Dr. Frank Buchman, in Frank N. D. Buchman, *Remaking The World*. New and Rev. ed. (London: Blandford Press, 1961), p. 72: "Direct messages come from the Mind of God to the mind of man—definite, direct, decisive. God speaks." Buchman often spoke of the Voice of God, saying, for example: "The Voice of God must become the voice of the people." See Buchman, *Remaking The World*, p. 91.

[39] Bill Pittman learned from Lois in an interview with her that "she and Bill frequently read *My Utmost for His Highest* by Oswald Chambers." See Bill Pittman, *AA The Way It Began* (Seattle: Glen Abbey Books, 1988), p. 183. From his own research, the author learned that Chambers was not connected with the Oxford Group at all, but that Oxford Group people, as well as Dr. Bob, Anne Smith, and Henrietta Seiberling, used Chambers' Bible devotional a great deal. It was also used in Akron meetings of the "alcoholic squad of the Oxford Group."

[40] This is an expression that Dr. Frank Buchman used quite often. It is covered at length in an important Oxford Group book that was widely read in early Akron A.A. and recommended by Dr. Bob and Anne. See A. J. Russell, *For Sinners Only* (London: Hodder & Stoughton, 1932), pp. 318-19.

8. "True democracy is Tom, Dick & Harry under God Control" (p. 12).[41]

9. "Oxford Group is spiritual revolution whose concern is vital Christianity under dictatorship of spirit of God" (p. 12).[42]

10. "Sunday—AM. Leader Shep [Cornell]. Making for better human relationship for unselfish cooperation, for cleaner business, cleaner politics, elimination of political, industrial, & racial antagonisms. A new spirit is abroad in the world, a new illumination can bring men & women of every social situation back to the basic principles of the Christian faith" (pp. 13-14).

11. "Speak from experience. Guidance no substitute for hard thinking. The beauty of country & the inspiration of so many people working toward such a purpose & the fellowship meant the most to me at House Party" (p. 15).

12. "Help Margaret to get back to God. Let go of my possessiveness of Bill" (p. 17).

13. "There ain't no white lies. All sins have blue eyes & dimples when they are young" (p. 25).

14. "Helen Shoemaker—Surrender to God" (p. 26).

---

[41] This expression, "God Control" can be found throughout Dr. Frank Buchman's speeches and writings. See, for example, Buchman, *Remaking The World*, pp. 3, 18, 24, 25, 28-30, 35-36, 39, 42, etc.

[42] In a manifesto in *Rising Tide*, in November of 1937, Buchman repeated this expression of his and said, "This is the dictatorship of the living Spirit of God, which gives every man the inner discipline he needs, and the inner liberty he desires." See Buchman, *Remaking The World*, p. 42.

15. "Fear of giving up that little special private citadel—oneself" (p. 28).[43]

16. "Fears of all kinds will disappear if self is forgotten" (p. 29).

17. "What do we say when someone asks us whether we think OG [Oxford Group] is the only way to God, that they have their own God perfectly satisfying?" "What do we say to agnostics?" (p. 35).

A number of Lois Wilson's notes related to two houseparties she and Bill attended. Noting the "Pocono House Party Dec 4-6," Lois mentioned Garrett Stearly, Garth Lean, Ted Watt, Alex Smith [Shoemaker's father-in-law], and Jim Newton-Florida. At pages 19 through 23, Lois listed a large number of well-known Oxford Group people, including: (1) James Newton-Florida; (2) Howard Davidson-businessman; (3) Garth Lean; (4) Irving Harris; (5) Ray and Elsa Purdy; (6) Vic Kitchen-advertising; (7) Philip Marshall Brown-Princeton; (8) James Watt-Scotland; (9) Cleveland Hicks. The reader may recall the context in which we have discussed these names—Newton, Lean, Harris, Purdy, Kitchen, Philip Marshall Brown, and Hicks.

Speaking of the "Houseparty at West Point-Jan 10/37," Lois mentioned: (1) Loudon Hamilton-Oxford; (2) Sam [Shoemaker]; (3) Frank [Buchman]; (4) James Newton-Firestone; (5) Eleanor Forde. We consider all these entries significant because they specifically name the following important Oxford Group people whom Bill and Lois either heard or met, or both, and whose lives are discussed in our book:

1. Jim Newton—who was so very much involved in Akron A.A.'s beginnings.

---

[43] Overcoming fear by abandoning self to God-control was a major Buchman theme. In *Remaking The World*, Buchman said: "What is the disease? Isn't it fear, dishonesty, resentment, selfishness? We talk about freedom and liberty, but we are slaves to ourselves" (p. 38).

2. Eleanor Forde, Jim Newton's wife-to-be, whose writings were much discussed in Anne Smith's workbook.

3. Garth Lean—Frank Buchman's close associate and biographer.

4. Irving Harris—Sam Shoemaker's assistant minister, who became a close friend of Bill Wilson's.

5. Ray and Elsa Purdy—important Oxford Group leaders, Ray being a member of the clergy.

6. Victor Kitchen—member of the Oxford Group business team and author of the Oxford Group book, *I Was A Pagan*—which tells of recovery from alcoholism through the Oxford Group.

7. Professor Philip Marshall Brown, who met with the Oxford Group business team, of whom Shoemaker spoke so highly, and who wrote the important Oxford Group book, *The Venture of Belief.*

8. Reverend Cleveland Hicks, who conducted many of the Oxford Group houseparty Bible sessions, according to Julia Harris.

9. A. S. Loudon Hamilton, the omnipresent Oxford Group business team member, who warmed the group up on Friday nights with "Scotch" stories.

10. Reverend Sam Shoemaker, who became Bill Wilson's close friend, and to whom Bill W. attributed much material for the Steps.

11. Dr. Frank Buchman, founder of the Oxford Group.

Brief though they are, we believe these "Oxford Group Notes" of Lois Wilson's provide much additional evidence of the nature and extent of Bill Wilson's exposure to Oxford Group principles and practices, to the Bible, and to some of the most important Oxford Group personages and writers of the 1935-1935 period of which Lois wrote. Entries in Lois Wilson's diary for 1937, which is also located at Stepping Stones and which the author inspected, indicated she frequently talked of Guidance, "being convicted," God's plan, and quiet times—all major Oxford Group ideas as to which Bill Wilson was also, presumably, informed and familiar.

The Calvary Episcopal Church Staff

Bill Wilson's associations with staff members of Reverend Sam Shoemaker's Calvary Episcopal Church were substantial. Leaving aside any personal contacts that might have occurred outside church environs, the places where Bill made contact were three:

1. *Calvary House*—where many Oxford Group meetings were held, where the Oxford Group bookstore was located, where several staff members and Dr. Shoemaker lived, and where the American headquarters of the Oxford Group was located. The Calvary House address was 61 Gramercy Park, and many Oxford Group pamphlets bore that address. Staff members known to have been or possibly in touch with Bill Wilson and who lived there were Reverend J. Herbert Smith and his family; Reverend John P. Cuyler, Jr. and his family; Miss Olive M. Jones, Director of Calvary House, Superintendent of Calvary Church School, and Oxford Group leader and writer;[44] Reverend W. Irving Harris and his

---

[44] Of Miss Olive M. Jones, Shoemaker had these things to say in *Calvary Church Yesterday And Today*: 1) She was a great educator, having begun work in the New York City schools for 'problem' boys and been a past president of the National Education Association (p. 258). 2) She was the director of Calvary House and lived there (pp. 258-259). 3) She was superintendent of the Calvary Church School and "made of it the means by which children found God" (pp. 258-59). 4) She wrote *Inspired Children*, which

(continued...)

wife-to-be Julia;[45] and Walter T. Biscoe, a member of the vestry who led some of the meetings.

2. *Calvary Mission*, located at 346 East Twenty-third Street,—"down in the Gas-House District," where, as its staff liked to say, "There is a place near-by, where a Carpenter [Jesus] still mends broken men." Thousands attended services held there every night of the year. Thousands received a night's lodging, and free meals. Its first Superintendent was Henry Harrison Hadley, II; and he was succeeded by Taylor "Tex" Francisco, who was Superintendent of Calvary Mission during the years Bill Wilson was involved there.

3. *Calvary Church*, which was located on Fourth Avenue (now renamed Park Avenue South) at 21st Street. There is a question whether Bill ever attended more than one or two church services at Sam Shoemaker's Calvary Church. Bill's secretary and close friend, Nell Wing, told the author at a personal interview in September, 1991 that she did not believe either Bill or Lois attended Shoemaker's church.[46]

---

[44] (...continued)
Shoemaker said "has been the [Oxford] Group classic on the training of children in religion" (pp. 274, 258). 5) By 1936, she had "traveled in many countries during the past few years as a valued member of international teams of the Oxford Group" (p. 259). As shown in our news accounts of the 1933 Akron Oxford Group events, Miss Jones was with Frank Buchman and the Oxford Group team in Akron in January of 1933. The name of Olive Jones frequently appeared on the programs and invitations of "A First Century Christian Fellowship" in the 1930's, as did the name of Eleanor Napier Ford (who became the wife of Jim Newton).

[45] In a telephone interview with the author from her home in October, 1991, Mrs. Irving Harris informed the author that she was in charge of the Oxford Group bookroom at Calvary House for several years in the mid-1930's and distributed its literature to many parts of America.

[46] Bill appears to have been at a Calvary Church service at least once; for in *Alcoholics Anonymous Comes of Age* (New York: Alcoholics Anonymous World Services, Inc., 1957), he wrote at page 261, "How well I remember that first day I caught sight of him [Shoemaker]. It was at a Sunday service in his church. I was still rather gun-shy and diffident about churches. I can still see him standing there before the lectern. His utter honesty, his tremendous forthrightness, struck me deep. I shall never
(continued...)

At the three Calvary Episcopal Church locations, Bill's contacts with its staff were of this nature:

1. *At Calvary Mission*, he made a decision for Christ.[47] He

---

[46] (...continued)
forget it." Of Bill Wilson's interest in church, Nell Wing wrote in *Grateful To Have Been There*, at pages 48-49: "I think Bill was essentially nonreligious, although he was deeply spiritual. . . . Bill was not a churchgoer and avoided joining any particular denomination. . . . He was open to all spiritual thinking and did not want to confine himself to one interpretation or creed. As Bill expressed more than once, he 'shopped the pie counter' of religion and philosophy."

[47] Mrs. Samuel Moor Shoemaker, Jr., informed the author on the telephone in an interview from her home in October, 1991, that she had been present at the Mission when Bill "made his decision for Christ." James D. Newton and Eleanor Forde Newton, both of whom were members of Calvary Church in 1934 and closely involved in its activities, told the author in his interviews with them in August, 1992, that they did not doubt the likelihood that Mrs. Shoemaker was present in Calvary Mission and that her recollection concerning Bill was correct. We are not aware of any direct accounts, by Bill or otherwise, as to *precisely* what Bill did when he made this decision. At the archives at Stepping Stones, there are copies of two letters from Billy Du Vall, who stated he was the Assistant Superintendent at Calvary Mission. His letter has been partially quoted in A.A. literature, but some important aspects have not been mentioned: a) The mission meetings involved a Bible lesson, hymns, and testimonials. b) Billy was present when Bill Wilson gave his testimonial. c) Ebby Thatcher was *not* [This possible absence of Ebby from an event at which he was reported to have been present has been explained by one historian as due to the fact that Bill was drunk when he made his decision and couldn't remember the details and Ebby was drunk when he was later interviewed as to details]. d) Spoons Costello, the cook, was present. e) Bill Wilson was in the company of Johnson, a Swede. f) Bill announced that he had been at Calvary Church the previous Sunday night and saw Ebby get up in the pulpit and give witness to the fact that with the help of God he had been sober a number of months. g) Bill Wilson said he felt he could get help. h) When the invitation to the altar was given at the close, Bill and Johnson went forward and knelt down. h) Those present suggested that Bill go on to Towns Hospital. A February, 1927, issue of the *Calvary Evangel*, celebrating the First Anniversary of Calvary Mission, described a typical conversion in which one of the first converts in Calvary Mission "praised God for eleven months free from sin and drink." Another said he had "come into the Mission and asked Christ to do for him what he couldn't do for himself." Another said he had come in so drunk and dirty "that you wouldn't have known me for the same man . . . . I knelt down there in front and asked the Lord, Jesus Christ, to help me and he has." In *Calvary Church In Action*, Reverend John P. Cuyler, Jr. gives these descriptions of conversions at Calvary Mission—"The Carpenter's Shop"—in the 1932-1933 period: 1) "This man [a man who could help the
(continued...)

definitely was in touch with its Superintendent, "Tex Francisco."[48] He was known to its Assistant Superintendent, Bill Du Vall. And he spent long hours talking to alcoholics at the Mission.[49]

2. *At Calvary House*, there do not seem—at this writing—to be exact details as to people on the staff with whom Bill talked, worked with, or heard leading meetings at any *particular* time or place. But the record is clear as to who the staff people were at that time and where they might have been. Bill definitely had contacts with Reverend J. Herbert ("Jack") Smith, the Associate Rector at Calvary Church.[50] Also with Reverend W. Irving Harris and his wife Julia.[51] Possibly

---

[47] (...continued)
person Cuyler described as "J"], J. sought out at the mission, in frank spiritual need. Almost at once he found him [J. did], and began to understand what he had to do: he must face his sins honestly, ask God's forgiveness and give Him complete control over his future. He did that simply and earnestly and found complete freedom from drink" (pp. 63-64). 2) "One man, S., who had been a bartender . . . . noticed several men going into the Mission , and followed . . . . Something in what was said by the men who spoke gave him a new idea, and he went forward at the end of the service to give himself to God. He had started out that evening to get; he ended by giving" (p. 64).

[48] See *Pass It On*, p. 117; *Alcoholics Anonymous Comes of Age*, p. 59; Cuyler, *Calvary Church in Action*, p. 67; Harris, *The Breeze of the Spirit*, p. 49.

[49] *Pass It On*, p. 131; Wing, *Grateful To Have Been There*, p. 68; Thomsen, *Bill W.*, p. 232; *Alcoholics Anonymous Comes of Age*, p. 64, 74; *The Language of the Heart* (New York: The A.A. Grapevine, Inc., 1988), p. 198; *Lois Remembers*, p. 91.

[50] See *Pass It On*, p. 169; Dick B., *The Oxford Group & Alcoholics Anonymous*, p. 105; Cuyler, *Calvary Church in Action*, pp. 30-44; Harris, *The Breeze of the Spirit*, p. 27; Mel B., *New Wine* (Minnesota: Hazelden, 1991), p. 90.

[51] See Dick B., *The Oxford Group & Alcoholics Anonymous*, pp. 105-06, 81-84, 95-97. In an article by Bill Wilson, published in *Faith at Work* Magazine, July-August, 1963, entitled "A.A.'s Debt to Its Friends," Bill wrote: "Who could furnish us the wherewithal to construct this spiritual edifice which today houses our world-wide brotherhood? Sam Shoemaker and his wonderful co-workers, among whom were Irving and Julie Harris, were the people who were given this critical assignment. Where there had been silence and guilt among us alcoholics, they brought us to confession. Where there had been misunderstanding and anger, they guided us toward restitution. They themselves exemplified the kind of love that makes no demands. They taught us to pray
(continued...)

with Walter T. Biscoe in his office or at the Tuesday afternoon meetings where sixty to eighty men met for sharing and witness.[52] Possibly with an Assistant Minister, Reverend John Potter Cuyler, Jr.[53] Certainly with Shoemaker and probably several of his assistants—Smith, Cuyler, Harris, or Biscoe on Sunday afternoons when Bill is known to have attended and even witnessed.[54] And there were, of course, many other Oxford Group meetings at Calvary House. Mr. and Mrs. James Newton informed the author that, though Shoemaker often "presided" at meetings, there were usually several speakers who shared—including the foregoing staff members, who participated in leading meetings. As to these meetings, we know for sure that Bill, Lois, Ebby and Shep Cornell attended meetings "constantly" and "regularly."[55]

3.   *At Calvary Church*, to the extent that Oxford Group meetings were held in the sanctuary and attended by Bill. The people apparently would be the same as those at Calvary House.

---

[51] (...continued)
for light, and light came. This was faith at work, the brand of dedication that so long ago began to set us free" (p. 24).

[52] According to Cuyler, *Calvary Church in Action* at page 57, both Shep Cornell and Walter Biscoe had a turn at leading the Tuesday meetings; and it is clear that Bill attended Tuesday Oxford Group meetings and then went to Stewart's Cafeteria after the meetings. See Thomsen, *Bill W.*, pp. 231-232; *Lois Remembers*, p. 94. In *Calvary Church Yesterday And Today*, Shoemaker said, "It would be hard to estimate how many men found an experience of Christ through coming into Mr. Biscoe's office, or getting into contact with him in other ways" (p. 277).

[53] See Cuyler, *Calvary Church In Action*, where Cuyler says at page 33, "the work of bringing people to the Lord Jesus Christ and His Body, the Church, was not left entirely to the clergy, Mr. Smith and Mr. Cuyler." The implication is that Smith and Cuyler did a good deal in that realm. The author has also seen Cuyler's name on an Oxford Group houseparty invitation though he has found no evidence that Cuyler and Wilson were or were not present at the same time at the houseparties Bill and Lois attended.

[54] *Lois Remembers*, p. 94.

[55] See Cuyler, *Calvary Church in Action*, pp. 49, 55-57; *Lois Remembers*, p. 91, 98.

Bill Wilson And Sam Shoemaker: 1934-1939

Much more research needs to be done, by this author at least, to be sure of the nature of Bill Wilson's personal contacts with Reverend Samuel Moor Shoemaker, Jr., in the period between November, 1934, and April, 1939, when 5,000 copies of the Big Book were actually printed and published. We are very hopeful that Shoemaker's own family, Oxford Group or Calvary Church oldtimers, archive materials, and even some eye-witness recollections may produce an accurate picture. We have dealt in a preliminary way with this problem which we have called the "Shoemaker puzzle."[56] But the problem remains in need, for its solution, of further investigation and evidence. This is largely because of Bill Wilson's insistence, through the years, that Sam Shoemaker played an extremely large role in teaching and inspiring him and Dr. Bob, and in contributing to the Twelve Steps.[57]

Shoemaker cautioned Bill in later years about this overly enthusiastic view and pointed out that he (Shoemaker) and his Calvary Church group had really viewed Bill's work at Calvary Church as being "off on your own spur."[58] We are not aware that Dr. Bob had any significant personal contact with Sam Shoemaker at all. Finally, much of Bill's focus on Shoemaker's contribution seemed part of Bill's avowed effort to distance A.A. from what Wilson considered to be some very controversial aspects of the Oxford Group practices and reputation.[59]

---

[56] See Dick B., *The Oxford Group & Alcoholics Anonymous*, pp. 92-109.

[57] See, for example, Bill's comments reported in *Alcoholics Anonymous Comes of Age* at pages 38-39, 44, 261; *Pass It On*, p. 174; *The Language of the Heart*, pp. 177-179, 298, 368, 379-80.

[58] See excerpt in *Pass It On*, at page 178, note 1, from Shoemaker's letter to Bill.

[59] See *Pass It On*, pp. 169-174. Aside from issues as to whether Roman Catholics could participate in an Oxford Group program, the Oxford Group itself was involved in three major controversies which could have caused Wilson to want space from his Oxford Group connections: (1) John Hibben, President of Princeton University, became involved in a long-standing series of accusations against Buchman, Buchmanism, and Buchman's

(continued...)

We see no value in this book in attempting to unravel the reasons for A.A.'s departure from the Oxford Group and from Sam Shoemaker's Calvary Episcopal Church, nor in delving into the reasons for Sam Shoemaker's break with his former close friend, Dr. Frank Buchman, the founder of the Oxford Group. We are simply attempting to establish an adequate factual picture of the spiritual resources Bill Wilson brought to Akron, to the Big Book, and to the Twelve Steps as a result of any one-on-one contacts he might have had with Shoemaker, his books, or his teachings.

---

[59] (...continued)

alleged abnormal and morbid emphasis on sex and conducting unwarranted inquisition into men's private lives while Buchman was connected with Princeton. This prompted Hibben at one point to announce to the press, "there is no place for Buchmanism in Princeton." Though the events had occurred in the 1920's, the "Princeton Enquiry" plagued Buchman's reputation for many years. See Garth Lean, *On the Tail of a Comet* (Colorado Springs: Helmers & Howard, 1988), pp. 88-89, 124-29. (2) In the years leading up to World War II, Buchman told a New York reporter, "I thank heaven for a man like Adolph Hitler." While the remark was taken out of context, the press never let the public forget it. Thus when Buchman got in his controversy with Sam Shoemaker in 1941, *Newsweek* for November 24, 1941 was quick to dredge up the past, stating, "The widespread suspicion that he [Buchman] likes Hitler has undoubtedly weakened Dr. Buchman's influence in this country. He himself inspired the suspicion five years ago when he told a New York reporter, 'I thank heaven for a man like Adolph Hitler.'" As so often happens when the press recalls the sordid files from the morgue, *Newsweek* gave no further details—just the statement out of context and the "suspicion." (3) In November, 1941, Sam Shoemaker evicted Frank Buchman and the Oxford Group Headquarters from Calvary House; and, whatever may have been the Shoemaker-Buchman quarrel, the press was quick to amplify this dispute. *Time* for November 24, 1941, wrote: "Buchmanism's recent disasterous decline in both Britain and America was high-lighted this month when it lost both its U.S. headquarters and its chief U.S. exponent. Rector Samuel Moor Shoemaker of Manhattan's Calvary Episcopal Church did this double job by ousting the cult from his parish house and declaring that "after careful thought and prayer" he himself had quit the movement because of his "increasing misgivings." The author is reluctant to dignify these brief excerpts by repeating them here; for there is much more to the history of the Oxford Group, Moral Re-Armament, Dr. Frank Buchman, Reverend Sam Shoemaker, and Calvary Church's Oxford Group involvement that has to be examined for an accurate historical picture. And much of the history shows activities of great worth. But the important thing here is not the truth of the foregoing charges. It is the effect they might have had on Bill Wilson as he himself was pulling away from the Oxford Group, attempting to promote the Big Book and Alcoholics Anonymous, and trying to differentiate between his connection with Reverend Sam Shoemaker and A.A.'s very clear connections with the Oxford Group itself.

Certain facts have been established very clearly. Perhaps the most recent one is the author's discovery at the Stepping Stones Archives in his visit there in August, 1992, of a letter that Reverend Sam Shoemaker wrote to Bill Wilson on January 22, 1935—less than a month after Bill had gotten sober at Towns Hospital, and only a short time after Bill had begun carrying the Oxford Group message to drunks. Writing on a Calvary Rectory letterhead, addressing his letter to "Dear Bill," and signing it, "Yours ever, Sam S.," Shoemaker wrote:

> I hope you realize the guided-ness of your having known Jim [name intentionally deleted in our book] previously, as I understand you did, in business. His wife, M [name deleted in our book], is full time in the Group and he has held out for a long while. You may be just the person that cracks the shell and brings him over. He drinks a lot and is desperately unhappy and inferior and needs what you have got for him. I am grateful for what you did for B [name deleted in our book].

The existence of this letter startled the author. We have never seen it quoted or discussed. It flies in the face of the opinion of some that Shoemaker and Wilson never corresponded until about 1943. It shows that Shoemaker was familiar with and supportive of Wilson's work with alcoholics. And, remarkably, it was written when Bill was barely getting started. One historian suggested indirectly to the author that the date could be in error and should have been "January 22, 1936." Even if this were true, the letter still shows personal, Wilson-Shoemaker contact early on, Shoemaker respect for Wilson, and Shoemaker's interest in Wilson's work with alcoholics. The latter fact is not really surprising since Shoemaker himself had, for example, worked with Russell Firestone, an alcoholic; had personally tried to help other alcoholics to recover; and had, with the assistance of Shep Cornell, worked with Charles Clapp, Jr., as recorded in Clapp's book, *The Big Bender*.

There are still more established facts about Wilson and Shoemaker in the early days of 1935-1937. Bill attended Oxford

Group meetings that were led by Sam Shoemaker and his assistants.[60] Bill attended houseparties at which Shoemaker was present and no doubt participated.[61] Bill met personally with Shoemaker in his study at Calvary House.[62] Bill also sent a multilith copy of the Big Book to Shoemaker before the book was printed in April of 1939.[63] And Shoemaker himself said he had been in closest touch with Bill since Bill's first connection with the Oxford Group in 1934.[64] Yet Bill and Lois departed from the Oxford Group and Calvary Church scene in 1937.

Some seem to suggest that Sam Shoemaker had a very real part in the writing of the Twelve Steps and thus perhaps even the Big Book. These people include Shoemaker's widow, Helen Smith Shoemaker, and Mrs. W. Irving Harris, widow of Shoemaker's close associate, Irving Harris, who, with Mrs. Harris, was a friend of Bill Wilson.[65] Bill Wilson's own statements about Shoemaker's contributions to the Steps seem to suggest that possibility.[66] But the fact remains that no eye witness accounts, correspondence, Shoemaker journal entries, or notes in diaries have yet surfaced that can pinpoint personal exchanges between Shoemaker and

---

[60] *Lois Remembers*, p. 94; *Pass It On*, p. 132.

[61] See discussion above of Lois Wilson's Oxford Group Notebook.

[62] See Dick B., *The Oxford Group & Alcoholics Anonymous*, pp. 101-04.

[63] Knippel, pp. 69-70; Dick B., *The Oxford Group & Alcoholics Anonymous*, p. 97, 99.

[64] Letter from Samuel H. Shoemaker to H. H. Brown, 13 March, 1952, quoted in Knippel, p. 69.

[65] See Helen Smith Shoemaker, *I Stand By The Door* (New York: Harper & Row, 1967), p. 192. As to Mrs. Harris, see Dick B., *The Oxford Group & Alcoholics Anonymous*, pp. 95-96.

[66] See, for example, Bill's comments in *The Language of the Heart*, pp. 379-380; and the language adjacent to Shoemaker's picture in *Pass It On*, stating at page 128, "The Rev. Samuel Shoemaker helped lead early members toward the spiritual principles embodied in Twelve Steps."

Wilson on the subject of the Big Book, the Steps, or even the specific biblical or Oxford Group ideas that influenced them.[67]

Our most recent conclusion is that such evidence may well exist. This is partly because of the remarkable number of phrases that seem attributable to Shoemaker and that can be found in the Big Book[68] and partly because of the insistent remarks by Bill Wilson that there was a close connection between Shoemaker teachings and A.A. principles. Thus Bill is quoted as follows:

> Where did the early AAs find the material for the remaining ten Steps? Where did we learn about moral inventory, amends for harm done, turning our wills and lives over to God? Where did we learn about meditation and prayer and all the rest of it? The spiritual substance of our remaining ten Steps came straight from Dr. Bob's and my own earlier association with the Oxford Groups, as they were then led in America by that Episcopal rector, Dr. Samuel Shoemaker.[69]

Notice that Bill did *not* say the steps came from Shoemaker. He *did* say, with some apparent care in the language used, that the *material* for the Steps existed in and thus was *found* in the Oxford Groups; that his and Dr. Bob's *learning* came from the Oxford Groups, that the substance of ten steps came from the *association* of Dr. Bob and Bill with the Groups, and that the groups "were then led" by Shoemaker in America. As we point out in our study of the Oxford Group, it is debatable whether Bill was correct in stating that the Oxford Group in America was "led" by Sam Shoemaker, as distinguished from his being an important leader and associate of Dr. Frank Buchman, its leader and founder.[70] It does, however, seem correct that Shoemaker was the one whose

---

[67] See Knippel, pp. 63-93; Dick B., *The Oxford Group & Alcoholics Anonymous*, pp. 92-109.

[68] See Appendix Nine.

[69] *The Language of the heart*, p. 298.

[70] See Dick B., *The Oxford Group & Alcoholics Anonymous*, pp. 73-84.

very strong influence was felt in the New York Oxford Group circles traveled by Bill. And we know that it was from Shoemaker's Calvary House that a large amount of Oxford Group literature was disseminated and apparently selected for use in America.[71]

A Summary Of Bill's Resources

When Bill met Dr. Bob, he had been traveling in the company of some very dedicated Oxford Group members in New York City—both lay people and clergy. He had been working with alcoholics, albeit with no effective results. He had been "preaching" the Oxford Group message;[72] and the word "preaching" certainly implies he had heard and known the message. He had been in personal contact with Calvary Church leaders, certainly including Sam Shoemaker, who were very much involved with the Oxford Group. He may have had close contacts with Shoemaker, though not necessarily over any extended period; and he had heard Shoemaker lead at Oxford Group meetings and possibly at the Oxford Group houseparties where he and Shoemaker were both present. He certainly had substantial knowledge about the disease of alcoholism. And he must have had a much better perspective—derived from Dr. Carl Jung, Professor William James, and Rowland Hazard—as to the spiritual solution than did the original Akron AAs. From that standpoint, though new to the Oxford Group and new to sobriety, Bill had a leg up on the Akron people to whom he was introduced in 1935. They had been to far more meetings than he. They had heard the Oxford Group's trumpet cry of success in 1933. They had done a vast

---

[71] Harris, *The Breeze of the Spirit*, p. 72; Dick B., *The Oxford Group & Alcoholics Anonymous*, pp. 81-84; Samuel M. Shoemaker, *God's Control* (New York: Fleming H. Revell, 1939), pp. 87-88.

[72] See *Pass It On*, p. 131.

amount of Bible, Oxford Group, and Christian reading whereas Bill appeared to have done little or none. But they had not been working with alcoholics and, as far as Dr. Bob was concerned and speaking for himself at least, had not adequately grasped the Oxford Group concept of service.[73]

The Akron crucible, therefore, was ready for Bill's experience and input. And Bill appeared in awe of the spiritual preparation that awaited him as he sought out Dr. Bob, participated in the Akron "alcoholic squad" meetings, and began to study, with Dr. Bob, Anne, Henrietta, T. Henry, Clarace, and the others, the biblical principles and Oxford Group program of action that would become the spiritual tools of Alcoholics Anonymous.

---

[73] As Ernest Kurtz pointed out in *Not-God*, a more accurate statement would be that Dr. Bob had not *heard* the Oxford Group service message (p. 317, n72). The Oxford Group was very much dedicated to witnessing and service from its earliest beginnings in YMCA groups to the First Century Christian Fellowship, Oxford Group, and Moral Re-Armament teams that travelled all over the world, both before and after World War II. The Group accomplished enormous amounts of altruistic service work—however controversial their work might have been considered to be.

9

The Oxford Group Crucible: 1933-1935

We've seen the elements in the Akron Genesis.

Akron was the place where A.A. was to be founded. Jim Newton brought to the City an Oxford Group message and compassion for an alcoholic friend, Bud Firestone. The message led to Bud's "miraculous" recovery from alcoholism. The message and the recovery were broadcast to an interested community by a grateful father, Harvey Firestone, Sr., and by widespread press accounts. And the progenitors were assuming their roles. A kindly and missionary oriented couple, the Williams's, had been impressed with the Oxford Group message and had a home to offer. A gifted and compassionate lady named Henrietta Seiberling, who had mastered some Oxford Group and biblical principles, had her eye on using the biblical principles to help her good friend, Dr. Bob, with his drinking problem. A lady of faith and love, Anne Smith, was busy assembling, recording, and sharing some important spiritual principles from the Bible, the Oxford Group, and Christian writers, all-the-time praying for a solution to her husband's seemingly hopeless tussle with alcoholism. A talented and very alcoholic surgeon, who was to be the object of focus by these people, was engaged in refreshing and enhancing his knowledge of the Bible, Christian literature, and prayer. But he was staying drunk.

Onto the Akron scene bounded the "rum hound from New York," moved by what both Bill Wilson and Henrietta Seiberling felt was the guidance of God.[1] Bill had recovered from his disease and was determined to stay sober by seeking out and helping another drunk and avoiding "preaching" to him. The rum hound named Bill "just happened" to bring to Akron: (1) some important knowledge about the disease of alcoholism that had been accumulating through the work of Dr. Silkworth at Towns Hospital in New York; (2) an important solution to the problem of alcoholism that had been known to Dr. Carl G. Jung and passed on to Rowland Hazard and passed on to Bill; (3) a validation of the spiritual solution by the scholarly studies of Professor William James; and (4) the linkage between the problem of alcoholism and the solution that God could and would solve the problem if a relationship were sought with him by practicing the Oxford Group's practical program of action.

The linkage had really been established by the Oxford Group miracle that Rowland Hazard and his friend, Ebby Thatcher, had themselves experienced when they followed the Oxford Group program. This same miracle had been experienced by other Oxford Group people of the day—people who had had no contact with A.A.—some of whom had been in contact with Bill. These included Shep Cornell, Victor Kitchen,[2] and Charles Clapp, Jr.[3] Bill appeared to have adopted the Oxford Group idea that "you

---

[1] Henrietta Seiberling recalled some of Bill's very words about this experience. She stated, "He said a prayer. He got the guidance to look in a ministers' directory. . . ." She pointed out that Bill, an Oxford Group member, put his finger on just one name—Tunks—, an Oxford Group member. Tunks, in turn, put Bill in touch with a friend of Henrietta's, who put Bill in touch with Henrietta, also an Oxford Group member. She concluded, "That is the way that God helps us if we let God direct our lives." See John Seiberling, *Origins of Alcoholics Anonymous* (A transcript of remarks by Henrietta B. Seiberling: transcript prepared by Congressman John F. Seiberling of a telephone conversation with his mother, Henrietta, in the spring of 1971): Employee Assistance Quarterly, 1985; (1); p. 8.

[2] See Victor C. Kitchen, *I Was A Pagan* (New York: Harper & Brothers, 1934).

[3] See Charles Clapp, Jr., *The Big Bender* (New York: Harper & Brothers, 1938).

have to give it away to keep it"[4] In the words of Frank Buchman, "The best way to keep an experience of Christ is to *pass it on.*"[5] Bill felt, and later incorporated into A.A. language, the conviction that the spiritual solution would be of little lasting effect if it were not made of service to God and to others, particularly alcoholics.[6] And this is what, with what the Oxford Group felt was divine guidance, propelled Bill Wilson to a phone booth and into the expectant Gatehouse home of Henrietta Seiberling where Bill met Dr. Bob on May 11, 1935.

The Oxford Group Meetings in Progress

We know that when Bill met Dr. Bob, Bill had been going to Oxford Group meetings in New York from almost the day of his release from Towns Hospital in December of 1934. At some point after that, Bill began keeping company with some very knowledgeable Oxford Group business people—Hanford Twitchell, Shep Cornell, and Rowland Hazard. He also went to Oxford Group houseparties that these men attended. We know too that Dr. Bob had been attending Oxford Group meetings in Akron with Henrietta, Anne, and others since the departure of Dr. Frank Buchman and his team in January of 1933. We believe it important to dwell briefly on the probable format of those meetings in New

---

[4] See Samuel M. Shoemaker, Jr., *One Boy's Influence* (New York: Association Press, 1925)—a book studied and quoted by Anne Smith in her workbook—in which Shoemaker said at page 15: "I told him that the only way to keep religion is to give it away. . . . Give what you can right away; it will increase as you give it." See the following later expressions of this by Shoemaker in *They're On The Way* (New York: E. P. Dutton, 1951), p. 159; *How To Become A Christian* (New York: Harper & Brothers, 1953), p. 80; *The Church Alive* (New York: E.P. Dutton, 1950), p. 139.

[5] Frank Buchman, *Remaking The World* (London: Blandford Press, 1961), p. x (emphasis added).

[6] See Big Book, p. 77: "Our real purpose is to fit ourselves to be of maximum service to God and the people about us."

York and in Akron because it was that format which had much to do with the sharing of experience, strength, and hope that is the heart of A.A.'s meetings today.

East Coast Meetings

We will not attempt to state that this or that specific thing happened at the meetings that Bill, Lois, Ebby, and Shep Cornell were attending in New York area. But we can list a few elements known to have been involved. From Julia Harris, friend of Bill W. and wife of Shoemaker's associate, Rev. W. Irving Harris, came the details that most meetings involved Sharing, also called witnessing. Sometimes they were led by Sam Shoemaker. Shoemaker would welcome people. Those present would sing a song or two. And the leader would call on people to share their spiritual experiences. Meetings would close with the Lord's Prayer.[7]

Reverend John Cuyler, Jr., gives us more details through his description of some of the sharing meetings:

> [Speaking of the Advent Mission of Personal Witness.] Every night during the first week in Advent six or eight lay-people told at a simple service held at the church, the story of their own experience of Christ, relating it to the larger problems of the world in such a way as to show how new individuals are the only possible foundation for a new world. Those who came to hear the evidence (and there were two to three hundred every night) saw instanced in the lives of those who spoke many of their own problems and the solution of them, and some passed that week from a religion of aspiration to one of possession. Possibly greater value, however, lay in the training of those who spoke. To convey a real experience of Christ to others in these days requires

---

[7] Telephone interview by the author with Julia Harris at her New Jersey home on October 5, 1991.

naturalness rather than forensic ability; evidence rather than argument; experience rather than theology. A man must learn to recognize the significance of what has happened to himself before he can proceed to estimate and record it with sensitiveness, with humour, and in a language "understanded [sic] of the people." Excerpts from what was said may bring out some of this quality: one man said, "Surrender costs you something; and since I thought a whole lot of myself, it cost me a whole lot." "Religion is like a talent," said another, "if you don't use it, you lose it; I find that I have to keep witnessing to people I meet every day." One woman confessed that the summer before she had "unbuckled the whole armour of God, and just relaxed." Another declared that she had found that "Sin was not just an inconvenience to me, but an insult to God."[8]

Week after week during 1932 and 1933 the capacity of Calvary Hall was taxed, with an average attendance of 232 persons in the first of these years and 301 in the second. They came to give and to receive the quality of life that derives from full commitment to our Lord Jesus Christ. Ordinarily there are about ten speakers, of varied type, mostly lay people, who tell in simple terms what He has done in their own lives and in the situations where they are placed. On any given night, one is likely to hear from a staff-member or two, some of the guests in the house, the telephone-girl or engineer or housekeeper or Rector, visitors from Oxford Group centres elsewhere, and a constant stream of new people, business, professional, young and old, employer and employee and unemployed, who have found in Christ the answer to their needs and want to "speak that they do know and testify that they have seen.". . . In quiet and in sharing, the plan of the Holy Spirit emerges; the emphasis varies from week to week, but there is always one theme, illustrated in experience after concrete experience, that Jesus Christ changes lives, and builds a new world with them.[9]

---

[8] John Potter Cuyler, Jr., *Calvary Church in Action* (New York: Fleming H. Revell, 1934), pp. 32-33.

[9] Cuyler, *Calvary Church in Action*, p. 56.

Sam Shoemaker had these things to say about some earlier meetings:

> For here was found the sharing of spiritual experience by ordinary individuals, confronted with the common problems and situations of life; they talked about these things naturally; the emphasis was on the will being given to God, and on what He could do to guide and use a life so given to Him.[10]

> Advent Missions have been held before in Calvary parish as this record attests; but in 1926 we held one where the speaking was done by laymen. . . . Through seven successive nights a simple service of hymns, prayers and Scripture led on to the witness of three or four men and women who spoke out of their experience. There was no preaching, no exposition—just the sharing of experience. The sequence of themes of the services was:

> > Spiritual Hunger
> > The Failure of Conventional Christianity
> > Sin, the Hindrance to Christ
> > The Living Christ
> > Self-surrender, the Turning Point
> > Witness from Those Changed at the Mission.[11]

Lois Wilson said this of meetings:

> The Oxford Group, as we knew it back in the early months of 1935, worked in teams of six to a dozen, sitting quietly together like a Quaker meeting and listening for the guidance of God for each one. Bill belonged to a team for a while, but I didn't. The rest of the team would get guidance for him to work with such and such a person in order to "bring him to God." . . . The

---

[10] Samuel M. Shoemaker, Jr., *Calvary Church Yesterday And Today* (New York: Fleming H. Revell, 1936), p. 245

[11] Shoemaker, *Calvary Church Yesterday And Today*, p. 251. For an interesting comparison with "Self-surrender, the Turning Point," see Big Book, p. 59, "We stood at the turning point. We asked His protection and care with complete abandon."

Oxford Group meetings on Sunday afternoons were usually led by Sam Shoemaker or one of his two assistants, and various members of the congregation were asked to speak. One Sunday Bill had been chosen to "share" or "witness," as it was often called. He recounted his alcoholic story, ending with his dramatic spiritual awakening. When he had finished, a big, florid-faced man jumped up and said he would like to talk to Bill later. . . . He needed Bill's help.[12]

Occasionally we [Lois and Bill] went to OG weekend house-parties. A house-party was a cross between a convention and a retreat. People came from far and near to be with one another, to worship, to meditate, to ask God's guidance and to gain strength from doing so together. Usually two or three well-known persons would lead the meetings, inspiring the rest of us to do as they had done.[13]

As to Oxford Group houseparties, Julia Harris said to the author in her telephone interview in 1991 that houseparties often had choir time in the morning; then small groups; and then a big chunk in the morning on the Bible. Bible studies lasting one and a half hours were often led by Cleve Hicks [who was one of those on the Oxford Group team that went to Akron in January, 1933]. Then there would be reading with individual people questioning and sharing.

The Church of England Newspaper published a little pamphlet by The Bishop of Leicester, Chancellor R. J. Campbell, and its own Editor, entitled "Stories of our Oxford House Party." The event occurred in 1931. Dr. Cyril Bardsley, The Bishop of Leicester, had the following to say of the emphasis:

---

[12] See *Lois Remembers* (New York: Al-Anon Family Headquarters, Inc., 1988), pp. 93-94. See also our discussion of Lois Wilson's Oxford Group Notebook, which contained a number of the points that were made by the Oxford Group at meetings attended by Bill and Lois.

[13] *Lois Remembers*, p. 103.

Three words are specially emphasized by the Groups—surrender, sharing, guidance. Complete surrender to Christ is urged if any person is to receive in fulness God's gifts of life and power. It is taught that this surrender involves absolute and unhesitating obedience—that the surrendered and consecrated life day by day is only possible through use of the means of grace, and great emphasis is laid upon the importance of the morning watch. "Sharing" is the word that has attracted most attention and called forth most criticism. . . . By "sharing" is meant the making known to others of personal failures and defeats, and of help and strength received in Christ. I must immediately say that any confession of acts—e.g., immoral acts or habits—at a group meeting is not allowed. . . . The possibility and need of constant guidance by the Holy Spirit is much stressed. This is to be sought and looked for in daily life and work.

Chancellor R. J. Campbell, D.D., said:

Being intensely in divine guidance they are accustomed to begin the day with what they call a "quiet time," wordless waiting upon God. They believe, and with good reason, that we spend too much time in asking God for things and too little listening to what He may have to say to us. . . . They practice daily Bible study for the nurture of the spiritual life. I listened to the conducting of one such study circle by a young clergyman. . . . He did very little talking himself. With the Greek Testament on his knees he would give the literal meaning of a passage and then wait for members of the circle to give their several ideas of its spiritual value before adducing his own. . . . The most distinguishing feature of the gathering was what its members called "sharing"—in other words the frank and unreserved statement of what faith in Christ and experience of the operation of the Holy Spirit had done for them severally in changing their lives. It is this changing of lives that is the chief aim of the movement. The name we all know it by is conversion, but it is conversion that goes to the very root of what is morally wrong.

Jim Newton provided the author with an invitation to an Oxford Group houseparty conference at The Hotel Hawthorne in Salem,

Massachusetts from January 25-31, 1929. The following description of such events was contained in the invitation:

> For the past decade or so there has been developing a unique variety of religious gathering known as a "houseparty." The name has held because it best describes the atmosphere of these gatherings, which, in their general setting, more closely resemble a secular houseparty than the "religious conference" or "convention." A prominent editor has called these meetings "the church in the house." They range in size from twenty to one hundred and fifty or more people. The place is a country inn, a hotel, or a private residence according to the demand for space. The period of time extends from a week-end to a week or ten days. They are attended by people of all ages and all professions—young people, parents, teachers, younger business men, men and women in every walk of life. Group meetings are held and people are free to go or not as they choose. There is time for quiet with one's self, for conversation with one's friends, and for the larger meetings. The object of the houseparty is frankly to relate modern individuals to Jesus Christ in terms which they understand and in an environment which they find convenient. The fundamentals of the principles of the message are covered in a series of informal talks. Bible study takes up an important part of each day. Separate groups for men and women, often divided as to age and profession, provide an opportunity for discussion of various problems relating to different aspects of the Christian life. Each morning opens with a time of united quiet during which thought is directed toward God in full conviction that, to a mind and heart eager to discover it, He can make known His will. The evening provides a period when anyone can talk who wants to.

Another houseparty invitation by "The Groups—A First Century Christian Fellowship" to Briarcliff Lodge at Briarcliff Manor in New York, from May 2-12, 1930 contained the following:

Emphasis will be laid on methods of Bible study. To this end, Miss Mary Angevine, of the biblical seminary in New York, will conduct Bible classes during the conference.

The movement of the houseparty will include a consideration of the following problems as related to the main topics:

> Spiritual diagnosis.
> The place of the guidance of God in human lives.
> The principles of sharing Christian experiences.
> The methods of helping those in difficulties.
> The place of possessions.
> The principles involved in developing a national and international fellowship.

Bill Wilson gave this description of some of the things he had heard at meetings:

> [*Pass It On* said that it appeared to Bill that social, class, and racial barriers were almost nonexistent in the Oxford Group, and even religious differences had been forgotten. Bill said:] Little was heard of theology, but we heard plenty of absolute honesty, absolute purity, absolute unselfishness, and absolute love. . . . Confession, restitution, and direct guidance of God underlined every conversation. They were talking about morality and spirituality, about God-centeredness versus self-centeredness.[14]

Akron Meetings

There is no particular reason to suppose the Akron Oxford Group meetings differed much from New York meetings. The Akron Oxford Group meetings were launched by teams which included

---

[14] *Pass It On* (New York: Alcoholics Anonymous World Services, Inc., 1984), p. 127.

Dr. Buchman himself, his contingent from the Calvary Church Oxford Group scene—a contingent which, in 1933, in Akron, included Hanford and Kenaston Twitchell (Shoemaker's brother-in-law), Olive Jones, Jim Newton, Walter Biscoe, and Cleve Hicks—and Oxford Group team leaders from the eastern and midwestern part of the United States, England and the Continent. The possible difference in the subsequent Akron meetings simply had to do with the absence of the star-studded cast of 1933 or of the actual Calvary Church setting in New York. But there certainly were distinguished clergy in Akron who participated in the Oxford Group activities there—not the least of whom was Dr. Walter F. Tunks.

In a talk he gave in later years, Dr. Bob's sponsee, Clarence S.—who organized A.A. in Cleveland—summarized the later Akron Oxford Group meetings about as succinctly as possible. He said they involved Quiet Time with the writing down of thoughts, Prayer, Scripture reading, and witness.[15] *DR. BOB and the Good Oldtimers* supplies these additional details:

Members of the Oxford Group sought to achieve spiritual regeneration by making a surrender to God through rigorous self-examination, confessing their character defects to another human being, making restitution for harm done to others, and giving without thought of reward—or, as they put it: "No pay for soul surgery." They did, however, accept contributions. Emphasis was placed on prayer and on seeking guidance from God in all matters. The movement also relied on study of the Scriptures and developed some of its own literature as well. At the core of the program were the "four absolutes":—absolute honesty, absolute unselfishness, absolute purity, and absolute love. . . . In addition to the four absolutes, the Oxford Group members had the "five C's" and the "five procedures." The C's were confidence, confession, conviction, conversion, and continuance, while the procedures were: Give in to God; listen to God's direction; check

---

[15] See also *DR. BOB and the Good Oldtimers* (New York: Alcoholics Anonymous World Services, Inc., 1980), pp. 139-40.

guidance; restitution; and sharing—for witness and for confession (pp. 54-55).

Much of the meeting discussion in *DR. BOB* concerns the way the Oxford Group meetings were conducted at the T. Henry Williams home from 1935 on; and we will discuss those details shortly. However, there is little reason to suppose the format was much changed from the meetings at the West Hill Group that were attended between 1933 and 1935. The meetings at the Williams home would open with a prayer; the leader would read Scripture; there would be witnessing by the leader and then from the floor; there was Quiet Time to permit listening for guidance; and the meetings closed with the Lord's Prayer.[16]

---

[16] See *DR. BOB*, pp. 137-42.

Part 3

The Alcoholic Squad of
the Oxford Group in Action

The events that occurred shortly before Mother's Day, 1935 have been told so many times in so many books that they do not need to be detailed here. However, many might see God at work in the rush of events that began with the Wednesday night meeting at the home of T. Henry and Clarace Williams shortly before Mother's Day, 1935.

Anne Smith's friend and fellow Oxford Group member, Delphine Weber, had apprised Henrietta Seiberling of Dr. Bob's drinking problem. Henrietta felt guided by God that the Oxford Group members should have a meeting for Bob Smith. T. Henry and Clarace provided their home. Dr. Bob confessed to his being a "secret drinker;" and all present joined him on his knees in prayer on T. Henry's living room carpet. The assistance of God was asked for the solution to Bob's drinking problem. Next morning Henrietta asked God for guidance and help; and said, "Something said to me—I call it 'guidance'; it was like a voice in my head—'Bob must not touch one drop of alcohol.'" In a matter of weeks, Bill Wilson was in Akron, troubled, but anxious to maintain his sobriety by seeking out another alcoholic with whom to talk.

Oxford Group member Bill Wilson was led to call Oxford Group member, Dr. Walter Tunks. Through a series of calls, Bill was led to Oxford Group member Henrietta Seiberling's phone. Henrietta welcomed the call as "manna from heaven." With some difficulty, she arranged for Dr. Bob to come to her home the next day, Mother's Day, to meet with Bill. What Dr. Bob had grudgingly scheduled as a "15 minutes tops" meeting turned into a mutual sharing between two drunks for some six hours. The result was electric. Dr. Bob and Bill saw mutual deliverance in their teaming up. Dr. Bob was Bill's first "evangelistic" success, largely because Bill had deferred the timing of his evangelistic talk and simply shared his own experience, his deliverance by God, and his own need to help others.

All the previous experience of Bill and Dr. Bob with the Oxford Group and all of the Bible study and spiritual reading in Akron began at once to gel. The two set out to help drunks recover. After Dr. Bob's Atlantic City "slip," Dr. Bob resolved, on June 10, 1935, to go through with the Oxford Group program. After sobering up that day with Bill's help, Bob and Bill began again. Dr. Bob never drank thereafter. And A.A. was founded![1]

---

[1] The story is told in greatest detail in *DR. BOB and the Good Oldtimers* (New York: Alcoholics Anonymous World Services, Inc., 1980), pages 53-75. For additional accounts, see Big Book, pp. xv-xvii, 153-56, 178-80; *Alcoholics Anonymous Comes of Age* (New York: Alcoholics Anonymous World Services, Inc., 1957); pp. 65-71; *The Language of the Heart* (New York: The A.A. Grapevine, Inc., 1988), pp. 355-57, 199; *Pass It On* (New York: Alcoholics Anonymous World Services, Inc., 1984), pp. 139-45; and John Seiberling, *Origins of Alcoholics Anonymous* (A transcript of remarks by Henrietta B. Seiblerling; transcript prepared by Congressman John F. Seiberling of a telephone conversation with his mother, Henrietta, in the spring of 1971); Employee Assistance Quarterly, 1985; (1); pp. 8-12.

10

The Laboratories

Three major activities began in the Akron crucible after Dr. Bob's and Bill's Mother's Day Meeting in May of 1935. All involved "laboratories" where the recovery *experiment* was perfected into a recovery *program*.

The most important experimentation occurred at Dr. Bob's home at 855 Ardmore. Bill Wilson moved in with the Smiths around the first of June. In July, Lois visited there for two weeks, and Bill remained until the end of August or early September.[1] It was there that Bill and Dr. Bob talked on night after night. It was there that drunks began to meet, to eat, to stay, and to take in spiritual nourishment. Ernest Kurtz put it: "It would appear in hindsight that most of their waking lives was a continuous A.A. meeting."[2] Much of this centered at Dr. Bob's home. It was there that Bill and Bob and Anne Smith engaged in two-way prayer. They read, studied, and discussed the Bible, the Oxford Group, Christian literature, and the Oxford Group program. It was there that Henrietta Seiberling frequently visited and contributed important ideas. And it was from there that work with alcoholics began.

---

[1] See Robert Thomsen, *Bill W.* (New York: Harper & Row, 1975), p. 249; Ernest Kurtz, *Not-God*. Expanded ed. (Minnesota: Hazelden, 1991), p. 42.

[2] Kurtz, *Not-God*, p. 56.

The next major experimentation scene was at the meetings, the principal of which was held on Wednesdays at the T. Henry Williams home. It was at T. Henry's that the educational process was furthered, that group Bible study, exchange of spiritual literature, two-way prayers, and witnessing occurred, and that alcoholics were led to surrenders if that had not already occurred at a hospital or at Dr. Bob's. There were social affairs there and also at the homes of Henrietta, Bob and Anne, and others to keep the drunks filled with coffee, food, and sober activity.

The final experimentation area involved the forays into hospitals and institutions where Dr. Bob and Bill became adept at "oxidizing" [a phrase which could have meant "Oxfordizing"—carrying the Oxford Group message]. Dr. Bob and Bill learned how to approach drunks. They developed the technique of hospitalizing them; anesthetizing them with paraldehyde; and then, later, in the hospital room, introducing them to the Bible as the only literature they could have. Later still, in the room, teams of early AAs would visit the hospital and share their stories with the new person. And the new man was often brought to surrender and to God at the ward.

Let's look at these three laboratories.

Dr. Bob's Home: 1935-1939

There are many accounts of what occurred at A.A.'s first "half-way" house from the day Bill Wilson began his stay there in June of 1935 until the day late in 1939 when the small home had become so filled with alcoholics and their wives (an estimated 80 people) and their meetings that the group began meeting at King

School and became Akron No. 1.[3] Here is a sketch of those events.

First, as to Dr. Bob and Bill, there was study and discussion of the Bible and its principles almost every evening until the wee morning hours. Our review of Dr. Bob's Library illustrates biblical ideas that could have been discussed. In the mornings, Bill would make the coffee; and there were quiet times presided over by Anne Smith. She would read and interpret Scripture and other Christian literature. We believe she may also have read from her workbook to Bill and Dr. Bob, but direct evidence of this is not presently available. In any event, our review of Anne Smith's Spiritual Workbook shows Anne's interest and focus. In the Quiet Times, there was ample opportunity to pray, listen for guidance, write down luminous thoughts, check Guidance, study the Bible, and cover the 28 Oxford Group principles Dr. Bob and Bill had heard and, in some cases read, and which Anne had studied and analyzed in her workbook. There were times when Anne discussed principles with Bill when Bob was not present. And then there were the daily visits with or phone calls from Henrietta. We have seen the scope of Henrietta's interests and resources in the Bible and Christian literature. All the founders were availing themselves of Scriptural guidance from *The Upper Room, My Utmost For His Highest*, and the other daily Bible devotionals Dr. Bob, Anne, Bill, and Henrietta used.[4]

Then there were the drunks they brought home to Ardmore; the surrenders that took place there; the long discussions of the Bible and Christian ideas by alcoholics and their wives with Anne Smith; and the daily, sober chit-chat amongst the alcoholics who stayed there. Of course, there was the riotous behavior of out-of-control drunks who kept the scene lively and their helpers sober. In the

---

[3] *DR. BOB and the Good Oldtimers* (New York: Alcoholics Anonymous World Services, Inc., 1980), pp. 76-89, 95-107; *Pass It On* (New York: Alcoholics Anonymous World Services, Inc., 1984), pp. 147, 151-59.

[4] See examples from the devotionals in Appendices Four, Five, Six, and Seven.

Chapter, "Working With Others," the Big Book itself tells the kind
of things that could have taken place:

> Helping others is the foundation stone of your recovery. A kindly
> act once in a while isn't enough. You have to act the Good
> Samaritan every day, if need be. It may mean the loss of many
> nights' sleep, great interference with your pleasures, interruptions
> to your business. It may mean sharing your money and your
> home, counseling frantic wives and relatives, innumerable trips to
> police courts, sanitariums, jails and asylums. Your telephone may
> jangle at any time of the day or night. Your wife may sometimes
> say she is neglected. A drunk may smash the furniture in your
> home, or burn a mattress. You may have to fight with him if he
> is violent. Sometimes you will have to call a doctor and
> administer sedatives under his direction. Another time you may
> have to send for the police or an ambulance. Occasionally you
> will have to meet such conditions (p. 97).

Did these things happen at the Ardmore Avenue laboratory?
Dr. Bob's children have given some indication of the scene in their
book, *Children Of The Healer.*[5] Here are some informative
excerpts:

> On the morning of June 10, 1935, Dr. Bob took his last drink, a
> beer given to him by Bill to steady his hands before he performed
> surgery. On that day Alcoholics Anonymous was born, at 855
> Ardmore Avenue in Akron, Ohio. The two men knew they had
> to help other drunks if they were to stay sober themselves. Bill
> decided to stay for the summer so they could work together. They
> began a vigorous campaign to find and treat other drunks. There
> followed a long, hot summer of enthusiastic recruiting and
> fearless experimentation. As Dr. Bob's son recalls, "Those early
> ones had a rugged time." The first one, Eddie R., was a failure
> because of underlying mental illness that only presented itself
> when he dried out. The next one, Bill D., was a success. A

---

[5] Bob Smith and Sue Smith Windows, *Children of the Healer* (Illinois: Parkside
Publishing Corporation, 1992).

succession of others followed, with varying degrees of success and failure. The two men didn't have a program. They were groping their way toward one, putting together an eclectic amalgam of Carl Jung, the Oxford Group, biblical sources, Wilson's spiritual experience, Anne Smith's practical applications of spiritual principles, Dr. Bob's personal and medical experience of alcoholism, and many other diverse influences. Slowly, Bill and Bob developed a little group of recovering people who formally met at Oxford Group meetings but kept in constant communication with each other at get-to-gethers in their homes. The Smith's house on Ardmore Avenue was the hub of the Akron group. . . (pp. 5-6).

[Sue Windows said:] There wasn't any program then. The restitution idea was one of the things he [Dr. Bob] got from the Oxford Group. Mom's notebook [*Anne Smith's Spiritual Workbook*] shows how much of A. A. came from there—restitution, surrendering, and so forth. Later on, they did the surrendering, for the new ones, right upstairs in Dad's room where it would be more private. . . . Dad was trying to get his practice back. He'd be gone to the hospital in the morning . . . and after 4 p.m. he'd usually come home. Then Bill would go downtown with him, or sometimes Bill would go over to Henrietta's with Mom and talk, or Dad and Bill would sit in the kitchen and talk. . . . Finally, they were getting a bit restless. They needed someone to work on. They got Eddie R., of course, and that was a little excitement. He was the first drunk they tried to fix. He was the one that shinnied down the drainpipe and chased Mom with the butcher knife. . . . He was their first attempt and it was a complete flop. . . . They needed someone to work with because I'd heard them say it. But it wasn't anything they told me directly. I just lost my room and slept on the davenport. . . . When Dad got the idea of getting drunks to fix from the hospital, things kind of picked up. . . . At that time I was getting involved with the quiet times they had in the morning. The guys would come, and Mom would have her quiet time with them. There was a cookie salesman and he'd bring the stale cookies over, and we'd take up a collection for three pounds of coffee for 29 cents. Then they'd have their quiet time, which is a holdover from the Oxford Group, where they read the Bible, prayed, listened, and got guidance. This was early in the morning, when the sky was just starting to get light. Sometimes they'd get us out of bed to do this (pp. 41-44).

[Bob Smith said:] When the other drunks started coming into the house that summer, that was fun. . . . These were three very determined people—Bill W., my mother, and my father. They worked on Bill D., and he was a success. And then more came. But you have to remember this thing was not an instant victory. It was a tough, tough row, with lots of heartaches, lots of egos. We were very unpopular. We had taken these drunks into our home because of the Depression, and it was like someone had moved a halfway house next door. You can imagine how popular they were in the neighborhood. . . . I didn't resent sleeping in the attic at home (pp. 126-129).

In other words, 855 Ardmore Avenue was a beehive of recovery activity ranging from Bible study to alcoholic tantrums to social gatherings to respite from the ravages of the Great Depression. As Dr. Bob said, "All of us were broke." And he felt that too was Providential.[6] It gave the alcoholics and their families time to share their woes, their trust in God, and their spiritual experiences.

The Meetings at T. Henry's

DR. BOB and the Good Oldtimers describes in part the meetings that were structured around the T. Henry Williams home commencing in the summer of 1935. But there is much more to be

---

[6] See his last major address, recorded in *The Co-Founders of Alcoholics Anonymous: Biographical sketches; Their last major talks* (New York: Alcoholics Anonymous World Services, Inc., 1972, 1975), p. 9

learned from taped interviews and other accounts by some of the oldtimers themselves.

The meetings were Oxford Group meetings. They were attended by alcoholics, their wives, and family members, as well as by Oxford Group people. Bill V. H., who got sober in early 1937, estimated the proportion of Oxford Group to non-Oxford Group people at about 50-50.[7] He said Oxford Group literature was passed out, and he remembered well "how we all challenged ourselves on the Four Absolutes of the Oxford Movement."[8] Wally G., who got sober in late 1938, said, "T. Henry's meetings ran more or less along Oxford Group lines. . . . Early meetings used Oxford Group terminology—witnessing, stories, restitution, shared confessions."[9] The regulars were Dr. Bob and Anne Smith. Both "Smitty" and "Sue," their children, came to a few meetings. Henrietta Seiberling was there, and her children had all attended Oxford Group meetings. Of course, there were T. Henry and Clarace.[10] Dr. Bob said they were "A Christian Fellowship."[11]

---

[7] From a transcript of the interview of Bill V. H. at Akron, Ohio, by Bill Wilson on June 17, 1954.

[8] From the transcript of the Bill V. H.-Bill Wilson interview. In a taped interview by Bill Wilson at Stepping Stones on August 30, 1954, Dorothy S. M., former wife of Clarence S., remembered her first meeting at T. Henry's shortly after February 12, 1938. She said, "one of the things that struck me the most was that somebody handed me a book, "Life Began Yesterday" [This book by Stephen Foot, *Life Began Yesterday* (New York: Harper & Brothers, 1935), was one of the most popular Oxford Group books of the day]. It was an Oxford Group book. I don't remember what it said now, life began for me that night."

[9] From a taped interview of Wally and Annabelle G. by Bill Wilson in Akron in December, 1954.

[10] *DR. BOB*, p. 100.

[11] *DR. BOB*, p. 118. Bob E. confirmed the fact that Dr. Bob told his business friends that the alcoholic squad people were "a Christian Fellowship." Bob E. wrote this to Nell Wing in his letter to her of March 14, 1975; and he wrote Lois Wilson to the same effect in a memo to Lois that was written on an Akron "Four Absolutes" Pamphlet. The author has copies of each document in his possession. The name, "A First Century Christian Fellowship," was much in use in the Oxford Group in America [See Samuel M. Shoemaker's introduction in Olive M. Jones, *Inspired Children* (New York: Harper &

(continued...)

The alkies who attended commonly called themselves "the alcoholic squad of the Oxford Group."[12] And, since some Oxford Group people in Akron may have looked down on the Williams meeting and its alcoholics, one member indicated that the meeting at T. Henry's was "sort of a clandestine lodge of the Oxford Group."[13]

There was preparation for the Wednesday meetings. In our discussion of T. Henry's role, we pointed out that there was a set-up meeting on Monday.[14] In today's A.A. parlance and spillover from this, it could be said that these were "steering committee" meetings which were focused on the "primary purpose," which was to carry the message to the person still suffering. Surrenders were a pre-requisite to full participation. Wally G. said:

> On the business of surrender which I think was probably the most important part of this whole thing, Dr. Smith took my surrender the morning of the day that I left the hospital. At that time it was the only way you became a member—you became a member by a definite act or prayer and surrender, just as they did in the Group. I'm sorry it has fallen by the wayside. Getting back to the business of how the thing operated: We took the "Upper Room" seriously. We took the meetings seriously, and we very seldom missed a set-up meeting.[15]

Bob E., who got sober in April of 1937, said of the surrender requirement:

---

[11] (...continued)
Brothers, 1933), p. ix]; in Shoemaker's books [See Samuel M. Shoemaker, *Twice-Born Ministers* (New York: Fleming H. Revell, 1929), p. 23; *Calvary Church Yesterday And Today* (New York: Fleming H. Revell, 1936), p. 270]; and in the houseparty programs and invitations of the 1928-1934 period. See also, Irving Harris, *The Breeze of the Spirit* (New York: The Seabury Press, 1978), p. 58.

[12] *DR. BOB*, pp. 117, 137, 156, 100.

[13] *DR. BOB*, p. 121.

[14] *DR. BOB*, pp. 138-139.

[15] Transcript of Wally G.-Bill Wilson interview. Wally's story, "Fired Again," is in the First Edition of the Big Book, at pages 325-331.

Sharing completely—have to be done with another person. Pray and share out loud. The act of surrender. . . . Yes, this was very important at that time. There were no exceptions. You couldn't attend a meeting unless you had gone through that. This-you couldn't go to a meeting—you had to go through the program of surrender.[16]

As nearly as we can piece together, the Wednesday night meetings took on the following format: They opened with a prayer and closed with a prayer—the latter prayer being the Lord's Prayer.[17] T. Henry often took care of the prayers with which the meeting was opened and closed.[18] There was reading from the Bible.[19] In fact, the Bible was stressed as reading material.[20] These were specific recollections by oldtimers of three different people, who led the first part of meetings, reading from the Bible before them:

Alex M. said [of meetings at a later point], "Doc talked much at regular meetings. He would come just at a regular meeting and speak. About 40 minutes, and he was a simple talker. He had the Bible in front of him and wasn't afraid to read from it. It [the Bible] was at King School. It was always on the podium.[21]

Wally G. said, "I remember the first meeting I attended was led by Dick S. He opened the meeting with a short prayer, read a passage from the Bible which I do not recall, and talked about that in its relationship to the everyday life of those present.[22]

---

[16] Transcript of the tape of Bob E. by Bill Wilson at Akron, Ohio, on June 18, 1954.

[17] This was confirmed by many of the transcripts and tapes of Akron oldtimers that the author reviewed.

[18] *DR. BOB*, p. 142.

[19] *DR. BOB*, pp. 139-41.

[20] *DR. BOB*, p. 151.

[21] Taped interview of Alex M. in Akron by Niles P. Alex got sober August, 1939.

[22] Transcript of Wally G.-Bill Wilson interview.

Earl T. said, "I remember most distinctly the first meeting that I attended—Bill D. [A.A. Number Three] sat with the Holy Bible in his lap. The meeting had been opened with a prayer. Bill read excerpts from the Bible and translated them into everyday life. After half an hour of this, the meeting was thrown open to everyone in the room and they in turn picked up some of these passages from the Bible that he had discussed and gave their interpretation."[23]

Dr. Bob would often announce at a meeting, "There's a pigeon in Room so-and-so who needs some attention." And this referred to the newcomer who was still hospitalized.[24]

There certainly were long "Quiet Time" periods in the early meetings in which those attending were listening for guidance from God.[25] According to Ernie G., those present used pencils and papers to record luminous thoughts; and this was in accordance with the Oxford Group practice.[26] Henrietta D., wife of A.A. Number Three, remembered that she and Anne Smith also engaged in this practice of writing down guidance.[27]

The topic for meetings often came, not only from the Bible, but also from the Bible devotionals—*The Upper Room* and *My Utmost For His Highest*—or from other Christian literature that was being studied and recommended at the time. Member after member of the early meetings confirmed the importance and use of the Bible

---

[23] Taped transcript of Earl T. by Bill Wilson in 1954. Earl got sober in early 1938 and founded A.A. in Chicago. See *Alcoholics Anonymous Comes of Age* (New York: Alcoholics Anonymous World Services, Inc., 1957), p. 22. See other details in his story in the Big Book, pp. 287-96.

[24] *DR. BOB*, p. 146.

[25] *DR. BOB*, p. 139; Seiberling, *Origins of Alcoholics Anonymous*; Bob E., transcript of his taped interview with Bill Wilson in 1954.

[26] Transcript of interview of Ernie G. by Bill Wilson in 1954. Ernie's story, "The Seventh Month Slip," is in the First Edition of the Big Book at pages 282-286.

[27] *DR. BOB*, p. 86. See Dick B., *The Oxford Group & Alcoholics Anonymous* (Seattle: Glen Abbey Books, 1992), pp. 242-47.

devotionals, particularly *The Upper Room.*[28] Henrietta Seiberling was the person who most stressed Oswald Chambers' *My Utmost For His Highest*, which—though Chambers was not affiliated with the Oxford Group—was a favorite in the Oxford Group.[29] Wally G. said:

> Henrietta Seiberling talked a great deal about Oswald Chambers and his books, which was a little mystic for the average A.A., but we bought his "My Utmost For His Highest." By the time we read the thing for a year, we began to understand a little of what Henrietta was talking about. The spiritual phase or phases of this thing gradually began to penetrate, and we took it seriously and used it.[30]

According to Henrietta, at the earlier meetings: "Every Wednesday night I would speak on some new experience or spiritual idea I had read."[31] Others who led meetings would take something from *The Upper Room*, *My Utmost For His Highest*, or the other spiritual literature as the subject of the meeting.[32] And there was, of course, the sharing of experience. Sometimes all present would

---

[28] Transcripts and tapes of interviews by Bill Wilson of (1) Wally G. (December, 1954). (2) J. D. H. (June, 1954). J. D. got sober in December of 1936. (3) William V. H. (June, 1954). William V. H. got sober in February of 1937. His story, "A Ward of the Probate Court," is in the First Edition of the Big Book, at pages 296-302. (4) Bob E. (June, 1954). (5) Dorothy S. M. (August, 1954). Dorothy was the first wife of Clarence S., who got sober in February of 1938, who organized A.A. in Cleveland in 1939, and whose story, "Home Brewmeister," is in the First Edition and also the Third Edition of the Big Book, the latter being at pp. 297-303. To the same effect was an interview of Al L. by Niles P. In his interview with Sue Windows, Dr. Bob's daughter, the author learned in June of 1991 of the wide usage of *The Upper Room* and that it was brought to meetings by Sue's mother-in-law, Lucy G.

[29] In a telephone interview with the author in November of 1991, Julia Harris, who was in charge of the Oxford Group bookstore at Calvary Church, informed the author that Chambers was not connected with the Oxford Group but that his book was very popular and widely used by Group members.

[30] Transcript of Wally G.-Bill Wilson interview.

[31] Seiberling, *Origins of Alcoholics Anonymous*, p. 9.

[32] *DR. BOB*, p. 139.

"witness" in this fashion.[33] As to discussion of drinking, Wally G. had this to say:

> You would be surprised at how little talk there was of drinking experiences. That was usually kept for interviews in the hospital at that time, or interviews with a prospect who wasn't too sure. We were more interested in our everyday life than we were in reminiscing about drinking experiences and that type of thing. Anyway we followed this "Upper Room" which was a quarterly publication of the Methodist Church South, I believe, although it was non-sectarian in character and consisted of a verse and a story in support of the verse from the Bible for each day, and a thought for the day, together with a suggestion as to our reading.[34] Incidentally we all had either Good [?] or Moffatt's [Bible] because it was much easier to understand than some of the King James translation. Sharing was self-analysis—preliminary to a surrender and quite frequently it was very much glossed over—I'm not sure that it was too important to make a complete exposition of all your faults and such things. If the man is really sincere in making a surrender and asking God for help and guidance, and doing it on a continuing daily basis, those things gradually fade into the background. Really, there is not much point in telling another person what a heel you have been—most of us know it anyhow, about all we need to do is to look at ourselves.[35]

Surrenders and the Book of James

Surrenders were a critical part of the meeting structure. As oldtimers pointed out, no one was allowed to participate in the Wednesday night meetings without having made surrender. And

---

[33] *DR. BOB*, p. 139-140.

[34] See Appendix Four.

[35] Transcript of Wally G.-Bill Wilson interview.

far too little has been written about what happened in a surrender. Recently, the author has been able to piece together information about the surrenders which seems not to have been mentioned in any published account. The information concerns the use of the Bible and the Book of James as the format for the surrender process.

The connection between A.A. and the Book of James is well documented. Dr. Bob said older members considered James an absolutely essential part of the recovery program.[36] The Book of James was a favorite with early AAs.[37] It was one of the three books of the Bible on Dr. Bob's "required reading list."[38] Some early AAs favored "The James Club" as a name for the A.A. Fellowship.[39] In the Smith home, Anne often read to Dr. Bob and Bill from the Book of James.[40] Bill Wilson said, "We much favored the Apostle James."[41] And the Big Book itself several times quotes "Anne Smith's favorite verse" which was from James—"Faith without works is dead."[42] But there is a new point that needs to be explored here.

James 5:13-16 reads as follows:

Is any among you afflicted? let him pray. Is any merry? let him sing psalms.
Is any sick among you? let him call for the elders of the church; and let them pray over him, anointing him with oil in the name of the Lord:
And the prayer of faith shall save the sick, and the Lord shall raise him up; and if he shall have committed sins, they shall be forgiven him.

---

[36] *DR. BOB*, p. 96.

[37] *DR. BOB*, 71.

[38] Bill Pittman, *AA The Way It Began* (Seattle: Glen Abbey Books, 1988), p. 197.

[39] *DR. BOB*, p. 71; *Pass It On*, p. 147.

[40] *DR. BOB*, p. 71; *Pass It On*, p. 147; *Alcoholics Anonymous Comes of Age*, p. 7.

[41] Kurtz, *Not-God*, p. 320, n11.

[42] Big Book, pp. 14, 76, 88.

Confess your faults one to another, and pray for one another, that ye may be healed. The effectual fervent prayer of a righteous man availeth much.

The Book of James stated that if any were sick, the elders should be called, should pray over the sick person, and should anoint him with oil in the name of the Lord [Jesus]. Jesus Christ several times taught that if prayers were made *in His name*, those prayers would be answered.[43] Glenn Clark explained in several of his books the effectiveness of praying in the name of Jesus Christ.[44] We know Clark's books were favorites with Dr. Bob, Henrietta, and in early A.A.[45] Whether the verses from Gospel of John about asking in the name of Jesus Christ, or the Clark books on prayer were the foundation for part of the Akron surrender prayer, we do not know. But there is clear evidence from Clarence S. that the foregoing verses from James 5:13-16 directly influenced surrenders as part of what Clarence S. described as the "healing ministry in James."

Clarence S. was Dr. Bob's sponsee. Clarence got sober in February of 1938 and remained, throughout his sober life, a controversial but leading member of A.A. Clarence informed his own sponsee, Mitch K., who lives in New York, about the precise

---

[43] John 14:13 said, "And whatsoever ye shall ask in my name, that will I do, that the Father may be glorified in the Son." John 14:14 said, "If ye shall ask any thing in my name, I will do it." John 16:23 said, ". . . . verily, verily I say unto you, Whatsoever ye shall ask the Father in my name, he will give it to you." John 16:24 said, "Hitherto have ye asked nothing in my name; ask, and ye shall receive, that your joy may be full." In Acts 4:7, the crowd asked Peter by what power, or by what name, he had healed the impotent man. In Acts 4:10, Peter replied, "Be it known unto you all, and to all the people of Israel, that by the name of Jesus Christ of Nazareth, whom ye crucified, whom God raised from the dead, even by him doth this man stand here before you whole."

[44] Glenn Clark, *The Soul's Sincere Desire* (Boston: Little, Brown, and Company, 1927), pp. 63-86; *I Will Lift Up Mine Eyes* (New York: Harper & Row. 1937), pp. 18-20.

[45] See Pittman, *AA The Way It Began*, p. 192; Dick B., *Dr. Bob's Library* (West Virginia: The Bishop of Books, 1992), pp. 35, 58-62; and our chapter in this book on Henrietta Seiberling.

details of Clarence's own surrender, as he said it was conducted by Dr. Bob, T. Henry, and the early AAs. Mitch K. provided the author with the following description of Clarence's surrender at T. Henry's, which Clarence had told Mitch was the way Dr. Bob conducted the Akron surrenders:

> T. Henry, Doc, and a couple of other Oxford Group members went into T. Henry's bedroom. They all, including Clarence, who by now was used to this kneeling, got down on their knees in an attitude of prayer. They all placed their hands on Clarence and then proceeded to pray. They introduced him to Jesus as Lord and Savior. They had him pray to Jesus and had him dedicate his life to Him. They then anointed him with oil and once again laid hands on him. They did this just as did First Century Christianity and then prayed for a healing and removal of his sickness, especially his alcoholism. When he arose, Clarence once again felt like a new man.[46]

Clarence S. also provided his sponsee, Mitch, with a three-page description of how to take the 12 Steps and said it was based on the method used by Dr. Bob and the Akron oldtimers from the Book of James. As to Step Three, with both on their knees, the sponsor directed the sponsee to repeat:

> Jesus, this is (name). He is coming to you in all humility to ask you to guide and direct him. (name) realizes that his life is messed up and unmanageable. (name) is coming to you Lord in all humility to ask to be one of your children—to work for you, to serve and dedicate his life to you and to turn his will over that he may be an instrument of your love.
>
> Lord, I ask that you guide and direct me, and that I have decided to turn my life and will over to you. To serve you and to dedicate my life to you. I ask all this in the name of Jesus Christ. I thank

---

[46] Interview with Mitch K. by the author on August 13, 1992 at Charleston, West Virginia.

you Lord. I thank you Lord. I thank you Lord. I believe that if
I ask in prayer, I shall receive what I have asked for. Thank you
Jesus. Thank you Jesus. Thank you Jesus. Amen. Amen. Amen.

The Step Seven procedure was described by Clarence in writing
as:

Both on knees: Lord, here is your child (name). He is coming to
you in all humility to humbly ask your forgiveness, believing that
anything he asks in prayer, he humbly shall receive.

I (name) humbly ask you oh Lord, to remove my shortcomings
and forgive me my sins and trespasses and ask in all humility that
you will remove my defects and shortcomings because I am one
of your children and I truly believe. Thank you Jesus. Thank you
Jesus. Thank you Jesus. Amen. Amen. Amen. (Sponsor—Your
sins are removed in the name of the Father, the Son, and the Holy
Spirit—if you truly believe. Healing Baptism with oil).
Both—Thank you Jesus. Thank you Jesus. Thank you Jesus.
Amen. Amen. Amen.[47]

As the reader can see, the details were very precise; but the
author had not heard of this procedure before. As a consequence,
the author has inquired of Dr. Bob's children and sent letters to
oldtimers to see if the James—anointing—with—oil procedure
could be verified by others. One oldtimer, Larry B., of Cleveland,
Ohio, replied in writing to the author on September 18, 1992.
Larry said he was in and out of A.A. between 1939 and 1944. He
stated that "oil never used by Doc, Clarence, or any others in
early days of Oxford Group." Larry believed Mitch K. was
incorrect though not disputing Clarence may have used oil on
Mitch. Of his own surrender, Larry said, "They took me and that
man upstairs to be a born again human being and be God's helper

---

[47] The author has in his possession of copy of the three-page, Twelve Step instruction
sheet given to Mitch K. by his sponsor, Clarence S. It is entitled, "GOING THROUGH
THE STEPS TO RECOVERY."

to alcoholics." And so the quest for more information goes on. The author is hopeful others will come forward with information as to whether Dr. Bob, Clarence, and the early Akron AAs did or did not use the James procedure.

Compare the more general language T. Henry gave in his description of the surrenders which occurred either before or after the Wednesday meeting was over:

> We might take the new man upstairs, and a group of men would ask him to surrender his life to God and start in to really live up to the four absolutes and also to go out and help other men who needed it. This was in the form of a prayer group. Several of the boys would pray together, and the new man would make his own prayer, asking God to take alcohol out of his life, and when he was through, he would say, "Thank you, God, for taking it out of my life." During the prayer, he usually made a declaration of his willingness to turn his life over to God.[48]

A Meeting Overview

In 1975, Bob E. an Akron oldtimer whom Dr. Bob sponsored, wrote A.A.'s then archivist, Nell Wing, and described a typical Akron meeting as follows:

> The general set up [of] a meeting was done by Dr. Smith & a few others in an upstairs bed room just before the regular 8:30 meeting & it usually followed a page of the Upper Room which was supplied to us by Ernie G.'s mother (@ 5 cents a piece) & we all carried them. They fit in our side pocket, they were the size of a Reader's Digest only not so thick. Each page was called a "thought for the day," 1st there was a short quote of scripture, next a short prayer, next the short story for the day was read.[49]

---

[48] *DR. BOB*, pp. 139-41.

[49] See Appendix Four for an example of a daily devotional in *The Upper Room*.

Next if the group was still small enough we would hold hands in a circle and have a short quiet time during which we silently asked God for guidance. Then we shared or witnessed whatever we felt guided to talk about, a problem or an experience with a point worth sharing. If it didn't help anybody it helped you. Then came instructions from Dr. Smith & announcements and asking for help or suggestions in handling a new man.[50]

A custom that persists in a somewhat different form in A.A. today was inaugurated then with the handing out of address books with everybody's name in it. If the member had a phone, his number was there; and people were urged to drop in or telephone.[51] Copies of *The Upper Room* were made available at the meetings for all the members to study.[52] The meetings were followed by social activity where the men went to the kitchen for coffee, and most of the women sat around talking to each other. At a later point in the early days, members went to Kistler's Donut Shop.[53]

As can be seen from some of the variations in descriptions, the meetings of the alcoholic squad did not always follow an identical form. Apparently most of the time, prayers were conducted by T. Henry. Invariably, it seems, meetings opened with prayer and with reading from the Bible, whether from the Bible itself or from Scripture in the Bible devotionals. The person who read from the Bible or who led the meetings varied. Sometimes the topic would be on a Bible subject, sometimes on a matter in the devotionals, and occasionally on some other topic vital to the lives of those present. The drinking experience stories that predominate in A.A. meetings today were apparently not a part of the Akron meetings. There was quiet time, prayer, and listening for guidance.

---

[50] Letter from Bob E. to Nell Wing, dated March 14, 1975, a copy of which was made available to the author during his visit to Stepping Stones in September of 1991.

[51] *DR. BOB*, pp. 145-46.

[52] See Dick B., *Dr. Bob's Library*, pp. 33-34; *DR. BOB*, pp. 151, 139, 71, 178, 220, 311.

[53] *DR. BOB*, p. 141 [incorrectly spelled "Kessler's" in that text].

Literature of the Oxford Group and literature, such as the devotionals, was discussed and passed out to those present or was exchanged. Dr. Bob kept the meeting focussed on the need of a newcomer, usually making an announcement on that topic. The meeting closed with the Lord's Prayer. Names, phone numbers, and addresses were often exchanged. And a social time followed.

The author has attended more than 1,500 A.A. meetings during his sobriety. And certain aspects of the Akron meetings bear a remarkable resemblance to the format of today's A.A. meetings, both before, during, and after the meetings. AAs often have Steering Committee meetings to focus on organization and content of the group's regular meetings. At regular meetings, literature is announced as available; and coffee and cookies are often furnished by the group. Meetings open and close with prayer—usually opening with the "Serenity Prayer" and closing with the "Lord's Prayer." The meetings open with "a moment of silence, to do with as you wish"—perhaps an abbreviated remnant of the old Quiet Time. There is often the reading of A.A.'s Preamble, reading from a portion of the Big Book, and the reading of the Twelve Traditions. New members are introduced; and the main focus of most meetings then becomes the sharing of experience, strength and hope by some member who has achieved recovery. Stories do focus on drinking experience before sobriety, the entry into A.A., and the speaker's current life situation.[54] Before and after the meetings, names, phone numbers, and sometimes addresses are made available to new members who are urged to keep in contact. The meetings are often followed by social get-togethers, usually for coffee, where the program and sobriety are frequently discussed in some detail. The lightheartedness that prevailed at alcoholic squad functions usually can be found in the noise, laughter, and friendliness at A.A. meetings today.

---

[54] Compare Big Book, p. 58.

Hospitals and Institutions

Bill set the stage in New York for locating prospects, "pigeons," "cookies," or "babies," as they were sometimes called. No sooner did Bill leave Towns Hospital in December of 1934 than he feverishly sought out drunks with whom to talk at Towns Hospital, Calvary Mission, and Oxford Group meetings. Though he modified his "preaching" approach when he arrived in Akron, Bill passed the Oxford Group's "working with others," concept on to Dr. Bob. Bill and Dr. Bob at once set out to "oxidize" drunks with their evolving recovery ideas. But there was a difference from the New York approach. We would summarize the Akron approach as follows:

> Often, wives would call. The alcoholic squad would find out about the prospect, his family situation, his job situation, and the nature of his drinking. Then the prospect himself would be approached; and there was a sharing of experience—just as Bill did with Dr. Bob and Ebby did with Bill. Following this preliminary questioning, the new prospect would be hospitalized and "defogged" for five to ten days—often with substantial doses of paraldehyde. Patients were given only a Bible as reading material. They would then be visited by several alcoholics who shared their experience. Dr. Bob emphasized hospitalization. He was hospitalization-oriented, and believed alcoholism to be a disease. The recovered alcoholics who visited the new person had a captive audience. Dr. Bob would often visit; and his part centered around three items: a) He would explain the medical and disease aspects to the new person. b) He would inquire about the person's belief in God—a God of love. c) He usually asked the newcomer to make a decision. If the newcomer agreed to go along, he was required to admit that he was powerless over alcohol and then to surrender his will to God—on his knees—with prayer—in the presence of one of more of the alcoholic squad.[55]

---

[55] See *DR. BOB*, pp. 109-11, 113, 118, 142-44, 146, 101-05, 81-87; Big Book, pp. 289-91.

Some of these same techniques are now described in detail and suggested in the Big Book's Chapter, entitled, "Working With Others," at pages 89 to 98. Others became part of Steps One, Two, Three, and Seven. In fact, A.A.'s remaining steps—those following the surrender and involving inventory and admission of character defects—were taken within a matter of days in the early days, sometimes all in one day.[56]

About the time the alcoholic squad left T. Henry's to begin meeting in part in Cleveland and in part at Dr. Bob's home, the approach was made to Sister Ignatia at St. Thomas Hospital to admit alcoholics there. Since the real work at St. Thomas did not begin until after our story ends, namely, in January of 1940, we leave the details of St. Thomas Hospital and Sister Ignatia to Mary C. Darrah's book, *Sister Ignatia*. However, we do point to the transition chronology: (1) Clarence S. announced on May 10, 1939, at T. Henry's, the formation of the Cleveland group—for alcoholics. (2) Dr. Bob and Anne left the Oxford Group the next night.[57] (3) Dr. Bob approached Sister Ignatia for a hospital bed at St. Thomas on August 14, 1939. (4) By the early fall of 1939, the treatment of alcoholism had an official but small beginning at St. Thomas, but the hospitalization of alcoholics had not become a regular admitting policy. (5) According to Sister Ignatia, it was not until January of 1940, when the alcoholics in Akron were finally meeting at the King School, that "a definite working agreement was achieved with the knowledge of my [Sister Ignatia's] superior, Sister Clementine, Dr. Bob, and probably the Chief of Staff.[58] The upshot of this bit of history is that the story of early A.A., its hospitalization activities, and the part these played in the Big Book and Twelve Steps were all in place and consummated by the time the Sister Ignatia-St. Thomas Hospital epoch had its significant beginnings.

---

[56] See *DR. BOB*, p. 102; Big Book, pp. 291-92.

[57] Smith and Windows, *Children of the Healer*, p. 49.

[58] See Darrah, *Sister Ignatia*, pp. 79-87.

The First Success with Bill D.
—A.A. Number Three

The Bill D. story has been told in detail before;[59] but we consider it important to see how the evolving Akron techniques were applied in bringing about sobriety for Bill D.—Bill Wilson's and Dr. Bob's first success story in the Akron recovery endeavors.

After what may have been their first failure—working with Eddie R.—Dr. Bob and Bill decided to look for alcoholics down at Akron City Hospital. The admissions nurse told them of Bill D., the lawyer who had been hospitalized many times, and was in an almost hopeless state. Prior to this, Bill D.'s wife had prayed with her pastor "that someone her husband could understand would visit him in City Hospital." The admissions nurse phoned Henrietta D., Bill's wife, and told her that Dr. Bob had found a way to help men with a drinking problem and wanted to talk to her. The wife agreed. Bill and Dr. Bob met with her at the hospital and learned some details of Bill D.'s life and drinking problem. With that, they arranged for Bill D. to have a private hospital room at no expense to the patient. Bill and Bob visited him and heard his drinking story, told him of their own experience, and asked if he could quit drinking of his own accord. This is the record in *DR. BOB*:

> He was there about five days before they could make him say that he couldn't control his drinking and had to leave it up to God. Well, he believed in God, but he wanted to be his own man. They *made* him get down on his knees at the side of the bed right there in the hospital and pray and say that he would turn his life over to God (p. 85).

Bill D. had gone to God, without reservation, admitting he was powerless over alcohol. He affirmed his willingness to let God take over his life and to find out what God's will was for him. As soon as Bill D. did that, he felt a great release. He knew he had

---

[59] See *DR. BOB*, pp. 76-89; Big Book, pp. 182-92.

a helper he could rely upon, and who wouldn't fail him. When Bill and Bob returned, he told them he had gone to this "Higher Power" [a term he may not have used at the time] and had told Him that he was willing to put His world first. He then made the surrender described above. He made a moral inventory, was told about the first drink, the 24-hour program, and the fact that alcoholism was an incurable disease. He also remembered he was told to go out and carry the message of recovery to someone else. Bill Wilson told Bill D.'s wife:

> Henrietta, the Lord has been so wonderful to me, curing me of this terrible disease, that I just want to keep talking about it and telling people.[60]

Bill D. pointed out that Bill Wilson was grateful for his release from alcoholism, had given God the credit, and wanted to tell others about it. He said that Bill Wilson's sentence became "sort of a golden text for the A.A. program and for me." He concluded his story in the Big Book by stating, "I came into A.A. solely for the purpose of sobriety, but it has been through A.A. that I have found God."[61]

What the Akron AAs Did in Their Homes for Recovery

Recovery was, in part, maintained by hanging out together; searching for and helping drunks; and attending the Wednesday night meetings at T. Henry's. But the Akron alcoholics were actually holding meetings of some sort all the time. And the real key to their *spiritual* program is perhaps best attributed to their quiet time and reading. Recall from our discussion of the twenty-

---

[60] Big Book, p. 191.
[61] Big Book, pp. 191-92.

eight Oxford Group principles that Quiet Time, Daily Surrender, and Continuance all were words that comprehended not only witnessing and church attendance but listening, praying, Bible study, and reading.

Quiet Time With Two-Way Prayer

The following was an exchange between Bill Wilson and Dorothy S. M., Clarence S.'s first wife, during an interview of Dorothy by Bill on August 30, 1954:

> DOROTHY: Did you know that he [Dr. Bob] prayed three times a day regularly?

> BILL WILSON: He [Dr. Bob] went up to his room three times a day on the hour. I think it was about 9, 11, and 4, as I recall, that he prayed not only for his own understanding but for a different group of people who requested him to pray for them. I was always glad that I was included in those prayers and sort of depended upon him to get me into heaven or something or other.

Paul S. described Dr. Bob's own morning quiet time as follows:

> Dr. Bob's morning devotion consisted of a short prayer, a 20-minute study of a familiar verse from the Bible, and a quiet period of waiting for directions as to where he, that day, should find use for his talent. Having heard, he would religiously go about his Father's business, as he put it.[62]

Henrietta D., wife of A.A. Number Three, described Anne Smith's practices and those of the oldtimers:

> Anne would call me every single morning and ask me if I'd had my quiet time. You see, we had a quiet time when you were supposed to go by yourself with a pad and pencil and put down

---

[62] *DR. BOB*, p. 314.

anything that came into your mind. Just anything. Later on in the day, it might come to you why that came into your mind. Probably for a year she called me every single morning: "Did you have your quiet time? Did you get anything out of it?" She was wonderful.[63]

William V. H. said:

This "Upper Room" was a little daily reading booklet that I've used ever since. It's published by the Methodist Church authority down in Nashville, Tennessee. At first, when there were quite a few in the group, each member was furnished a copy which was good for three months of daily readings by the mother of one of our fellowship, Ernie. . . . I am greatly indebted to her because here's a tool that I stuck by, and I start each day by reading this service. I credit my success to a lot of the daily readings. . . . I bought many books and tried to help myself upon their advice. I kept up my daily devotions reading the "Upper Room." Paul S. came along one day when I was feeling quite low, and he said, "Bill, don't forget there's One that's all loving and all forgiving." And I said, "Who's that, Paul?" He said, "That's your God." So I continued reading the "Upper Room" and the references in the Good Book. Finally, I got to the point where I could make a practical adaptation for myself, or could see them as concrete examples, as you might say. The reference one day was to the second book of Corinthians, the fifth chapter, and the seventeenth verse. It said there, "Therefore if a man be in Christ, he becomes a new creature, all things are passed away, behold, all things are new."[64] I applied that to myself, and the first, if I followed the A.A. program, I would become a new creature. The next part which said, "all things are passed away," I latched on to that authority to forget a lot of skeletons in my closet. The lawyer has his statutes on the shelf there to render decisions. The Bible, I

---

[63] Transcript of taped interview of Henrietta D., on file in A.A. Archives in New York.

[64] 2 Corinthians 5:17, to which William V. H. referred, says: "Therefore if any man be in Christ, he is a new creature; old things are passed away; behold, all things are become new."

figured, was my statute now. I immediately got a release from things I thought I would never forget. So, continuing with the wonderful help, I latched on to the keynote that I found in this "Upper Room". . . . and I have had many victories, which we used to cite in the early days. This keynote which I found through my application to the "Upper Room," I appreciated that I needed to discipline myself, so I've never failed to start a morning without this spiritual reading and guidance. . . . I lay out my Good Book, and the "Upper Room" in hotels and they were really company for me, for I knew back in Akron, Ohio, were a little group of people that was applying and using the same things. . . . I tried to attack any books that Doc was reading or that Henrietta [Seiberling] recommended. Some of them were a little over my head. Henrietta recommended the Twenty-seventh Psalm. Well, I dug that out, and that was very helpful too, because I had a lot of personal trouble.[65]

The following is an exchange which took place between Bill Wilson and Wally and Annabelle G., in his taped interview of them in December of 1954:

BILL WILSON: They [Wally and Annabelle] were the pioneers in the A.A. work here in Akron since the very early days, and it was in their house that so many people were rehabilitated after having been taken from the hospital here in Akron. Under the tutelage and inspiration of these folks, probably more people have recovered than in any A.A. home in the world. They were the first to make it a success. Lois and I tried the same thing in New York, but actually failed so far as the people were concerned.

WALLY G.: In our home we had a quiet time for them here in the morning. Maybe we'd sit at the breakfast table until noon. We'd have our quiet time, and then we'd talk. Tom and Maybelle L. had about fifteen people, and Paul S. must have had about 25 or so. Clarence and Dorothy S. in Cleveland had quite a success.

---

[65] Transcript of interview of William V. H. by Bill Wilson at Akron, Ohio, on June 17, 1954.

DR. BOB describes the importance of Quiet Time—which involved both talking to God and listening—as follows:

> Morning quiet time continued to be an important part of the recovery program in 1938-1939, as did the spiritual reading from which the early members derived a good deal of their inspiration. "Here in Los Angeles, they now emphasize meetings," said Duke P., who used to live in Toledo and was one of the pioneering members there. "I guess that's because there are so many of them. When I started, they stressed morning quiet time, daily reading, and daily contact."[66]

Reflecting on why Wally and Annabele G. had so many successes, Bill Wilson said:

> I think there may have been times when we attributed it to their morning meditation. I sort of always felt that something was lost from A.A. when we stopped emphasizing the morning meditation.[67]

Here is how Dr. Bob, Anne, and Bill had quiet times together in the beginning:

> Each morning, there was a devotion, he [Bill] recalled. After a long silence, in which they awaited inspiration and guidance, Anne would read from the Bible. "James was our favorite," he said. "Reading from her chair in the corner, she would softly conclude, 'Faith without works is dead.'" This was a favorite quotation of Anne's much as the Book of James was a favorite with early A.A.'s—so much so that "The James Club" was favored by some as a name for the Fellowship. Sue also remembered the quiet time in the mornings—how they sat around reading from the Bible. Later, they also used *The Upper Room*, a Methodist publication that provided a daily inspirational

---

[66] *DR. BOB*, pp. 150-51.

[67] *DR. BOB*, p. 178.

message, interdenominational in its approach. "Then somebody said a prayer," she recalled. "After that, we were supposed to say one to ourselves. Then we'd be quiet. Finally, everybody would share what they got or didn't get. This lasted for at least a half hour and sometimes went as long as an hour." Young Smitty was aware of the early-morning prayers and quiet time, but didn't attend.[68]

Bible Study

The Oxford Group, Dr. Bob, Anne Smith, Henrietta, and the Williams's were all strong on the Bible.[69] Dr. Bob read the Bible from cover to cover three times and could and did quote favorite passages verbatim.[70] Dr. Bob's "required reading list" had the Bible at the head of the list.[71] As we have said, he felt that the Sermon on the Mount best expressed A.A.'s underlying philosophy and that the Sermon on the Mount, the 13th chapter of First Corinthians, and the Book of James were absolutely essential parts

---

[68] *DR. BOB*, pp. 71-72.

[69] As we previously pointed out, T. Henry had been a Bible teacher for many years; and he had participated in the Oxford Group business team meetings where Mary Angevine, a Bible instructor, was helping team members become thoroughly familiar with Scripture. An early newspaper headline that announced the arrival of an Oxford Group team in the community, was headlined: "Bible Christianity." This article is in the Hartford Seminary archives at Hartford, Connecticut; and the author has a copy of the article. The Oxford Group's founder, Dr. Frank Buchman's recipe for Bible-reading was, "Read accurately, interpret honestly, apply drastically" (See Garth Lean, *On The Tail of A Comet* (Colorado Springs: Helmers & Howard, 1988), p. 157. Reverend Sherwood Day wrote: "The principles of 'The Oxford Group' are the principles of the Bible" (See Sherwood Sunderland Day, *The Principles of the Group* (Oxford: University Press, n.d.), p. 1. Shoemaker wrote: "Read and know the Bible, and all else, including public worship, will fall into its place." See Samuel M. Shoemaker, *Realizing Religion* (New York: Association Press, 1923), p. 62.

[70] *DR. BOB*, p. 310.

[71] Bill Pittman, *AA The Way It Began* (Seattle: Glen Abbey Books, 1988), p. 197.

of the A.A. recovery program.[72] He believed the Oxford Group's Four Absolutes, which were derived primarily from the Sermon on the Mount, were the only and the proper yardsticks early A.A. had for behavior consistent with God's will.[73] He believed the basic ideas for the Twelve Steps came from A.A.'s study of the Bible.[74] In fact, Clarence S. recalled, and told his sponsee, Mitch K., that Dr. Bob said that the Sermon on the Mount was the source of two of A.A.'s best known slogans. Dr. Bob told Clarence S.:

"First Things First" came from Matthew 6:33: "But seek ye first the kingdom of God, and his righteousness; and all these things shall be added unto you."[75]

"One Day At A Time" came from Matthew 6:34: "Take therefore no thought [be not anxious] for the morrow: for the morrow shall

---

[72] *DR. BOB*, pp. 228, 96. Mitch K. supplied the author with a pamphlet given him by Clarence S., and which is entitled, "A Manual for Alcoholics Anonymous." It states: "This pamphlet was written and edited by members of Alcoholics Anonymous Akron Group No. 1, popularly known as the King School Group. Akron Group No. 1 is the original chapter of Alcoholics Anonymous and includes in its active membership one of the organization's founders, the first person to accept the program, and a large number of other members whose sobriety dates back five, six and seven years. The text of this pamphlet has been approved by the membership." The pamphlet states on page 9, "There is the Bible you haven't opened for years. Get acquainted with it. Read it with an open mind. You will find things that amaze you. You will be convinced that certain passages were written with you in mind. Read the Sermon on the Mount (Matthew V, VI and VII.) Read St. Paul's inspired essay on love (I Corinthians XIII.) Read the Book of James. These readings are brief but so important."

[73] *DR. BOB*, p. 54. The author has in his possession several copies of the *Central Bulletin*, published in Cleveland, Ohio, in 1942 and 1943. The *Central Bulletin* for November, 1942, carries as its banner: Unselfishness-Honesty-Truth-Love. The *Central Bulletin* for December, 1942, and for July, 1943, carries the logo: "Unselfishness-Honesty-Purity-Love A-A." These bulletins were given to Mitch K. by his sponsor, Clarence S.

[74] *DR. BOB*, p. 97.

[75] Interview of Mitch K., Clarence's sponsee, by the author at Charleston, West Virginia, in August, 1992. See also *DR. BOB*, pp. 144, 192.

take thought for the things of itself. Sufficient unto the day is the evil thereof."[76]

Dr. Bob donated his own Bible to A.A.'s first group at King School in Akron, where it still rests on the podium at every meeting (This author personally observed that Bible on the podium when he attended the King School Group with Dr. Bob's daughter in June of 1992).

Anne Ripley Smith, Dr. Bob's wife, was no less devoted to the Bible as her source for inspiration and for education as to God's will. As we have said, she wrote in her workbook: "Of course the Bible ought to be the main Source Book of all. No day ought to pass without reading it."[77] She said, "One should by all means read at least one book on the life of Christ a year for a while. More would be better."[78] And the 64 pages of her spiritual workbook are filled to overflowing with quotations from the Bible, books about it, and her own thoughts as to its meanings. Bill Wilson's most vivid recollections of Anne were of her Scripture reading in the mornings when he lived with Dr. Bob and Anne. Anne, of course, seems much remembered for her frequent use of the Bible verses defining God as love and emphatically stating that "faith without works is dead." This latter Bible verse is firmly lodged in the pages of the Big Book.[79]

Henrietta Seiberling was a Bible reader, and she spoke of and quoted from the Good Book quite often. She did this in her personal life, in family conversations, and in meetings. Her Bible was at her bedside and was thoroughly read, underlined, and annotated.[80] T. Henry Williams was a Bible teacher for many

---

[76] Interview of Mitch K. by the author, August, 1992.

[77] Dick B., *Anne Smith's Spiritual Workbook* (Corte Madera, Ca: Good Book Publishing Company, 1992), pp. 11-12.

[78] Dick B., *Anne Smith's Spiritual Workbook*, p. 14.

[79] See Big Book, pp. 14, 76, 88.

[80] Dorothy Seiberling showed her mother's Bible to the author at a personal interview in New York in October, 1992; and the facts above were confirmed.

years; and his wife was trained for missionary work. They were
no strangers to the Good Book either. Hence the alcoholic squad
of the Oxford Group were sitting in a spiritual community where
the Bible was not only stressed as reading matter, but also as the
source for their ideas. And if Sam Shoemaker was, as Bill Wilson
often said, the prime source of inspiration and teaching for the
A.A. principles and program, Reverend Irving Harris's words
about Shoemaker and the Bible should be noted:

> The Scriptures formed the basis of Sam Shoemaker's preaching.
> He was a "Bible Christian."
>
> Consider the implications of Shoemaker's major
> premise—"Christianity is a religion that works."
>
> So, as Calvary's program developed, two interesting points
> became ever more apparent: (1) Here was a place to learn the
> how of faith, both in sermons and in groups—How to find God.
> How to pray. How to read the Bible. How to pass faith on.[81]

If Dr. Frank Buchman and the Oxford Group as a whole were
the source for A.A.'s principles and program, consider this
description of Buchman:

> Buchman was, as Thornton-Duesbury often said, "soaked in the
> Bible," and made certain it formed the basis of the training given
> in Oxford.[82]

If, as Dr. Bob said and as we believe, A.A.'s basic ideas came
from the Bible itself, then it is important to remember that almost
every spiritual source material that was used by early AAs in

---

[81] Irving Harris, *The Breeze of the Spirit* (New York: The Seabury Press, 1978), pp.
18, 10, 25.

[82] Garth Lean, *On The Tail of A Comet* (Colorado Springs, Helmers & Howard,
1988), p. 157.

Akron involved a source that focused on the Bible. There were the daily Bible devotionals:

1. *The Upper Room*,[83]
2. *My Utmost For His Highest*,[84]
3. *Daily Strength For Daily Needs*,[85] and
4. *Victorious Living*.[86]

All of these were owned and read by Dr. Bob and Anne, and all commenced the page for each day with a Bible verse. Two of the devotionals—*The Upper Room* and *My Utmost For His Highest*—were very much used in the Oxford Group, the homes of A.A.'s progenitors—Henrietta, the Smiths, and the Wilsons, and in the Akron area.[87] We have included in Appendices Four, Five, Six, and Seven copies of a page from each of these devotionals to illustrate the biblical guidance AAs were receiving from this literature on a daily basis. Interestingly, not one of these daily Bible meditation books was an Oxford Group or Shoemaker book!

The Spiritual Literature They Read

Our books—*Dr. Bob's Library, Anne Smith's Spiritual Workbook*, and *The Oxford Group & Alcoholics Anonymous*—as well as our review in this book of Henrietta Seiberling's, Dr. Bob's and Anne's books, and our Appendix Three should make clear that Dr. Bob, Anne, and Henrietta read an immense amount of spiritual literature. They shared their books and their interest in the books.

---

[83] A Methodist quarterly whose issues commenced in the spring of 1935.

[84] Oswald Chambers, *My Utmost For His Highest* (London: Simpkin Marshall Ltd., 1927).

[85] Mary Wilder Tileston, *Daily Strength for Daily Needs* (New York: Grosset & Dunlap, 1928).

[86] E. Stanley Jones, *Victorious Living* (New York: The Abingdon Press, 1936).

[87] As to *My Utmost For His Highest*, see comments in Pittman, *AA The Way It Began*, p. 183; Dick B., *Dr. Bob's Library*, pp. 30-34; Mark Guldseth, *Streams* (Fritz Creek, Alaska: Fritz Creek Studios, 1982), p. 160.

Both Dr. Shoemaker and the Oxford Group itself, as well as its adherents, wrote a large number of books on Oxford Group principles and personalities.[88] Such books as Dr. Bob owned were widely loaned out to alcoholics he worked with. The Bible devotionals were used in meetings. And the Christian literature was read and discussed in the Akron meetings, read and discussed in Dr. Bob's home, interpreted by Anne Smith, and read by many people in early A.A.[89]

DR. BOB and the Good Oldtimers mentions some of the principal books that were popular: (1) Henry Drummond's *The Greatest Thing In The World*—a study of 1 Corinthians 13 and love;[90] (2) *The Upper Room*, the Methodist quarterly that was widely used in meetings and in homes;[91] and (3) Emmet Fox's *The Sermon on the Mount*.[92] Bob E., Clarence S., and Al L., all Akron oldtimers of the 1930's, mentioned the importance of James Allen's *As A Man Thinketh*;[93] Fox's *Sermon*; and Drummond's book on Corinthians.[94] *RHS*, the Grapevine's memorial issue published at Dr. Bob's death, mentions the James Allen book and *The Runner's Bible*, which Dr. Bob owned and loaned.[95] The author viewed part of Dr. Bob's library at the home of his daughter, Sue, and part at Dr. Bob's Ardmore home. The author

---

[88] See Appendix One, listing the Oxford Group books disseminated from Calvary House and also listing other popular Oxford Group writings of the 1930's.

[89] See Kurtz, *Not-God*, p. 32; *Pass It On*, p. 147; *DR. BOB*, pp. 71-72; Dick B., *Anne Smith's Spiritual Workbook*, pp. 6-7; *Dr. Bob's Library*, pp. 7-12, 18-19; *The Oxford Group & Alcoholics Anonymous*, pp. 88-89.

[90] Henry Drummond, *The Greatest Thing In The World* (New Jersey: Spire Books, Fleming H. Revell, 1968), first written about 1884. See *DR. BOB*, pp. 151, 310-11.

[91] See *DR. BOB*, pp. 151, 139, 71, 178, 220, 311.

[92] *DR. BOB*, p. 151.

[93] James Allen, *As A Man Thinketh* (New York: Peter Pauper Press, Inc., n.d.).

[94] Information from transcriptions of interviews of Bob E. by Bill Wilson in 1954; Al L. by Niles P.; and information as to Clarence S. supplied to the author by Clarence's sponsee, Mitch K. in their August, 1992, interview.

[95] Nora Smith Holm, *The Runner's Bible* (New York: Houghton Mifflin Company, 1915). See *RHS*, p. 34.

confirmed that the Oxford Group's most important books were being circulated in Akron. Several of the oldtimers whose tapes or transcripts were reviewed by the author mentioned the presence and circulation of Oxford Group literature at the T. Henry meetings. The OG books in Dr. Bob's possession, and which indicated (by the notation "Please return") that he was circulating them, were Russell's *For Sinners Only, What Is The Oxford Group?*, Walter's *Soul Surgery*, Begbie's *Life Changers*, and Foot's *Life Began Yesterday*.[96] Sue Smith Windows told the author that the Glenn Clark books were favorites with Dr. Bob; and the author verified with Mrs. Windows that these Clark books also were in circulation in Akron. Nell Wing, A.A.'s first archivist, and Bill Wilson's second secretary, confirmed that all of Glenn Clark's books were popular with early AAs.[97] Nell Wing compiled a list of at least ten books that were read by Bill Wilson and others between 1935 and 1939. They were Allen's *As A Man Thinketh*; Lewis Browne's *This Believing World* and *The Conversion Experience*; Glenn Clark's *I Will Lift Up Mine Eyes* and *This Changing World*; Emmet Fox's *The Sermon on the Mount*; William James's *The Varieties of Religious Experience*; Richard Peabody's *The Common Sense of Drinking*; A. J. Russell's *For Sinners Only*; and Thomas Troward's *The Edinburgh Lectures on Mental Science*.[98]

The significance of all these book lists is that early AAs were readers.[99] Dr. Bob said of himself that he did an immense amount of reading; and our research and the materials in Appendix Three bear this out. His wife, Anne Ripley Smith, also read widely; and

---

[96] See A. J. Russell, *For Sinners Only* (London: Hodder & Stoughton, 1932); The Layman with a Notebook, *What Is The Oxford Group?* (London: Oxford University Press, 1933); Howard A. Walter, *Soul-Surgery*. 6th Ed. (Oxford: Printed at the University Press by John Johnson, Printer to the University. 1st ed. published 1919); Harold Begbie, *Life Changers* (New York: G. P. Putnam's Sons, 1927).

[97] Pittman, *AA The Way It Began*, p. 182.

[98] Pittman, *AA The Way It Began*, pp. 182-83, 192.

[99] See Foreword by Dr. Ernest Kurtz to Dick B., *Dr. Bob's Library*, pp. ix-x.

the details can be found in our book, *Anne Smith's Spiritual Workbook.* Our research on Henrietta Seiberling's reading shows that she also read widely and that the books were pretty much the same as those read by the Smith family. Finally, there were a large number of Oxford Group and Shoemaker books available to early AAs in New York and in Akron. One need only look at the language of A.A.'s Big Book, Twelve Steps, and Fellowship literature to see the similarities between the language of the Oxford Group, Shoemaker, and Anne Smith's workbook and the language in A.A. literature.

Somehow, a great deal was transposed. As Bill's secretary, Nell Wing put it:

> No one knew better than Bill himself that "nobody invented A.A." "Everything in A.A. is borrowed from somewhere else," he often stated.[100]

Bill himself said:

> As a society we must never become so vain as to suppose that we are authors and inventors of a new religion. We will humbly reflect that every one of A.A.'s principles has been borrowed from ancient sources.[101]

> A.A. was not invented! Its basics were brought to us through the experience and wisdom of many great friends. We simply borrowed and adopted their ideas.[102]

---

[100] Nell Wing, *Grateful To Have Been There* (Illinois: Parkside Publishing Corporation, 1992), p. 25.

[101] *As Bill Sees It* (New York: Alcoholics Anonymous World Services, Inc., 1967), p. 223.

[102] *As Bill Sees It*, p. 67.

11

Frank Amos Reviews the Evidence

In an effort to raise money for a possible hospital in Akron and for other monies that were felt to be needed, Bill Wilson approached John D. Rockefeller, Jr., who dispatched Frank Amos to Akron to see what was going on. Amos left for Akron on February 1, 1938. He did a thorough job of investigating what he called the "self-styled Alcoholic Group of Akron, Ohio." He called on Dr. Bob and attended meetings. He questioned members and nonmembers, including professional associates of Dr. Bob. And he looked at the vacant house that A.A.'s wanted to convert into a hospital. In February of 1938, Amos rendered his report to Rockefeller; and a good many details are reported in *DR. BOB and the Good Oldtimers* at pages 129-135. He said that the alcoholic group comprised "some 50 men and, I believe, two women former alcoholics—all considered practically incurable by physicians—who have been reformed and so far have remained teetotalers." Amos said he had met with a number of men, their wives, and, in some cases, their mothers—hearing varying stories, "many of them almost miraculous." He noted that when it came to recovery, the stories were all remarkably alike in the Christian technique used[1] and the system followed. He described the "Program" as follows:

1. An alcoholic must realize that he is an alcoholic, incurable from a medical viewpoint, and that he must never again drink anything with alcohol in it.

2. He must surrender himself absolutely to God, realizing that in himself there is no hope.

3. Not only must he want to stop drinking permanently, he must remove from his life other sins such as hatred, adultery, and others which frequently accompany alcoholism. Unless he will do this absolutely, Smith and his associates refuse to work with him.

4. He must have devotions every morning—a "quiet time" of prayer and some reading from the Bible and other religious literature. Unless this is faithfully followed, there is grave danger of backsliding.

5. He must be willing to help other alcoholics get straightened out. This throws up a protective barrier and strengthens his own willpower and convictions.

6. It is important, but not vital, that he meet frequently with other reformed alcoholics and form both a social and a religious comradeship.

7. Important, but not vital, that he attend some religious service at least once weekly.[2]

---

[1] As to the description of Akron's A.A. technique as a "Christian technique," see *DR. BOB and the Good Oldtimers* (New York: Alcoholics Anonymous World Services, Inc., 1980), p. 128; *Pass It On* (New York: Alcoholics Anonymous World Services, Inc., 1984), p. 184—"lst century Christianity;" and Robert Thomsen, *Bill W.* (New York: Harper & Row, 1975), p. 282—"based on Christian doctrine."

[2] *DR. BOB*, p. 131.

Amos indicated that Dr. Robert H. Smith was the Akron-Cleveland leader by common consent and that all looked to Dr. Bob for leadership. Amos added, "Nonalcoholics, Christian ministers, Oxford Group members, Christian Scientists, and others have tried and failed. Apparently, with most cases, it takes a former alcoholic to turn the trick with an alcoholic—and a fine physician of excellent standing, himself formerly an alcoholic and possessed of natural leadership qualities, has proven ideal."

Amos was said to have reported at a later point in 1938:

1. Members did not want the movement connected directly or indirectly with any religious movement or cult; they stressed the point that they had no connection with any so-called orthodox religious denomination, or with the Oxford Movement.[3] It was also emphasized that they were in no way practicing medicine but were cooperating with physicians and psychiatrists.

2. Of the 110 members then in the program, 70 were in the Akron-Cleveland area and "in many respects, their meetings have taken on the form of the meetings described in the Gospels of the early Christians during the first century."[4]

---

[3] The author of *DR. BOB* added, "Obviously, Amos meant the Oxford Group; the older, Anglican movement played no part in A.A. history" (p. 135). While that author may have been correct in his assumption, we do not think it "obvious." In February, 1938, the Akron people were calling themselves a "Christian Fellowship" and calling the alcoholic members "the alcoholic squad of the Oxford Group." They continued to meet as part of the Oxford Group at T. Henry's for more than a year thereafter. It was only in New York that Bill and his tiny group of alcoholics had parted company with the Oxford Group meetings. See, for example, *DR. BOB*, pp. 118, 117, 169. It is remotely possible that the reference to the "Oxford Group Movement" meant the Oxford Movement of 1833, which had an entirely different course from that of Buchman's Oxford Group and was often confused with Buchman's later movement. See Rev. Robert H. Murray, *Group Movements Throughout The Ages* (New York: Harper And Brothers, n.d.), pp. 291-303.

[4] The use of this "First Century Christianity" language is not surprising since Dr. Bob referred to the alcoholic squad fellowship in that manner and the Oxford Group had often been known as and called "A First Century Christian Fellowship," particularly in

(continued...)

On March 21, 1939, Frank Amos, Treasurer of The Alcoholic Foundation, was preparing the Foundation for the future and for the expeditious publishing, advertising, and distribution of the book *ALCOHOLICS ANONYMOUS*, then in multilith form. He wrote as follows to the Trustees and Advisory Committee Members:

> About fifteen (15) months have now passed since fifteen of us first gathered to consider ways and means to promote the work among alcoholics. This period has convinced some, perhaps all, of us that the methods used are sound, practical and successful in a sufficiently large percentage of cases to justify our efforts to get the Foundation and this work on a better organized basis. Fifteen months ago, there were probably sixty alcoholics who had been straightened out. It is now estimated that there are at least 150, with many more apparently approaching that condition. The work was then confined to New York City and Akron. It has now spread to New England, Upper New York State, Pennsylvania, Washington D.C., Cleveland and several other Ohio cities, close

---

[4] (...continued)

America. See Walter Houston Clark, *The Oxford Group: Its History and Significance* (New York: Bookman Associates, 1951), p. 35; James D. Newton, *Uncommon Friends* (New York: Harcourt Brace Jovanovich, 1987), p. 157; Garth Lean, *On The Tail of a Comet* (Colorado Springs: Helmers & Howard, 1988), p. 97; Samuel M. Shoemaker, *Twice-Born Ministers* (New York: Fleming H. Revell, 1929), pp. 23, 90, 95, 101, 122, 147, 148; *Calvary Church Yesterday and Today* (New York: Fleming H. Revell, 1936), p. 270; John Potter Cuyler, Jr., *Calvary Church in Action* (New York: Fleming H. Revell, 1934), p. 11; Irving Harris, *The Breeze of the Spirit* (New York: The Seabury Press, 1978), pp. 47, 58; Stephen Foot, *Life Began Yesterday* (New York: Harper & Brothers, 1935), p. 139; Olive M. Jones, *Inspired Children* (New York: Harper & Brothers, 1933), p. ix; Harold Begbie, *Life Changers* (London: Mills & Boon, Ltd, 1932), p. 122; Dick B., *The Oxford Group & Alcoholics Anonymous*, pp. 63-65; *DR. BOB*, pp. 118-119. In June of 1991, Sue Smith Windows, Dr. Bob's daughter, informed the author that Dr. Bob described every King School Group meeting (of A.A.) as a "Christian Fellowship." As previously stated, Akron Oldtimer, Bob E., both in a letter to Nell Wing and in a memo to Lois Wilson, said Dr. Bob referred to A.A. as a "Christian Fellowship."

to Akron, to Detroit and other cities. Apparently there is almost an unlimited field.[5]

There are what could be called two postscripts to the Amos review. In May of 1939, Dr. Bob had written Frank Amos stating his difficult financial situation. In an effort to assist Dr. Bob, Bill Wilson responded with a letter to Dr. Bob stating he was approaching the Guggenheim Foundation for help. He enclosed a letter he had written to them on Dr. Bob's behalf. It said:

> At Akron, Ohio, there is a physician, Dr. Robert H. Smith, who has been responsible during the past four years for the recovery of at least 100 chronic alcoholics of types hitherto regarded by the medical profession as hopeless. . . . For more than four years, without charge to sufferers, without fanfare and almost without funds, Dr. Smith has carried on work among alcoholics in the Akron-Cleveland area. In this human laboratory, he has proved that any alcoholic, not too mentally defective, can recover if he so desires. The possible recovery among such cases has suddenly been lifted from almost nil to at least 50 percent, which, quite aside from its social implications, is a medical result of the first magnitude. Though, as a means of our recovery, we all engage in the work, Dr. Smith has had more experience and has obtained better results than anyone else.[6]

In Bill W.'s last major talk on the occasion of the celebration of the 35th anniversary of his sobriety, Bill said:

> This story goes back to one day in Dr. Bob's living room. And here I might interject that my partnership with Dr. Bob was a perfect one. We never had a hard word between us, and the credit is all due to him. His quiet counsel kept me on the track.

---

[5] Memo obtained by the author in September, 1992, from the archives at Bill Wilson's home at Stepping Stones.

[6] *DR. BOB*, pp. 173-74.

It had been decided that Bob would attend mostly to the questions of hospitalization and the development of our Twelfth Step work. Between 1940 and 1950, in the company of that marvelous nun, Sister Ignatia, he had treated 5,000 drunks at St. Thomas Hospital in Akron, and he never charged a cent for his medical care. So Dr. Bob became the prince of all twelfth-steppers. Perhaps nobody will ever do such a job again.[7]

Did something occur in Akron that just happened long ago and left no trace of anything significant thereafter? The foregoing facts that were summarized by Frank Amos, reported out by Bill Wilson, and euologized in the appellation given Dr. Bob—Prince of Twelfth-Steppers—should provide adequate answer.

---

[7] *The Co-Founders of Alcoholics Anonymous. Biographical sketches. Their last major talks* (New York: Alcoholics Anonymous World Services, Inc., 1972, 1975), p. 27. The Big Book states, at page 171, "To 1950, the year of his death, he [Dr. Bob] carried the A.A. message to more than 5,000 alcoholic men and women, and to all these he gave his medical services without thought of charge."

12

Akron's Part in the Big Book

There are three important aspects of Akron's role in the writing of the Big Book: (1) Its part in the *decision* to write the book; (2) Its participation in the *writing of the text*—the first 164 pages; and (3) Its contribution to the *personal stories* in the back of the book. In each case, the Akron role was substantial and perhaps much different than has been thought, in view of the many statements that there were battles over the Big Book's content and that Bill Wilson was a self-characterized "umpire."[1]

---

[1] In a speech he delivered at Fort Worth, Texas in 1954, Bill described his going into A.A. meetings in *New York* with some chapters in the rough. He said, "I suddenly discovered I was in this whirlpool of arguments. I was just the umpire—I finally had to stipulate, 'Well boys, over here you got the Holy Rollers who say we need all the good old-fashioned stuff in the book, and over here you tell me we've got to have a psychological book, and that never cured anybody, and they didn't do much with drugs in the missions, so I guess you'll have to leave me just to be the umpire.' . . . . So, we fought, bled and died our way through one chapter after another. We sent them out to Akron and they were peddled around and there were terrific hassles about what should go in this book and what not."

The Decision to Write a Book
about the Recovery Program

First, let's look at the *decision* to write and publish the Big Book. From a geographical viewpoint, the decision was made in Akron. Thomsen's *Bill W.* phrases the situation this way:

> In November [of 1937] Bill had to make a trip to the Midwest.
> . . . [and] the trip gave him an opportunity to visit Dr. Bob in Akron. Bill had been sober almost three years, Bob two and a half, and this, they figured, should be ample time for them to see where they were and even make some sort of informal progress report.
> . . . There had been failures galore. Literally hundreds of drunks had been approached by their two groups [in Akron and in New York] and some had sobered up for a brief period but then slipped away. . . . But as the afternoon wore on and they continued going over lists, counting noses, they found themselves facing a staggering fact. In all, in Ohio and in New York, they knew forty alcoholics who were sober and were staying sober, and of this number at least twenty had been completely dry for more than a year. Moreover, every single one of them had been diagnosed a hopeless case. . . . There were forty names representing forty men whose lives had been changed, who actually were alive tonight because of what had started in this very room [in Dr. Bob's kitchen at 855 Ardmore Avenue in Akron]. The chain reaction they had dreamed about—one alcoholic carrying the word to another—was a reality. It had moved onward, outward from them.[2]

Bill Wilson had this to say, as quoted in *RHS*, the memorial issue in A.A.'s Grapevine commemorating Dr. Bob's death:

> Our eyes glistened. Enough time had elapsed on enough cases to spell out something new, perhaps something great indeed.

---

[2] Robert Thomsen, *Bill W.* (New York: Harper & Row, 1975), pp. 266-67.

Suddenly the ceiling went up. We no longer flew blind. A beacon had been lighted. God had shown alcoholics how it might be passed from hand to hand. Never shall I forget that great and humbling hour of realization, shared with Dr. Bob. But the new realization faced us with a great problem, a momentous decision. It had taken nearly three years to effect forty recoveries. The United States alone probably had a million alcoholics. How were we to get the story to them? Wouldn't we need paid workers, hospitals of our own, lots of money? Surely we must have some sort of textbook. Dare we crawl at a snail's pace whilst our story got garbled and mayhaps thousands would die? What a poser that was![3]

And, of course, Bill—the organizer and promoter—*did* think in grandiose terms about books, pamphlets, hospitals, drying-out establishments, staffs to man them, and thousands, even millions of dollars to be raised. Dr. Bob, though conservative, was not far behind in following this kind of thinking. As Thomsen's *Bill W.* recounts it:

For two-and-a-half years their little word-of-mouth program had worked, and worked magnificently, but they could hardly expect every active alcoholic to make his way to Akron, Ohio, or Clinton Street in Brooklyn. And yet they also realized that any decision about new approaches or new methods of spreading their knowledge was not a thing they could take alone. Any changes such as they were beginning to contemplate would require not only the approval but the support of the entire fellowship. Without wasting any time, Bob got on the phone to arrange a special meeting of the Akron group. . . . Listening to his [Bill's] plans, Dr. Bob was more than a sounding board. He was—he would continue to be—a very necessary balance. He liked the idea of a book and saw it as a valuable way of codifying their beliefs, but as to running hospitals, having their own staffs and raising millions of dollars, he had his doubts. Sitting in Annie Smith's

---

[3] *RHS*, Memorial Issue of the Grapevine, issued in January, 1951, on the occasion of Dr. Bob's death (New York: The A.A. Grapevine, Inc.), p. 8.

kitchen, they discussed the pros and cons of each proposition, and by the night of the meeting, Bill had his arguments well lined up. He felt in good form that night and was raring to go. . . . There were eighteen members present and the meeting began promptly at eight o'clock. They were still talking at midnight. . . . But as he [Bill] went on, warming to his subject, it became clear . . . first, that . . . now his full concentrations were on their responsibility to the world of alcoholics and how best to reach them. And second, the men gathered before him now were anything but inarticulate. . . . They went at him and his suggestions from every conceivable angle, and at first there seemed no unanimity in their arguments; they disagreed heartily with him and with each other. . . . It was quite a meeting. Every suggestion was challenged, every idea thoroughly examined. Going into the hospital business they said would be regarded as—and, considering who they were, would soon become—a commercial racket, and what, they demanded, would this do to the spirit of the group and their principle of carrying the message to other drunks with no strings and no money attached? Bill's point that word of mouth was not only too slow and too limited a way of carrying the message, but that it might also lead to the program's being twisted out of shape, seemed to make sense. But some could see no reason for having a book or even a pamphlet. . . . And as for raising money and subsidizing missionaries, they were convinced it would spell the end of the fellowship. It was a long night and arguments grew loud and heated, but always, and this was apparent with each man who spoke, their concentration was focused on just one thing: on finding the best way to get the word across to drunks who wanted help. In the end—and it was well after midnight before they broke up—Bob and Bill found they'd been more persuasive than they'd known. The proposals were put to a vote and by a majority of two Bill was authorized to go ahead with his plan, return to New York and, if he felt it necessary, to start raising money. . . . As a few of the Akron group who had been at the meeting saw Bill off at the station, they were admittedly deeply concerned. It was there, before Bill stepped on the train, that Dr. Bob put his hand on Bill's arm and said just one thing, "For God's sake, Billy, keep it simple" (pp. 267-271).

So the *decision* was made in Akron; but the plan was not simple. And Bill really could not, and certainly did not keep it simple. We do not propose to go into the oft-told stories about the approaches to Rockefeller—involving the plans for missionaries, drunk tanks, subsidies, and the book. And of Rockefeller's pointed question, "But isn't money going to spoil this thing?" And of the end result, which was the formation of the Alcoholic Foundation in the spring of 1938 with all its unsuccessful pleas for money. To the Foundation and others, including Dr. Bob, Bill had submitted two proposed chapters of the book. Finally, there was a decision to keep the book out of the hands of *Harper's* and let Bill go on with his own promotion—"Works Publishing Company." Akron can claim no particular part in these activities except that Dr. Bob was on the Board of the Alcoholic Foundation. But Akron could claim that the decision was made at Akron to have a book and move the message-carrying out of the hands of a few drunks working on a one-to-one basis and make it available through publication.

Akron's "Warm Support" for the Big Book's Basic Text

Whatever else may be thought, Bill Wilson wrote all or almost all of the Big Book. Thomsen's *Bill W.* describes the beginning:

> Still they went on and in April the Alcoholic Foundation was established. Dreams of hospitals and paid workers had to be left in abeyance, but there was nothing to stop them from moving ahead with the projected book. So every morning, in the little office in Newark, Bill began dictating to Hank's [Henry Parkhurst's] secretary, Ruth Hock (p. 277).

The author has examined the first two chapters of Bill's efforts in various of their draft forms. The material is available at the archives at Stepping Stones. Much of the material in the drafts at Stepping Stones resembles that in the first two chapters of the Big Book as it was published in 1939. The major difference is that the order of the first two chapters is reversed. "There is a Solution"—now essentially Chapter Two of the Big Book—was the first chapter. And "Bill's Story"—now essentially Chapter One of the Big Book—was the second chapter. In the summer of 1938, Bill wrote to Dr. Bob:

> As a starting point I have, with the help of the folks here, dictated and mimeographed two chapters of the proposed book, one in the nature of an introduction, and the second my own story. These I inclose to you together with a rough outline of the other chapters.[4]

We have found no reply by Dr. Bob, in writing or otherwise, in which Dr. Bob indicated disagreement with the first two chapters.

Bill fed the other chapters to Dr. Bob as they were being written. For example, on September 27, 1938, Bill wrote Dr. Bob, "2 more chapters are close to completion: 'More about alcoholism.' The Chapter, 'We Agnostics,' I do not like so much. It is still 'too preachy' and rather disconnected." These chapters obviously refer to what presently are Chapters Three and Four of the Big Book—"More About Alcoholism" (Chapter 3) and "We Agnostics" (Chapter 4), respectively. Again, we found no reply by Dr. Bob, in writing or otherwise, indicating any disagreement of his or of the Akron Group.

On November 3, 1938, Bill wrote to Dr. Bob enclosing 5 chapters. On November 9, 1938, Bill wrote Dr. Bob, stating, "Glad to hear you liked the chapters I sent you. I have but two more of the General Chapters to write, and then I shall come out." On December 13, 1938, Bill wrote to Dr. Bob, stating, "It's practically complete, and I will send you the rest of the chapters

---

[4] Author obtained a copy of this letter from the Stepping Stones Archives during his visit there in October, 1991.

within two or three days."[5] Again we found nothing to show that either Dr. Bob or the Akron Group dissented. Notes in A.A. Archives in New York, and the record of Historical Events in *Lois Remembers*, at page 198, indicate that in December of 1938, Bill wrote the famous Chapter 5 which contains the Twelve Steps. Considering the fact that it was an early chapter, it seems unlikely that this was one of the two chapters still to be sent to Dr. Bob. Hence it would appear that Chapter 5 and the Steps were approved by Akron as presented.

What does history record of Akron's part as to the *writing of the text* of the Big Book—the first 164 pages? *Pass It On* states:

> Bill wrote at least ten of the opening chapters of the book; there is some reason to believe that "To Employers" [Chapter 10, the next to the last Chapter of the text] may have been written by Hank [Henry G. P.]. But there is no doubt about the authorship of "To Wives." Of that chapter, Lois said, "Bill wrote it, and I was mad."[6]

There are many indications that Dr. Bob and the Akron AAs, so far as they were apprised of the drafts, were supportive. Thus *Pass It On* says:

> While Bill received "nothing but the warmest support" from Akron, he got what he called "a real mauling" from the New York members. Possibly, the Akron members were strongly attuned to Bill's spiritual ideas, while the New York group contained members who were either agnostic or skeptical.[7]

---

[5] Copies of the letters referred to in this and the preceding paragraph are on file at the A.A. Archives in New York City.

[6] *Pass It On* (New York: Alcoholics Anonymous World Services, Inc., 1984), p. 200.

[7] At A.A.'s Archives in New York, there are questionnaires filled out by Bill Wilson, James B., and Henry G. P.. These three had much to do with the New York arguments. Jim B.'s questionnaire says: "religious history after left the influence of the childhood home. None. Made it a point to keep out of church and prayer." A.A.

(continued...)

Another possible reason was Dr. Bob's enormous influence and stature; his support of the book virtually guaranteed that most of the Akron members would also support it (p. 196).

Bob E., who was an early Akron oldtimer in A.A. and a man sponsored by Dr. Bob, spoke on a tape to Bill Wilson on June 18, 1954. In response to Bill's questions about Bob E.'s impressions of the time the Big Book came out, Bob E. said:

> Well, of course, you started coming through with these rough drafts—we didn't show them to too many people—I was one of the chosen few. . . . Well, of course, we were very serious about the thing [the rough drafts of the Big Book]. We were quite awed by the realization that it was beginning to take form. There wasn't much we could do to add or subtract the information that you put down. Doc Smith was driving down to New York in those days and would keep in touch with you that way. I can remember going over the draft with Doc in his home there and down at Hildreth and Paul S.'s and Tom L.'s. Those were the main fellows looking at the draft.
> . . . There were no stories in the picture at that time. There had been some talk about the boys getting their stories boiled down—just a couple of pages very brief. But Jim S. had come into the picture and he was staying—he was taken away from the Salvation Army and staying with Tom L. So he would—if you didn't write one—he'd just listen to you recite your story and he'd write it for you and he edited all of them.[8]

---

[7] (...continued)
Oldtimer, Lyle B. of Nebraska, informed the author in a telephone interview in 1991 that he had many times heard Jim B. describe himself in a meeting as one who was an "atheist" when he came into A.A. Henry G. P. listed himself in his answers to the questionnaire as "agnostic." Wilson said: "religious background as a child—slight. Rarely inside church. Christian Science & metaphysical—no results. Attitude couldn't accept."

[8] The author was provided with a copy of this transcript by Ray G., Archivist at Dr. Bob's Home in Akron.

Why this support in Akron? We think that recent research on A.A.'s spiritual roots and histories about them provides much of the answer. Bill frequently referred to the many ideas from the Oxford Group that he said were incorporated in the A.A. program. Later he said all the material for "the remaining ten steps" [other than One and Twelve] came straight from the Oxford Group and directly from Reverend Sam Shoemaker. Further, there is a remarkable similarity between the language of the Big Book and that used by Shoemaker and other Oxford Group writers.[9] A.A. oldtimer and historian Mel B. sets forth in his book, *New Wine*, many similarities he found between A.A. concepts and those of Harold Begbie, Dr. Robert E. Speer (author of the Four Absolutes), Henry B. Wright (Frank Buchman's mentor, who was a Professor at Yale), Harry Emerson Fosdick (who endorsed the Big Book), Mary Baker Eddy (whose Christian Science textbook was studied by both Dr. Bob and Bill), William James (whose name and book, *The Varieties of Religious Experience*, are mentioned in the Big Book), Ralph Waldo Trine, Brother Lawrence (whose *The Practice of The Presence of God* ideas seem involved), and Emmet Fox.[10] We believe we have shown in our books, *Dr. Bob's Library*, *Anne Smith's Spiritual Workbook*, and *The Oxford Group & Alcoholics Anonymous*, and in the portion of this book on Henrietta Seiberling's "spiritual infusion," the tremendous amount of Christian literature, Oxford Group books, and Shoemaker teachings that were being fed into the Akron Group. There is even more research and writing to be done on the contributions from the Bible. A few of the Bible's direct contributions can be seen today in the verbatim quotes from it in the text of the Big Book.[11]

---

[9] See Appendix Nine.

[10] See Mel B., *New Wine: The Spiritual Roots of the Twelve Step Miracle* (Minnesota: Hazelden, 1991), pp. 101-16, 127-53.

[11] See, for example, Big Book, page 88: "Thy will be done" and "Faith without works is dead." Compare Matthew 6:10: "Thy will be done" and James 2:26: "faith without works is dead." See, for example, Big Book, page 153: "Love thy neighbor as thyself." Compare James 2:8: "Thou shalt love thy neighbor as thyself."

As all these materials show, Bill and Dr. Bob seemed very much in agreement that the sources of A.A. were in the Bible and in the Oxford Group. Though others may disagree, the author believes Bill did not stray far from these concepts in his language and approach in the Big Book. All of these spiritual resources were the subject of regular reading and study by Dr. Bob, Anne, Henrietta, Bill and the Akron AAs in those early quiet times, meetings, and discussions. We therefore are not surprised that there was "warm support" in Akron for Bill's efforts and very little disagreement over their content. Not so in New York where Bill was running the hurdles manned by Henry G. P., who characterized himself as an agnostic, and Jim B., who characterized himself as an atheist. Even when Bill added the phrase "Power greater than ourselves" to Step Two, inserted the words "God as we understood Him" in Steps Three and Eleven, and deleted "on our knees" from Step Seven, he did little that would, *at that point of time*, have irritated the Bible-Oxford Group oriented AAs of Akron.[12] Ruth Hock, Bill's first secretary, was

---

[12] For a succinct review of these changes, see Ernest Kurtz, *Not-God*. Expanded ed. (Minnesota: Hazelden, 1991), pp. 70, 76. We will note two aspects of the changes: *FIRST*, as to "Power greater than ourselves" and "God," Anne Smith herself had used language speaking about a "stronger power" and said, "God provided that power through Christ." See Dick B., *Anne Smith's Spiritual Workbook* (Corte Madera, CA: Good Book Publishing Company, 1992), pp. 73-74. Shoemaker, the "Bible Christian," had spoken of God in terms of "a Force outside himself, greater than himself." See Samuel Moor Shoemaker, Jr., *If I Be Lifted Up* (New York: Fleming H. Revell, 1931), p. 176. And Harold Begbie, a noted Christian writer who had influenced Frank Buchman, had written of a "first idea of God. . . . as a Rescuer, some indefinable Power capable of turning his unhappiness into happiness." See Harold Begbie, *Twice-Born Men* (New York: Fleming H. Revell, 1909), p. 164. In his chapter on "The Solution," Stephen Foot several times wrote of a "Power," a "Power that can change human nature," and stating that "through this Power problems are being solved." See Stephen Foot, *Life Began Yesterday* (New York: Harper & Brothers, 1935), p. 22. In the same breath, Foot was talking of "a surrender of all that I knew of self, to all that I know of God," "the standards of Jesus Christ," and a "decision to surrender to God." See Foot, *Life Began Yesterday*, pp. 12-13, 15, 175, 44. Though Bill Wilson changed "God" to "Power greater than ourselves" at one place, Bill kept the remaining Big Book language consistent with the idea that the "Power" was God—just as the noted Oxford Group writer, Stephen Foot had done. Thus
(continued...)

present when these changes were made. Ruth, a nonalcoholic, may have suggested the phrase "God as we understood Him," which is the language that resulted; and which she didn't "think had much of a negative reaction anywhere."[13]

So what was Akron's part in the *writing of the text* of the Big Book? "Warm support!" And why not? The Bible, the Oxford Group writings and teachings, the words of Sam Shoemaker, and the ideas of so many of the other Christian writings that were studied in Akron became very much a part of the ideas *in* and, to some extent, the very language of the Alcoholics Anonymous text book that Bill Wilson wrote in New York in 1938 and early 1939.[14]

Akron and the Big Book's Personal Stories

Henry G. P. prepared an outline of the proposed Big Book, and the format consisted primarily of stories about the experiences of

---

[12] (...continued)
Bill wrote of "a Power greater than ourselves. . . . [stating] that Power *which is God*" (emphasis added). See Big Book, p. 46. Furthermore, the word "God" and pronouns describing Him in capital letters are specifically used in the Big Book 212 times. See Stewart C., *A Reference Guide To The Big Book* (Seattle: Recovery Press, Inc., 1986), pp. 115-116. These specific references to God were in addition to the biblical names for God such as Creator, Maker, Father, Spirit, and Friend which are frequently used in the Book and spelled with capital letters. See Dick B., *The Oxford Group & Alcoholics Anonymous* (Seattle: Glen Abbey Books, 1992), pp. 117-120. *SECOND*, "God as we understood Him" would not particularly have shocked Akron AAs because such Oxford Group writers as Stephen Foot, and Bill's "mentor," Sam Shoemaker, and Anne Smith were all adherents to the idea that one should "surrender as much of himself as he knows to as much of God as he knows." See again Foot, *Life Began Yesterday*, pp. 12-13, 175; Samuel M. Shoemaker, *Children of the Second Birth* (New York: Fleming H. Revell, 1927), p. 25; Dick B., *Anne Smith's Spiritual Workbook*, p. 28.

[13] *Pass It On*, p. 199. Jim B. laid claim to being the person who contributed the phrase "God as you understand Him" to A.A. books. The author has a copy of a letter from Jim B. to Bill Wilson, dated May 15, 1965, in which Jim B. makes this statement.

[14] See Appendix Nine for examples.

the alcoholics.[15] The Multilith draft of the Big Book said this, of the resultant stories:

> There is a group of personal narratives. Then clear-cut directions are given showing how an alcoholic may recover. These are followed by more than a score of personal experiences. Each individual, in the personal stories, describes in his own language and from his own point of view the way he found or rediscovered God. These give a fair cross section of our membership and a clear-cut idea of what has actually happened in their lives. We hope no one will consider these self-revealing accounts in bad taste.[16]

The First Edition of the Big Book, as published, changed the language to read as follows:

> Further on clear-cut directions are given showing how we recovered. These are followed by more than a score of personal experiences. Each individual, in the personal stories, describes in his own language, and from his own point of view the way he established his relationship with God. These give a fair cross section of our membership and a clear-cut idea of what has actually happened in their lives. We hope no one will consider these self-revealing accounts in bad taste.[17]

The Multilith draft has this additional material on the personal stories:

> Our stories disclose in a general way what we used to be like, what happened, and what we are like now. . . . Our description of the alcoholic, the chapter to the agnostic, and our personal

---

[15] The author obtained a copy of Henry G. P.'s outline from the archives at Stepping Stones during his visit there in September, 1991.

[16] Multilith Copy of the Original Manuscript, p. 13.

[17] *Alcoholics Anonymous* (New York City: Works Publishing Company, 1939), pp. 39-40.

adventures before and after, have been designed to sell you three pertinent ideas:

   a. That you are an alcoholic and cannot manage your own life.
   b. That probably no human power can relieve your alcoholism.
   c. That God can and will.

If you are not convinced on these vital issues, you ought to re-read the book to this point or else throw it away.[18]

This somewhat imperious language was toned down in the first edition that was actually published. But the importance of personal stories remained in those early drafts and editions and remains in the Third Edition of the Big Book that has today sold more than 10 million copies.

The idea of recounting stories of conversion experiences that produced deliverance from alcoholism was certainly not new. William James's, *The Varieties of Religious Experience*, was vitally important to Bill W., was popular with Dr. Bob, and is even mentioned in the Big Book.[19] And the James book certainly recounted personal stories of conversion experiences. So did Harold Begbie's books, *Twice-Born Men* and *Life-Changers*. So did Russell's *For Sinners Only* and Reynold's *New Lives for Old*. So also Shoemaker's books, *Children of the Second Birth* and *Twice-Born Ministers*. In her spiritual workbook, Anne Smith recommended these books specifically, stating, "Biographies, or stories of changed lives are very helpful for the young Christian."[20]

This sharing of personal stories certainly was the technique the Oxford Group used in personal evangelism. Willard Hunter wrote:

---

[18] Multilith draft, pp. 26-27.

[19] *Pass It On*, pp. 124-25, 197, 199; *DR. BOB and the Good Oldtimers* (New York: Alcoholics Anonymous World Services, Inc., 1980), p. 306; Big Book, p. 28.

[20] Dick B., *Anne Smith's Spiritual Workbook*, p. 13.

He [Dr. Frank N. D. Buchman] was very much a pioneer, perhaps *the* pioneer, of the school of "story theology," in recent years advocated by Harvey Cox and others. "When the life experience dimension is excluded nowadays," Cox writes, "people feel cheated." Buchman's whole message began and ended with life experience. He forbade his people to speak or write "one inch" beyond their experience.[21]

Sam Shoemaker wrote in his first book:

This may take time, the loan of books, introduction to someone who may be able to answer very hard problems—though we ought soon to be arriving where we can ourselves give account of the faith that is in us—prayer, and very earnest pressing upon them of the *fact* of our conversion and our own fundamental beliefs. Moody said, "Do not talk an inch beyond your experience," but use that for everything there is in it. It is the one thing *you* can be perfectly sure of, and you are on unassailable ground, for only yourself and God know what happened.[22]

In *The Conversion of the Church*, Shoemaker wrote:

The difference between true sharing and formal confession lies primarily in the open willingness of the person who is trying to help, to share himself. St. Paul tells the Thessalonians, ". . . we were willing to have imparted unto you, not the gospel of God only, but also our own souls" (1 Thess. 2:8). He may have reason to think that he knows about what your difficulty is, and he may share something parallel in his own life. Or he may share in general what sort of person he was before his conversion, and how Christ came to him and changed him. In any case, he will

---

[21] T. Willard Hunter, *World Changing Through Life Changing* (Thesis, Newton Center, Mass: Andover-Newton Theological School, 1977), p. 111.

[22] Samuel M. Shoemaker, *Realizing Religion* (New York: Association Press, 1923), pp. 81-82.

create the sort of atmosphere in which you can talk without fear, reserve, or hurry.[23]

In her spiritual workbook, Dr. Bob's wife, Anne, wrote pointedly on the necessity for receiving a spiritual experience before being qualified to witness effectively. She said:

A general experience of God is the first essential, the beginning. We can't give away what we haven't got. We must have a genuine contact with God in our present experience. Not an experience of the past, but an experience in the present—actual, genuine. When we have that, witnessing to it is natural, just as we want to share a beautiful sunset. We must be in such close touch with God that the whole sharing is guided.[24] The person with a genuine experience of God and with no technique will make fewer mistakes than one with lots of technique and no sense of God. Under guidance, you are almost a spectator of what is happening. Your sharing is not strained, it is not tense. We must clearly see and understand our own experience, and clearly articulate it, so as to be ready to know what to say, or to use parts of it, when the need comes to share with others in order to help them.[25]

Henrietta Seiberling adjured AAs to give "news, not views" of what God had done. At the last A.A. dinner she went to, she complained of the witnesses who spoke. She said:

---

[23] Samuel M. Shoemaker, *The Conversion of the Church* (New York: Fleming H. Revell, 1932), p. 39.

[24] Compare the statement in Eleanor Napier Forde, *The Guidance of God* (Oxford: University Press, 1930), p. 8, in which Miss Forde also points out that it is the person with an experience of God who will make the better witnessing person because that person has the experiential knowledge that the Holy Spirit is the great Teacher and guides the process.

[25] Dick B., *Anne Smith's Spiritual Workbook*, pp. 60-61.

And I spoke to Bill afterwards and I said there was no spirituality
there or talk of what God had done in their lives. They were
giving views, not news of what God had done.[26]

In a letter to the author, John Seiberling said his mother frequently
stressed the importance of sharing "news, not views." *DR. BOB
and the Good Oldtimers* points out that "Give news, not views"
was an Oxford Group slogan (p. 55).

The sharing of personal experience (which the Oxford Group
called Sharing or Sharing for Witness)—both in written stories and
in meetings, was a part of the early A.A.'s Oxford Group heritage
in New York and in Akron. The Oxford Group handbook that Dr.
Bob owned, studied, and loaned said this:

> Personal proof of experience can do more than the best of
> theories. These Oxford Group witnesses have felt Christ working
> in their own lives and the Spirit of Christ has walked beside them.
> They tell of what they themselves know as a positive truth.
> Generalization and guess-work are not in their programme. . . .
> People in need are more inclined to tell us the truth about
> themselves if they know we are telling them the truth about
> ourselves. This is the foundation of the mutual trust which is
> essential when we witness in order to bring others to a Life
> Change.[27]

It is not surprising, then, that the first chapter of A.A.'s Big Book
is entitled "Bill's Story." And the First Edition of the Big Book
was filled with personal stories in the back of the book, the first
of which was Dr. Bob's personal story. The author has assembled
from archival material, at the homes of Dr. Bob in Akron and Bill
W. at Stepping Stones in Bedford Hills, New York, and from a

---

[26] John F. Seiberling, *Origins of Alcoholics Anonymous*, Employer Assistance
Quarterly, p. 12.

[27] The Layman with a Notebook, *What It The Oxford Group?* (London: Oxford
University Press, 1933), p. 37. Concerning Dr. Bob's use of this book, see Dick B., *Dr.
Bob's Library* (West Virginia: The Bishop of Books, 1992), p. 48.

collection owned by A.A. Oldtimer, Earl H. of Oklahoma, a list of the authors of the stories in the First Edition of the Big Book, together with titles of their stories, their home group—whether Akron or New York—and, where possible, their sobriety dates. There were 29 stories. Seventeen of these were the stories of people from Akron. Eleven were New Yorkers' stories. And one is supposed, according to many, to have come from a Californian who was drunk when he arrived in New York and whose story was removed from all but the red copy of the First Edition. *Akron stories thus played a major role* in the First Edition of Alcoholics Anonymous.

In a document entitled "Bill's history," which the author located at Stepping Stones, Bill wrote these things about the Akron stories:

> Helped by an Akron newspaper man, Jim S. [name deleted in our book], Doc Smith began to ship the stories to us. Meanwhile the chapters of the book were sent to him for debate and inspection out there. He never passed them around very much, merely writing me saying he thought they were all right. . . .
>
> By late January, 1939, we had got in the stories from Akron and all of the book chapters were done.

From this brief material and the comments we quoted earlier from Bob E. as he was interviewed by Bill, we can see that Akron's support for the Big Book extended not only to the Big Book's textual portion, but also to the personal experiences. The stories of the Akron people predominated in the Big Book's personal adventure accounts. And this seems to have been due to the fact that most of A.A.'s sober people at that time were from Akron.

13

The Alcoholic Squad in Akron Becomes Alcoholics Anonymous

We need only briefly review the transition of the alcoholic fellowship from the Oxford Group to Alcoholics Anonymous. There are four aspects. Most have been covered or will be covered in other historical reviews.

The first aspect occurred in 1937 when Bill and Lois Wilson and their New York area alcoholics left the Oxford Group meetings in New York and began meeting solely on their own.[1] There were a number of reasons given for this situation. In one account, Lois said the "Oxford Group kind of kicked us out."[2] In another, there were indications that Calvary Church staff people considered that Bill was "off on your [Bill's] own spur" in working only with alcoholics rather than participating in the mainstream Oxford Group team efforts.[3] In still another, the fact that Bill had been meeting with alcoholics at Stewart's Cafeteria after Oxford Group meetings and in his home on Clinton Street made the transition from the Oxford Group to an alcoholic group

---

[1] *Pass It On* (New York: Alcoholics Anonymous World Services, Inc., 1984), p. 171.

[2] *Pass It On*, p. 174.

[3] *Pass It On*, pp. 178, 174.

a predictable one.[4] Finally, Bill later gave many reasons why the participation of alcoholics in the Oxford Group was no longer acceptable.[5] Whatever the view, the fact is that New York alcoholics severed all connection with Calvary House and the New York Oxford Group meetings about August of 1937.[6]

The second aspect occurred when Clarence S. announced at the Akron meeting at T. Henry's house on May 10, 1939, that the Cleveland contingent would no longer be coming to Akron, but would meet in Cleveland at a meeting just for alcoholics.[7] The principal reason given was that the Roman Catholics who were coming down to Akron from Cleveland could not be comfortable in a meeting of the Oxford Group because their church frowned on participation by Catholics in the Oxford Group.[8] In any event, the Cleveland people began holding their meetings in Cleveland. The first was held on May 11, 1939, at the home of Abby G., at 2345 Stillman Road, in Cleveland Heights. Shortly, another group was meeting at the home of T. F. Borton, a non alcoholic friend of Clarence S.'s. This location was at 2427 Roxboro Road in Cleveland. And on November 20, 1939, the "Orchard Group" split off from the Borton Group. By November of 1939, there was a group in Cleveland composed only of alcoholics—the old Borton Group.[9] That group had no connection with the Oxford Group. The Clevelanders borrowed as *their* name the name, "Alcoholics

---

[4] *Pass It On*, p. 169.

[5] *Pass It On*, pp. 171-73.

[6] *Lois Remembers* (New York: Al-Anon Family Headquarters, Inc., 1987), pp. 103, 197.

[7] *DR. BOB and the Good Oldtimers* (New York: Alcoholics Anonymous World Services, Inc., 1980), p. 164.

[8] *Pass It On*, p. 173; *DR. BOB*, pp. 161-167; Ernest Kurtz, *Not-God*. Expanded ed. (Minnesota: Hazelden, 1991), pp. 77-78; Mary C. Darrah, *Sister Ignatia* (Chicago: Loyola University Press, 1992), pp. 26, 28, 30-33.

[9] *DR. BOB*, p. 169.

Anonymous," from the Big Book "Alcoholics Anonymous," which had been published in April of 1939.[10]

The third aspect occurred in late October of 1939.[11] At that time, the Akron alcoholics decided to meet at Dr. Bob's home instead of T. Henry's home. There are a variety of accounts as to the reasons for the break. Dr. Bob seemed very reluctant to make the break and remained very loyal and friendly to T. Henry and Clarace Williams.[12] Some attributed the break to arguments among the women.[13] Others indicated that there had been a growing dissatisfaction with Oxford Group meetings and practices.[14] In any event, the alcoholic squad moved to Dr. Bob's home. But the home soon became so overcrowded with "between seventy to eighty people" in the Smith's small livingroom and diningroom that the alcoholics had to move.[15] And the meeting was moved to King School, where Delphine Weber's husband was superintendent. At that point, Akron A.A. apparently became Alcoholics Anonymous. Bill Wilson called it "our first group, Akron Number One."[16] And that King School Group exists to this day though it has been moved to another location.

The final aspect—the aftermath of the breaks—seemed salutary. A few alcoholics in Akron continued to go to Oxford Group meetings at T. Henry's.[17] There was not a momentous growth in Akron or in New York. But the efforts of Clarence S. and the

---

[10] Kurtz, *Not-God*, p. 78; *DR. BOB*, p. 164. The use in Cleveland of the name "Alcoholics Anonymous" has given rise to the belief that this was the first use of that name and therefore was a "founding" of sorts of the Fellowship of Alcoholics Anonymous. However, there are other references in the fellowship to the name of Alcoholics Anonymous that predate the Cleveland split-off from Akron in May of 1939. See Kurtz, *Not-God*, p. 74.

[11] Kurtz, *Not-God*, p. 81.

[12] *DR. BOB*, pp. 161, 171.

[13] Kurtz, *Not-God*, p. 81.

[14] *DR. BOB*, pp. 157-65.

[15] Kurtz, *Not-God*, p. 81.

[16] *The Language of the Heart* (New York: The A.A. Grapevine, Inc., 1988), p. 353.

[17] Taped interview by Bill Wilson of Bob E., June, 1954.

Cleveland members soon spurred a real outreach. The Cleveland group had expanded to about 30 groups and several hundred members in about a year.[18] And A.A. had begun to spring up in other cities. In New York, Shoemaker broke with Dr. Frank Buchman, asking him to move his personal possessions and office from Calvary House which had been Buchman's American Oxford Group headquarters.[19] We will not speculate as to the reasons for the break. But a simple answer would be that Buchman chose to emphasize Oxford Group—then called Moral Re-Armament—activities on the world life-changing scene, while Shoemaker chose to continue working within the framework of the church and pushed on with his own Faith at Work movement.[20] As to the reasons for the Shoemaker-Buchman split, there are, of course, numerous versions of the controversy; but we see no profit in unraveling them in this A. A. history. Our story of the Akron Genesis ends after the Big Book was published and before Shoemaker and Buchman broke relations.

---

[18] *DR. BOB*, p. 211.

[19] Garth Lean, *On The Tail of a Comet* (Colorado Springs: Helmers & Howard, 1988), p. 304.

[20] See Dick B., *The Oxford Group & Alcoholics Anonymous* (Seattle: Glen Abbey Books, 1992), pp. 70-71.

Part 4

The Akron Taproot

Webster's Ninth New Collegiate Dictionary defines a taproot as: (1) a primary root that grows vertically downward and gives off small lateral roots, (2) the central element or position in a line of growth or development.[1]

---

[1] For the phrase, "the Akron taproot," the author is indebted to Ray G., Archivist at Dr. Bob's Home—the birthplace of A.A.

14

Akron as One Part of the Picture

We start this discussion with a firm belief that early A.A. cannot and should not be divided into separate parts—geographical or otherwise. The Akron contribution to A.A. was not a "we or they" proposition. The evidence is clear that Bill Wilson and Dr. Bob worked well together, were loyal to each other, and remained close in A.A.'s formative years and thereafter.[1] To speak of Akron roots and New York roots as being at variance with each other does not do justice to the facts. To be sure, Bill and Bob had differing beliefs, backgrounds, and emphasis. They were perhaps working with two varieties of core people. Dr. Bob's Akron associates seemed more biblically and religiously inclined, though there were exceptions.[2] Bill's New York associates seemed, for the most part, more skeptical and, with at least two men, irreligious or unbelieving.[3] Again, however, there were

---

[1] *Pass It On* (New York: Alcoholics Anonymous World Services, Inc., 1984), p. 155; *The Co-Founders of Alcoholics Anonymous* (New York: Alcoholics Anonymous World Services, Inc., 1972, 1975), p. 27.

[2] See, for example, the story of Norman H. of Akron, Ohio, in the First Edition of the Big Book at pages 351-356, entitled, "Educated Agnostic."

[3] In a memorandum prepared by Henry G. P. on the promotion of the Big Book, Parkhurst said, speaking for himself at least, that the society was "irreligious." The author obtained a copy of this memo during his 1991 visit to the archives at Bill's home
(continued...)

exceptions.[4] But the historical evidence concerning A.A.'s two co-founders gives a picture of two dedicated men, working together to: (1) Help drunks by understanding how these people could be relieved of their alcoholism; (2) Develop a message as to how-to-do-it, based on their own trial and error studies and experiences; (3) Perfect a means of communicating their message to insure that the technique would work. We believe fairness dictates the conclusion that each cofounder was working with associates in his respective area who had the same three objectives, whatever their other beliefs or motivations might have been.[5] So the following review should be considered in the context of Akron as part of a common objective, whatever the difference might have been in information assembled and emphasis placed.

Akron's Biblical Emphasis

One could fairly say that the focus on the Good Book as the primary source of A.A.'s ideas was in Akron. We will deal with the specifics shortly. But Dr. Bob emphatically stated his belief that A.A.'s basic ideas came from their study of the Bible.[6] By

---

[3] (...continued)
at Stepping Stones. In *Alcoholics Anonymous Comes of Age* (New York: Alcoholics Anonymous World Services, Inc., 1957), at page 17, Bill Wilson said that Henry G. P. and Jim B. were both former atheists.

[4] As we previously stated, *Pass It On* says, at page 199, that "Fitz" insisted that the Big Book express Christian doctrines and use Biblical terms and expressions. In *AA Comes of Age*, Bill Wilson said that "Fitz wanted a powerfully religious document; Henry and Jimmy would have none of it. They wanted a psychological book" (p. 17).

[5] There is, of course, the whole story of the business and profit aims and objectives of Wilson and Henry G. P. in their "Works Publishing Company," which published the Big Book. There were also criticisms of the payment of royalties to the founders, an arrangement that produced substantial money for Wilson and his wife for life.

[6] *DR. BOB and the Good Oldtimers* (New York: Alcoholics Anonymous World Services, Inc., 1980), pp. 96-97, 228, 54, 100.

contrast, we are not aware that Bill Wilson ever gave such emphasis or recognition to the Bible.

To be sure, Bill said he treasured his three months of living with Dr. Bob and his wife, Anne, when Anne was reading and interpreting Scripture.[7] Bill also said, "I sort of always felt that something was lost from A.A. when we stopped emphasizing the morning meditation."[8] These meditations included Bible study and use of daily Bible devotionals such as *The Upper Room* and *My Utmost For His Highest.*[9] And Bill and Lois continued this practice together until his death in 1971, apparently often using Chambers' *My Utmost For His Highest.*[10] But we have found no written memorandum or statement by Bill Wilson acknowledging A.A.'s debt to the Bible, nor any statement even remotely resembling Dr. Bob's acknowledgments of Good Book sources.

Akron and Akron area remarks emphasizing the Bible, Bible study, and Bible sources will be found in:

1. Dr. Bob's own statements.[11]
2. Anne Smith's statements and spiritual workbook.[12]

---

[7] E.g., James 2:26. There is even more to this story than seems thus far to have been told. Eddie S., an oldtimer from Colorado, wrote the author in September of 1992 that Bill often spoke to her not only about Anne's reading from the Book of James, but also of Anne's reading the sermon on the mount from Matthew.

[8] *DR. BOB*, p. 178.

[9] *DR. BOB*, p. 178. In a personal interview with the author in June of 1991 at Akron, Dr. Bob's daughter, Sue Smith Windows, stated that both her mother and her father used *The Upper Room* and *My Utmost For His Highest* in their meditations. As previously stated, the Seiberling children confirmed to the author that their mother read both of these books. And Julia Harris confirmed to the author in a telephone interview from her New Jersey home in October, 1991, that Oxford Group members frequently used *My Utmost For His Highest* in their meditations.

[10] *DR. BOB*, p. 178; Bill Pittman, *AA The Way It Began* (Seattle: Glen Abbey Books, 1988), p. 183.

[11] *DR. BOB*, pp. 96-97, 228, 54-55.

[12] *DR. BOB*, pp. 116-17; Dick B., Anne Smith's *Spiritual Workbook* (Corte Madera, CA: Good Book Publishing Company, 1992), pp. 12-13.

3. Henrietta Seiberling's studies and quotes.[13]
4. The personal stories of Ohio oldtimers.[14]
5. The pages of *DR. BOB and the Good Oldtimers.*[15]
6. The biblical surrender procedures that were said by Clarence S. to have been used by Dr. Bob, Akron AAs, and Clarence's own sponsees.[16]

We have found no such references in the accounts of Bill's life, writings, or remarks. But the reader should bear in mind the biblical language Bill used in the Big Book and his repeated stress on Shoemaker—the "Bible" Christian—as the main source of the spiritual principles in A.A.'s program. Recall too the many Oxford Group meetings at Calvary House and perhaps elsewhere in New York, as well as those in Akron, where the Bible was a major item of discussion. Considering these facts, the Bible as a source for Bill's thinking and writing simply cannot be ignored.

Bill Wilson was a major and vital part of the Akron research and development team. And Akron chose to emphasize A.A.'s Good Book connection. To this author, Bill's lack of mention of the Bible does not disprove its major influence on A.A.'s roots. It means, simply, that Bill chose not to mention that which was very much in evidence, and he quite apparently did not wish to give this source the emphasis it was given in Akron.

---

[13] See Part Two, Chapter Two of this book.

[14] See Big Book, pp. 257-59, 268, and the many remarks about the Bible that we have included in this book from transcripts of Ohio oldtimers.

[15] *DR. BOB*, pp. 71, 96-97, 102, 111, 116, 136, 139, 140-141, 144, 148, 151, 162, 187, 198, 218, 224, 228, 252, 276, 306, 308, 310, 314.

[16] While disputing the statement by Mitch K. that Dr. Bob and Clarence had used the "anointing with oil" procedure in James, Larry B., a Cleveland oldtimer, did speak of the use of the Bible in connection with the surrenders.

Akron's Specificity about the
Religious Books They Read

In several different ways, Bill Wilson referred to the written, religious sources of A.A. ideas. In *Twelve Steps And Twelve Traditions*, he wrote:

> The basic principles of A.A., as they are known today, were borrowed mainly from the fields of religion and medicine.[17]

A few years later, he said in *Alcoholics Anonymous Comes of Age*:

> [Of "the Episcopal clergyman Sam Shoemaker"] It was from him that Dr. Bob and I in the beginning had absorbed most of the principles that were afterward embodied in the Twelve Steps of Alcoholics Anonymous, steps that express the heart of A.A.'s way of life.[18]

> [Of "the men of religion"] Yet they have taught us all that we know of things spiritual. It is through Sam Shoemaker that most of A.A.'s spiritual principles have come. He has been the connecting link: it is what Ebby learned from Sam, and then told me, that makes the connection between Sam, a man of religion, and ourselves (p. 261).

> [Of the Oxford Groups and Sam Shoemaker] The early A.A. got its ideas of self-examination, acknowledgment of character defects, restitution for harm done, and working with others straight from the Oxford Groups and directly from Sam Shoemaker, their former leader in America, and from nowhere else (p. 39).

---

[17] *Twelve Steps And Twelve Traditions* (New York: Alcoholics Anonymous World Services, Inc., 1952), p. 16.

[18] *Alcoholics Anonymous Comes of Age* (New York: Alcoholics Anonymous World Services, Inc., 1957), pp. 38-39.

[Of several sources] Since Ebby's visit to me in the fall of 1934 we had gradually evolved what we called the "word of mouth program." Most of the basic ideas had come from the Oxford Groups, William James, and Dr. Silkworth (p. 160).

Recall Bill's even broader statement in a Grapevine article that "The spiritual substance of our remaining Steps came straight from Dr. Bob's and my own earlier association with the Oxford Groups, as they were then led in America by that Episcopal rector, Dr. Samuel Shoemaker"[19]

We do not think the foregoing statements by Bill either fully or correctly depict A.A.'s religious sources; and we suggest consideration of the following facts for a more complete picture:

1. Despite efforts to do so, we have found no evidence that Dr. Bob *ever* had any significant *personal* contact with Sam Shoemaker—in person, in correspondence, or by phone. But Dr. Bob *did* read Shoemaker's books—many of them.

2. We are not aware that Dr. Bob ever made a statement which attributed A.A. ideas to Shoemaker. Nor have we thus far found any mention of Shoemaker or his books in *DR. BOB and the Good Oldtimers*, in any accounts by Akron oldtimers, or in any of the writings of Dr. Bob's children. However, Anne Smith *specifically referred* in her workbook to Shoemaker books; and *Dr. Bob's family have or had a number of Shoemaker books* in their collection of Dr. Bob's books.

3. Dr. Bob and Anne Smith both read, studied, and recommended to alcoholics they worked with a large number of books by non-Oxford Group, Christian writers; and Akron oldtimers specifically mentioned many of these books. Given special mention were *The Upper Room*, and books by James Allen, Oswald Chambers, Glenn Clark, Henry Drummond,

---

[19] *The Language of the Heart*, p. 298.

Emmet Fox, E. Stanley Jones, and Toyohiko Kagawa, to name those most frequently discussed.

4. Dr. Bob did not merely specify the *Bible* as the source of A.A.'s basic ideas. He pointed to specific parts—the Sermon on the Mount, 1 Corinthians 13, and the Book of James—as being "absolutely essential." He frequently stressed the importance of the "Four Absolutes"—which were taken not merely from the Sermon on the Mount, but also from other books of the New Testament.[20] Dr. Bob did stress the importance of the Sermon on the Mount and studied several books specifically devoted to that topic—the works of Oswald Chambers, Glenn Clark, Emmet Fox, and E. Stanley Jones, none of whom was an Oxford Group member, and none of whom had any connection with Sam Shoemaker's teachings.[21]

5. There have been convincing statements made, some by Bill himself, that A.A. ideas came from such non-Oxford Group spiritual sources as Mary Baker Eddy, Professor William James, Dr. Carl G. Jung, Lewis Browne, Charles M. Sheldon, Ralph Waldo Trine, Harry Emerson Fosdick, Brother Lawrence, St. Augustine, Thomas A'Kempis, Bruce Barton, General William Booth, Charles Finney, and Dwight Moody.[22] Dr. Bob read and recommended the books of most of these people.

Was there a conflict or disagreement here between Dr. Bob and Bill W. as to the source of A.A.'s spiritual ideas? We don't know! Nor have we found any A.A. historians who have chosen to study that issue. But we do know that early AAs read, studied, discussed, and used a wide variety of Christian books, together

---

[20] See Dick B., *The Oxford Group & Alcoholics Anonymous* (Seattle: Glen Abbey Books, 1992), pp. 219-30.

[21] See Appendix Three.

[22] See Mel B., *New Wine* (Minnesota: Hazelden, 1991), pp. 7, 9-26, 103-06, 110-11, 130-37, 152-53.

with the Bible, as the source of their ideas, growth, and spiritual nourishment. *DR. BOB and the Good Oldtimers* says:

> This was the beginning of A.A.'s "flying blind period." They had the Bible, and they had the precepts of the Oxford Group. They also had their own instincts. They were working, or working out, the A.A. program—the Twelve Steps—without quite knowing how they were doing it (p. 96).

A statement in the 1939 Multilith copy of the Big Book may have referred to the broader sources. It says:

> There are many helpful books also. If you do not know of any, ask your priest, minister, or rabbi, for suggestions. Be quick to see where religious people are right. Make use of what they offer (p. 40).[23]

Akron A.A. itself was specific about suggested reading, not only in the Bible, but also in a wide number of spiritual books and sources that did not involve the writings or teachings of either Shoemaker or the Oxford Group. However, many of the ideas in these writings did harmonize with the ideas of the Oxford Group; and some did occasionally refer to Oxford Group writings.[24]

What contributions to A.A.'s ideas came from the spiritual books that only Akron AAs read, emphasized, and recommended? We believe they may have been substantial, and will touch on

---

[23] In her spiritual workbook, Dr. Bob's wife had made two similar comments: "If you do not know what books to read, see someone who is surrendered and who is mature in the Groups" (p. 16) and "See your ministers for others [books on the life of Christ] if you desire. But get those biographies of the Master which bring out his humanity" (p. 16). See Dick B., *Anne Smith's Spiritual Workbook* (Corte Madera, Ca: Good Book Publishing Company, 1992), pp. 11-14.

[24] See Glenn Clark, *Fishers Of Men* (Boston: Little Brown & Company, 1928), pp. 6, 21, 48-49, 98-99; *I Will Lift Up Mine Eyes* (New York: Harper & Row, 1937), p. 64. Compare E. Stanley Jones, *Victorious Living* (New York: The Abingdon Press, 1936), p. 36. Both Dr. Bob and Anne Smith read and recommended the Jones books, as did Henrietta Seiberling.

them in our portion on the Big Book. We also believe, however, there were reasons for Dr. Bob and even for Anne to emphasize the importance of the Bible over specific, spiritual books. The reasons might have been:

1. The Bible is the source for such Christian writings.

2. It was regarded as the "Word of God," *rather than just an interpretation of that Word.*

3. It was the book most likely to be read and accepted by people of all Judeo-Christian faiths—Jews, Roman Catholics, Christian Scientists, and those from varied Protestant denominations—who were then seeking help in Akron.

4. It was the least controversial source when it came to the concerns of their Roman Catholic friends who had some objections to Oxford Group practices and ideas.

However, one need only examine the reading of, and books recommended by, Dr. Bob, Anne, and Henrietta to see that they believed writings, other than the Bible, were necessary and valuable for an interpretation and understanding of the Good Book.[25] Again, we do not believe it possible for Bill Wilson to have been so much in the company of Dr. Bob, Anne, Henrietta, T. Henry, Clarace, and the Akron AAs without absorbing material from the Christian books these people were reading and discussing so much.

---

[25] Compare also Acts 8:28-38.

Comparisons of Statements about
A.A.'s Early "Six Steps"

Bill Wilson made the following record of his thoughts, as he prepared, in December of 1938, to write the Twelve Steps:

> Though subject to considerable variation, it [the "word of mouth program"] boiled down into a pretty consistent procedure which comprised six steps. These were approximately as follows:
>
>   1. We admitted that we were licked, that we were powerless over alcohol.
>   2. We made a moral inventory of our defects or sins.
>   3. We confessed or shared our shortcomings with another person in confidence.
>   4. We made restitution to all those we had harmed by our drinking.
>   5. We tried to help other alcoholics, with no thought of reward in money or prestige.
>   6. We prayed to whatever God we thought there was for power to practice these precepts.

This was the substance of what, by the fall of 1938, we were telling newcomers.[26]

Of another and possibly earlier time, Bill wrote as follows in a Grapevine article:

> As we commenced to form a Society separate from the Oxford Group, we began to state our principles something like this:
>
>   1. We admitted we were powerless over alcohol.
>   2. We got honest with ourselves [moral inventory].
>   3. We got honest with another person, in confidence [confession].

---

[26] *AA Comes of Age*, p. 160.

4. We made amends for harms done others [restitution].
5. We worked with other alcoholics without demand for prestige or money.
6. We prayed to God to help us to do these things as best we could.[27]

Lois Wilson described "the Oxford Group precepts" as:

1. Surrender your life to God.
2. Take a moral inventory.
3. Confess your sins to God and another human being.
4. Make restitution.
5. Give of yourself to others with no demand for return.
6. Pray to God for help to carry out these principles.[28]

---

[27] *The Language of the Heart*, p. 200.

[28] *Lois Remembers* (New York: Al-Anon Family Group Headquarters, 1987), p. 92. *Pass It On* contains this statement in Footnote 2 on page 206: "In later years, some A.A. members referred to this procedure as the six steps of the Oxford Group. Reverend T. Willard Hunter, who spent 18 years in full-time staff positions for the Oxford Group and M.R.A., said, 'I never once saw or heard anything like the Six Tenets. It would be impossible to find them in any Oxford Group-M.R.A. literature. I think they must have been written by someone else under some sort of misapprehension.'" In the past two years, the author has heard statements that A.A.'s six steps came from the "six steps of the Oxford Group." After reviewing thousands of pages of Oxford Group-Shoemaker writings, the author has found no reference to such six steps or six tenets. However, Lois's summary does comprehend *six of some twenty-eight* principles the author found in Oxford Group-Shoemaker writings. And, the "licked," "powerless," and "deflation" ideas do bear some resemblance to the countless stories in Oxford Group-Shoemaker writings that start with the helpless, hopeless condition of some "twice-born" person before he had his religious experience; and Shoemaker does speak of "spiritual misery," the "unhappiness of spiritual people," and the spiritual "malady" which is "estrangement from God." See Samuel M. Shoemaker, *Realizing Religion* (New York: Association Press, 1923), pp. 4-5. This spiritual problem prompted Shoemaker to say, "What you want is simply a vital religious experience. You need to find God. You need Jesus Christ" (p. 9). The concept of "estrangement from God" is not only biblical, but is frequently found in the Oxford Group-Shoemaker writings. However—except for the accuracy of Lois's summary and of the resemblance to "spiritual misery" in the first of A.A.'s original six steps—we would agree with Willard Hunter's opinion that there were no relevant steps or tenets, "six in number," in the Oxford Group.

Earl T., who got sober in Akron in 1937, who formed the Chicago nucleus of A.A., and whom Bill Wilson described as "soundly indoctrinated by Dr. Bob and the Akronites," wrote this description of Dr. Bob's six steps:

1. Complete deflation.
2. Dependence and guidance from a Higher Power.
3. Moral inventory.
4. Confession.
5. Restitution.
6. Continued to work with alcoholics.[29]

We summarize here the Akron "program" as Frank Amos reported its "vital" parts to Rockefeller in February of 1938:

1. An alcoholic must realize that he is an alcoholic, incurable from a medical standpoint, and that he must never again drink anything with alcohol in it.
2. He must surrender himself absolutely to God, realizing that in himself there is no hope.
3. He must remove from his life other sins such as hatred, adultery, and others which frequently accompany alcoholism.
4. He must have devotions every morning—a "quiet time" of prayer and some reading from the Bible and other religious literature.
5. He must be willing to help other alcoholics get straightened out.[30]

If we eliminate the "First Step," or "alcohol" aspects from the foregoing summaries, each contains ideas found in Oxford Group language, or that evidence an Oxford Group influence upon them. Four summaries specifically describe: (1) Moral inventory; (2) Confession; and (3) Restitution. In effect, Frank Amos combined

---

[29] Big Book, p. 292; See also *AA Comes of Age*, pp. 22-23.

[30] *DR. BOB*, p. 131.

all three of these ideas in his third point, dealing with removal of "character defects." Speaking of "removal" of sins, Amos was using language similar to language Bill would later use in Steps Six and Seven of the subsequent Twelve Steps. Earl T. did not include in his description of Dr. Bob's six steps the "removal" or "housecleaning" aspects of "character defects." But he did go on as follows to explain what Dr. Bob did:

> We went over these [bad personality traits or character defects] at great length and then he finally asked me if I wanted these defects of character removed. When I said yes, we both knelt at his desk and prayed, each of us asking to have these defects taken away.[31]

Earl T.'s description of Dr. Bob's procedure, like Amos's summary, seemed to forecast Bill's Step Six and Step Seven language—involving removal of character defects.

The Eleventh Step ideas of prayer and meditation were specified in the Frank Amos report. They seemed to be involved in Dr. Bob's talk of dependence upon and guidance of a "Higher Power;" and also in Bill and Lois Wilson's discussions of prayer to God.

As can be seen, all five summaries described the Twelfth Step service concept. Bill and Lois both, in effect, mentioned "practicing the principles," and Dr. Bob *and* Akron were stressing such practice by using the "Four Absolutes" as "yardsticks" to measure behavior.[32]

---

[31] Big Book, p. 292.

[32] See *Alcoholics Anonymous Comes of Age*: "In Akron and vicinity they still talked about the Oxford Group's absolutes: absolute honesty, absolute purity, absolute unselfishness, and absolute love" (p. 161). As quoted in *The Language of the Heart* at page 200, Bill said: "Though these principles were advocated according to the whim or liking of each of us, and though in Akron and Cleveland they still stuck by the O.G. absolutes of honesty, purity, unselfishness, and love, this was the gist of our message to incoming alcoholics up to 1939, when our present Twelve Steps were put to paper."

Was there, then, a special Akron influence on the "six step" program? We think that a comparison of the foregoing five summaries will show that the procedures in New York and Akron were essentially the same, except that Akron's descriptions also comprehended ideas that were to appear in Steps 2, 3, 6, 7, and 12, as Bill ultimately wrote them. In fact, Bill himself finally said he felt the ideas of the Absolutes were incorporated into the Sixth and Seventh Steps when he wrote them.[33] And the foregoing summaries show that Bill and Bob, as well as New York and Akron, were working pretty much along the same lines, with individual variations based largely on Akron's great focus on the Bible and the Oxford Group as the sources of their ideas.

Differences Between New York and Akron Views of Bill's Twelve Steps

Bill Wilson indicated that the Twelve Steps, as he originally drafted them, were essentially approved and accepted by Akron as written, but that they received a "mauling" in New York.[34] That may have been an overstatement in terms of the end result. *Pass It On* states that the very first draft of the Twelve Steps, as Bill wrote them while lying in bed at his home on 182 Clinton Street, has been lost.[35] *Pass It On* presented the following reconstruction of the lost draft, and the reconstruction closely resembles the language in the 1939 multilith:

---

[33] See Ernest Kurtz, *Not-God*. Expanded ed. (Minnesota: Hazelden, 1991), pp. 242-243.

[34] See *Alcoholics Anonymous Comes of Age*, pp. 162-64, 17; *The Language of the Heart*, p. 201; and his speech at 1954 Fort Worth, Texas on the writing of the Big Book, a transcript of which is in the author's possession.

[35] *Pass It On*, pp. 197-98.

1. We admitted we were powerless over alcohol—that our lives had become unmanageable.
2. Came to believe that God could restore us to sanity.
3. Made a decision to turn our wills and our lives over to the care and direction of God.
4. Made a searching and fearless moral inventory of ourselves.
5. Admitted to God, to ourselves, and to another human being the exact nature of our wrongs.
6. Were entirely willing that God remove all these defects of character.
7. Humbly on our knees asked Him to remove these short-comings—holding nothing back.
8. Made a complete list of all persons we had harmed, and became willing to make amends to them all.
9. Made direct amends to such people wherever possible, except when to do so would injure them or others.
10. Continued to take personal inventory and when we were wrong promptly admitted it.
11. Sought through prayer and meditation to improve our contact with God, praying only for knowledge of His will for us and the power to carry that out.
12. Having had a spiritual experience as the result of this course of action, we tried to carry this message to others, especially alcoholics, and to practice these principles in all our affairs.[36]

Was there a special Akron influence on this language?
Remember that even when he attributed the Steps to Shoemaker, Bill usually stated that he *and* Dr. Bob were indebted to Shoemaker. Further, as can be seen from an examination of the twenty-eight Oxford Group principles, the ideas in the Twelve Steps, as originally drafted, could have come from New York, from Akron, or from both. As we mentioned in our discussion of the six steps, many of the ideas, involving surrender to God, removal of character defects, and improving spiritual condition through prayer and meditation, were in place well *before* the

---

[36] *Pass It On*, pp. 198-99.

Twelve Steps were written in December of 1938. As Oxford
Group and Shoemaker books show, people were uttering an
unmanageability prayer, conducting an experiment of faith based
on their belief in God, surrendering their wills and lives to God's
direction, examining and confessing their shortcomings, asking
Him to take away their "sins," making restitution, utilizing quiet
time with two-way prayer and Bible study, serving others, and
trying to practice the principles of the Four Absolutes, the Sermon
on the Mount, and the 13th Chapter of 1st Corinthians before there
was an A.A. And even before there *was* an Oxford Group. We
believe that is why Bill Wilson so often said that nobody invented
A.A., that its spiritual ideas were the "common property of
mankind," and that its spiritual principles were borrowed mainly
from religion.

Whence came the spiritual ideas and answers? Bill Wilson said
this in *Alcoholics Anonymous Comes of Age*:

> Always better versed in spiritual matters than I, he [Dr. Bob] had
> paid little attention to that aspect of my story [the spiritual
> matters]. Even though he could not make them work, he already
> knew what the spiritual answers were. What really did hit him
> hard was the medical business, the verdict of inevitable
> annihilation. And the fact that I was an alcoholic and knew what
> I was talking about from personal experience made the blow a
> shattering one (pp. 69-70).

The foregoing remarks were characteristic of Bill when he spoke
of Dr. Bob's immense reading about and knowledge of the
spiritual answers they discussed and developed. From Bill's
statements, then, we can certainly conclude that Dr. Bob's and
Anne's spiritual resources were listened to with respect by Bill. It
is highly probable that Bill, the great assimilator, incorporated
those resources in the crucible from which A.A.'s ideas were
formed.

Let's briefly review the Akron and/or Oxford Group
influences—whether from the Bible, the Group itself, or from
Shoemaker—that seem apparent in the Twelve Steps as Bill first

drafted them. The reader can then join us in pondering just how Bill Wilson put them together, wherever he may have seen or heard them:

Step One: [We admitted we were powerless over alcohol—that our lives had become unmanageable] The unmanageable life!

We believe this concept bears the unmistakable influence of a prayer that was used, in varying forms, by Dr. Frank Buchman; by Oxford Group leader—writer, Professor Philip M. Brown; by A. J. Russell in *For Sinners Only*; at Calvary Church—where it was known as "Charlie's prayer;" and by Dr. Bob's wife, Anne, in her workbook. This, in words or substance, was the prayer:

O God, if there be a God, take command of my life; I cannot manage it myself.[37]

Our belief that this "manage me" prayer influenced the First Step is buttressed by these words in Big Book Multilith page 27:

a. That you are alcoholic and cannot manage your own life.
b. That probably no human power can relieve your alcoholism.
c. That God can and will.

Step Two: [Came to believe that God could restore us to sanity] Came to believe, God, and the concept of a Power greater than ourselves—the concept which replaced "God" in a later draft.

---

[37] See Garth Lean, *On The Tail of a Comet* (Colorado Springs: Helmers & Howard, 1988), p. 113; Philip M. Brown, *The Venture of Belief* (New York: Fleming H. Revell, 1935), pp. 29-30; A. J. Russell, *For Sinners Only* (London: Hodder & Stoughton, 1932), p. 79; Irving Harris, *The Breeze of the Spirit* (New York: The Seabury Press, 1978), p. 10; Dick B., *Anne Smith's Spiritual Workbook*, p. 73.

The Oxford Group emphasized the necessity for belief in God *before you began.*[38] So did Shoemaker.[39] So did Dr. Bob and the Akron AAs.[40] So apparently did Bill when he first became active in the Oxford Group.[41] And so did the Bible itself as exemplified by Hebrews 11:6—often quoted by the other A.A. sources.

The idea of "came to believe" was a concept designed to meet the needs of the agnostics; and we believe it also was grounded in the experiment of faith found in Oxford Group and Shoemaker sources.[42]

The concept of God as God, Creator, Maker, Friend, Father, and Spirit, was a concept that was, of course, in the Bible, in the Oxford Group, in Shoemaker writings; and—even after the God idea was "mauled" by the New Yorkers—in the Big Book. The foregoing names for God, with capital letters, that spoke of and described the God of the Bible or, the "God of the preachers," as Bill called Him, remained in the Big Book.[43] Despite objections by at least two New Yorker's to the word "God," it was retained throughout the Big Book except in Step 2.

"God" was replaced in the Second Step with "Power greater than ourselves." But this change did not take place in Akron. It was the result of arguments by Bill with his partner, Henry P., and

---

[38] See Brown, *The Venture of Belief,* p. 24; Philip Leon, *The Philosophy of Courage* (New York: Oxford University Press, 1939), p. 19; Leslie D. Weatherhead, *How Can I Find God?* (London: Hodder & Stoughton, 1933), p. 72.

[39] Samuel M. Shoemaker, *National Awakening* (New York: Harper & Brothers, 1936), p. 40; *The Gospel According To You* (New York: Fleming H. Revell, 1934), p. 47; *Religion That Works* (New York: Fleming H. Revell, 1928), p. 55; *Confident Faith* (New York: Fleming H. Revell, 1932), p. 187.

[40] *DR. BOB,* pp. 144, 239; Big Book, p. 181.

[41] Big Book, p. xvi.

[42] Garth Lean, *Good God, It Works! an experiment of faith* (London: Blandford Press, 1974). Compare Samuel M. Shoemaker, *The Experiment of Faith* (New York: Harper & Brothers, 1957), p. 36—citing John 7:17 and Matthew 5:8.

[43] See Dick B., *The Oxford Group & Alcoholics Anonymous,* pp. 114-20; *Pass It On,* p. 121.

a newcomer named Jim B., each of whom—said Bill—was "an ex salesman and former atheist." In Henry's case, there *was* belief in *some sort* of "universal power;" but Bill said Jim B. was "denouncing God at our meetings."[44] Bill substituted the word "Power" for God in the Second Step; yet he still called the Power God.[45] And the idea of reliance on a "greater" or "stronger" power which was, in fact, God can be found in Begbie's *Twice-Born Men*; in Foot's *Life Began Yesterday*, in Shoemaker's *Children of the Second Birth*, in Shoemaker's *If I Be Lifted Up*; and in Anne Smith's workbook.[46]

> ***Step Three***: [Made a decision to turn our wills and our lives over to the care and direction of God] Decision to surrender wills and lives to God's direction.

The idea that surrender starts with a *decision* can be found in Oxford Group and Shoemaker writings and in Anne Smith's spiritual workbook.[47]

Handing, turning, giving, or casting one's will and life over to God is part of the surrender idea that went back to William James and his *Varieties of Religious Experience*. It appears much in Oxford Group language, and it appears in *Anne Smith's Spiritual*

---

[44] *Alcoholics Anonymous Comes of Age*, pp. 17, 163.

[45] Big Book, p. 46.

[46] See Harold Begbie, *Twice-Born Men* (New York: Fleming H. Revell, 1909), p. 164; Stephen Foot, *Life Began Yesterday* (New York: Harper & Brothers, 1935), p. 22; Samuel M. Shoemaker, *Children of the Second Birth* (New York: Fleming H. Revell, 1927), pp. 45-46; *If I Be Lifted Up* (New York: Fleming H. Revell, 1931), pp. 175-176; Dick B., Anne *Smith's Spiritual Workbook*, p. 73.

[47] Henry Wright, *The Will of God and a Man's Lifework* (New York: The Young Men's Christian Association, 1909), pp. 43-116; The Layman with a Notebook, *What Is The Oxford Group?* (New York; Oxford University Press, 1933), pp. 46-48; Brown, *The Venture of Belief*, p. 26; Foot, *Life Began Yesterday*, pp. 10, 44; Samuel M. Shoemaker, *The Conversion of the Church* (New York: Fleming H. Revell, 1932), pp. 39-40, 77; *The Church Can Save The World* (New York: Fleming H. Revell, 1938), p. 120; *Religion That Works*, pp. 46-47; Dick B., *Anne Smith's Spiritual Workbook*, p. 74.

Workbook.[48] For a close parallel in language, see Shoemaker's *Twice-Born Ministers*: "with the decision to cast my will and my life on God, there came an indescribable sense of relief, of burdens dropping away."[49]

Oxford Group writer, Stephen Foot said, "Our job . . . is to serve the world as God shall direct.[50] The idea of God-direction, God-control, and God-led is certainly Buchman oriented.[51]

Step Four: [Made a searching and fearless moral inventory of ourselves] Moral Inventory.

Self-examination was a strong Oxford Group, Shoemaker, and Bible concept.[52] The Oxford Group and Anne Smith spoke of this as making the "moral test."[53] The idea of taking an "inventory," a "business inventory that looked at the books," can certainly be found in Oxford Group writings.[54]

Step Five: [Admitted to God, to ourselves, and to another human being the exact nature of our wrongs] Confession of faults in honesty to God and another human being.

---

[48] At page 4 of her spiritual workbook, Anne wrote, "This is the turning to God, the decision, the surrender." At page 42, she wrote, "Surrender is a complete handing over of our wills to God."

[49] Samuel M. Shoemaker, *Twice-Born Ministers* (New York: Fleming H. Revell, 1929), p. 134; See also V. C. Kitchen, *I Was A Pagan* (New York: Harper & Brothers, 1934), pp. 74, 104, 145, Dick B., *Anne Smith's Spiritual Workbook*, p 75.

[50] Foot, *Life Began Yesterday*, p. 60.

[51] See Frank N. D. Buchman, *Remaking The World* (London: Blandford Press, 1961), pp. 3, 12, 24-25, 30, 35.

[52] Henry Drummond, *The Ideal Life* (New York: Hodder & Stoughton, 1897), pp. 316; Buchman, *Remaking The World*, p. 24; Shoemaker, *The Conversion of the Church*, pp. 30-34. See Matthew 7:3-5—"look for the log in your own eye."

[53] Howard Walter, *Soul-Surgery*. 6th ed. (Oxford at the University Press, by John Johnson, 1940), pp. 43-44; Dick B., *Anne Smith's Spiritual Workbook*, pp. 32-33.

[54] Clarence I. Benson, *The Eight Points of the Oxford Group* (London: Humphrey Milford. Oxford University Press, 1936), pp. 44, 162, 18, 7; Cecil Rose, *When Man Listens* (New York: Oxford University Press, 1937), pp. 17-19.

This was one of the Oxford Group's 5 C's; and it was based on James 5:16.[55]

Step Six: [Were entirely willing that God remove all these defects of character] Willingness to change.

The concept of "willingness" as expressed by obedience to God's known will can be found throughout Oxford Group writings and in John 7:17.[56] We also believe this Step involves the Oxford Group concept of Conviction.[57]

Step Seven: [Humbly on our knees asked God to remove these shortcomings—holding nothing back] Humbly—on the knees—asking God to remove.

We shall have more to say about "humility" at a later point. But it was and is a clearly recognizable biblical, Oxford Group, and Shoemaker concept.[58]

While New York AAs apparently did kneel to pray and make surrenders, the practice was not as rigid as in Akron, where such surrender "on their knees" was an absolute must.[59]

---

[55] See Walter, *Soul-Surgery*, pp. 41-64; Begbie, *Life Changers*, pp. 37, 102-104, 169; *What Is The Oxford Group?*, pp. 25-35. In *The Conversion of the Church*, Shoemaker said, "Of course confession, in the absolute sense, is to God alone: but where there is a human listener, confession is found to be both more difficult and more efficacious" (p. 36). See James 5:16 and Dick B., *Anne Smith's Spiritual Workbook*, pp. 33-34, 82-83.

[56] See Dick B., *The Oxford Group & Alcoholics Anonymous*, pp. 19, 34, 48, 50, 153, 160, 205, 234, 248, 261, 304-05, 312.

[57] See Dick B., *The Oxford Group & Alcoholics Anonymous*, pp. 162-68.

[58] Brown, *The Venture of Belief*, pp. 29, 32; Geoffrey Allen, *He That Cometh* (New York: The Macmillan Company, 1933), pp. 45-68; Shoemaker, *National Awakening*, pp. 78-88; *Confident Faith*, p. 72; *The Church Can Save The World*, p. 55. See, for example, James 4:10: "Humble yourselves in the sight of the Lord, and He shall lift you up."

[59] See Kurtz, *Not-God*, pp. 326,n 54; pp. 54-56; and the descriptions in our book by such oldtimers as Bob E. and Clarence S.

That God can *remove* shortcomings is an idea that can be found in the Oxford Group writings and in Anne Smith's workbook.[60]

Step Eight: [Made a complete list of all persons we had harmed, and became willing to make amends to them all] A restitution list and willingness to set things right.

As to a list, see Dick B., *Anne Smith's Spiritual Workbook*, p. 75. As to "willingness," see our discussion of Step Six. As to amends, see the next Step (Nine), but note also how often A.A. sources cited the verse in the Sermon on the Mount from Matthew 5:23-24 on being reconciled with a brother.[61]

Step Nine: [Made direct amends to such people wherever possible, except when to do so would injure them or others] Restitution.

Amends, also called Restitution, were a vital Oxford Group and Shoemaker concept.[62] And the Oxford Group people cited several Bible authorities in support of their ideas about restitution.[63]

Step Ten: [Continued to take personal inventory and when we were wrong promptly admitted it] Daily surrender!

---

[60] See Allen, *He That Cometh*, p. 147; V. C. Kitchen, *I Was A Pagan*, p. 73; Dick B., *Anne Smith's Spiritual Workbook*, p. 74

[61] See Benson, *The Eight Points*, p. 30; Shoemaker, *The Conversion of the Church*, p. 47; Leslie D. Weatherhead, *Discipleship* (London: Student Christian Movement Press, 1934), p. 113; *DR. BOB*, p. 308; *RHS*, The A.A. Grapevine Memorial Isssue for January, 1951 (New York: A.A. Grapevine, Inc.), front page and page 44.

[62] See Dick B., *The Oxford Group & Alcoholics Anonymous*, pp. 180-86; Russell, *For Sinners Only*, pp. 119-35; Shoemaker, *The Conversion of the Church*, pp. 41-43; Dick B., *Anne Smith's Spiritual Workbook*, p. 75.

[63] Numbers 5:6-7; Matthew 5:23-24; Luke, Chapter 15; Luke 19:1-10.

This Step was based on the Oxford Group idea of Continuance or Conservation—maintaining and growing in the spiritual condition already obtained.[64]

> *Step Eleven*: [Sought through prayer and meditation to improve our contact with God, praying only for knowledge of His will for us and the power to carry that out] Prayer. Meditation. Contact with God. Knowledge of His Will. Power to carry that out.

These ideas are so ponderous and so very much a part of Oxford Group, Shoemaker, and Bible writings and concepts that we will not do more here than refer to our extensive treatment of these ideas in our book about the Oxford Group and A.A.[65]

However, there is a striking resemblance between the language and idea in Step Eleven and that in Stephen Foot's *Life Began Yesterday*, where Foot expounds on the idea that "God had a plan for every individual in the world." . . . that "I will ask God to show me His purpose for my life and claim from Him the power to carry that purpose out." . . . and that "Contact with God is the necessary fundamental condition, and that is made through prayer and listening. . . ."[66]

> *Step Twelve*: [Having had a spiritual experience as the result of this course of action, we tried to carry this message to others, especially alcoholics, and to practice these principles in all our affairs] A spiritual experience. Carrying the message. Practicing the principles.

---

[64] Dick B., *The Oxford Group & Alcoholics Anonymous*, pp. 199-257; *Anne Smith's Spiritual Workbook*, p. 75.

[65] In Dick B., *The Oxford Group & Alcoholics Anonymous*, as to: (1) Prayer, see pp. 239-42; (2) Meditation, quiet time, and listening, see pp. 230-57; (3) Contact with God, see pp. 265-78; (4) Knowledge of God's Will, see pp. 258-65; (5) The Power of God, see pp. 187-99. See also *Anne Smith's Spiritual Workbook*, pp. 70, 75-76.

[66] Foot, *Life Began Yesterday*, pp. 4-5, 11, 13.

Again, the amount of material is too great to cover even in summary form. But we would emphasize that the end of the Oxford Group procedures was a life-changing spiritual experience.[67] The Group's whole focus was on witnessing or sharing by witness to bring about life-changing experiences in others—"passing it on."[68] We will have more to say about the principles later. For now, suffice it to say that the Absolutes of honesty, unselfishness, and love were principles found throughout the Twelve Steps and that the concept of purity—"pure in heart"—may have become lodged in house-cleaning ideas.

What was the Akron contribution to the Twelve Steps as Bill wrote them? We believe we have already answered satisfactorily. The Akron emphasis was on the Bible and the Oxford Group; and it seems very likely that the spiritual input from Dr. Bob, Anne, Henrietta and the Akron AAs was present in Bill's mind as he drafted the steps in New York.

---

[67] Dick B., *The Oxford Group & Alcoholics Anonymous*, pp. 265-78; Buchman, *Remaking The World*, pp. 19, 24, 35, 54; Shoemaker, *Twice-Born Ministers*, pp. 10, 61, 156

[68] Dick B., *The Oxford Group & Alcoholics Anonymous*, pp. 290-95; Buchman, *Remaking The World*, p. x; Russell, *For Sinners Only*, p. 62; Shoemaker, *Religion That Works*, pp. 72-73; Acts 5:32 (See *What Is The Oxford Group?*, pp. 36-37); Acts 26:22-23 (*What Is The Oxford Group?*, p. 25); 2 Corinthians 5:20 (*What Is The Oxford Group?*, p. 35); 1 John 1:2 (*What Is The Oxford Group?*, p. 38).

15

Traces of Akron in the Big Book

Again we start with the caution that Akron did not stand alone. Alcoholics in New York, including Bill, read or were exposed to the Bible. Bill's Oxford Group business team friends— Rowland, Shep, and Hanford—were regularly receiving Bible instruction from Mary Angevine, the Bible teacher Frank Buchman provided for the business team. We know Bill's friend, Fitz, stood for having the Big Book express Christian doctrines and use biblical terms and expressions.[1] We also know Bill read Bible devotionals such as *The Upper Room* and *My Utmost For His Highest*.[2] For at least two years in New York, the alcoholics with whom Bill worked at Calvary House and Calvary Mission heard Dr. Sam

---

[1] *Pass It On* (New York: Alcoholics Anonymous World Services, Inc., 1984), p. 199.

[2] As to *The Upper Room. Daily Devotions for Family and Individual Use* (Nashville, Tennessee: Issued Quarterly by the General Committee on Evangelism Through the Department of Home Missions, Evangelism, Hospitals, Board of Missions, Methodist Episcopal Church, South; 1st quarterly issue was for April, May, June, 1935), see discussion in Dick B., *Dr. Bob's Library* (West Virginia: The Bishop of Books, 1992), pp. 33-34. The *Upper Room* was widely used in early Akron A.A. And Bill Wilson attended Akron meetings regularly in the summer of 1935 where this pamphlet was used. As to *My Utmost For His Highest* by Oswald Chambers (London: Simpkin Marshall, Ltd., 1927), see Dick B., *Dr. Bob's Library*, pp. 32-33; and Bill Pittman, *AA The Way It Began* (Seattle: Glen Abbey, 1988), p. 183, for a discussion of the use of this devotional by Dr. Bob and Anne Smith, *and* by Bill and Lois Wilson.

271

Shoemaker, his staff, and his lay assistants talk about the Bible, both in and outside of Oxford Group meetings.[3] Bill said they heard much about the Four Absolutes from these same New York sources; and Dr. Shoemaker often wrote about the Four Absolutes. So what we say here about Akron has to do with *emphasis rather than source.* Akron AAs gave special emphasis to the Sermon on the Mount, the Lord's Prayer, the Corinthians chapter on love, and the Book of James.[4] Oxford Group writers also gave these Bible sources important emphasis.[5] They stressed and often mentioned the Four Absolutes, which were based not only on the Sermon on the Mount, but also on a number of Pauline Epistles.[6] In fact, Akron A.A. still holds to the Four Absolutes.[7] So our review here will be of those items Akron emphasized in the foregoing specific Bible materials, from the Bible in general, and the literature we know was read in Akron, and very possibly in New York. It will

---

[3] In Irving Harris, *The Breeze of the Spirit* (New York: The Seabury Press, 1978), Harris said, "The Scriptures formed the basis of Sam Shoemaker's preaching. He was a 'Bible Christian'" (p. 18). Calvary's program, said Harris, "was a place to learn the how of faith, both in sermons and in groups—How to find God. How to pray. How to read the Bible. How to pass faith on" (p. 25).

[4] *DR. BOB and the Good Oldtimers* (New York: Alcoholics Anonymous World Services, Inc., 1980), pp. 96-97, 228; Pittman, *AA The Way It Began*, p. 197; Dick B., *Dr. Bob's Library*, pp. 40-42, 44-45.

[5] See, for example, Stephen Foot, *Life Began Yesterday* (New York: Harper & Brothers, 1935), pp. 142-43; V. C. Kitchen, *I Was A Pagan* (New York: Harper & Brothers, 1934), p. 28; The Layman with a Notebook, *What Is The Oxford Group?* (London: Oxford University Press, 1933), pp. 17, 36, 47-50, 106.

[6] For mention of the Four Absolutes, see *DR. BOB*, pp. 54, 139, 163. For discussion of the source of the Four Absolutes, see Garth Lean, *On The Tail of a Comet* (Colorado Springs: Helmers & Howard, 1988), p. 76; Samuel M. Shoemaker, *How You Can Help Other People* (New York: E. P. Dutton & Co., 1946), p. 59; Helen Smith Shoemaker, *I Stand By The Door* (New York: Harper & Row, 1967), p. 24; Robert E. Speer, *The Principles of Jesus* (New York: Fleming H. Revell, 1902), pp. 33-35; Henry Wright, *The Will of God and a Man's Lifework* (New York: The Young Men's Christian Association Press, 1909), pp. 167-218.

[7] *The Four Absolutes* (Cleveland: Cleveland Central Committee of A.A., n.d.). This is a pamphlet that is currently available both in Cleveland and through the Akron Inter-Group Office, 774 Elma Street, Akron, Ohio 44310.

cover those traces that can be identified with reasonable certainty in the language of the Big Book today. We will, where appropriate, cite Oxford Group and other references from the Christian books that early AAs used, to illustrate where AAs could have gained information about the specific Bible verses and ideas they studied.

From the Book of James

Many might have started this review with a discussion of the Sermon on the Mount in the Book of Matthew. The Sermon survives in A.A. today in emphasis and in the frequent recommendations within A.A. of Emmet Fox's book on that topic.[8] But we will start with the Book of James because that was said to be the favorite in Akron A.A.;[9] and "New Thought" philosophies and "mind cure" religions *may* not have been quite as popular in Akron as they were in New York.[10] The Sermon itself was; and Dr. Bob studied and recommended a number of books that analyzed and interpreted it.[11] We are aware of no such comprehensive studies or interpretive books on James that were utilized in early A.A. Akron AAs simply read James, found frequent references to it in their source literature, mentioned it in their own lingo, perhaps utilized it in their surrenders, and counted it their favorite.

Let's review the Book of James, chapter by chapter. As we do so, we will point to traces of that book which we believe can be found in the text of the Big Book.

---

[8] See Mel B., *New Wine* (Minnesota: Hazelden, 1991), pp. 111-14. The author has also observed many A.A. sponsors in his area recommending Fox's book. See Emmet Fox, *The Sermon on the Mount* (New York: Harper & Row, 1934).

[9] *DR. BOB*, p. 71.

[10] See *DR. BOB*, p. 306.

[11] See Dick B., *Dr. Bob's Library*, pp. 40-42.

James Chapter 1

1. *Patience*. Chapter One is not the only chapter in the Book of James which mentions patience.[12] Nor is it the only portion of the Bible that stresses patience.[13] But James was a favored Bible source in early A.A. James 1:3-4 states:

> Knowing this, that the trying of your faith worketh patience. But let patience have her perfect work, that ye may be perfect and entire, wanting nothing.

Patience certainly wound up as one of the most frequently mentioned spiritual principles in the Big Book.[14]

2. *Asking wisdom of God with unwavering believing*. James 1:5-8 states:

> If any of you lack wisdom, let him ask of God, that giveth to all men liberally, and upbraideth not; and it shall be given him.
> But let him ask in faith, nothing wavering. For he that wavereth is like a wave of the sea driven with the wind and tossed.
> For let not that man think that he shall receive anything of the Lord.
> A double minded man is unstable in all his ways.[15]

---

[12] See also James 5:7-11: "Be *patient*, therefore, brethren, unto the coming of the Lord. . . . Be ye also *patient*; stablish your hearts; for the coming of the Lord draweth nigh; Take, my brethren, the prophets, who have spoken in the name of the Lord, for example of suffering affliction, and of *patience*; Behold, we count them happy which endure. Ye have heard of the *patience* of Job, and have seen the end of the Lord: that the Lord is very pitiful, and of tender mercy" (emphasis added).

[13] See, for example, Hebrews 10:36: "For ye have need of *patience*, that, after ye have done the will of God, ye might receive the promise" (emphasis added).

[14] Big Book, pp. 67, 70, 83, 111, 118, 163.

[15] Dr. Bob owned and loaned Nora Smith Holm's *The Runner's Bible* (New York: Houghton Mifflin Company, 1915), where these verses are discussed at pages 51 and 60. See another favorite of Dr. Bob's, also much read by Henrietta Seiberling: Glenn Clark, *The Soul's Sincere Desire* (Boston: Little, Brown, 1927), p. 59.

Asking for God's direction and strength and receiving "Guidance" from Him, are major themes in both the Old and New Testaments, and were important Oxford Group ideas. We discussed them at length in our books on the Oxford Group and on Anne Smith's spiritual workbook.[16] And the Big Book, including the Eleventh Step itself, is filled with such Guidance concepts.[17]

3. *Every good and perfect gift comes from God, the Father of lights.* James 1:17 states:

> Every good gift and every perfect gift is from above, and cometh down from the Father of lights, with whom is no variableness, neither shadow of turning.

Bill seemed to be referring to this verse when he wrote on page 14 of the Big Book:

> I must turn in all things to the Father of Light [sic] who presides over us all.[18]

---

[16] Dick B., *The Oxford Group & Alcoholics Anonymous* (Seattle: Glen Abbey Books, 1992), pp. 207-18, 230-57; *Anne Smith's Spiritual Workbook* (Corte Madera, CA: Good Book Publishing Company, 1992), pp. 44-47, 50-53. See also Holm, *The Runner's Bible*, pp. 126-130; Chambers, *My Utmost For His Highest*, pp. 4, 155, 319; *The Upper Room*, April 22, 1935.

[17] Big Book, pp. 13, 46, 49, 62-63, 67, 69-70, 76, 79-80, 83, 84-88, 100, 117, 120, 124, 158, 164.

[18] Note that at the conclusion of the "Long Form" Twelve Traditions in Appendix One of the Big Book, Bill wrote: "To the end that our great blessings may never spoil us; that we shall forever live in thankful contemplation of Him who presides over us all" (Big Book, p. 568). Dr. Bob perhaps mentioned this concept of God as a good and loving provider in his last major address in 1948, stating: "Christ said, 'Of Myself, I am nothing—My strength cometh from My Father in heaven.' If He had to say that, how about you and me?" See *The Co-Founders of Alcoholics Anonymous* (New York: A.A. World Services, Inc., 1972, 1975), p. 15. Compare 1 John 1:5: "This then is the message which we have heard of Him, and declare unto you, that God is light, and in Him is no darkness at all."

The Big Book often describes God as a loving and providing God.[19] Possibly confirming his convictions about God's goodness, and thus possibly relying on the idea he quoted from James 1:17, Bill wrote:

> We are sure God wants us to be happy, joyous, and free (Big Book, p. 133).

4. *Be ye doers of the word, and not hearers only.* James 1:21-22 states:

> Wherefore lay apart all filthiness and superfluity of naughtiness and receive with meekness the engrafted word, which is able to save your souls.
> But be ye doers of the word, and not hearers only, deceiving your own selves.

Shoemaker devoted an entire chapter to this verse, stating:

> I think St. James' meaning is made much clearer in Dr. Moffatt's translation, "Act on the Word, instead of merely listening to it." Try it out in experiment, and prove it by its results—otherwise you only fool yourself into believing that you have the heart of religion when you haven't.[20]

Shoemaker also pointed out that prayer is often more a struggle to find God than the enjoyment of Him and cooperation with His will. He added that "God is and is a Rewarder of them that seek Him."[21] We cannot find a specific reference to James 1:21-22 in the Big Book; but A.A. stresses over and over that it is a program

---

[19] Big Book, pp. 10-11, 13, 25, 28, 49, 52, 56-57, 59, 63, 68, 76, 83, 85, 100, 117, 120, 124, 130, 133, 158, 161, 164.

[20] Samuel M. Shoemaker, *The Gospel According To You* (New York: Fleming H. Revell, 1934), pp. 45-55.

[21] Hebrews 11:6.

of *action*,[22] that probably no human power can relieve a person of alcoholism, but "That God could and would if He were sought" (p. 60). A.A.'s program emphasizes action—*seeking* by *following* the path that leads to a relationship with God.[23] The James verse stresses *doing* God's will as expressed in His Word—not merely listening to it. In view of James as an Akron favorite and Shoemaker as a Wilson favorite, it seems possible that the action stress in A.A. might have derived from James 1:21-22.

James Chapter 2

Chapter Two of the Book of James may have made two direct and major contributions to the language of the Big Book and also to A.A.'s philosophy. The concepts were "Love thy neighbor as thyself" and "Faith without works is dead."

1. *Love thy neighbor as thyself.* James 1:8 states:

> If ye fulfill the royal law according to the scripture, Thou shalt love thy neighbor as thyself, ye do well.

This commandment, "Love thy neighbor," is also stated in other parts of both the Old and New Testaments. Thus, when the Big Book uses this phrase, we cannot say for sure whether the quote is from James or from one of the other Bible verses to the same effect.[24] In any event, the Big Book states:

---

[22] Big Book, pp. 14-15, 19, 25, 57, 59-60, 63-64, 72, 75-77, 85, 87-88, 89-103.

[23] As to relationship with God, see Big Book, pp. 13, 28-29, 72, 100, 164, 452. As to the path, see Big Book, pp. xxii, 15, 58, 72, 100, 116, 349.

[24] See Matthew 5:43; 19:19; 22:39; Mark 12:31; 12:33; Luke 10:27; Romans 13:9; Galatians 5:14; Leviticus 19:18.

Then you will know what it means to give of yourself that others may survive and rediscover life. You will learn the full meaning of "Love thy neighbor as thyself" (p. 153).[25]

James seems the probable source of this Bible quote since Dr. Bob favored the "love" concept *and* the Book of James.[26]

2. *Faith without works is dead.* Said to be the favorite verse of Anne Smith and perhaps the origin of many expressions in A.A. concerning "works," this expression, or variations of it, appear several times in Chapter Two of the Book of James.[27] For example, James 2:20 states:

But wilt thou know, O vain man, that faith without works is dead?

The "faith without works" phrase and its action concept are quoted or referred to many times in the Big Book.[28] The Oxford Group people also put emphasis on these James verses, using them in connection with the importance of witnessing.[29]

James Chapter 3

1. *Taming the tongue.* In his Farewell Address to A.A., Dr. Bob said:

---

[25] See also Big Book, p. 236.

[26] *DR. BOB*, pp. 338, 110.

[27] James 2:14, 17-18, 20, 22, 26. See Nell Wing, *Grateful To Have Been There* (Illinois: Parkside Publishing Corporation, 1992), pp. 70-71.

[28] Big Book, pp. 14-15, 76, 88, 93, 97.

[29] The Layman with a Notebook, *What Is The Oxford Group?* (London: Oxford University Press, 1933), pp. 35-38.

Let us also remember to guard that erring member the tongue, and if we must use it, let's use it with kindness, consideration and tolerance.[30]

A major portion of James, Chapter Three, is devoted to the trouble that can be caused by an untamed tongue.[31] These are a few of the verses:

Even so the tongue is a little member and boasteth great things. Behold, how great a matter a little fire kindleth! And the tongue is a fire, a world of iniquity; so is the tongue among our members that it defileth the whole body, and setteth on fire the course of nature; and it is set on fire of hell. . . . But the tongue can no man tame; it is an unruly evil, full of deadly poison.
. . . Out of the same mouth proceedeth blessing and cursing. My brethren, these things ought not to be.

These verses from James are not quoted in the Big Book. But, in paraphrasing them, Dr. Bob seemed to be speaking of tolerance, courtesy, consideration, and kindness. James said that good *conversation* should be a focus—conversation, we believe, laced with consideration, kindness, and tolerance.[32] And these principles *are* very much stressed in the Big Book.[33]

2. *Avoidance of envy, strife, and lying.* James 3:14-16 makes clear that a heart filled with envy, strife, and lies is not receiving wisdom from God, but rather from devilish sources. The verses state:

But if ye have bitter envying and strife in your hearts; glory not, and lie not against the truth.

---

[30] *DR. BOB*, p. 338.

[31] James 3:1-13.

[32] See James 3:13.

[33] Big Book, pp. 67, 69-70, 83-84, 97, 118, 125, 135.

This wisdom descendeth not from above, but is earthly, sensual, devilish.

For where envying and strife is, there is confusion and every evil work.

We do not find "envy" as much decried in the Big Book as jealousy; but a more modern translation of these King James verses equates "envy" *with* "jealousy."[34] And the Big Book most assuredly condemns jealously.[35] In fact, it states as to jealousy *and* envy:

Keep it always in sight that we are dealing with that most terrible human emotion—jealousy (p. 82).

The greatest enemies of us alcoholics are resentment, jealousy, envy, frustration, and fear (p. 145).

As to strife, the Big Book states:

After all, our problems were of our own making. Bottles were only a symbol. Besides, we have stopped fighting anybody or anything. We have to (p. 103)!

On the lying and dishonesty counts, we might point to the Four Absolutes, and suggest the frequency with which the Big Book emphasizes A.A.'s requirement of grasping and developing a manner of living which "demands rigorous honesty" (p. 58). In the case of James 3:14-16, however, we move farther from the level of certainty that these particular verses were an exclusive or even major source for the traits of envy, jealousy, strife, and dishonesty, decried also in many other parts of the Bible.

---

[34] *The Revised English Bible* (London: Oxford University Press, 1989), p. 208.

[35] Big Book, pp. 37, 69, 82, 100, 119, 145, 161.

James Chapter 4

1. *Asking amiss for selfish ends.* We shall have much more to say about selfishness and self-centeredness. But we do point to the following in James 4:3:

> Ye ask, and receive not, because ye ask amiss, that ye may consume it upon your lusts.

Some Christian sources that were favorites of Dr. Bob's discuss this verse at some length.[36] And the Big Book authors may have obtained from James 4:3 their inspiration for the following:

> We ask especially for freedom from self-will, and are careful to make no request for ourselves only. We may ask for ourselves, however, if others will be helped. We are careful never to pray for our own selfish ends. Many of us have wasted a lot of time doing that and it doesn't work (p. 87).

2. *Humility.* The Big Book is filled with discussions of humility, of humbling one's own self before God, and of humbly asking for His help. Examples include:

> There I humbly offered myself to God, as I understood Him, to do with me as He would (p. 13).

> He humbly offered himself to his Maker—then he knew (p. 57).

> Just to the extent that we do as we think He would have us, and humbly rely on Him, does He enable us to match calamity with serenity (p. 68).

---

[36] See Clark, *The Soul's Sincere*, p. 35; Holm, *The Runner's Bible*, p. 60

We constantly remind ourselves we are no longer running the show, humbly saying to ourselves many times each day "Thy will be done" (pp. 87-88).[37]

The Book of James has no corner on the biblical injunction to be humble.[38] But the importance of James, and the remarks of Shoemaker under Item 3 immediately below, suggest that the following verses from James may have been a source of the foregoing Big Book ideas. James 4:7, 10 state:

Submit yourselves therefore to God. Resist the devil, and he will flee from you.
Humble yourselves in the sight of the Lord, and he shall lift you up.[39]

3. *Trusting God and cleaning house.* James 4:8 states:

Draw nigh to God, and he will draw nigh to you. Cleanse your hands, ye sinners; and purify your hearts, ye double minded.[40]

The Big Book says on page 98:

Burn the idea into the consciousness of every man that he can get well regardless of anyone. The only condition is that he trust in God and clean house.

Pointing out that one can establish conscious companionship with God by simply, honestly, and humbly seeking Him, the Big Book says at page 57:

---

[37] See also Big Book, pp. 59, 63, 73, 76, 85, 164.

[38] See Matthew 18:4; 23:12; 1 Peter 5:6; Micah 6:8; 2 Kings 22:19; 2 Chronicles 33:23.

[39] See also, Holm, *The Runner's Bible*, pp. 59, 94.

[40] See for discussion, Chambers, *My Utmost For His Highest*, p. 309.

He has come to all who have honestly sought Him. When we drew near to Him He disclosed Himself to us!

In Step Seven, the Big Book relates "cleaning house" of character defects to "humbly asking" God to remove them. The verses in James, which speak of drawing near to God, cleansing our hearts, humbling ourselves in His sight, and then being "lifted" up by God, seem directly involved in the Big Book's Seventh Step language. In fact, many years after the Big Book was written, Sam Shoemaker wrote about his understanding of the Seventh Step and said in A.A.'s *Grapevine* in 1964:

Sins get entangled deep within us, as some roots of a tree, and do not easily come loose. We need help, grace, the lift of a kind of divine derrick.[41]

James Chapter 5

1. *Patience*. In our discussion of James, Chapter One, we have already covered the verses on patience in James 5:7, 8, 10, 11.

2. *Grudge not one another*. James 5:9 reads:

Grudge not one against another, brethren, lest ye be condemned; behold, the judge standeth before the door.

A major portion of the Big Book's Fourth Step discussion is devoted to resentment, about which page 64 says:

Resentment is the "number one" offender. It destroys more alcoholics than anything else. From it stem all forms of spiritual disease.

---

[41] Samuel M. Shoemaker, *Those Twelve Steps as I Understand Them*; Volume II, *Best of the Grapevine* (New York: The A.A. Grapevine, Inc., 1986), p. 130.

The Big Book then suggests putting resentments on paper—making a *"grudge list"* (p. 64). Oxford Group member Ebenezer Macmillan wrote at length on the importance of eliminating resentments, hatred, or the *"grudge"* that "blocks God out effectively."[42] Shoemaker specified "grudges" as one of the "sins" to be examined in an inventory of self.[43] Since the Big Book lists resentments or "grudges" as one of the four major "character defects" which *block us from God*,[44] we think it quite possible that the "grudge" language in the Big Book was influenced by Akron's interest in James, and perhaps James 5:9.

3. *The "Healing Ministry of James."* James 5:14-15 states in part:

> Is any sick among you? let him call for the elders of the church; and let them pray over him, anointing him with oil in the name of the Lord:
> And the prayer of faith shall save the sick, and the Lord shall raise him up. . . .

We have already discussed our recent discovery through Mitch K., a sponsee of Clarence S.'s, that the foregoing verses might have been the basis for surrender prayers and procedures in Akron and in some of Cleveland. Recovered AAs had the newcomer get down on his knees, prayed over him, anointed him with oil, and had him make his request in the name of Jesus Christ that alcohol be taken out of his life and that he be healed. As far as we know from our extensive review of Oxford Group literature, the praying and

---

[42] Ebenezer Macmillan, *Seeking and Finding* (New York: Harper & Brothers, 1933), pp. 96-98. There is a copy of Macmillan's book in the library of Bill's home at Stepping Stones; and it is one of the very few Oxford Group books to be found anywhere at Stepping Stones.

[43] Samuel M. Shoemaker, *Twice-Born Ministers* (New York: Fleming H. Revell, 1929), p. 182; *How To Become A Christian* (New York: Harper & Brothers, 1953), pp. 56-67.

[44] See Big Book discussions at pages 71-72, 64-65, 84, 86.

anointing with oil in the name of Jesus Christ had no counterpart in Oxford Group surrenders although we hope more information on the "healing ministry of James" will surface at least from A.A. sources and, if the verses were used in the Oxford Group, from Oxford Group sources.

4. *Asking God's forgiveness for sins.* We repeat James 5:15, partially quoted above. The entire verse says:

> And the prayer of faith shall save the sick, and the Lord shall raise him up; and if he have committed sins, they shall be forgiven him.

The Big Book says this of asking God's forgiveness when we fall short:

> If we are sorry for what we have done, and have the honest desire to let God take us to better things, we believe we will be forgiven and will have learned our lesson (p. 70).

> When we retire at night, we constructively review our day. . . . After making our review, we ask God's forgiveness and inquire what corrective measures should be taken (p. 86).

The foregoing Big Book quotes show that its authors believed they could, after surrender, still gain forgiveness from God for their shortcomings after surrender. Here again, James has no corner on the statement that God makes it possible, through forgiveness, for a believer to regain fellowship with Him. 1 John 1:9 may also have been a source of these Big Book ideas:

> If we confess our sins, he is faithful and just to forgive us our sins, and to cleanse us from all unrighteousness.

See also our discussion of forgiveness, in a moment, in connection with the Sermon on the Mount. The Books of James, 1 John, or

Matthew could have been the basis for the Big Book forgiveness concept.

4. *Confess your sins one to another.* It has often been noted that the Oxford Group concept of confession and Step Five in the Big Book were derived from James 5:16:

> Confess your faults one to another, and pray for one another, that ye may be healed.[45]

5. *Effectual, fervent prayer works.* James 5:16 states:

> The effectual fervent prayer of a righteous man availeth much.

The Big Book abounds with prayers. And it states:

> Step Eleven suggests prayer and meditation. We shouldn't be shy on this matter of prayer. Better men than we are using it constantly. It works, if we have the proper attitude and work at it.

James 5:16, being, as it is, part of the "healing ministry" portions of James, that were referred to by Clarence S., could well have been a major foundation for the Big Book's statements about the effectiveness of prayer.

We believe the foregoing review of a good many verses in the Book of James suggests why Dr. Bob felt this particular book of the Bible was an essential part of the program that early AAs were shaping.

---

[45] See Dick B., *The Oxford Group & Alcoholics Anonymous* (Seattle: Glen Abbey Books, 1992), pp. 158-62, 312.

1 Corinthians 13 and Love

Dr. Bob stressed, perhaps even "required," the reading of the 1 Corinthians 13—known as the "Love" Chapter.[46] And he was equally strong, as were other Akron AAs, in his enthusiasm for Henry Drummond's study and analysis of 1 Corinthians 13.[47] Bill Wilson said, "The definition of love in Corinthians also played a great part in our discussions."[48] For the sake of brevity, we have included the text of the 13th Chapter in Appendix Eight of this book. Here we will utilize Drummond's study in *The Greatest Thing In The World* because his words and concepts can very possibly be identified in the language of the Big Book.[49] This is the case whether those concepts came from the Bible itself, from the host of Christian writers that were read by early AAs, or from Drummond's book.

Drummond said the spectrum of love, as it is set out in Corinthians, has nine ingredients. He listed these in "modern" English as of the 1880's and placed alongside each ingredient the equivalent King James language from 1 Corinthians 13. He listed love's nine ingredients as follows:[50]

1. Patience   "Love suffereth long."[51]
2. Kindness   "And is kind."[52]

---

[46] See *DR. BOB*, page 96, where he said the chapter was "absolutely essential." See also Dr. Bob's "required reading list" set forth in Pittman, *AA The Way It Began*, p. 197.

[47] *DR. BOB*, pp. 310-11; 150-51; Pittman, *AA The Way It Began*, p. 197.

[48] Kurtz, *Not-God*, p. 320 n11.

[49] Henry Drummond, *The Greatest Thing In The World and other addresses* (World Bible Publishers, Inc., n.d.).

[50] Drummond, *The Greatest Thing in the World*, p. 26

[51] See our discussion of "patience" as to the Book of James where we cite the frequent occurrences of this principle in the Big Book.

[52] See Big Book, pp. 67, 83, 86.

3.	Generosity	"Love envieth not."[53]
4.	Humility	"Love vaunteth not itself, is not puffed up."[54]
5.	Courtesy	"Doth not behave itself unseemly."[55]
6.	Unselfishness	"Seeketh not her own."[56]
7.	Good Temper	"Is not easily provoked."[57]
8.	Guilelessness	"Thinketh no evil."[58]
9.	Sincerity	"Rejoiceth not in iniquity, but rejoiceth in truth."[59]

We've pointed out that Dr. Bob stressed that A.A.'s steps simmered down to love and service.[60] He presented God as a God of love.[61] Dr. Bob's wife, Anne, frequently quoted the "God is love" verses in 1 John 4:8,16.[62] Dr. Bob and Anne studied

---

[53] See our discussion of "envy" and "jealousy" as to the Book of James, with citations of the occurrence of these issues in the Big Book.

[54] See our discussion of humility as to the Book of James, with citations of the occurrences of this principle in the Big Book.

[55] Drummond said at page 31: "Courtesy is said to be love in little things." He equates it with being considerate. And the Big Book stresses this principle (p. 69).

[56] "Unselfishness" was one of the four principles in the Oxford Group's Four Absolutes. And the Big Book decries "selfishness" many times (pp. 62, 69, 84, 86).

[57] Drummond wrote at length on the vice of "ill temper," pointing out that it involved want of patience, want of kindness, want of generosity, want of courtesy, want of unselfishness. He said all are instantly symbolized in one flash of Temper. Certainly one aspect of this Temper is *lack of tolerance*. And the Big Book stressed the principle of tolerance and used the slogan, "Live and let live," to symbolize the importance of tolerance (Big Book, pp. 19, 67, 70, 83-84, 125, 118, 135).

[58] Drummond essentially equates this with looking on the bright side, looking for the best in others. Perhaps this equates with unselfishness and with tolerance and certainly with love.

[59] Here is a cardinal A.A. spiritual principle—*honesty*. Honesty was one of the Four Absolutes of the Oxford Group; and it appears throughout the Big Book as a vital spiritual principle (Big Book, pp. xiv, xxvii, 13, 26, 28, 32, 44, 47, 55, 57-58, 63-65, 67, 70, 73, 117, 140, 145).

[60] *DR. BOB*, p. 338.

[61] *DR. BOB*, p. 110.

[62] *DR. BOB*, p. 117.

Kagawa's book on love.[63] The Big Book talks repeatedly of the principle of love.[64]

Jesus Christ's greatest message, as stated in Mark 12:30-31, concerned the two great commandments about love:

> And thou shalt love the Lord thy God with all thy heart, and with all thy soul, and with all thy mind, and with all thy strength; this is the first commandment.
> And the second is like, namely this, Thou shalt love thy neighbor as thyself. There is none other commandment greater than these.[65]

These verses were given as the explanation for the standard of "Absolute Love," as it was discussed in Akron's "A Manual for Alcoholics Anonymous," from which we have previously quoted. That same manual referred to the importance of 1 Corinthians 13—the chapter on "how to" love and "of what" the love of God consisted. The Old Testament contained the same commandments that Jesus gave on loving God and loving one's neighbor.[66]

Once again, then, we think we can see from an examination of 1 Corinthians 13, a chapter that Dr. Bob and Akron AAs emphasized, where this second portion of the Bible could have influenced the Big Book.

---

[63] See Dick B., *Dr. Bob's Library*, pp. 43-44; *Anne Smith's Spiritual Workbook*, pp. 11, 14-17.

[64] Big Book, pp. 83-84, 86, 118, 122, 153.

[65] See also Luke 10:27.

[66] Deuteronomy 6:5; Leviticus 19:18.

Matthew Chapters 5-7: The Sermon on the Mount

Jesus Christ's Sermon on the Mount—as presented in Matthew 5-7—was a primary influence on A.A. As we pointed out, Dr. Bob said the Sermon contained A.A.'s underlying philosophy. He said it was one of the essential sections of the Bible that early AAs read. Oxford Group members, including Sam Shoemaker, wrote on many of its topics. Every major Christian writer studied by Dr. Bob and the Akron AAs wrote about the Sermon; and four of these writers—Oswald Chambers, Glenn Clark, Emmet Fox, and E. Stanley Jones—wrote major books or studies of the Sermon.[67]

Emmet Fox and the Sermon on the Mount

Any discussion of A.A. and the Sermon on the Mount would seem to require comment on Emmet Fox's study of the Sermon. Emmet Fox's *The Sermon on the Mount* has been thought by some to be an important source of A.A. principles and is read by many AAs today, as it was by Dr. Bob and some other early AAs.[68] But ours is a book about the Akron Genesis; and there is another side of the Emmet Fox story.

The Fox book may not have been as popular among Akron AAs as it was in the east.[69] Fox is not mentioned in *Anne Smith's Spiritual Workbook*, though most of the other Christian writers that AAs read—Oxford Group and otherwise—are. Not one of the three Seiberling children mentioned to the author that Fox was a person whose books were read by Henrietta Seiberling. We are not aware

---

[67] Dick B., *Dr. Bob's Library*, pp. 40-42.

[68] Emmet Fox, *The Sermon on the Mount* (New York: Harper & Row, 1934). See *DR. BOB*, pp. 310-11; Pittman, *AA The Way It Began*, p. 197; Mel B., *New Wine* (Minnesota: Hazelden, 1991), pp. 5, 105-06, 111-14; Igor Sikorsky, Jr., *AA's Godparents* (Minnesota: CompCare Publishers, 1990), pp. 19-23.

[69] See *DR. BOB*, p. 306, where there is a possible suggestion that "new thought" philosophies" and "mind cure" religions may not have been as popular a subject for study among Akron AAs as they were with Dr. Bob.

that Fox is mentioned in any Oxford Group or Shoemaker book. And there may be a substantial reason: Succinctly put to the author by Mrs. Irving Harris, widow of Shoemaker's close associate, Reverend Irving Harris, "we were not sure Fox was a Christian."[70] And Fox's writings might have given rise to such concerns among many Christians. In his *The Sermon on the Mount*, Fox put a lot of distance between himself and Christianity as it is described in the New Testament.[71] He wrote:

The "Plan of Salvation" which figured so prominently in the evangelical sermons and divinity books of a past generation is as completely unknown to the Bible as it is to the Koran (p. 5).

What has happened is that certain obscure texts from Genesis, a few phrases taken here and there from Paul's letters, and one or two isolated verses from other parts of the Scriptures, have been taken out and pieced together by divines to produce the kind of teaching which it seemed *ought* to have been found in the Bible. Jesus knows nothing of all this (p. 5).

Jesus has been sadly misunderstood and misrepresented in other directions too (p. 5).

Many modern Christians do, however, realize that there is no system of theology in the Bible unless one likes to put it there deliberately (p. 7).

The story of Adam and Eve and the Garden of Eden is a case in point. . . . It was never intended by its author to be taken for

---

[70] Mrs. Harris made this observation in a telephone interview with the author from New York to her home in Princeton, New Jersey on October 5, 1991. Later on, she phoned the author to say that Fox had performed a marriage ceremony for her brother and also that she had heard Fox lecture at Carnegie Hall. On November 6, 1991, she wrote the author, as to Fox, and said "I never thought the Oxford Group crowd were connected in any way" [with Fox].

[71] References in the following paragraphs are to Fox, *The Sermon on the Mount*.

history, but literal-minded people did so take it, with all sorts of absurd consequences (p. 13).

We have not researched for critiques of the foregoing remarks. But the statements would have been unacceptable to most in the 1930's who regarded the Bible as the Word of God and God as its author—the author who moved holy men to write as they were given revelation.[72] Nor would the statements have been acceptable to the many Christians who look upon Jesus as Savior, as most assuredly the Oxford Group and Shoemaker did.[73] Nor would the statements have been acceptable to any denomination which believed that Jesus was, as He himself said, the way, the truth, and the life, and the only way by which man could come to His Father.[74] So we leave further discussion of Emmet Fox to other analysts and to those who do subscribe to "New Thought."

---

[72] See, for example, Galatians 1:11-12; 2 Peter 1:20-21; 2 Timothy 3:16-17; discussion in *New Bible Dictionary*. 2d ed. (Illinois: Tyndale House Publishers, 1987), p. 1259; *The Abingdon Bible Commentary* (New York: The Abingdon Press, 1929), pp. 1287-88, 1347-48; W. E. Vine, *Vine's Expository Dictionary of Old and New Testament Words*, Vol. IV (New York: Fleming H. Revell, 1981), pp. 229-30.

[73] Matthew 1:21; Luke 2:11; John 4:42; Acts 5:31; 13:23; Ephesians 5:23; Titus 1:4; 2 Peter 1:11; 1 John 4:14. See, for example, Howard A. Walter, *Soul-Surgery*. 6th ed (Oxford: Printed at the University Press by John Johnson, Printer to the University, 1940), p. 85; Clarence Benson, *The Eight Points of the Oxford Group* (London: Oxford University Press, 1936), pp. 158-159; Burnett Hillman Streeter, *The God Who Speaks* (London: Macmillan & Co., 1943), pp. 148-149; Philip Leon, *The Philosophy of Courage or The Oxford Group Way* (New York: Oxford University Press, 1939), p. 75; Ebenezer Macmillan, *Seeking and Finding* (New York: Harper & Brothers, 1933), pp. 216, 279; V. C. Kitchen, *I Was A Pagan* (New York: Harper & Brothers, 1934), p. 152; Samuel M. Shoemaker, *Religion That Works* (New York: Fleming H. Revell, 1928), p. 74. See also Oswald Chambers, *Studies in the Sermon on the Mount* (London: Simpkin Marshall, Ltd., n.d.), p. i; E. Stanley Jones, *Christ At The Round Table* (New York: Grosset & Dunlap, 1928), p. 108; Glenn Clark, *Touchdowns For the Lord* (Minnesota: Macalester Park Publishing Co., 1947), pp. 44-45.

[74] John 14:6. See Shoemaker, *Religion That Works*, pp. 28-29; Brown, *The Venture of Belief*, p. 49; Benson, *The Eight Points of the Oxford Group*, p. 125; Olive Jones, *Inspired Children* (New York: Harper & Brothers, 1933), p. 150; Holm, *The Runner's Bible*, pp. 12-13; E. Stanley Jones, *The Christ of the Indian Road* (New York: The Abingdon Press, 1925), pp. 178-79.

But such "New Thought" teachings did not seem to be the focus of the alcoholics of Akron, nor of the people in the Oxford Group or Calvary Church. Nor do we believe that the distancing of Jesus Christ from a plan of salvation was acceptable to any major denomination of that time.[75]

On the other hand, A.A. historian Mel B. stated that Bill Wilson freely acknowledged the importance of Fox's book to A.A. and that Bill and other early A.A. members attended Fox's lectures in New York City in the late 1930's.[76] There *are* some ideas in the Big Book which resemble Fox's ideas; and one of them is that *all* people always have direct access to an all-loving, all-powerful Father-God, who will forgive them, and supply His own strength to them to enable them to find themselves again.[77] Such thinking certainly offers a "Higher Power" to anyone who works the Steps, rather than limiting access to God to those who have been "converted" and saved.[78] But A.A.'s claim to the Sermon on the Mount was not limited to what might have been said in the teachings of Emmet Fox.

Our discussion here will not deal with this or that interpretation of Matthew Chapters 5-7. It will be of the Sermon on the Mount

---

[75] The World Council of Churches states in Article I of its Basis: "The World Council of Churches is a fellowship of Churches which confess the Lord Jesus Christ as God and Saviour according to the Scriptures." See Nigel Turner, *Grammatical Insights into the New Testament* (Edinburgh: T & T Clark, 1965), p. 14. The Roman Catholic Church considers the official statement of the Council of Chalcedon (A.D. 451) to be authoritative for its members. See John Ziesler, *The Jesus Question* (London: Lutterworth, 1980), p. 104. The "Definition of Chalcedon" states: "We all with one accord teach men to acknowledge one and the same son, our Lord Jesus Christ . . . . begotten for us men and for our salvation." See Henry Bettenson, ed. *Documents of the Christian Church*, 2d ed. (London: Oxford, 1963), p. 51. For further analysis, see Kenneth Charles Burns, *The Rhetoric Of Christology: A Content Analysis Of Texts Which Discuss Titus 2:13*, San Francisco State University, 1991. Unpublished Master's Thesis.

[76] Mel B., *New Wine*, p. 111.

[77] Fox, *The Sermon on the Mount*, p. 5; Compare Big Book, p. 28.

[78] See Romans 10:9-10, which assures salvation only to those who confess with their mouth that Jesus is Lord and believe in their heart that God raised him from the dead. See also John 3:3, 7, 16-18.

itself; for this Sermon which Jesus gave was not the property of some particular writer. The fact that Dr. Bob read the Matthew chapters themselves and many interpretations of them seems to show his belief that the Sermon itself *was* "the common property of mankind," whatever the theology behind it. So we give the Sermon a review here, not because it was the peculiar property of Akron, but rather because Dr. Bob emphasized it as a biblical source of A.A. ideas. And we will now review some major points we believe found their way into the thinking behind the Big Book.

The Lord's Prayer—Matthew 6:9-13

Oxford Group meetings closed with the Lord's Prayer—in New York and in Akron.[79] The author has attended at least fifteen hundred A.A. meetings, and almost every one closed with the Lord's Prayer. At the 1990 International A.A. Conference in Seattle, which this author attended, some 50,000 members of Alcoholics Anonymous joined in closing their meetings with the Lord's Prayer. So it has not been Dr. Bob Smith alone who has stressed this prayer. The question here concerns what parts of the Lord's Prayer found their way into the Big Book; and we do point out here that the prayer is *part of the Sermon on the Mount.*

Here are the verses of the Lord's Prayer (King James Version) as found in Matthew 6:9-13. Jesus instructed the Judeans, "After this manner therefore pray ye":

> Our Father which art in heaven. Hallowed be thy name.
> Thy kingdom come. Thy will be done in earth as it is in heaven.
> Give us this day our daily bread.
> And forgive us our debts as we forgive our debtors.[80]

---

[79] Telephone interview by the author with Mrs. Julia Harris, October 5, 1991; *DR. BOB*, pp. 137-42.

[80] AAs substitute the word "trespasses" for "debts," as do many Christian denominations.

And lead us not into temptation, but deliver us from evil: For thine is the kingdom, and the power, and the glory, for ever. Amen.

Dr. Bob studied books on the Sermon by Chambers, Clark, Fox, and Jones. And these writers extracted a good many teachings, prayer guides, and theological ideas from these verses. But there are a few concepts and phrases in the Lord's Prayer which either epitomize A.A. thinking or can be found in its language—whether the A.A. traces came from the Lord's Prayer itself of from other portions of the Bible.

The Big Book used the word "Father" when referring to God; and the context of the usage shows that the name came from the Bible.[81] The Oxford Group also used the term "Father," among other names, when referring to God.[82] The concept and expression of God as "Father" is not confined to the Sermon on the Mount. It can also be found in many other parts of the New Testament.[83] But AAs have given the "Our Father" prayer a special place in their meetings. So the Lord's Prayer seems the likely source of the word "Father."

The phrase "Thy will be done" is directly quoted in the Big Book and underlies its contrast between "self-will" and "God's will."[84] The Oxford Group stressed, as do A.A.'s Third and Seventh Step prayers, that there must be a *decision to do God's*

---

[81] Thus the Big Book, at page 14, speaks of "Father" and "God" in the context of "Father of Light" from James 1:17; and, at page 62, of "Father" and "God," stating "He is the Father, and we are His children." See, for example, 1 John 3:2, "Beloved, now are we the sons of God;" and 1 John 5:2, "By this we know that we love the children of God, when we love God, and keep his commandments."

[82] Dick B., *The Oxford Group & Alcoholics Anonymous*, p. 117.

[83] See, for example, Matthew 10:20; 11:25; 12:50; 15:13; 18:35; 26:39; John 10:25; 12:28; 16:27; 17:24; Acts 1:4; 2:33; Romans 1:7; 1 Corinthians 8:6; Ephesians 2:18; Colossians 1:12; 1 Thessalonians 3:13; James 1:27; 1 Peter 1:17; 1 John 2:1.

[84] Big Book, pp. 67, 85, 88. See also p. 63: "May I do Thy will always." And pp. 86-87, "we ask God to direct our thinking. . . . We ask especially for freedom from self-will."

will and to surrender to His will. They said these ideas were often symbolized in the prayer, "Thy will be done."[85]

Finally, "Forgive us our debts" or "trespasses" clearly implies that God can and will "forgive;" and these concepts can be found in the Big Book, whether they came from the Lord's prayer or from other biblical sources such as the Book of James.[86]

The Sermon on the Mount—Matthew Chapters 5-7

This will not be a study of all of the Sermon on the Mount. We plan another book to trace into A.A. the entirety of those biblical ideas that appear to have influenced it. Here, therefore, we simply review some principal thoughts that Dr. Bob may have had in mind when he spoke of the Sermon and the philosophy of A.A. Dr. Bob studied a book on the Sermon by E. Stanley Jones, which outlined the Sermon's contents in this fashion:

1. The goal of life: To be perfect or complete as the Father in heaven is perfect or complete (5:48) with twenty-seven marks of this perfect life (5:1-47).

2. A diagnosis of the reason why men do not reach or move on to that goal: Divided personality (6:1-6; 7:1-6).

3. The Divine offer of an adequate moral and spiritual re-enforcement so that men can move on to that goal: The Holy Spirit to them that ask him (7:7-11).

4. After making the Divine offer he gathers up and emphasizes in two sentences our part in reaching that goal. Toward others—we are to do unto others as we would that they

---

[85] Wright, *The Will of God*, pp. 50-51; Macmillan, *Seeking and Finding*, p. 273; Samuel Moor Shoemaker, *Children of the Second Birth* (New York: Fleming H. Revell, 1927), pp. 58, 175-87; *If I Be Lifted Up* (New York: Fleming H. Revell, 1931), p. 93.

[86] Big Book, pp. 70, 86.

should do unto us (7:12); toward ourselves—we are to lose ourselves by entering the straight gate (7:13).

5. The test of whether we are moving on to that goal, or whether this Divine Life is operative within us: By their fruits (7:15-23).

6. The survival value of this new life and the lack of survival value of life lived in any other way: The house founded on rock and the house founded on sand (7:24-27).[87]

Matthew Chapter 5

1. *The Beatitudes*. The *Beatitudes* are in Matthew 5:3-11. The word "beatitudes" refers to the first word "Blessed" in each of these verses. Webster's Ninth New Collegiate Dictionary says "blessed" means "enjoying the bliss of heaven." "Bliss" is defined as "complete happiness." The word in the Greek New Testament from which "blessed" was translated means, according to Ethelbert Bullinger, a Greek Bible scholar, "happy."[88] *Vine's Expository Dictionary of Old and New Testament Words* explains the word "blessed" as follows: "In the beatitudes the Lord indicates not only the characters that are blessed, but the nature of that which is the highest good."[89] We have italicized Webster's definitions for the key words in each verse, quoting also the King James Version, which was the version Dr. Bob and Akron AAs most used.

The Sermon says: "Blessed" are: (v. 3) the poor (*humble*) in spirit: for theirs is the kingdom of heaven; (v. 4) they that mourn (*feel grief or sorrow*): for they shall be comforted; (v. 5) the meek (*enduring injury with patience and without resentment*); for they

---

[87] E. Stanley Jones, *The Christ of the Mount* (New York: The Abingdon Press, 1931), pp. 36-37.

[88] Ethelbert W. Bullinger, *A Critical Lexicon and Concordance to the English and Greek New Testament* (Michigan: Zondervan Publishing House, 1981), p. 104.

[89] W. E. Vine, *Vine's Expository Dictionary of Old and New Testament Words*. Vol. I (New York: Fleming H. Revell, 1981), p. 132-33.

shall inherit the earth; (v. 6) they which do hunger and thirst after righteousness (*acting in accord with divine law*): for they shall be filled; (v. 7) the merciful (*compassionate*): for they shall obtain mercy; (v. 8) the pure (*spotless, stainless*) in heart: for they shall see God; (v. 9) the peacemakers: for they shall be called the children of God; (v. 10) they which are persecuted for righteousness sake (*acting in accord with divine or moral law*): for theirs is the kingdom of heaven; (v. 11) ye when men shall revile you, and persecute you, and shall say all manner of evil against you falsely, for my sake (*because of me*): for great is your reward in heaven: for so persecuted they the prophets which were before you.

Did Dr. Bob, Anne, or Henrietta study these verses and extract and utilize them?[90] We do not know. But we do see some ideas common to A.A. ideas in the phrases: (1) Humility; (2) Suffering and comfort; (3) Patience and tolerance to the end of eliminating resentment; (4) Harmonizing actions with God's will; (5) Compassion, which Webster defines as "sympathetic consciousness of others' distress together with a desire to alleviate;" (6) "Cleaning house;"[91] (7) Making peace; (8) Standing for and acting upon spiritual principles because they are God's principles, whatever the cost. We can see Twelve Step ideas in the Beatitudes; and we believe A.A. founders probably saw them too.

----

[90] Dr. Bob and his wife, and Bill and his wife, and Henrietta all read Chambers' *My Utmost For His Highest*; and Chambers says at page 207, "the Beatitudes contain the dynamite of the Holy Ghost. . . . The Sermon on the Mount is not a set of rules and regulations: it is a statement of the life we will live when the Holy Spirit is getting His way with us."

[91] In *My Utmost For His Highest*, Chambers wrote: "the pure in heart see God. . . . If we are going to retain personal contact with the Lord Jesus Christ, it will mean there are some things we must scorn to do or to think, some legitimate things we must scorn to touch" (p. 86). Dr. Frank Buchman used the verse "blessed are the pure in heart, for they shall see God," in the context of getting people to change—to "hate sin, confess sin, and forsake sin." See A. J. Russell, *For Sinners Only* (London: Hodder & Stoughton, 1932), p. 63. This was part of the 5 C process of life-changing. See also *The Runner's Bible*, at page 77: "The pure in heart see only God. . . . only Good, hence their conversation is not of evil, of imperfection, destruction, death; but of things that are perfect, that make for peace and happiness and spiritual growth."

2. *Letting your light shine.* The verses in Matthew 5:13-16 extol glorifying the Heavenly Father by letting others see your good works. The suggestion is that "letting your light shine" is not to glorify yourself, but rather to glorify God by letting others see the spiritual walk in action—see the immediate results of surrender to the Master.[92] Perhaps these verses found their way into the Big Book's statement: "Our real purpose is to fit ourselves to be of maximum service to God" (p. 77). But we have discovered no evidence on that point.

3. *The Law of Love in action.* In Matthew 5:17-47, Jesus confirms the Law of Love as fulfilling the Old Testament Law and the Ten Commandments. He rejects anger without cause, unresolved wrongs to a brother, quibbling with an adversary, lust and impurity, adultery, retaliation, and hatred of an enemy. We won't discuss these ideas in detail because many are covered in our discussion of the Twenty Eight Oxford Group principles.[93] But certain of these verses appear to have made their mark on A.A. language: (1) Overcoming resentments;[94] (2) Making

---

[92] See *The Upper Room* for April, May, June, 1935 (Nashville: Methodist Episcopal Church South), verse for May 2nd.

[93] See Dick B., *The Oxford Group & Alcoholics Anonymous*, pp. 111-296.

[94] Matthew 5:21-22. See Holm, *The Runner's Bible*, p. 82, for discussion.

restitution;[95] (3) Avoidance of retaliation for wrongdoing by others;[96] and (4) Making peace with our enemies.[97]

Matthew Chapter 6

1. *Anonymity.* Matthew 6:1-8, 16-18, dealing with almsgiving "in secret," praying "in secret," fasting "in secret," avoidance of "vain repetitions," and hypocrisy, may possibly have had something to do with A.A.'s spiritual principle of anonymity. Jesus said, "for your Father knoweth what things ye have need of, before ye ask him" and "thy Father, which seeth in secret, shall reward thee openly." The vain practices Jesus was condemning were not practices that walked the ways of God, but practices that focused on inflation of self—something A.A. disdains.[98] However, we have no evidence that these verses were an actual source of A.A.'s anonymity principle.

---

[95] Matthew 5:23-24 reads: "Therefore if thou bring thy gift to the altar, and there rememberest that thy brother hath ought against thee; leave there thy gift before the altar, and go thy way; first be reconciled to thy brother, and then come and offer thy gift." Oxford Group writers commonly cited this verse in connection with their writings on restitution. See Benson, *The Eight Points of the Oxford Group*, p. 30; Russell, *For Sinners Only*, p. 120; Leslie D. Weatherhead, *Discipleship* (London: Student Christian Movement Press, 1934), p. 113; Macmillan, *Seeking and Finding*, p. 176; Samuel M. Shoemaker, *The Conversion of the Church* (New York: Fleming H. Revell, 1932), pp. 47-48; *DR. BOB*, p. 308. Matthew 5:25 says: "Agree with thine adversary quickly." As stated, Dr. Bob used and recommended Nora Smith Holm's *The Runner's Bible*; and Dr. Bob, Bill, and Henrietta all read and used Oswald Chambers' *My Utmost For His Highest*. Both *The Runner's Bible* at page 67, and *My Utmost For His Highest* at page 182, stressed this verse in connection with making amends. *My Utmost For His Highest* also referred to Matthew 5:26—paying "the uttermost farthing"—with regard to the amends concept (p. 183).

[96] Matthew 5:38-41; See Chambers, *My Utmost For His Highest*, p. 196, for discussion; and see Big Book, pp. 62, 77-78.

[97] Matthew 5:43-47; See *The Upper Room* for May 22, 1935, for discussion; and see Big Book, pp. 77-78, 103, 135.

[98] Big Book, pp. 62, 292. See Ernest Kurtz, *Not-God*. Expanded ed. (Minnesota: Hazelden, 1991), pp. 20-21.

2. *Forgiveness*. Matthew 6:14-15 stressed forgiving men their trespasses; and Emmet Fox makes some emphatic statements about these verses which may well have influenced the A.A. amends process. He wrote:

> The forgiveness of sins is the central problem of life. . . . It is, of course, rooted in selfishness. . . . We must positively and definitely extend forgiveness to everyone to whom it is possible that we can owe forgiveness, namely, to anyone who we think can have injured us in any way. . . . When you hold resentment against anyone, you are bound to that person by a cosmic link, a real, tough metal chain. You are tied by a cosmic tie to the thing that you hate. The one person perhaps in the whole world whom you most dislike is the very one to whom you are attaching yourself by a hook that is stronger than steel.[99]

We are not aware of any proof that Fox's writing on this point found its way into the Big Book; for many other writers that were read by AAs used similar language as to forgiveness of enemies.[100] Nor is the Sermon on the Mount the only place in the New Testament where forgiveness is stressed. Thus, after Christ had accomplished remission of past sins, Paul wrote in Colossians 4:13:

> Forbearing one another, and forgiving one another, if any man have a quarrel against any; even as Christ forgave you, so also do ye.

---

[99] Fox, *The Sermon on the Mount*, pp. 183-88. Compare Big Book, page 66: "It is plain that a life which includes deep resentment leads only to futility and unhappiness. . . . We found that it is fatal. . . . If we were to live, we had to be free of anger. The grouch and the brainstorm were not for us. They may be the dubious luxury of normal men, but for alcoholics these things were poison."

[100] See, for example, Glenn Clark, *I Will Lift Up Mine Eyes* (New York: Harper & Row, 1937), p. 32: "Your first duty is to forgive others. Turn to all those who have trespassed against you and forgive them. . . . So, first of all, take up these sins that others have committed against you, and forgive them one by one. Forgive them completely and utterly."

As we pointed out, Henrietta Seiberling taught her children 1 John 4:20:

> If a man say I love God, and hateth his brother, he is a liar; for he that loveth not his brother whom he hath seen, how can he love God whom he hath not seen.

In any event, the Big Book states at page 77:

> The question of how to approach the man we hated will arise. It may be he has done us more harm than we have done him and, though we may have acquired a better attitude toward him, we are still not too keen about admitting our faults. Nevertheless, with a person we dislike, we take the bit in our teeth. It is harder to go to an enemy than to a friend, but we find it more beneficial to us. We go to him in a helpful *and forgiving spirit*, confessing our former ill feeling and expressing our regret. Under no condition do we criticize such a person or argue. Simply we tell him that we will never get over drinking until we have done our utmost to straighten out the past (emphasis ours).

3. *Seek ye first the kingdom of God.* Matthew 6:24-34 seems to have had tremendous influence on A.A. Its substance is that man will be taken care of if he seeks God first and puts God's commandments first. Verse 33 says:

> But seek ye first the kingdom of God, and his righteousness; and all these things shall be added unto you.

As previously discussed, Dr. Bob emphasized the A.A. slogans "Easy Does It" and "First Things First."[101] When he was asked the meaning of "First Things First," he replied, "Seek ye first the kingdom of God and His righteousness, and all these things shall be added unto you."[102] He told his sponsee, Clarence S., that

---

[101] *DR. BOB*, p. 192. See Big Book, p. 135.

[102] *DR. BOB*, p. 144.

"First Things First" came from Matthew 6:33 in the Sermon on the Mount. And this verse was widely quoted in the books that Dr. Bob and the Akron AAs read and recommended.[103] On page 60, the Big Book states A.A.'s solution: "God could and would if He were sought." We believe the concept of "seeking" results by reliance on God instead of self is a bedrock idea in the Big Book and appears to have been much influenced by the "seeking God first" idea in Matthew 6:33. We say this because Dr. Bob emphasized the verse and seemed to put God first in his own life, as did his wife.

Matthew Chapter 7

1. *Taking your own inventory.* Much of A.A.'s Fourth, Ninth, Tenth, and Eleventh Step procedures involve looking for your own part, for your own fault, as part of the house-cleaning and life-changing process which, in Appendix II of the Third Edition of the Big Book, became described as "the personality change sufficient to bring about recovery from alcoholism" (Big Book, p. 569).[104] Matthew 7:3-5 states:

And why beholdest thou the mote [speck] that is in thy brother's eye, but considerest not the beam [log] that is in thine own eye? Or how wilt thou say to thy brother, Let me pull the mote [speck] out of thine eye; and, behold, a beam [log] is in thine own eye. Thou hypocrite, first cast out the beam [log] out of thine own eye; and then shalt thou see clearly to cast out the mote [speck] out of thy brother's eye.

---

[103] Russell, *For Sinners Only*, p. 36; Clark, *The Soul's Sincere Desire*, p. 16; Samuel M. Shoemaker, *National Awakening* (New York: Harper & Brothers, 1936), p. 41; *A Young Man's View of the Ministry* (New York: Association Press, 1923), p. 80; Chambers, *My Utmost For His Highest*, p. 142; Holm, *The Runner's Bible*, p. 127; Mary Wilder Tileston, *Daily Strength for Daily Needs* (New York: Grossett & Dunlap, 1928), p. 327.

[104] See the inventory procedures described in the Big Book, pp. 67, 69-70, 76, 84, 86, 98.

These verses were very frequently cited by A.A.'s spiritual sources as biblical authority for self-examination and finding one's own part, one's own erroneous conduct in a relationship problem.[105]

2. *Ask, seek, knock.* Matthew 7:7-11 states:

Ask, and it shall be given you; seek, and ye shall find; knock, and it shall be opened unto you;
For every one that asketh receiveth; and he that seeketh findeth; and to him that knocketh it shall be opened.
Or what man is there of you, whom if his son ask bread, will he give him a stone?
Or if he ask a fish, will he give him a serpent?
If ye then, being evil, know how to give good gifts unto your children, how much more shall your Father which is in heaven give good things to them that ask him?

Shoemaker wrote:

Our part [in the crisis of self-surrender] is to ask, seek, knock. His [God's] part is to answer, to come, to open.[106]

The Runner's Bible has an entire chapter entitled, "Ask and Ye shall receive."[107] *My Utmost For His Highest* says about these verses beginning with Matthew 7:7

The illustration of prayer that Our Lord uses here is that of a good child asking for a good thing. . . . It is no use praying

---

[105] Samuel M. Shoemaker, *God's Control* (New York: Fleming H. Revell, 1939), pp. 62-72; Chambers, *My Utmost For His Highest*, pp. 169, 174; Russell, *For Sinners Only*, pp. 309-16; Geoffrey Allen, *He That Cometh* (New York: The Macmillan Company, 1932), p. 140; Kitchen, *I Was A Pagan*, p. 110-11.

[106] Shoemaker, *Realizing Religion*, p. 32.

[107] Holm, *The Runner's Bible*, pp. 59-65.

unless we are living as children of God. Then, Jesus says—"Everyone that asketh receiveth."[108]

We believe the following paragraph from the Big Book indicates a possible influence of these verses on A.A.:

God will constantly disclose more to you and to us. Ask Him in your morning meditation what you can do each day for the man who is still sick. The answers will come *if your own house is in order*. But obviously you cannot transmit something you haven't got. *See to it that your relationship with Him is right*, and great events will come to pass for you and countless others. This is the Great Fact for us (emphasis added).[109]

In this same vein, Dr. Bob's wife, Anne, had written in her workbook:

We can't give away what we haven't got. We must have a genuine contact with God in our present experience. Not an experience of the past, but an experience in the present—actual, genuine.[110]

3. *He that doeth the will of my Father*. The author believes that the bottom line, in terms of what A.A. might have derived from the Sermon on the Mount, can be found in Matthew 7:21:

Not every one that saith unto me, Lord, Lord, shall enter into the kingdom of heaven; but he that doeth the will of my Father which is in heaven.[111]

---

[108] Chambers, *My Utmost For His Highest*, p. 237. See also our discussion of James 4:3, as to asking amiss to consume it on self.

[109] Big Book, p. 164.

[110] Dick B., *Anne Smith's Spiritual Workbook*, p. 60.

[111] See Henry Drummond, *The Ideal Life* (New York: Hodder & Stoughton, 1897), p. 243; Wright, *The Will of God*, p. 43; Allen, *He That Cometh*, p. 140.

The author believes that the Big Book offered and described a path to a relationship with God.[112] We believe also that the path involved the removal and destruction of the blocks to the relationship—the removal of self-will, selfishness, and self-centeredness—sins, as they were called in the Oxford Group and in early A.A.[113] The end was surrendering to and doing "the will of the Father"—God.[114]

Some may find themselves asking how valid it is to relate phrases, verses, and concepts in the Sermon on the Mount to similar ideas in the Big Book. One oldtimer in the author's A.A. community frequently circulates a card showing the number of different religions and belief systems which contain ideas similar

---

[112] The Big Book says, on page 58, "Rarely have we seen a person fail who has thoroughly followed our *path*" (emphasis added). On page 59, it says, "Here are the *steps* we took. . . ." (emphasis added). On page 28, it says, "all of us, whatever our race, creed, or color are children of a *living Creator with whom we may form a relationship* upon simple and understandable terms as soon as we are willing and honest enough to try" (emphasis added). And on page 29, "Each individual, in the personal stories, *describes* in his own language and from his own point of view *the way he established his relationship with God*" (emphasis added). The author believes the steps describe the Big Book's path to a relationship with God. Many of A.A.'s spiritual source books carry a message as to how to establish a relationship with God; and they use that phrase. See Weatherhead, *Discipleship*, p. 18; Walter, *Soul-Surgery*, p. 72; Brown, *The Venture of Belief*, p. 11; Benson, *The Eight Points of the Oxford Group*, pp. 48, 92; Macmillan, *Seeking and Finding*, p. 99; Kitchen, *I Was A Pagan*, p. 113; Samuel M. Shoemaker, *Children of the Second Birth* (New York: Fleming H. Revell, 1927), p. 16; Oswald Chambers, Studies in the Sermon on the Mount (London: Simpkin, Marshall, Ltd., n.d.), p. 48. Anne Smith wrote at page 37 of her spiritual workbook, "A stronger power than his was needed. God provided the power through Christ, so that we could find a new kind of relationship with God."

[113] See Big Book, pp. 14, 60-62, 64, 71. For an excellent comparable discussion of the need for removal of the blocks of self-will, self-seeking, self-centeredness, self-sufficiency, and self management—getting self out of the way, see Kitchen, *I Was A Pagan*, pp. 39, 69-71, 81, 87; Foot, *Life Began Yesterday*, pp. 9, 47, 67. See *Pass It On*, p. 197.

[114] As to "Thy will be done," see Big Book, pp. 67, 88. And see p. 59—"praying only for knowledge of His will for us and the power to carry that out." Compare Kitchen, *I Was A Pagan*: "'I am the master of my fate' gave way to 'Thine is the kingdom and the power.' 'Thy will be done' was substituted for 'I am the captain of my soul'" (p. 67).

to the language in the "Golden Rule."[115] But we are not seeking in this study to ascertain the compatibility of A.A. ideas with those of specific religions or specific belief systems, nor to establish their acceptability to all religions. For in many instances today, the trend is in exactly the opposite direction as far as analyses go.[116] But we do take A.A.'s founders at their word. Dr. Bob stressed the Bible as the primary source of A.A. ideas, the Sermon as containing A.A.'s underlying philosophy, and Matthew 5-7 as "required reading." Bill stressed the Oxford Group in general and Shoemaker in particular as the primary source; and neither source was scanty in its references to the Sermon on the Mount.[117] For

---

[115] Matthew 7:12.

[116] For example, one Christian physician decries A.A as a solution to alcoholism, stating: "There are two primary reasons I oppose sending the non-Christian to the recovery industry. He will be told his sin is sickness; he will never be confronted with his real and most basic moral and spiritual problems. And he will more than likely be introduced to the *any god* of Twelve Stepdom, who is, by Biblical criteria, a false god. These are the very same reasons I oppose utilizing the recovery industry for Christians. Where in Scripture do we find the rationalization, 'Don't call this or that what it really is (sin) because someone may be unbelieving or reject the truth?' Nowhere! Where in Scripture do we find Christians telling non-Christians that any god will do?" See William L. Playfair, M.D., *The Useful Lie* (Illinois: Crossway Books, 1991), pp. 174-175. The contrast to this kind of Christian criticism of A.A. can be found in the writings of those who criticize A.A. for its "religiosity" and who favor *secular* alternatives to A.A. See, for example, Charles Bufe, *Alcoholics Anonymous. Cult or Cure?* (San Francisco: Sharp Press, 1991). Then, there are the Christian writers who endeavor to harmonize Twelve Step ideas with Christianity. See, for example, Paul Barton Doyle, *In Step With God* (Tennessee: New Directions, 1989). Doyle states: "The consistency of these steps [Twelve Steps] with New Testament teaching makes it possible to use them without any fear of their leading to a violation of the Word of God. . . . I am convinced that A.A.'s 12 step program was inspired primarily by the Holy Bible, especially New Testament teaching." See Doyle, *In Step With God*, pp. 1, 3. Finally, there are Christian writers who distinguish present-day A.A. concepts from Christian principles, but conclude A.A. has useful ideas and a successful program in spite of their objections. See Tim Stafford, "The Hidden Gospel of the 12 Steps," *Christianity Today*, July 22, 1991.

[117] See, for example, Foot, *Life Began Yesterday*, p. 142; Allen, *He That Cometh*, p. 139; Macmillan, *Seeking and Finding*, p. 273; *What Is The Oxford Group?*, pp. 47-48; Samuel M. Shoemaker, *National Awakening*, p. 41; *God's Control*, p. 63; *Realizing Religion* (New York: Association Press, 1923), pp. 42-43, 46, 51; *The Church Can Save The World* (New York: Harper & Brothers, 1938), p. 100.

these reasons, therefore, we have done our best to show the ideas in the Sermon most likely to have found their way to A.A.

The Four Absolutes

Bill Wilson said he had heard plenty about the Four Absolutes at the Oxford Group meetings he attended.[118] However, he and Lois left the Oxford Group in the fall of 1937. And by October 30, 1940, Bill had developed a list of some eight objections he had to the Oxford Group as far as alcoholics were concerned. Item 3 read as follows:

> The principles of honesty, purity, unselfishness, and love are as much a goal for A.A. members and are as much practiced by them as by any other group of people; yet we found that when the word "absolute" was put in front of these attributes, they either turned people away by the hundreds or gave a temporary spiritual inflation resulting in collapse.[119]

That was Bill's opinion.

But in 1948, when Dr. Bob gave to A.A. his last major address, he spoke very favorably about the Four Absolutes, stating:

> The four absolutes, as we called them, were the only yardsticks we had in the early days, before the Steps. I think the absolutes still hold good and can be extremely helpful. I have found at times that a question arises, and I want to do the right thing, but the answer is not obvious. Almost always, if I measure my decision carefully by the yardsticks of absolute honesty, absolute unselfishness, absolute purity, and absolute love, and it checks up

---

[118] *Pass It On*, p. 127.

[119] *Pass It On*, pp. 171-73.

pretty well with those four, then my answer can't be very far out
of the way. If, however, I do that and I'm still not too satisfied
with the answer, I usually consult with some friend whose
judgment, in this particular case, would be very much better than
mine.[120] But usually the absolutes can help you to reach your
own personal decision without bothering friends.[121]

In an interview with the author in June of 1991, Dr. Bob's
daughter, Sue Smith Windows, stated she felt her father tried to
live by those absolutes throughout his life and that her mother did
also.

As we have shown, the Four Absolutes were spoken of with
frequency in Akron before the Big Book was written; they were
spoken of with favor by Dr. Bob up to the time of his farewell
message; and they are still publicized and spoken of with favor in
the Akron area and in a few other areas such as Cleveland. And
we think it fair to say that the influence of the Four Absolutes on
A.A. came primarily from the emphasis they were given by Akron
AAs. What was that influence?

1. *Absolute honesty.* Virtually the first message that Bill Wilson
got from his "sponsor" and Oxford Group friend, Ebby Thatcher,
concerned the Four Absolutes and particularly Absolute Honesty.
Ebby told Bill what Rowland Hazard had told him; and *Pass It On*
recorded the point as follows:

Rowland impressed upon him [Ebby] the four principles of the
Oxford Group: absolute honesty, absolute purity, absolute
unselfishness, absolute love. "He was particularly strong in

---

[120] Compare Eleanor Napier Forde, *The Guidance of God* (Oxford: Printed at the
University Press by John Johnson, Printer to the University, 1930), p. 21: "The fifth
signpost, 'What say others to whom God speaks?' is the unwritten law of fellowship."
On page 31 of her spiritual workbook, Anne wrote, "What makes us ineffective: . . .
unwillingness to check plans with someone else."

[121] *The Co-Founders of Alcoholics Anonymous* (New York: Alcoholics Anonymous
World services, Inc., 1972. 1975), pp. 12-13.

advocating absolute honesty," Ebby said. "Honesty with yourself, honesty with your fellowman, honesty with God." And these things he followed himself, and thereby, by example, he made me believe in them again as I had as a young man" (p. 114).

In a *Grapevine* article, Bill confirmed that such emphasis on honesty continued to the time of his writing of the Twelve Steps. He outlined the existing six principles, as he then saw them, two of which said:

We got honest with ourselves.
We got honest with another person in confidence.[122]

As to absolute honesty, Dr. Bob said in his last address:

Suppose we have trouble taking the First Step; we can't get quite honest enough to admit that John Barleycorn really has bested us.[123]

We believe the Big Book's repeated emphasis on rigorous honesty came straight from the Four Absolutes of the Oxford Group. See, for example, the three times that honesty is mentioned on page 58 of the Big Book—the first page of the Chapter, entitled "How It Works." And see the numerous other references in the Big Book to honesty.[124] "Rigorous honesty" said the Big Book at page 58. "Rigorous honesty" said the Big Book at page 145. The theme was the same throughout!

2. *Absolute purity.* In his last address, Dr. Bob saw this principle involved in the First Step. He said:

---

[122] *The Language of the Heart* (New York: The A.A. Grapevine, Inc., 1988), p. 200.

[123] *Co-Founders*, p. 13.

[124] Big Book, pp. xiv, xxvii, 13, 26, 28, 32, 44, 47, 55, 57-58, 63-65, 67, 70, 73, 83, 117, 140, 145.

The lack of absolute purity is involved here—purity of ideas, purity of motives.[125]

And as we have previously discussed, the Oxford Group saw the beatitude, "Blessed are the pure in heart for they shall see God," as the foundation for "hating, confessing, and forsaking" sin—the housecleaning process involved in the 5 C's. We believe this same housecleaning process is involved in A.A.'s Steps 4 through 9.

3. *Absolute unselfishness.* Dr. Bob said:

Absolute unselfishness includes the kind of service I have been talking about—not the dime or two bits to the bum, but actually giving of yourself.[126]

The Big Book says:

Helping others is the foundation stone of your recovery. A kindly act once in a while isn't enough. You have to act the Good Samaritan every day, if need be (p. 97).[127]

Similar language emphasizing selfless giving can be found throughout the Big Book.[128] And, of course, the Big Book stresses that selfishness and self-centeredness are the root of the alcoholic's spiritual malady.[129]

---

[125] *Co-Founders*, p. 13.

[126] *Co-Founders*, p. 13.

[127] There are frequent references to the story of the Good Samaritan in Oxford Group writings. See, for example, Foot, *Life Began Yesterday*, pp. 177-80; and Shoemaker, *Realizing Religion*, p. 80.

[128] Big Book, pp. 89, 94-95, 97, 102.

[129] Big Book, p. 62. In "Bill's Story," Bill Wilson wrote: "Simple, but not easy; a price had to be paid. It meant destruction of self-centeredness" (Big Book, p. 14).

4. *Absolute Love*. We have adequately discussed the Big Book's emphasis on love. But we would add that *What Is The Oxford Group?* said very simply that Absolute Love is best lived by the principles of 1 Corinthians 13.[130] The significance of 1 Corinthians 13 to Dr. Bob, to Akron, and to A.A. has already been covered. But we will close with this excerpt from Dr. Bob's last major talk at Detroit, Michigan in December, 1948:

> As you well know, absolute love incorporates all else. It is very difficult to have absolute love. I don't think any of us will ever get it, but that doesn't mean we can't *try* to get it. It was extremely difficult for me to love my fellow-man. I didn't dislike him, but I didn't love him, either. Unless there was some special reason for caring, I was just indifferent to him. I would be willing to give him a little bit *if* it didn't require much effort. I never would injure him at all. But love him? For a long time, I just couldn't do it.
>
> I think I overcame this problem to some extent when I was forced to do it, because I had to either love this fellow or attempt to be helpful to him, or I would probably get drunk again. Well, you could say that was just a manifestation of selfishness, and you'd be quite correct. I was selfish to the extent of not wanting Bob hurt; so, to keep from getting Bob hurt, I would go through the motions of trying to be helpful to the other fellow. Debate it any way you want to, but the fact remains that the average individual can never acquire absolute love.[131]

In his short farewell address to AAs, Dr. Bob was still seeing things in their simplest form and still seeing them in terms of loving and being of help. He said:

---

[130] *What Is The Oxford Group?*, p. 107. Compare Shoemaker, *Realizing Religion*, p. 50.

[131] *Co-Founders*, p. 13.

Our Twelve Steps, when simmered down to the last, resolve themselves into the words "love" and "service."[132]

Akron emphasized the Oxford Group's four absolute standards—honesty, purity, unselfishness, and love, which were grounded, in part, in the Sermon on the Mount. Its favorites were "God is love" and "faith without works is dead." It stressed the Bible itself, quiet time, prayer, guidance, healing, the surrender technique of James, the "seek ye first" message of the Sermon, the "doeth the will of the Father" message of Matthew, and the "humble yourselves" approach of James. It utilized the Lord's Prayer and, inevitably, "Thy will be done." It focussed on the patience, tolerance, kindness, and love message of 1 Corinthians 13. It taught reconciliation, forgiveness, and tolerance as expressed in the Sermon. Were these basic Bible ideas part of, or did they exemplify Akron as A.A.'s taproot? None of these principles came from Akron alone. They can be found in the Oxford Group-Shoemaker circles traveled by Bill and his small New York band. But we believe they received their greatest study, stress, and support in the Akron alcoholic recovery arena in which Bill Wilson was also participant and promoter in the pre-Big Book years.

---

[132] *DR. BOB*, p. 338.

16

Conclusion

Summary—Akron a Special Place

The author believes Akron was a very special place for A.A. to be born and that Akron made some very special contributions to A.A. The contributions had long-lasting effects. They might never been possible in another location. And they certainly hadn't been made prior to June 10, 1935.

Religion had long offered to alcoholics a solution that worked. Throughout the ages, many alcoholics had—prior to 1935—been relieved of their alcoholism through religious experiences. William James established that. But religion often failed to reach the alcoholic in a way that made him feel comfortable. He may have been a sinner that needed to be saved. But even the saved alcoholic sinner could not always throw off his feelings of guilt and inadequacy in a religious atmosphere that sometimes "talked down" to drunks. Many a drunk continues drinking while yielding to the very spiritual inadequacies religion makes painfully and pointedly clear to him.

Medicine had also succeeded with alcoholics. But A.A.'s medical mentor, Dr. William Silkworth, said that medicine itself had no tool to effect the needed "psychic change," except "some

315

form of moral psychology."[1] Medicine could not and did not offer to the alcoholic the "divine help" that some medical people were, in the 1930's, conceding was the only solution to the seemingly hopeless cases.[2]

Much has been said of A.A.'s "spiritual solution;" and we believe it was defined and refined primarily with the spiritual tools that were developed by the experimentation of drunks with drunks in Akron. Let's review what the author believes was "special" about Akron.

In the 1930's, Akron was uniquely prepared to foster the program that was about to be born. The Firestone family was prominent there, and the alcoholic plight of one of its members was either very much known or would soon attract wide attention once the family's solution had been achieved. Jim Newton, who helped to bring the solution to Akron and to witness to it, was a youthful dynamo—in Florida, at Firestone Tire and Rubber, with Bud Firestone, and in Newton's own Oxford Group work which continues to this day. The Akron newspapers were the catalysts that made a witnessing attempt come alive in Akron. The message-carrying was done primarily by the Firestones and by an Oxford Group team. T. Henry, Clarace, Henrietta, Dr. Bob, and Anne all had urgent needs for life-changing experiences. And all ears were tuned to hear of a successful spiritual solution.

Akron's progenitors had a unique focus on helping drunks. T. Henry had expressed his compassion for them at any early age. Clarace was trained in and looking for a missionary goal. Henrietta's own needs began to be met in a significant way when she turned her attention to Dr. Bob's drinking and then to the problems of Akron alcoholics. Anne's need to overcome the family disease of alcoholism began to be met when she turned to the Oxford Group. Dr. Bob was focused on solving his drinking problem with a spiritual answer and was dedicated to that end when Bill arrived in Akron. Bill needed to avoid drinking by

---

[1] Big Book, pp. xxv-xxvii.

[2] Big Book, pp. 43, 571-72.

effectively carrying his spiritual message to another alcoholic. He had been taught in New York to do just that. But none of these elements had come together as a whole or was working in New York though many may have been present there. Akron, it seemed, was the place where the interests of all these people in helping drunks in a spiritual context could gel.

Akron provided a unique atmosphere for developing an effective spiritual solution to alcoholism. Its progenitors all possessed substantial capabilities and information in spiritual areas—the Bible, Christian belief systems, and the Oxford Group—where the spiritual path was to be fitted to the needs of alcoholics. All the progenitors dedicated their own homes to spiritual work with alcoholics. Their homes—those of Dr. Bob and Anne, T. Henry and Clarace, and Henrietta Seiberling—together with the homes of alcoholic squad members, Bill and Henrietta D., Wally and Annabelle G., Clarence and Dorothy S., Paul and Hildreth S., Tom and Maybelle L., and a number of others—were open to seemingly continuous meetings of and for alcoholics and their families. The broke and mostly jobless members of the alcoholic squad had the time and took the time to focus on a spiritual recovery program—one that stressed (1) prayer, (2) Bible study, (3) religious literature, and (4) Quiet Time listening. They had the time to fail and pick themselves up again as they experimented. And it took time for their efforts to succeed.

The Akronites offered splendid raw material that made Bill's writing of the Big Book a do-able project. They studied, knew, and believed the Bible. They were certain it contained spiritual answers as to the will and power of God. They exemplified service without thought of money or prestige. They learned to integrate their recovery ideas with hospitalization. They learned how to use their homes as centers for sober recovery. They utilized the Good Book with drunks in a way the author believes had not been done before, in the Oxford Group or elsewhere. The Bible was not used as an instrument of condemnation or preaching. In the Bible, the Akron people found and pointed to a God of love. From James and the Sermon on the Mount, they learned simple ideas for prayer.

From James, the Sermon, and 1 Corinthians, they gained specific ideas as to God's will concerning Himself and their fellow man. In James, they were enjoined to tap into God's power through prayer. From James, the Sermon, and particularly 1 Corinthians 13, they extracted some spiritual principles they found necessary to do God's will and to see that their relationship with Him was right. And from the Book of Acts, they found concrete illustrations of what First Century Christianity had accomplished through conversion, healing, and power when its apostles preached Jesus Christ as Lord and Savior and that God had raised him from the dead.[3] Anne Smith wrote and taught of these concepts in her Spiritual Workbook. The concepts concerned a gospel that Paul called "the power of God unto salvation to every one that believeth."[4]

The author believes Akron's unique spiritual resources crystallized many ideas that A.A. needed for its early successes.

---

[3] See Acts 4:10; 2:36, 38; 5:30-32, 42; 10:38-42.

[4] See Romans 1:16; 10:9-10. In Jack Winslow, *Why I Believe In The Oxford Group* (London: Hodder & Stoughton, 1934), Winslow said at page 17, "The Oxford Group has no new Gospel to proclaim. I wish for no other Gospel than that which the Apostles taught in the first Christian age, and which the Christian Church has taught from their days until ours. That is 'the power of God unto salvation to all who believe' and no new Gospel has taken its place." See Glenn Clark, *Touchdowns For The Lord* (Minnesota: Macalester Park Publishing Company, 1947). Clark had no connection with the Oxford Group. His books and ideas were favorites of Dr. Bob's and in early A.A.; and Dr. Bob and Anne attended and loved his "Camp Farthest Out." In *Touchdowns*, Clark said, "The Gospel Team work of that era ["Dad" Elliot's] was also a powerful instrument in influencing boys and young men to accept Jesus Christ as their Savior and Lord" (p. 44). At pages 55-57, Clark wrote: "Paul said, 'If thou shalt confess with thy mouth the Lord Jesus and shalt believe in thine heart that God hath raised him from the dead, thou shalt be saved' (Romans 10:9). The noted psychologist, William James, said, 'If you have an impulse and wish to make it permanent, seal it with the hardest, most difficult physical expression that is within your power to make.' . . . The student must feel the burden of his individual and social guilt and his need of salvation. . . . He must be brought to sincere repentance for *all* known sins; confession, forgiveness, assurance of salvation and full restitution that is within the power of the penitent to make, are absolutely necessary. 'Christ must be the Lord of all or He cannot be the Lord at all.' (Lamb). . . . Those principles enunciated by Paul and William James are sound and fundamental. A choice has to be made, action has to be taken."

From the Sermon on the Mount, Akron AAs learned to seek God first. From James they gained strong ideas about humility, prayer, healing, and "works" (service). From the books of the Bible they considered "absolutely essential," they learned principles for "cleaning house" of the things that had blocked them from God. They learned from the Sermon on the Mount to look for the log in their own eye before criticizing the speck in their brother's eye. From James, they learned to "confess" their own shortcomings. From the Lord's Prayer, they extracted ideas for surrendering to God's will, saying, "Thy will be done." From the Sermon they determined that God expected them to *correct* their wrongs, to forgive, and to reconcile with their brother *before* they went to the "altar." The Sermon specified the shortcomings as to which they were, with God's help, to seek removal. And all three "essential" books, Matthew 5-7, James, and particularly 1 Corinthians 13, showed them the principles they felt obliged to practice—patience, tolerance, kindness, forgiveness, and love.

Akron birthed and trained recovered alcoholics who carried the message of experience, strength and hope far beyond Dr. Bob's home and T. Henry's living room. True, people sent drunks to Dr. Bob from afar, and he helped them in Akron. But Bill disseminated the message from New York. Clarence S. (Dr. Bob's sponsee) and his wife, Dorothy S. M., along with Abby G. (who "joined" in Akron) and his wife, Grace G., moved the message in Cleveland where "results were of the best."[5] Earl T., who was "soundly indoctrinated by Dr. Bob and the Akronites," returned home to Chicago and eventually established a solid nucleus from which A.A.'s great growth could issue.[6] And Archie T., who "had been tenderly nursed back to sobriety in the home of Dr. Bob and Anne at Akron" set the stage in Detroit for its huge membership of later years.[7]

---

[5] *Alcoholics Anonymous Comes of Age* (New York: Alcoholics Anonymous World Services, Inc., 1957), pp. 19-22.

[6] *Alcoholics Anonymous Comes of Age*, pp. 22-23.

[7] *Alcoholics Anonymous Comes of Age*, p. 24.

Akron made the initial decision on, warmly supported the writing in, and contributed a large majority of the personal stories to the Big Book—the basic text which made the world-wide dissemination of A.A.'s message possible. Akron's support continued. Dr. Bob spent enormous amounts of time with the 5,000 alcoholics he helped in the ten years after the Big Book's publication. He also offered substantial and continuing support and counsel to Bill. In 1948, when Dr. Bob made his last major address to A.A., those present listened with respect to his words about A.A.'s beginnings in Akron, about the books of the Bible that produced A.A.'s basic ideas, and about the Oxford Group practices that provided the program's structure. Bill himself never stopped acknowledging A.A.'s debt to T. Henry, Clarace, Henrietta, Anne, and Dr. Bob.

Today's Challenge from an Historical Standpoint

Today, A.A. numbers its members in the millions. Its geographic outreach is world-wide. Its adherents include people of many faiths and many religions, some with no faith, and many with no religion. Its principles, program, and success are certainly not anonymous. Anonymity reposes, for the most part, with its members—who appear more than ever to subscribe to the belief that anonymity is the spiritual foundation of all A.A.'s traditions, challenging members to place principles before personalities.

But with all its rapid growth, large numbers, universal outreach, and diversity, A.A. today faces a challenge. We here mention again the phrase that A.A.'s current archivist often quotes in his extensive travels:

Whenever a society or civilization fails, there is always one condition present. They forgot where they came from.

Have AAs *and others* forgotten where A.A. came from?

A good example of the loss of historical perspective about A.A. can be found in this statement in *The Useful Lie*, a book which seems designed to steer Christians away from A.A. The author of that book states:

> Those *acknowledged* by A.A. to be the most important in shaping the many religious aspects of A.A. were anything but Christian believers in the orthodox sense.[8]

We hope our book will shed historical light on the accuracy of that statement.

Tim Stafford wrote in *Christianity Today*:

> The spiritual roots of the 12 steps are complex, tangled between experience-oriented evangelical Christianity and secularizing, psychological tendencies of American religious pluralism. Understanding how these sources produced the 12 Steps can help Christians know how to interact with them today.[9]

We hope our book will help Christians understand A.A.'s Akron roots before they make an historical judgment about what A.A.'s spiritual roots produced.

Dennis Morrein made the following assumptions about some amendments made in the Big Book's manuscript before it went to the printer. He pointed to the deletions of the word "God" in Step Two and the words "on our knees" from Step Seven. He pointed to the insertion of the words "as we understood Him" in Steps Three and Eleven. Morreim then states in *Changed Lives*:

> These final concessions to those who were atheists or agnostics broadened the spectrum so that more people who suffered from alcoholism could use the Twelve Steps regardless of their spiritual

---

[8] William L. Playfair, M.D., *The Useful Lie* (Illinois: Crossway Books, 1991), p. 95.

[9] Tim Stafford, "The Hidden Gospel of the 12 Steps" (*Christianity Today*, July 22, 1991), p. 14.

faith or lack of it. Certainly God was present in the Steps, but God was expressed in such terms that anyone, anyone at all, could accept and apply to his or her life.[10]

We hope our book will help readers determine from A.A.'s early history in Akron whether the AAs in that time period and in that setting ever were thinking along the lines Morreim suggests. Did they really intend people with lack of faith to use the steps without gaining faith? Was the God who was referred to specifically 220 times in the Big Book just an "any god" for "anyone" to accept and apply? We hope our book will put such questions in an historical context, whatever the answer may be in A.A. as it exists today.

Paul Barton Doyle stated the following in his book, *In Step With God*, concerning his beliefs about the Twelve Steps:

> The consistency of these steps with New Testament teaching makes it possible to use them without any fear of their leading to a violation of the Word of God.[11]

Doyle adds:

> This [Doyle's] manual was written to support the notion that the 12 step program has its roots in Christianity. Most existing 12 step programs go to great pains to stress and express spirituality rather than religion. Literature and language consistently refer to a "God of our Understanding," and/or "Higher Power." This manual was written for that element of the Christian community practicing a 12 Step Program.[12]

---

[10] Dennis C. Morreim, *Changed Lives* (Minneapolis: Augsburg Fortress, 1991), p. 106.

[11] Paul Barton Doyle, *In Step With God* (Tennessee: New Directions, 1989), p. 1.

[12] Doyle, *In Step With God*, p. 4.

Doyle then lays out twelve steps that insert the word "Christ" in Steps 2 and 3, delete "as we understood Him" from Steps 3 and 11, and add "Christian principles" to Step 12.

We hope our historical account of the Akron Genesis will help readers to evaluate the fruitfulness of attempts such as Doyle's [and there seem to be many today] to confirm the Twelve Steps, yet amend them by expressly inserting "Christ" and "Christian" language in those steps and discussions of them.[13] Can we look at Akron history and conclude that the basic ideas of the Steps are consistent with Christianity and capable of being utilized by Christians without having to adapt and amend the Steps with Christian words of art?

Charles Bufe writes in *Alcoholics Anonymous Cult or Cure?*:

> Still, remarkably little useful information about Alcoholics Anonymous is available to the public. . . . This has resulted in many false impressions becoming a part of "the conventional wisdom. . . ."[14]

> In order to understand Alcoholics Anonymous, it is first necessary to understand the movement which gave birth to A.A.: the Oxford Group movement. . . . Thus A.A.'s bible, *Alcoholics Anonymous*, the so-called Big Book, in large part reads like a piece of Oxford Group Movement literature, and the 12 Steps, the cornerstone of A.A. ideology, are for all intents and purposes a codification of Oxford Group principles.[15]

---

[13] See also A. Philip Parham, *Letting God. Christian Meditations For Recovering Persons* (New York: Harper & Row, 1987).

[14] Charles Bufe, *Alcoholics Anonymous Cult or Cure?* (San Francisco: Sharp Press, 1991), p. 9

[15] The problem with this statement is its factual and historical inaccuracy. First, Dr. Bob never met Oxford Group founder, Frank Buchman; apparently had no significant contact with Reverend Sam Shoemaker—an American Oxford Group leader to whom Bill Wilson gave credit for the Twelve Step ideas; and appears never to have credited the Oxford Group, Buchman, or Shoemaker with the basic ideas of A.A. Dr. Bob was emphatic that those ideas came from a study of the Bible and that A.A.'s underlying
(continued...)

Are the 12 Steps essential to recovery, and are alcoholics who reject them doomed to an early death from alcoholism? Fortunately, the answer is "no" to both parts of the question. If it were "yes," the many thousands of members of Secular Organizations for Sobriety, Rational Recovery, Women for Sobriety, and Men for Sobriety wouldn't be sober today, nor would the multitude—probably millions—of persons who have recovered from alcohol abuse without participating in *any* recovery program.[16]

In every respect, A.A.'s orientation passes the "duck" test: If it looks like a duck, waddles like a duck, and quacks like a duck, it's probably a duck. In this case the "duck" is A.A.'s religious nature.[17]

Despite ideological fossilization, it seems a foregone conclusion that A.A. will continue to expand both in the United States and abroad, not because it's an effective treatment for alcoholism—it isn't—but because its criteria for membership. . . . grows even

---

[15] (...continued)
philosophy was based on the Sermon on the Mount. Second, while Bill Wilson did state that A.A. got most of its ideas from the Oxford Group, as it was led in America by Sam Shoemaker, Wilson only met Frank Buchman once, and may have had very little personal contact with Sam Shoemaker before the Big Book was published. Wilson also stated frequently that A.A.'s ideas were ancient and universal ones—borrowed from many sources. Bufe devotes an entire chapter of his book to criticisms that were made about Dr. Frank Buchman over a period of many years. This appears to have been done so that Bufe could saddle A.A. with the burden of some bad publicity Frank Buchman had received over the years. For two other historical treatments of the incidents Bufe discussed, see: (1) Garth Lean, *On the Tail of a Comet* (Colorado Springs: Helmers & Howard, 1988)—a comprehensive biography of the life of Frank Buchman; and (2) Walter Houston Clark, *The Oxford Group: Its History and Significance* (New York: Bookman Associates, 1951)—a scholarly review of most of the matters Bufe discusses. In any event, neither history nor the facts will support the contention that A.A. ideas are merely a codification of Oxford Group principles and practices. They came from the Bible, from the Oxford Group, from non-Oxford Group Christian writings, and later from Roman Catholic influences stemming from Father Ed Dowling and Father John Ford, a Roman Catholic theologian.

[16] Bufe, p. 63. Bufe includes no citation supporting this statement.

[17] Bufe, p. 93.

broader, because it's developed a symbiotic relationship with the alcoholism treatment industry; because its religiosity and implied political quietism fit snugly into the existing social order; because it addresses (however inadequately) oftentimes real problems for which, all too frequently, no free or inexpensive alternative treatment is readily available; because it's widely and uncritically promoted in the media; because it provides relief from isolation and loneliness; and because it provides a quick and easy escape from the "torture" of critical thinking and individual decision-making—in other words, A.A. provides a substitute dependency, a quick and easy escape from the personal struggle necessary to achieve true independence from alcoholism.[18]

As well, the A.A. Steps almost certainly drive away far more alcoholics than they attract, and as noted in Chapter 5, they induce guilt, irrationality, and other-directness. For these reasons it seems probable that a set of steps embodying rational principles of recovery would be far more useful to recovering alcoholics than the strange melange of useful concepts and irrational religiosity offered in the 12 Steps of Alcoholics Anonymous.[19]

In the last decade of the 20th century, A.A. is a mass organization and one with great influence in both the United States and abroad. . . . The irony is that during its over 50 years of expansion and external changes, the core of A.A.'s program has remained virtually unchanged, and at present probably not one member in 100 of A.A. or other 12-Step groups has more than the foggiest concept of where the ideas contained in the 12-Step programs originated.[20]

Whether Bufe is right or wrong about A.A., we hope our book will help lift the fog from anyone—whether interested in a "secular

---

[18] Bufe, p. 120. Note that this paragraph contains no critique of A.A.'s emphasis on the power of God!

[19] Bufe, p. 128.

[20] Bufe, pp. 52-53.

alternative" or not—who wants to know where A.A.'s Twelve Step ideas originated.

The foregoing quotes present several different views, among them, those of: (1) a Christian who rejects the "any god" of A.A., (2) a Christian who believes A.A.'s ideas are religious and tangled, but useful, (3) Christians who think the ideas are just fine—even Christian—but need to have "Christ" added, and (4) an A.A. critic who doesn't like either A.A.'s history as he sees it or A.A.'s society as he finds it, believing that the Steps are neither Christian nor useful. All of the statements suggest a need for knowing just what AAs did study and believe as they worked together in what, in Akron, they themselves called a "Christian fellowship" and in what the Oxford Group called "A First Century Christian Fellowship" in New York and in Akron.

What the Founders Found

In his discussion of alcoholism at the beginning of the Big Book, Dr. William Silkworth pointed out that men and women drink essentially because they like the effect produced by alcohol. He went on to say that while they admit the sensation is injurious, they cannot after a time differentiate the true from the false. They are "restless, irritable and discontented," said Silkworth, unless they can again experience the ease and comfort that comes at once with a few drinks. The problem for the alcoholic is that the drinks produce disaster, a resolution not to drink again, and then still more drinking and disaster.[21] In his bottle, the real alcoholic finds only a false solution to his problem.

After a time, A.A.'s founders came to see the liquor, the bottle, and the drinking, as just symptoms of the real problem. The real problem, they said, was a spiritual malady, a spiritual

---

[21] Big Book, pp. xxvi-xxvii.

sickness, a spiritual disease. They called that malady selfishness—self-centeredness. They believed that the spiritual sickness produced states of anger, fear, dishonesty, and self-seeking that led inevitably to the very restlessness, irritability, and discontent that had previously led alcoholics to drink. They had sought to escape their self-inflicted spiritual misery through an illusory solution in the bottle.[22] The founders concluded they couldn't overcome the underlying self-centeredness by wishing or willing. They had to have God's help.[23]

In his very first book, published in 1923, Reverend Sam Shoemaker had written about the spritual malady—the spiritual misery. He said its root was estrangement from God—estrangement from Him in people that were made to be his companions. What was Shoemaker's solution? A bottle? No, Shoemaker implied, not even "rest cures and exercise and motor drives" will help. The answer, he said, could be found through religion. What you want, said Shoemaker, is "simply a vital religious experience. You need to find God. You need Jesus Christ."[24]

Some twelve years later, Bill and Dr. Bob agreed they needed the solution Shoemaker stressed—"a vital religious experience." And many years after that, Dr. Carl G. Jung explained the solution to Bill Wilson. Jung replied to a letter that Bill Wilson had written, and explained that man's craving for alcohol was the equivalent on a low level of the spiritual thirst of our being for wholeness, expressed in medieval language: *the union with God.* Jung quoted from the Bible to illustrate. He quoted Psalm 42:1: "As the hart panteth after the water brooks, so panteth my soul after thee, O God."[25]

---

[22] Big Book, pp. 61-64, 103.

[23] Big Book, p. 62.

[24] Samuel M. Shoemaker, *Realizing Religion* (New York: Association Press, 1923), pp. 4-5, 9.

[25] *Pass It On* (New York: Alcoholics Anonymous World Services, Inc., 1984), p. 384.

So, the solution, said Shoemaker, was finding God. The
solution, said Jung, was union with God. The solution, ultimately
said A.A.'s Big Book, was: "there is One who has all power—that
One is God. May you find Him now!"[26] Let's briefly take a look
at what A.A.'s founders had actually found before they decided at
Akron, Ohio, to write and publish their basic text, the Big Book.

When Bill Wilson reached his most desperate low point in
drinking, his alcoholic friend, Ebby Thatcher, popped on the
scene, "fresh-skinned and glowing," and "inexplicably different."
To Bill, who had theretofore been in a "bitter morass of self-pity,"
where he had found only loneliness and despair, Ebby carried a
message. Ebby said, "I've got religion." He shared with Bill, if
Bill cared to have it, that "God had done for him what he could
not do for himself."[27]

One has to work hard to piece together the facts as to
succeeding events. In fact, there are divergent accounts and
probably divergent views of the facts. But here are accounts from
eye witnesses: (1) Before long, Bill went to Calvary Mission,
"very drunk" and accompanied by a "Swede" named Johnson.
According to Billy Du Vall, the Assistant Superintendent, the
leader at the Mission meeting had just finished the Bible and
started to witness when Wilson insisted on speaking. Bill said that
if Ebby could get help there, he was sure he needed help and could
also get it at Calvary Mission.[28] (2) According to Bill Wilson's
own account, "There were hymns and prayers. Tex, the leader,
exhorted us. Only Jesus could save, he said. Certain men got up
and made testimonials. Numb as I was, I felt interest and
excitement rising. Then came the call. Penitents started marching
forward to the rail. Unaccountably impelled, I started too. . . .

---

[26] Big Book, p. 59.

[27] Big Book, pp. 8-11.

[28] This much is covered in two letters written to "Larry" by Billy Du Vall, the
Assistant Superintendent at Calvary Mission, who was present the night Bill Wilson made
the altar call. Copies of the two letters were obtained by the author from Bill Wilson's
home at Stepping Stones during the author's visit in August, 1992.

Soon I knelt among the sweating, stinking penitents. . . . Something touched me. I guess it was more than that. I was hit. I felt a wild impulse to talk. Jumping to my feet I began. Afterward, I could never remember what I said."[29] (3) According to Helen Smith Shoemaker, Reverend Sam Shoemaker's wife, and according to Bill's friend and Shoemaker's assistant, Reverend W. Irving Harris, Bill made a "decision for Christ" at the altar at Calvary Mission that night.[30] (4) Bill soon checked in to Towns Hospital where Dr. William D. Silkworth met him in the hall. Waving a bottle around, Bill said to Silkworth, "At last, Doc, I've found something."[31] (5) In a few days, Ebby visited Bill at Towns Hospital; and shortly thereafter, Bill had his famous "hot flash" religious experience. Bill's own words are as follows: "But what of the Great Physician? . . . If there be a Great Physician, I'll call on him." . . . [Bill did so, and said] "I became acutely conscious of a presence which seemed like a veritable sea of living spirit. I lay on the shores of a new world. 'This,' I thought, 'must be the great reality. The God of the preachers.'"[32] (6) Bill said, "For the first time I felt that I really belonged. I knew that I was loved and could love in return. I thanked my God who had given

---

[29] Bill Wilson, *W. G. Wilson Recollections*, a manuscript of Bill's dictation to Ed. B. on September 1, 1954, at the Hotel Bedford (Bedford Hills, N.Y.: Stepping Stones Archives), p. 121. The author inspected the manuscript during his visit to Bill's home at Stepping Stones in August, 1992. See also *Pass It On*, p. 118.

[30] In a telephone interview with the author from her home at Burnside in October, 1991, Reverend Sam Shoemaker's wife, Helen, said she was present when Bill made his decision for Christ at the Mission. In a memorandum typed by Reverend W. Irving Harris, friend of Bill Wilson and Assistant Minister at Calvary Church, Reverend Harris spoke of the same event and wrote: "and it was at a meeting at Calvary Mission that Bill himself was moved to declare that he had decided to launch out as a follower of Jesus Christ." See the Harris memorandum which was sent to the author by Mrs. Irving W. Harris, the full contents of which are set out in Dick B., *The Oxford Group & Alcoholics Anonymous* (Seattle: Glen Abbey Books, 1992), pp. 101-04.

[31] Wilson, *W. G. Wilson Recollections*, p. 124. *Pass It On* edited this account and added a statement by Silkworth that implied Bill had found something in two philosophy books. See p. 120.

[32] Wilson, *W. G. Wilson Recollections*, p. 129. A modified version of this quote is set forth in *Pass It On*, p. 121. Neither version is included in the Big Book.

me a glimpse of his absolute self."[33] (7) Bill then states, "For sure I'd been born again."[34] (8) In another manuscript located at Stepping Stones, entitled "Bill Wilson's Original Story," each line of which is numbered, Bill wrote at page 30, lines 966 to 969, "So then came the question—If I were no longer to be God then how was I to find and perfect the new relationship with my creator—with the Father of Lights who presides over all?"[35]

The foregoing statements, coming as they did either from eye witnesses or from the archives at Bill's own home at Stepping Stones, Bedford Hills, New York, indicate the following as to *what* Bill had found: (1) He had answered an altar call at Calvary Mission after hearing, "Jesus saves." (2) He knelt at the Mission altar and "made a decision for Christ." (3) He told Dr. Silkworth he had at last "found something." (4) At Towns Hospital, Bill called on the "Great Physician" for help. (5) He experienced what he believed to be the presence of God. (6) He said he felt he was loved and could love. (7) He said he had found the great reality—the God of the preachers. (8) He concluded positively that he had been "born again." (9) He then asked what he needed to do to find and perfect this new relationship with his creator—the "Father of Lights." Bill describes this Father in words identical to

---

[33] Wilson, *W. G. Wilson Recollections*, p. 129. The words in the September 1, 1954 manuscript at Stepping Stones Archives and in *Pass It On* at page 121 are identical. They were not included in the Big Book.

[34] Wilson, *W. G. Wilson Recollections*, p. 130. These words—"For sure, I'd been born again"—are Bill's exact words from the *W. G. Wilson Recollections*, September 1, 1954 manuscript at page 130. Another transcript of the September 1, 1954, dictations, also located at Stepping Stones Archives, contains identical words at page 103. Both were inspected by the author at Stepping Stones, and copies of both transcripts are in the author's possession. The quoted words were not included in the *Pass It On* account at page 121, nor in the Big Book.

[35] Bill Wilson, *Bill Wilson's Original Story*—a manuscript bearing no date, in which each line is numbered, going from line 1 to line 1180 (Bedford Hills, NY: Stepping Stones Archives), p. 30. The author obtained a copy of this manuscript from Bill's home at Stepping Stones during his October, 1991, visit there. The quote does not appear in *Pass It On* or in the Big Book.

those in James 1:17.[36] And note that Bill seems to have heard about the "Father of Lights" in New York in 1934 before he ever came to Akron and met Dr. Bob and Anne in 1935 and heard Anne reading from the Book of James.

Now let's try to determine what Dr. Bob found. In Dr. Bob's case, we cannot look for an answer to any such dramatic account of a religious experience as Bill's story. But we do know what Dr. Bob and his wife, Anne, frequently said about God. *DR. BOB and the Good Oldtimers* indicates Dr. Bob referred "simply and without ostentation to God."[37] And the earliest A.A.'s agreed that "Bob presented God to them as a God of love who was interested in their individual lives."[38] Dr. Bob's wife, Anne, was well remembered for reading and quoting from 1 John 4:8 that "God is love."[39] Both Dr. Bob and Anne were, of course, ardent Bible students and seemed very much to have found the God of love. But Bill Wilson seems also to have found and passed on this same conception of a loving God to the fellowship of Alcoholics Anonymous. In both the long and short forms of the Twelve Traditions that were adopted by A.A., Tradition 2 says: "For our group purpose there is but one ultimate authority—a loving God as He may express Himself in our group conscience."[40] And it was this God of love that the author found available to him when he came in the doors of Alcoholics Anonymous and saw on the wall of his second meeting, "God as we understood Him."[41]

---

[36] Interestingly, when this same phrase reached the Big Book some 4 years later, it had been rendered "Father of Light" at Big Book page 14. But Bill was still writing of this "Father of Light" who "presides over us all."

[37] DR. BOB, p. 228.

[38] *DR. BOB*, p. 110.

[39] *DR. BOB*, pp. 116-17; See a confirmation of this in Ernest Kurtz, *Not-God*. Expanded ed. (Minnesota: Hazelden, 1991), p. 55.

[40] Big Book, pp. 564-65.

[41] See the author's own story in Appendix 10 of this book, which explains how he related to "God as we understood Him."

And how was this loving God described in the Bible—the Good Book that was read and stressed so frequently in Akron, Ohio, during A.A.'s formative years?

Let's look at portions of Psalm 103:

> Bless the Lord, O my soul: and all that is within me, bless his holy name.
> Bless the Lord, O my soul, and forget not all his benefits;
> Who forgiveth all thine iniquities; who healeth all thy diseases;
> Who redeemeth thy life from destruction; who crowneth thee with lovingkindness and tender mercies. . . .
> The Lord is merciful and gracious, slow to anger, and plenteous in mercy. . . .
> He hath not dealt with us after our sins; nor rewarded us according to our iniquities.
> For as the heaven is high above the earth, so great is his mercy toward them that fear [reverence] him.
> As far as the east is from the west, so far hath he removed our transgressions from us. . . .
> For he knoweth our frame; he remembereth that we are dust.
> . . .
> Bless the Lord, all his works in all places of his dominion; bless the Lord, O my soul.

Psalm 103 describes a merciful God—one who forgives, heals, and delivers. We believe A.A.'s founders sought and found this same Almighty God as they studied the Good Book. Their Bible described the same God from Genesis to Revelation. God said in His own Word, "For I am the Lord, I change not."[42]

Bill called Him "the God of the preachers," the "Father of Lights," and "loving God."[43] He was Dr. Bob's God of love. He

---

[42] Malachi 3:6.

[43] Some may find Bill's own words hard to swallow in light of the amendments and deletions that were made in the Big Book, some at the hands of former atheists Henry G. P. and Jim B. We certainly cannot and do not present proof that Bill had a clear understanding of his own words or that he was or was not a Christian. But we do say

(continued...)

was the One of whom Anne said, "God is love," as she read from 1 John 4:8 and 16. And we believe He is the One of whom the Big Book spoke when it said, "There is One who has all power. That One is God." The Bible says He changes not, and that He remembers our frame—that we are dust. And that was how the author understood God—who provided the power he so much needed when he entered the rooms of Alcoholics Anonymous.

May the reader, like the founders in those early Akron days, find or return to fellowship with that loving God. And may the Akron Genesis help to show how A.A.'s founders did!

END

---

[43] (...continued)

that history requires a look at the facts. As Bill himself chose to add on the subject of Spiritual Experience, at page 570 of the Big Book: "There is a principle which is a bar against all information, which is proof against all arguments and which cannot fail to keep a man in everlasting ignorance—that principle is contempt prior to investigation." Bill attributes the quote to Herbert Spencer.

Appendix 1

Oxford Group Literature List

The following is the list of Oxford Group literature, with publication information added, that was included in the March, 1939, issue of *The Calvary Evangel*. The *Evangel* was a regular publication of Sam Shoemaker's Calvary Episcopal Church in New York. For a period of time, it also became virtually the "house organ" of Moral Re-Armament, the successor to the Oxford Group—which had its American Headquarters at Calvary House:

Allen, Geoffrey Francis. *He That Cometh*. New York: The Macmillan Company, 1933.
Brown, Philip M. *The Venture of Belief*. New York: Fleming H. Revell, 1935.
Foot, Stephen. *Life Began Yesterday*. New York: Harper & Brothers, 1935.
Forde, Eleanor Napier. *The Guidance of God*. Oxford: Printed at the University Press, 1930.
Holmes-Walker, Wilfred. *New Enlistment* (no publication data available to author).
Jones, Olive M. *Inspired Children*. New York: Harper & Brothers, 1933.
———. *Inspired Youth*. New York: Harper & Brothers, 1938.
Kitchen, V. C. *I Was A Pagan*. New York: Harper & Brothers, 1934.
Lean, Garth, and Martin, Morris. *New Leadership*. London: William Heinemann, 1936.
Rose, Cecil. *When Man Listens*. New York: Oxford University Press, 1937.
Rose, Howard J. *The Quiet Time*. New York: The Oxford Group at 61 Gramercy Park North, 1937.
Russell, A. J. *For Sinners Only*. London: Hodder & Stoughton, 1932.
Shoemaker, Samuel Moor, Jr. *Children of the Second Birth*. New York: Fleming H. Revell, 1927.
———. *Confident Faith*. New York: Fleming H. Revell, 1932.
———. *If I Be Lifted Up*. New York: Fleming H. Revell, 1931.
———. *National Awakening*. New York: Harper & Brothers, 1936.
———. *Realizing Religion*. New York: Association Press, 1921.
———. *Religion That Works*. New York: Fleming H. Revell, 1928.
———. *The Church Can Save The World*. New York: Harper & Brothers, 1938.
———. *The Conversion of the Church*. New York: Fleming H. Revell, 1932.
———. *The Gospel According To You*. New York: Fleming H. Revell, 1934.
Streeter, Burnett Hillman. *The God Who Speaks*. London: Macmillan & Co., 1943.
The Layman with a Notebook. *What Is The Oxford Group?* London: Oxford University Press, 1933.

335

Viney, Hallen. *How Do I Begin?* New York: The Oxford Group at 61 Gramercy
Park North, 1937.

Walter, Howard A. *Soul-Surgery.* 6th ed. Oxford: Printed at the University Press by
John Johnson, 1940.

Winslow, Jack. *Church in Action* (no publication data to the author).

————. *Why I Believe in the Oxford Group.* London: Hodder & Stoughton, 1934.

Books Known to Have Been Read,
But Not on Evangel List

The following are Oxford Group books known to have been read by one or more of
A.A.'s founders, but not included in the *Evangel* list.

Begbie, Harold. *Life Changers.* New York: G. P. Putnam's Sons, 1927.

————. *Twice-Born Men.* New York: Fleming H. Revell, 1909 (Begbie wrote the
book before the Oxford Group was underway, but his book was quite popular
with Group people).

Leon, Philip. *The Philosophy of Courage.* New York: Oxford University Press, 1939.

Macmillan, Ebenezer. *Seeking and Finding.* New York: Harper & Brothers, 1933.

Nichols, Beverley. *The Fool Hath Said.* Garden City: Doubleday, Doran, 1936.

Reynolds, Amelia S. *New Lives For Old.* New York: Fleming H. Revell, 1929.

Russell, A. J. *One Thing I Know.* New York: Harper & Brothers, 1933.

Weatherhead, Leslie D. *Discipleship.* London: Student Christian Movement Press,
1934 (Weatherhead was not actually a "member" of the Oxford Group, but he
wrote widely and sympathetically about it. His books were read by the
founders).

Other books by or about the Oxford Group are listed in our Bibliography. It is
probable that many were read by the early AAs in the case where the books bear
publication dates prior to 1940. Dr. Bob said he had done an "immense amount" of the
reading the Oxford Group had recommended. According to her son, John, Henrietta
Seiberling read "all" the Oxford Group books of the 1930's. According to his daughter,
Dorothy, T. Henry Williams had tables in the "furnace room" of his house, where boxes
of Oxford Group books and pamphlets were available to those attending meetings at the
Williams home.

Appendix 2

Twenty-Eight Oxford Group Principles
That Influenced A.A.

For more complete citations and discussions of the following principles, the reader is invited to read Dick B., *The Oxford Group & Alcoholics Anonymous* (Seattle: Glen Abbey Books, 1992), where the principles and discussions about them by Oxford Group writers are set forth in great detail. Also, in Dick B., *Anne Smith's Spiritual Workbook* (Corte Madera, Ca: Good Book Publishing Company, 1992), details are included showing what Dr. Bob's wife wrote about each of these principles. Here we will simply list the principles; a supporting Bible citation where appropriate; at least one place where the principle is discussed in Oxford Group writings; and, where appropriate, a citation to the Big Book or A.A. literature where a trace seems to exist in A.A. itself.

In the beginning, God.

1. *God*—Biblical descriptions of Him as Creator, Maker, Father, Spirit, Living God.

   See as to Creator (Isaiah 40:28; Big Book, pp. 13, 76);
   Maker (Psalm 95:6; Big Book, pp. 57, 63);
   Father (Matthew 5:45; Big Book, p. 62);
   Spirit (John 4:24; Big Book, p. 84);
   Living God (Acts 14:15; Compare Big Book, p. 28—an early draft spoke of the "living God").

   In Oxford Group writings, see Philip M. Brown, *The Venture of Belief* (New York: Fleming H. Revell, 1935), pp. 24-25; Geoffrey Allen, *He That Cometh* (New York: The Macmillan Company, 1933), pp. 222-223; Clarence I. Benson, *The Eight Points of the Oxford Group* (Oxford: Oxford University Press, 1936), p. 73; Frank Buchman, *Remaking The World* (London: Blandford Press, 1961), p. 13.

2. *God has a plan.*

See Buchman, *Remaking The World*, p. 48;
DR. BOB and the Good Oldtimers (New York: Alcoholics Anonymous World
Services, Inc., 1980), p. 145.

3. *Man's chief end.*

Acts 13:22;
See Samuel M. Shoemaker, *Christ's Words From The Cross* (New York:
Fleming H. Revell, 1933), p. 50;
Big Book, Step Eleven.

4. *Belief.*

Hebrews 11:6;
See Samuel M. Shoemaker, *National Awakening* (New York: Harper &
Brothers, 1936), pp. 40-41;
Big Book, p. 53.

Sin—Estrangement from God—The Barrier of Self.

5. *Sin, the self-centeredness that blocks man from God and from others.*

Romans 3:23;
See Benson, *The Eight Points*, pp. 20-21; Samuel M. Shoemaker, *They're On
The Way* (New York: E. P. Dutton, 1951), p. 154;
Pass It On (New York: Alcoholics Anonymous World Services, Inc., 1984),
p. 197;
Big Book, pp. 60-64, 66, 71, 76.

Finding or Rediscovering God.

6. *Surrender, the turning point.*

Acts 3:19;
See Benson, *The Eight Points*, p. 5; Samuel M. Shoemaker, *The Church Can
Save The World* (New York: Harper & Brothers, 1938), pp. 113-14;
Big Book, p. 59.

7. *Soul-Surgery, the "art."*

See Howard A. Walter, *Soul-Surgery*. 6th ed. (Oxford at the University Press,
1940);
DR. BOB, p. 54.

8. *Life-change, the result.*

John 3:3;
See Harold Begbie, *Life Changers* (New York: G. P. Putnam, 1927);
Big Book, pp. 63, 569-70.

The Path to the relationship with God.

9. *Decision.*

Matthew 6:10;
See Samuel M. Shoemaker, *Children of the Second Birth* (New York: Fleming H. Revell, 1927), pp. 58, 175-187; The Layman with a Notebook, *What Is The Oxford Group?* (London: Oxford University Press, 1933), pp. 46-48;
Big Book, pp. 60, 63.

10. *Self-examination.*

Matthew 7:3-5;
See Samuel M. Shoemaker, *God's Control* (New York: Fleming H. Revell, 1939), pp. 62-72;
Big Book, Step 4.

11. *Confession.*

James 5:16;
See Benson, The *Eight Points*, p. 18;
Pass It On, p. 128;
Big Book, Step 5.

12. *Conviction, readiness to change.*

Psalm 65:3;
See Samuel M. Shoemaker, *Realizing Religion* (New York: Association Press, 1923), p. 81; Walter, *Soul-Surgery*, pp. 64-78;
Mel B., *New Wine* (Minnesota: Hazelden, 1991), pp. 34-35.
Big Book, Step 6;

13. *Conversion, change.*

John 3:3-4;
See Shoemaker, *National Awakening*, pp. 55, 57-58; Allen, *He That Cometh*, pp. 19-43;
Big Book, pp. 63, 76.

14. *Restitution.*

Numbers 5:6-7; Matthew 5:23-24;
See Russell, *For Sinners Only*, p. 119; Shoemaker, *The Conversion of the Church* (New York: Fleming H. Revell, 1932), pp. 47-48;
Big Book, Steps 8 and 9.

Jesus Christ.

15. *Jesus Christ, source of power.*

John 14:6;
See Brown, *The Venture of Belief*, p. 49; Samuel M. Shoemaker, *With the Holy Spirit and With Fire* (New York: Harper & Brothers, 1960), pp. 29-33.
Compare Ernest Kurtz, *Not-God*. Expanded ed. (Minnesota: Hazelden, 1991), p. 50, with Dick B., *The Oxford Group & Alcoholics Anonymous* (Seattle: Glen Abbey Books, 1992), pp. 197-98.

Spiritual Growth—Continuance.

16. *Conservation.*

Samuel M. Shoemaker, *Religion That Works* (New York: Fleming H. Revell, 1928), pp. 14-15; *Realizing Religion*, p. 82;
Big Book, pp. 83, 85.

17. *Daily surrender.*

Samuel M. Shoemaker, *The Gospel According To You* (New York: Fleming H. Revell, 1934), pp. 81-91;
Big Book, pp. 84-88.

18. *Guidance.*

Psalm 32:8;
See Benson, *The Eight Points*, p. 80;
Big Book, Step Eleven.

19. *The Four Absolutes.*

John 8:44; Matthew 5:8; Luke 14:33; John 13:34;
See Robert E. Speer, *The Principles of Jesus* (New York: Fleming H. Revell, 1902), pp. 33-34; Garth Lean, *On The Tail of a Comet* (Colorado Springs: Helmers & Howard, 1988), p. 76;
DR. BOB, p. 54, 163.

20. *Quiet Time.*

> Psalm 46:10;
> Benson, *The Eight Points*, pp. 58-73; Shoemaker, *Realizing Religion*, pp. 65-66;
> Big Book, p. 86.

21. *Bible study.*

> Shoemaker, *Realizing Religion*, pp. 58-62; Dick B., *Anne Smith's Spiritual Workbook* (Corte Madera, Ca: Good Book Publishing Company, 1992), pp. 12-13;
> Compare Big Book, p. 87.

22. *Prayer.*

> James 5:16;
> See *What Is The Oxford Group?*, p. 69;
> Big Book, pp. 85-86.

23. *Listening to God.*

> Jeremiah 30:1-2; 1 Samuel 3:9;
> Buchman, *Remaking The World*, p. 36; Howard Rose, *The Quiet Time* (New York: The Oxford Group, 61 Gramercy Park North, n.d.);
> Big Book, pp. 86-87.

24. *Checking.*

> John 16:13;
> Russell, *For Sinners Only*, p. 94;
> Compare *Pass It On*, p. 172.

The Spiritual Experience or Awakening.

25. *Knowledge of God's Will.*

> John 7:17; Acts 9:6;
> See Shoemaker, *The Conversion of the Church*, pp. 49-50; *Religion That Works*, p. 36;
> Big Book, Step Eleven.

26. *God-consciousness.*

> John 3:7; Matthew 10:39; Matthew 6:33; Acts 2:1, 4;
> See Dick B., *The Oxford Group & Alcoholics Anonymous*, pp. 265-278;

Big Book, Step 12, pp. 569-570.

Fellowship with God and Believers, and Witness by Life and Word.

27. *Fellowship.*

1 John 1:3; Ephesians 2:1-22;
Benson, *The Eight Points*, pp. 102-113; Shoemaker, *Religion That Works*, pp. 66-76;
Compare Big Book, p. 164 and p. 565 (Tradition 2).

28. *Witness.*

Acts 5:32, 26:22-23;
See *What Is The Oxford Group?*, pp. 36, 26;
Big Book, Step 12.

Appendix 3

Dr. Bob's Library

Here we list by category the spiritual books that Dr. Bob read. Some additional books that Dr. Bob read in the religious field, not pertinent to the categories, can be found in Dick B., *Dr. Bob's Library* (West Virginia: The Bishop of Books, 1992).

1. *The Bible.*

2. *Books on Jesus Christ.*

   George A. Barton, *Jesus of Nazareth: A Biography* (New York: The Macmillan Company, 1922);
   Harry Emerson Fosdick, *The Man From Nazareth* (Harper & Brothers, 1949);
   ———. *The Manhood of the Master* (London: Student Christian Movement, 1924);
   T. R. Glover, *The Jesus of History* (New York: Association Press, 1930);
   Charles Whitney Silkey, *Jesus and Our Generation* (Chicago: University of Chicago Press, 1925);
   Robert E. Speer, *Studies of the Man Christ Jesus* (New York: Fleming H. Revell, 1896);
   Rev. James Stalker, *Life of Christ*. New & Rev. ed. (New York: Fleming H. Revell, 1891).

3. *Christian classics.*

   The Confessions of St. Augustine. Translated by E. B. Pusey. A Cardinal ed. (New York: Pocket Books, 1952);
   Thomas A Kempis, *The Imitation of Christ*. A New Reading of the 1441 Latin Autograph Manscript by William C. Creasy (Georgia: Mercer University Press, 1989);
   Brother Lawrence, *The Practice of the Presence of God* (Pennsylvania: Whitaker House, 1982).

4. *Bible devotionals.*

   Oswald Chambers, *My Utmost For His Highest* (London: Simpkin Marshall, Ltd., 1927);

Glenn Clark, *I Will Lift Up Mine Eyes* (New York: Harper & Brothers, 1937);

Lewis L. Dunnington, *Handles of Power* (New York: Abingdon-Cokesbury Press, 1942);

Harry Emerson Fosdick, *The Meaning of Prayer* (New York: Association Press, 1915);

Nora Smith Holm, *The Runner's Bible* (New York: Houghton Mifflin Company, 1915);

E. Stanley Jones, *Victorious Living* (New York: The Abingdon Press, 1936);

———. *Abundant Living* (New York: Abingdon-Cokesbury Press, 1942);

The Upper Room: Daily Devotions for Family and Individual Use. Quarterly. Grover Carlton Emmons, Editor (Nashville: General Committee on Evangelism through the Department of Home Missions, Evangelism, Hospitals, Board of Missions, Methodist Episcopal Church, South);

Mary W. Tileston, *Daily Strength For Daily Needs* (Boston: Roberts Brothers, 1893).

5. *Books on Prayer.*

Glenn Clark, *How To Find Health Through Prayer* (New York: Harper & Brothers, 1940);

———. *The Lord's Prayer and Other Talks on Prayer from The Camps Farthest Out* (St. Paul, MN: Macalester Park Publishing Co., 1932);

———. *The Soul's Sincere Desire* (Boston: Little, Brown, and Company, 1925);

Starr Daily, *Recovery* (St. Paul, Minnesota: Macalester Park Publishing Company, 1948);

Mary Baker Eddy, *Science and Health with Key to the Scriptures* (Boston: Published by the Trustees under the Will of Mary Baker G. Eddy, 1916);

Charles and Cora Filmore, *Teach Us To Pray* (Lee's Summit, Missouri: Unity School of Christianity, 1950);

Emmet Fox, *Getting Results By Prayer* (no data);

———. *The Sermon on the Mount* (New York: Harper & Row, 1934);

Gerald Heard, *A Preface to Prayer* (New York: Harper & Brothers, 1944);

Frank Laubach, *Prayer (Mightiest Force in the World)* (New York: Fleming H. Revell, 1946);

Charles M. Layman, *A Primer of Prayer* (Nashville, Tidings, 1949);

J. Rufus Mosely, *Perfect Everything* (St. Paul, MN: Macalester Park Publishing Co., 1949).

Dr. William R. Parker and Elaine St. Johns, *Prayer Can Change Your Life.* New ed. (New York: Prentice Hall Press, 1957);

F. L. Rawson, *The Nature of True Prayer* (Chicago: The Marlowe Company, n.d.);

6. *Books on Healing.*

Charles Filmore, *Christian Healing* (Kansas City: Unity School of Christianity, 1936);

James Moore Hickson *Heal the Sick* (London: Methuen & Co., 1925);

Ethel R. Willitts, *Healing in Jesus Name* (Chicago: Ethel R. Willitts Evangelists, 1931).

7. *Books on the Sermon on the Mount.*

Oswald Chambers, *Studies in the Sermon on the Mount* (London: Simpkin, Marshall, Ltd., n.d.);
Emmet Fox, *The Sermon on the Mount* (see above);
E. Stanley Jones, *The Christ of the Mount: A Working Philosophy of Life* (New York: The Abingdon Press, 1931);
Glenn Clark, *The Soul's Sincere Desire* (see above);
————. *I Will Lift Up Mine Eyes* (New York: Harper & Brothers, 1937).

8. *Books on Christian love.*

Toyohiko Kagawa, *Love: The Law of Life* (Philadelphia: The John C. Winston Company, 1929);
Henry Drummond, *The Greatest Thing In The World* (New York: Grosset & Dunlap, n.d.);
Glenn Clark, *The Soul's Sincere Desire* (see above).

9. *Oxford Group Books.*

Indications from the statements of both Dr. Bob and Henrietta Seiberling are that almost every Oxford Group book prior to 1940 was read by these two people. Hence the reader should consult Appendix 1 and our Bibliography for a complete list of the Oxford Group books prior to 1940. Those specifically mentioned by or found in the collection of Dr. Bob are as follows:

Geoffrey Allen, *He That Cometh* (New York: The Macmillan Company, 1933);
Harold Begbie, *Life Changers* (London: Mills & Boon, Ltd., 1932);
————. *Twice-Born Men* (New York: Fleming H. Revell, 1909);
Amelia S. Reynolds, *New Lives for Old* (New York: Fleming H. Revell, 1929);
A. J. Russell, *For Sinners Only* (London: Hodder & Stoughton, 1932);
————. *One Thing I Know* (New York: Harper & Brothers, 1933);
The Layman with a Notebook, *What Is The Oxford Group?* (London: Oxford University Press, 1933);
Howard A. Walter, *Soul-Surgery: Some Incisive Thoughts on Personal Work.* 6th Ed. (Oxford at the University Press by John Johnson, Printer to the University, 1940);

10. *Sam Shoemaker Books.*

Sam Shoemaker was, of course, an American leader in the Oxford Group, but we list his books here for convenience. Again, it is very probable that Dr. Bob read all the Shoemaker books prior to 1940; and the reader should consult Appendix 1 and the Bibliography for a complete list. However, those specifically mentioned by or found in the collection of Dr. Bob are:

Samuel Moor Shoemaker, Jr., *Children of the Second Birth* (New York: Fleming H. Revell, 1927);
———. *Confident Faith* (New York: Fleming H. Revell, 1932);
———. *If I Be Lifted Up* (New York: Fleming H. Revell, 1931);
———. *The Conversion of the Church* (New York: Fleming H. Revell, 1932);
———. *Twice-Born Ministers* (New York: Fleming H. Revell, 1929);
———. a pamphlet—What If I Had But One Sermon to Preach (on John 17:3)—which was also published in *Religion That Works* (New York: Fleming H. Revell, 1928).

11. *Books by A.A.'s "Founders":*

William James, *The Varieties of Religious Experience* (New York: Vintage Books/The Library of America Edition, 1990);
Dr. Carl G. Jung, *Modern Man in Search of a Soul* (New York: Harcourt Brace Jovanovich, Publishers, 1933).

12. *Books by Christian writers popular in the 1930's.*

James Allen, *As A Man Thinketh* (New York: Peter Pauper Press, Inc., n.d.);
———. *Heavenly Life* (New York: Grosset & Dunlap, n.d.);
Glenn Clark, *The Soul's Sincere Desire* (see above);
———. *Fishers of Men* (Boston: Little, Brown, 1928);
———. *I Will Lift Up Mine Eyes* (see above);
———. *Two or Three Gathered Together* (New York: Harper & Brothers, 1942);
———. *How To Find Health Through Prayer* (see above);
———. *The Man Who Talks with Flowers* (Minnesota: Macalester Park Publishing Company, 1939);
———. *The Lord's Prayer and Other Talks on Prayer from The Camps Farthest Out* (see above);
———. *God's Reach* (Minnesota: Macalester Park Publishing, 1951);
———. *Clear Horizons*. Vol. 2, Quarterly (Minnesota: Macalester Park Publishing, 1941);
Lloyd Douglas (mostly fictional, see Dick B., *Dr. Bob's Library*, pp. 62-63);
Henry Drummond, *The Greatest Thing in the World* (see above);
___. *Natural Law In The Spiritual World* (New York: John B. Alden, 1887);
Mary Baker Eddy, *Science and Health with Key to the Scriptures* (see above);
Charles Filmore, *Christian Healing* (see above);
———. *Teach Us To Pray* (see above);
Harry Emerson Fosdick, *The Meaning of Service* (London: Student Christian Movement, 1921);
———. *The Meaning of Prayer* (see above);
———. *The Manhood of the Master* (see above);

———. *As I See Religion* (New York: Grosset & Dunlap, 1932);

———. *On Being a Real Person* (New York: Harper & Brothers, 1943);

———. *A Great Time To Be Alive* (New York: Harper & Brothers, 1944);

———. *The Man From Nazareth* (New York: Harper & Brothers, 1949);

Emmet Fox, *The Sermon on the Mount* (see above);

———. *Find and Use Your Inner Power* (New York: Harper & Brothers, 1937);

———. *Power Through Constructive Thinking* (New York: Harper & Brothers, 1932);

———. *Sparks of Truth* (New York: Grosset & Dunlap, 1941);

———. *Alter Your Life* (New York: Harper & Brothers, 1950); and pamphlets:

———. *Getting Results By Prayer* (1933);

———. *The Great Adventure* (1937);

———. *You Must Be Born Again* (1936);

———. *Your Heart's Desire* (1937);

E. Stanley Jones, *The Christ of the Indian Road* (New York: Abingdon Press, 1925);

———. *The Christ of the Mount* (see above);

———. *Along The Indian Road* (New York: Abingdon Press, 1939);

———. *Victorious Living* (see above);

———. *Abundant Living* (see above);

———. *Christ at the Round Table* (New York: The Abingdon Press, 1928);

———. *The Christ of Every Road* (New York: The Abingdon Press, 1930);

———. *Christ and Human Suffering* (New York: The Abingdon Press, 1933);

———. *The Choice Before Us* (New York: The Abingdon Press, 1937);

———. *The Christ of the American Road* (New York: Abingdon-Cokesbury Press, 1944);

———. *Way To Power & Poise* (New York: The Abingdon Press, 1949);

Toyohiko Kagawa, *Love: The Law of Life* (see above);

Fulton Oursler (mostly fictional. See Dick B., *Dr. Bob's Library*, pp. 76-77);

Norman Vincent Peale, *The Art of Living* (New York: The Abingdon Press, 1937);

Vincent Sheean, *Lead Kindly Light* (New York: Random House, 1949);

Fulton J. Sheen, *Peace of Soul* (New York: McGraw Hill, 1949);

Charles M. Sheldon, *In His Steps* (Nashville: Broadman Press, 1935);

R. Lleweln Williams, *God's Great Plan, a Guide To the Bible* (Hoverhill Destiny Publishers, n.d.).

13. *Books on Christianity and the Mind.*

Dr. Carl G. Jung, *Modern Man in Search of a Soul* (see above);

Joshua Loth Liebman, *Peace of Mind* (New York: Simon & Schuster, 1946);

Ernest M. Ligon, *Psychology of a Christian Personality* (New York: Macmillan, 1935);

Dr. Henry C. Link, *The Rediscovery of Man* (New York: Macmillan, 1939);

Dilworth Lupton, *Religion Says You Can* (Boston: The Beacon Press, 1938);

Ralph Waldo Trine, *In Tune With The Infinite* (New York: Thomas Y. Crowell, 1897);

———. *The Man Who Knew* (New York: Bobbs Merrill, 1936).

14. *Books about the Bible and the Church Fathers.*

R. Llewlyn Williams, *God's Great Plan A Guide to the Bible* (see above); *The Fathers of the Church* (New York: CIMA Publishing, 1947).

15. *Books by modern Roman Catholic authors.*

Fulton J. Sheen, Peace of Soul (see above).

16. *Books about Quiet Time.*

S. D. Gordon, *The Quiet Time*, (London: Fleming, n.d.).

17. *Miscellaneous.*

See Dick B., *Dr. Bob's Library*, pp. 75-80.

Appendix 4

Excerpt from *The Upper Room*

The following is a verbatim excerpt of the contents of *The Upper Room*, the Methodist quarterly, for April 22, 1935:

APRIL 22

"I will instruct thee and teach thee in the way which thou shalt go: I will guide thee with mine eye." Ps. 32:8

He who created us in His own image desires that we fulfil His plans for our lives. Are we going His way, or do we follow our own ways? We may enjoy divine light if we will, but not by coaxing a friendly God to help us in ways we have marked out for ourselves. The secret of spiritual guidance is in finding God's plan for us and following it faithfully every day. Jesus declared, "I am the Way," and in Him we discover the directions life should take. He most knows God who best knows Christ.

Read Acts 10.

PRAYER

Heavenly Father, our fears vanish when we believe that Thou art near us for friendly guidance. We long for keener spiritual insight to know Thy will, and for greater moral power to walk in Thy ways. Evermore would we follow Thy Son, our Savior and Lord! Amen.

THOUGHT FOR THE DAY

Ought we not each day to remember that God constantly seeks through us to guide the broken, troubled lives into spiritual peace and power?

Richard L. Ownbey.

Appendix 5

Excerpt from *My Utmost for His Highest*

The following is a verbatim excerpt from the contents of *My Utmost For His Highest*, by Oswald Chambers, for May 21.

May 21st.

DIVINE REASONINGS OF FAITH

"But seek ye first the kingdom of God, and His righteousness; and all these things shall be added unto you." MATTHEW vi. 33.

Immediately we look at these words of Jesus, we find them the most revolutionary statement human ears ever listened to. "Seek ye *first* the kingdom of God." We argue in exactly the opposite way, even the most spiritually-minded of us—"But I *must* live; I *must* make so much money; I *must* be clothed; I *must* be fed." The great concern of our lives is not the kingdom of God, but how we are to fit ourselves to live. Jesus reverses the order: Get rightly related to God first, maintain that as the great care of your life, and never put the concern of your care on other things.

"Take no thought for your life. . . ." Our Lord points out the utter unreasonableness from His standpoint of being so anxious over the means of living. Jesus is not saying that the man who takes thought for nothing is blessed—that man is a fool. Jesus taught that a disciple has to make his relationship to God the dominating concentration of his life, to be carefully careless about everything else in comparison to that. Jesus is saying—"Don't make the ruling factor in your life what you shall eat and what you shall drink, but be concentrated absolutely on God." Some people are careless over what they eat and drink, and they suffer for it; they are careless about what they wear, and they look as they have no business to look; they are careless about their earthly affairs, and God holds them responsible. Jesus is saying that the great care of the life is to put the relationship to God first, and everything else second.

It is one of the severest disciplines of the Christian life to allow the Holy Spirit to bring us into harmony with the teaching of Jesus in these verses.

351

Appendix 6

Excerpt from *Victorious Living*

The following is a verbatim excerpt of the contents of *Victorious Living*, by E. Stanley Jones, for January 22.

FOURTH WEEK

JANUARY 22   Acts 17.23-28

-------------------------------------HOW   CAN I FIND GOD?-----------------------------------

We have seen that life will work only in one way—God's way. The statement of Augustine is oft repeated because oft corroborated: "Thou has made us for Thyself, and we are restless until we rest in Thee." Let that fact be burned into our minds. Let it save us from all trifling, all dodging, and bend us to the one business of finding God and His way.

In our quest for God let us look at a few preliminary things. *Hold in mind that the purpose of your very being, the very end of your creation is to find and live in God.* As the eye is fashioned for light, so you are fashioned for God. But many question this. A Hindu student once asked this question, "If there is a God, what . . . motive of His is seen in the creation of this universe, where 'to think is to be full of sorrow'?" At one morning-interview time, five students, one after the other, with no collusion, asked the question, in one form or another, "Why was I created?" It is the haunting question in many minds.

I could only answer thus: Of course we cannot see the whole motive of creation, for we are finite. But why does a parent create? Physical lust? Not in the highest reaches of parenthood. Does not a parent create because of the impulse of love—the impulse that would have an object upon which he can lavish his love and to whom he can impart himself in the development and growth of the child? Is parenthood different in God? Could God, being love, have done otherwise than create objects of that love? And having created us, will He not give Himself to us? If not, then the whole apparent good is stultified. With that thought in mind to think is not "to be full of sorrow," but to be full of hope and expectancy. The creative Lover is at the door.

Father God, Thou has come a long way through creation to the very door of my heart. I hear Thy very footsteps there. I let Thee in. Thrice welcome, Lover of my soul. Amen.

Appendix 7

Excerpt from *Daily Strength for Daily Needs*

The following is a verbatim excerpt of the contents of *Daily Strength For Daily Needs*, by Mary W. Tileston, for February 15:

FEBRUARY 15

If ye fulfil the royal law according to the Scripture, thou shalt love thy neighbor as thyself, ye do well.

JAMES ii, 8

COME, children, let us go
We travel hand in hand;
Each in his brother finds his joy
In this wild stranger land.
The strong be quick to raise
The weaker when they fall;
Let love and peace and patience bloom
In ready help for all.

G. TERSTEEGEN

It is a sad weakness in us, after all, that the thought of a man's death hallows him anew to us; as if life were not sacred too,—as if it were comparatively a light thing to fall in love and reverence to the brother who has to climb the whole toilsome steep with us, and all our tears and tenderness were due to the one who is spared that hard journey.

GEORGE ELIOT

Would we codify the laws that should reign in households, and whose daily transgression annoys and mortifies us, and degrades our household life,—we must learn to adorn every day with sacrifices. Good manners are made up of petty sacrifices. Temperance, courage, love, are made up of the same jewels. Listen to every prompting of honor.

R. W. EMERSON

355

Appendix 8

1 Corinthians 13

The following is a verbatim excerpt of the contents of 1 Corinthians 13 (King James Version):

> Though I speak with the tongues of men and of angels, and have not charity [love], I am becoming as sounding brass, or a tinkling cymbal.
> And though I have the gift of prophecy, and understand all mysteries, and all knowledge; and though I have all faith, so that I could remove mountains, and have not charity [love], I am nothing.
> And though I bestow all my goods to feed the poor, and though I give my body to be burned, and have not charity [love], it profiteth me nothing.
> Charity [love] suffereth long, and is kind; charity [love] envieth not; charity [love] is not puffed up.
> Doth not behave itself unseemly, seeketh not her own, is not easily provoked, thinketh no evil;
> Rejoceth not in iniquity, but rejoiceth in truth;
> Beareth all things, believeth all things, hopeth all things, endureth all things.
> Charity [love] never faileth: but whether there be prophecies, they shall fail; whether there be tongues, they shall cease; whether there be knowledge, it shall vanish away.
> For we know in part, and we prophesy in part.
> But when that which is perfect is come, then that which is in part shall be done away.
> When I was a child, I spake as a child, I understood as a child, I thought as a child; but when I became a man, I put away childish things.
> For now we see through a glass, darkly; but then face to face; now I know in part; but then I shall know even as also I am known.
> And now abideth faith, hope, charity [love], these three; but the greatest of these is charity [love].

[Note: the word "love" has been substituted for "charity," because the underlying Greek text, from which King James was translated, uses the Greek word *agapē* which is more correctly translated "love." See *New Bible Dictionary*. 2d ed. (Illinois: Tyndale House Publishers, 1987), pp. 711-12; Ethelburt W. Bullinger, *A Critical Lexicon and Concordance to the English and Greek New Testament* (Michigan: Zondervan Publishing

House, 1981), p. 145; W. E. Vine, *Vine's Expository Dictionary of Old and New Testament Words*. Volume 3 (New York: Fleming H. Revell, 1981), pp. 20-21. See also James Moffatt, *The Bible. A New Translation* (New York: Harper & Row, 1954), New Testament, pp. 217-18; *The Revised English Bible* (Oxford: Oxford University Press, 1989), New Testament, p. 156].

Appendix 9

Possible Spiritual Sources of Big Book Language

This Appendix will not set out all of the Big Book expressions that came from or bear a close resemblance to the portions of the Bible, Christian literature, and Oxford Group books that the Akron progenitors were reading. Nor will it list all of the places in the biblical literature Akron AAs used where the basic ideas can be found. We will, however, include enough illustrations to show just how much of the Big Book language seemed to come from the sources Akron AAs studied. We will list each expression, one or more of the sources where it can be found, and then one or more of the pages in the Big Book where the expression or an apparent counterpart appears. Abbreviations for the titles of the source books are as follows:

Explanation of Symbols

RTW	Samuel M. Shoemaker, *Religion That Works*.
SSD	Glenn Clark, *The Soul's Sincere Desire*.
CSB	Samuel M. Shoemaker, *Children of the Second Birth*.
WI	The Layman with a Notebook, *What Is The Oxford Group?*
SF	Ebenezer Macmillan, *Seeking and Finding*.
IWP	Victor C. Kitchen, *I Was A Pagan*.
EPOG	Clarence I. Benson, *The Eight Points of the Oxford Group*.
RW	Frank N. D. Buchman, *Remaking The World*.
RR	Samuel M. Shoemaker, *Realizing Religion*.
LBY	Stephen Foot, *Life Began Yesterday*.
YMV	Samuel M. Shoemaker, *A Young Man's View of the Ministry*.
FSO	A. J. Russell, *For Sinners Only*.
VB	Philip Marshall Brown, *The Venture of Belief*.
TBM	Samuel M. Shoemaker, *Twice-Born Ministers*.
WML	Cecil Rose, *When Man Listens*.
LC	Harold Begbie, *Life Changers*.
NA	Samuel M. Shoemaker, *National Awakening*.
CF	Samuel M. Shoemaker, *Confident Faith*.
ILU	Samuel M. Shoemaker, *If I Be Lifted Up*.
GATY	Samuel M. Shoemaker, *The Gospel According To You*.

CCS	Samuel M. Shoemaker, *The Church Can Save The World*.
GC	Samuel M. Shoemaker, *God's Control*.
ASWB	Dick B., *Anne Smith's Spiritual Workbook*.
IWL	Glenn Clark, *I Will Lift Up Mine Eyes*.
QT	Howard Rose, *The Quiet Time*.
PG	Sherwood Sunderland Day, *The Principles of the Group*.
GG	Eleanor Napier Forde, *The Guidance of God*.
FHS	Beverley Nichols, *The Fool Hath Said*.

Possible Spiritual Sources of Big Book Language

Abandon yourself to Him [God].
    RTW, pp. 19-20;
    Big Book, pp. 63, 164, 59.
Not my will but Thine be done.
    RTW, p. 19; CSB, p. 58, 182; SD, p. 40;
    Big Book, p. 85.
Thy will be done.
    CSB 175-187;
    Big Book, pp. 67, 88.
Contact with God.
    SSD, p. 15;
    Big Book, pp. 59, 87.
Faith without works is dead.
    WI, p. 36;
    Big Book, pp. 14, 76, 88.
First Things First.
    SF, p. 17;
    Big Book, p. 135.
I've got religion.
    CSB, p. 165;
    Big Book, p. 9.
Relationship with God.
    IWP, pp. 113; EPOG, pp. 48, 92;
    Big Book, pp. 28-29, 100, 164.
Higher Power.
    IWP, p. 85;
    Big Book, pp. 43, 100.
God-consciousness.
    IWP, pp. 28, 33, 41, 75, 96;
    Big Book, pp. 13, 85, 570.
Spiritual awakening.
    RW, pp. 19, 24, 28, 35;
    Big Book, p. 60.

Personal God.
  CSB, p. 61;
  Big Book, p. 10.
All-powerful God Who created man.
  IWP, p. 14;
  Big Book, p. 49.
Fear, dishonesty, resentment, selfishness.
  RW, p. 38;
  Big Book, pp. 84, 86.
Giving up self-will.
  IWP, p. 45; RR, p. 31;
  Big Book, pp. 60, 62, 87.
We were reborn.
  IWP, p. 68;
  Big Book, p. 63.
God simply lifted that desire [for alcohol] entirely out of my life.
  IWP, p. 74;
  Big Book, p. 85.
Selfish and self-centered.
  IWP, p. 103;
  Big Book, pp. 62.
He . . . produced a piece of yellow fool's-cap from his pocket, neatly divided into four quarters, one for each standard [each of the Four Absolutes], on which he had written down all the places where he felt he had fallen down on them.
  CCS, p. 119;
  Big Book, pp. 64-65, 68-70.
The minute Saul is really convinced that both his love and his hate are in the wrong place, the minute Saul is honest, God can flood his spirit with light, and speak truth into his soul.
  CF, p. 111,
  Compare Big Book, p. 66.
In God's hands.
  IWP, p. 108;
  Big Book, pp. 100, 120, 124.
The power of God to *remove* these fears and mental conditions [resentments, worry, possessiveness].
  IWP, p. 143;
  Big Book, pp. 71, 76.
We must first remove all the beams and motes of Self, with its vanity, covetousness, and egotism; of Anger, with its brood of jealousies, envies, and fault-finding; and of Worry, with its children of fear and cowardice.
  SSD 61;
  Big Book, pp. 62, 64, 67, 84, 86, 88.

What you want is simply a vital religious experience.
>   RR, p. 9;
>   Big Book, p. 27.

You need to find God.
>   RR, p. 9;
>   Big Book, p. 59.

For most men, the world is centered in self, which is misery.
>   RR, p. 11;
>   Big Book, pp. 61-62.

We are told that conversion is "gradual or sudden."
>   RR, p. 27;
>   Big Book, p. 569.

Self-surrender has always been and always must be regarded as the vital turning point of the religious life.
>   RR, p. 30; YMV, p. 55, CSB, p. 16, RTW, p. 48;
>   Big Book, p. 59.

God is and is a Rewarder of them that seek Him.
>   Hebrews 11:6;
>   GATY, p. 47;
>   Big Book, p. 60.

O Lord, manage me, for I cannot manage myself.
>   FSO, p. 79; VB, p. 30;
>   Big Book, pp. 59, 60.

It meant a handing over of our little in return for God's All-Sufficiency.
>   FSO, p. 29;
>   Big Book, pp. 52-53.

Self was the centre of my life, not God.
>   LBY, p. 9:
>   Big Book, pp. 61-62.

The first action is . . . a decision . . . that one has not controlled one's life particularly well hitherto, and that it had better be put under new management.
>   LBY, p. 10;
>   Big Book, pp. 62-63.

Contact with God is the necessary fundamental condition, and that is made through prayer and listening.
>   LBY, p. 13;
>   Big Book, pp. 59, 85-88.

A Power that can change human nature . . . and through this Power problems are being solved.
>   LBY, p. 22;
>   Big Book, pp. 45-46.

Fear may be the great paralyser; its effect a negation of action and not a stimulus. Fear may make us run away from a situation, or prevent us from taking action; fear cramps and hinders us, entangles our feet, enmeshes our arms, keeps us in ruts, dulls our imagination.

  LBY, p. 31;

  Big Book, pp. 67-68.

The Oxford Group is working for changed lives, God-centered in place of self-centered.

  LBY, p. 47;

  Big Book, p. 62.

Our job, whether it be in business or society, is to serve the world as God shall direct.

  LBY, p. 60.

  Big Book, p. 62.

Sin is anything that separates individuals from God or from one another.

  LBY, p. 67; CSB, p. 22; WI, p. 19; CC, p. 47;

  Big Book, pp. 64, 66, 71-72.

All testify to the irreducible minimum of religious experience, namely, the certainty of the "presence of God" in this universe.

  VB, p. 24;

  Big Book, pp. 51, 56, 162, 25.

Creator.

  Isaiah 40:28;

  LC, p. 16; VB, p. 25;

  Big Book, pp. 13, 25, 28, 56, 68, 72, 75-76, 80, 83, 158, 161.

Father.

  Matthew 5:45;

  VB, p. 25;

  Big Book, p. 62.

Infinite Power.

  VB, p. 25:

  Big Book, p. 68.

Father of Light.

  James 1:17 [Father of lights];

  Big Book, p. 14.

Maker.

  Psalm 95:6;

  Big Book, pp. 57, 63.

Friend.

  James 2:23;

  Big Book, p. 13.

Spirit.

  John 4:24;

  Big Book, p. 84.

Decision.
>   VB, p. 26;
>   Big Book, pp. 60, 62.

Willingness.
>   VB., pp. 28-29, 36; EPOG, p. 9;
>   Big Book, p. 46.

Grudges.
>   EPOG, p. x; TBM, p. 182;
>   Big Book, p. 65.

It means confessing our part in the sinning.
>   EPOG, p. 28;
>   Big Book, p. 67.

Before we can get right with God, we must leave no stone unturned to get right with men.
>   EPOG, p. 36;
>   Big Book, p. 77.

[Of self-examination] Every sensible man in business spends several days in the year checking his financial position. . . . If he does not make out an accurate balance sheet every year, he may be heading for financial ruin [has he] taken stock.
>   EPOG, p. 44;
>   Big Book, p. 64.

[Of self-examination] If, then, I want God to take control of my life, the first thing I must do is to produce the books. . . . A good way to begin this examination of the books is to test my life beside the Sermon on the Mount.
>   WML, pp. 17-18;
>   Big Book, p. 64, 68-70.

Nine-tenths of our misery is due to self-centeredness. To get ourselves off our hands is the essence of happiness.
>   EPOG, p. 56;
>   Big Book, p. 14.

Things begin to happen when we 'let go' and 'let God.' He is God—not you.
>   EPOG, p. 68;
>   Big Book, p. 62.

The Great Reality.
>   SSD, p. 30;
>   Big Book, pp. 55, 161.

No man can sound the depths of his own natural peace, or rise to the heights of his own natural bliss, who is not conscious of the presence and the companionship of God.
>   LC, p. 16;
>   Big Book, pp. 51, 56.

God comes to us when we ask Him.
>   LC, p. 37;
>   Big Book, p. 57.

God floods in when a man is honest.
> LC, p. 103;
> Big Book, p. 57.

They recognize that the [sex] instinct is at bottom a God-given one.
> LC, p. 176;
> Big Book, p. 69.

Confess therefore your sins one to another, and pray for one another, that ye may be healed.
> James 5:16;
> WI, p. 29;
> Big Book, pp. 72-73.

The first step for me was to be honest with God, the next to be honest with men.
> LBY, p. 11;
> Big Book, pp. 73-74.

It is the way of young-mindedness to treat one's spiritual defects as a problem, not a fate.
> TBM, p. 36;
> Big Book, p. 76.

My own life was disciplined. Almost daily new surrenders have to be made, but I can honestly say that nothing is left standing between God and myself, or other people and myself.
> TBM, p. 92;
> Big Book, p. 88.

That night I decided to 'launch out into the deep:' and with the decision to cast my will and my life on God, there came an indescribable sense of relief, of burdens dropping away.
> TBM, p. 134;
> Big Book, pp. 59-60, 62-63.

And we must honestly ask ourselves where lies our final security; whether it lies in people and things or whether it lies in God.
> NA 35;
> Big Book, p. 68.

God is, or He isn't. You leap one way or the other.
> CF, p. 187;
> Big Book, p. 53.

Completeness is really a matter of inner wealth and peace. It is a quality of self-sufficiency in the presence of the bafflements and perplexities and sufferings of life, or rather a matter of God-sufficiency.
> ILU, pp. 106-107;
> Big Book, pp. 52-53.

God in mercy strip up this day of the last vestiges of self-reliance, and help us to begin anew trusting to nothing but His grace!
> ILU, p. 166;
> Big Book, p. 68.

When you blow away the clouds of your self-pity, self-will, self-centeredness, all that you will find left is a universe of opportunity, with God to help you, and a miserable, petty little self sitting down in the midst of it, refusing to play.
> GC, p. 57;
> Big Book, pp. 62, 68.

Surrender of all one knows of self to all one knows of God.
> LBY, p. 175; CSB, p. 25; ASWB, p. 28;
> Big Book—God as you understand Him, pp. 12, 47, 59-60.

Love thy neighbor as thyself.
> Leviticus 19:18; Matthew 22:39; Romans 13:9; James 2:8;
> IWL, p. 63;
> Big Book, p. 153.

Peace, direction, power—the fullness of life—await the complete surrender of ourselves to God for His purposes.
> WML, p. 17;
> Big Book, p. 63.

The next practical result of my "willingness" will be that I shall take any Steps which God shows me to put right the wrong I have done.
> WML, p. 19;
> Big Book, pp. 76, 80, 83, 164.

The greater strength and peace [which] come when we have listened to God and received His directions for our day. And morning is emphatically the best time. The opening of the day with quiet thought, planning, and prayer, is so obviously the right start for the Christian.
> WML, pp. 36-37;
> Big Book, p. 86.

The guided life is a growth. Through the continuous experiment of listening to God, more and more of our thinking and action is freed from the guidance of self, hate, fear, indulgence, prejudice, ignorance, and all other forms of sin, and is made available to God.
> WML, p. 36;
> Big Book, pp. 86-88.

Self-giving will certainly mean that our time and money, and our strength, are entirely at the disposal of other people as God directs.
> WML, p. 46;
> Big Book, pp. 20, 77, 93, 97.

Our human impulse is to give advice, to point out the steps that other persons ought to take, to rearrange their life ourselves. . . . If they listen to us instead of God, they will depend on us instead of Him. That is fatal.
> WML, p. 62;
> Big Book, p. 98.

The more general results of the Quiet Time are: . . . A Christ-centered and unified life, issuing in joyous, spontaneous, God-directed service.
> QT, p. 4;
> Big Book, pp. 77, 164.

The fourth signpost is an intuitive conviction that a course of action is inherently right. . . . There is a sense of freedom from strain and worry, hurry and apprehension, which characterizes a life so led by the Spirit and lavishly trusting God.

GG, p. 21;

Big Book, pp. 83-84, 87-88.

A united front made up of varied personalities presenting a single message carries conviction where one individual may not appeal.

PG, p. 10;

Big Book, pp. 60, 93.

We really come to know God as we share Him with others. An experience that is not shared dies or becomes twisted and abnormal.

PG, p. 8;

Big Book, pp. 89, 102, 159, 161, 164.

Patience, tolerance, kindness, understanding, humility, forgiveness, honesty, unselfishness, love.

1 Corinthians 13; Philippians 4:8;

IWL, pp. 54-114;

Big Book, pp. 67, 70, 73-74, 83-84, 118, 125.

It works.

FHS, p. 171;

Big Book, p. 88.

Appendix 10

The Author's Story

This will not be a "drunkalog" that recites either the author's drinking story or his qualification as a real alcoholic. Suffice it to say that sometime between 1968 and 1972, he had had enough stress and fear and anger in his career, his marriage, and his life to have developed an abnormal, uncontrollable drinking pattern. Alcohol had become an illusory solution for his problems; and when he drank, he drank far too much. Later, neither sleeping pills, nor alcohol, nor a confused mixture of both did anything but cause trouble—trouble with his wife, his friends, his minister, his doctor, his psychiatrist, his career, his health, and eventually the law.

The author was not an alcoholic who came to A.A. to find God, to rediscover God, to establish a relationship with God, to understand God, or to become a Christian. He was a Christian who came to A.A. at age 59, a very sick person, physically, mentally, emotionally, and spiritually. He had a deep belief in God and in the accuracy and integrity of the Bible as God's Word. But he had been out of fellowship with God and under siege by his Adversary.[1]

Most assuredly, at that point, he knew nothing significant about his problem with alcohol, his alcoholism, or Alcoholics Anonymous. At the point of his greatest despair, having been in deep depression, and drinking hand over fist for 9 months, the author

---

[1] 1 Peter 5:8-10 states: "Be sober, be vigilant; because your adversary the devil, as a roaring lion, walketh about, seeking whom he may devour. Whom resist steadfast in the faith, knowing that the same afflictions are accomplished in your brethren that are in the world. But the God of all grace, who hath called us unto his eternal glory by Christ Jesus, after that ye have suffered a while, make you perfect, stablish, strengthen, settle you." Interestingly, Bill Wilson said of himself in his story in the Big Book, "If there was a Devil, he seemed Boss Universal, and he certainly had me" (p. 11). Many years after the Big Book was written, Dr. Carl G. Jung replied to a letter from Bill Wilson concerning the nature of A.A.'s spiritual solution, and said: "I am strongly convinced that the evil principle prevailing in this world leads the unrecognized spiritual need into perdition, if it is not counteracted either by a real religious insight or by the protective wall of human community. An ordinary man, not protected by an action from above, and isolated in society, cannot resist the power of evil, which is called very aptly the Devil." See *Pass It On* (New York: Alcoholics Anonymous World Services, Inc., 1984), p. 384.

found that his physician, his psychiatrist, and his fellow-believers in his Bible fellowship all endorsed his entry into A.A. "Endorsed" puts it mildly. He is sure they all heaved a sigh of relief when he put down his bottles and his sleeping pills and began seeking fellowship with God, help in A.A., and other alcoholics with whom to work.

There were difficulties in the spiritual realm. The author's first sponsor, though loving and helpful, discouraged the author from any connection with the Bible or his Bible fellowship. And, unfortunately, the author acquiesced, focusing instead on A.A. *and* his fears, resentments, health, and legal difficulties—professional, civil, tax, and criminal. He did ask for God's help in abstaining from drink and has not had a drop from his first day of sobriety. But the author was scarcely in the door of A.A. when—from several sources—the author, in his confused, frightened, anxious, forgetful, and shaking condition, began hearing talk of a "Higher Power," a "Power greater than ourselves," God as a "Group Of Drunks," God as "Good Orderly Direction," God as "the Group," and even God as a "door knob," the "Big Dipper," a "tree," and, yes, "Ralph!" To be sure, the expressions were more prevalent in the recovery center where the author was hospitalized for seizures, a 28 day program, and aftercare. But they were also painfully and confusingly present in the rooms of A.A.—particularly from the mouths of people the author respected and asked for help.

When he came into the rooms of A.A., the author understood God as the Father of his Lord and Saviour, Jesus Christ. He still does. The expressions "Higher Power," "Group Of Drunks," and "door knob" did little to help or enlighten him spiritually.[2] And they certainly confused him as he groped about A.A., blindly seeking help from people using such language. Worse—the author began at an early point, talking some of the same language, and even "passed it on." At four months of sobriety, he turned himself in to a V.A. psych ward and suffered there until he once again began studying the Word, reading about his deliverance and redemption, and believing it. Things changed. The fear left. Health began returning. And the other problems soon were resolved. During this time, the author was going to A.A. meetings and keeping in touch with his sponsor.

Before long, he was well enough to look to and study the Big Book with people who understood it. He saw in the Twelve Steps of Alcoholics Anonymous some important principles—seemingly Christian principles—for changing the way he had been living. From the Steps and the Big Book, he learned important facts about his then principal foe—alcohol, "cunning, baffling, powerful." He found people in A.A. who focused on living a day at a time without picking up a drink, who hung out together for that

---

[2] Compare: (1) John 14:6: "Jesus saith unto him, I am the way, the truth, and the life; no man cometh unto the Father, but by me;" (2) John 1:18: "No man hath seen God at any time, the only begotten Son, which is in the bosom of the Father, he hath declared him;" (3) John 3:3: "Jesus answered and said unto him, Verily, verily, I say unto thee, Except a man be born again, he cannot see the kingdom of God;" (4) Acts 2:36: "Therefore let all the house of Israel know assuredly, that God hath made that same Jesus, whom ye have crucified, both Lord and Christ;" and (5) Romans 10:9: "That if thou shalt confess with thy mouth the Lord Jesus, and shalt believe in thine heart that God hath raised him from the dead, thou shalt be saved."

purpose, who helped each other to that end, and whose fellowship enabled the author to find new friends and purpose in life.

The author's interest in and enthusiasm for the Akron Genesis began when a young friend, now dead of alcoholism, said, "Did you know that A.A. was based on the Bible?" The young man suggested reading A.A.'s *DR. BOB and the Good Oldtimers.* The author did, and found—from Dr. Bob's own words—that the young man's statement was basically true. This, in turn, led the author to pursue these questions: "What had Akron A.A. Oldtimers studied and found in the Bible?" "Did their findings reach A.A.?" If so, "What happened to the Bible and to Jesus Christ in the transition from Akron to the Big Book?" The answers became even more important to the author when he discovered that Dr. Bob was considered, by far, the most effective sponsor in early A.A. and was dubbed by his Co-founder, Bill W., as the "Prince of Twelfth Steppers." The author found Akron had produced substantial early successes and that New York had not. And he felt there may have been something in Akron's focus on the Bible and Christian belief in deliverance that was responsible for Akron's predominant success.

This, if true, would have been music to the ears of any Christian and Bible student who was as enthusiastic about A.A. and what it had done for him as the author believed himself to be. For the author studied the Big Book, worked and endeavored to practice the Twelve Steps, sponsored many men in their recovery, and involved himself in fellowship and in service.

The author did not enter Alcoholics Anonymous with a banner proclaiming, "Onward Christian Soldiers." He arrived, as most do, in the midst of a sea of health, family, tax, legal, law enforcement, and financial troubles. Like most, he wondered how it all had happened. Where did alcohol fit in this sordid picture? Why was he so sick he was having seizures, shaking like a leaf, wetting his pants at meetings, and unable even to remember his own phone number and address? Why was he lonely—and scared to death? Hearing about alcoholism and the plight of others who had recovered, the author quickly concluded that A.A. was where he belonged. He "reluctantly" discovered he had a "problem with alcohol." A.A.'s Preamble, that is read at almost every meeting, said that the only requirement for membership is a "desire to stop drinking"—something the author acquired rather soon, when he realized what a deadly drug he had been imbibing in uncontrollable excess. At the end of each meeting, the group stood with hands clasped, recited the Lord's Prayer, and suggested, "Keep coming back. It works!"

It did. But "what" worked was for the author yet to discover. That "it" worked became more evident each day the author asked God for help, strength, and guidance; stayed away from a drink and a sleeping pill; involved himself in the fellowship; worked at the Steps and the Big Book; and focused on helping other drunks. Almost at once, the alcohol problem was gone. Other troubles were eventually resolved. Life without a drink became a joy and a challenge. The challenge, for the author, was to keep in tune with God and to focus on others. The Bible suggests this in what Jesus Christ called the two great commandments: Love God and love your neighbor as yourself. The Bible also suggests:

Study to shew thyself approved unto God, a workman that needeth not to be ashamed, rightly dividing the word of truth.[3]

A.A.'s Eleventh Step speaks to "improving" one's relationship with God; and the author found that this was exactly what Dr. Bob, Anne, and the early AAs were doing in Akron with their Bibles, their Christian literature, and their daily devotionals.

To the author, this early history was important. For the author could have been lured from A.A. by statements such as these in *The Useful Lie*:

> Many within the Christian commnity believe the founders of A.A. were Christians and that A.A.'s Twelve Steps are based on the Bible. . . . However, nothing in A.A.'s history supports these beliefs. In fact, the myth is actually denied by the founders themselves as well as by the official literature of A.A. and spinoff organizations. . . . I have never read anything in A.A. literature or elsewhere to indicate that Bill W. or Dr. Bob were Christians in the Biblical sense. To call them Christian would, however, be the equivalent of calling a Buddhist or a Morman Christian.[4]

We believe our present book, and our previous three books, will demonstrate the fallacies in the foregoing statements.

The author's own experience is that he was able to survive the "any god" that certainly floats about in A.A., recovery center, and therapy talk. Looking back on his years of involvement with A.A. to date, the author sees the A.A. fellowship in this way: The twelve suggested steps for recovery require an honest acknowledgement of defeat at the hands of alcohol. They require recognition of an unmanageable life. They stress dependence upon God as one understands Him. They suggest a design for living based on spiritual principles, most of which came directly from the Bible. They leave to the individual alcoholic his own language and point of view in his establishment of "a relationship with God." They demand no theology or denominational bias. And they insist that those who recover must pass on their experience to a still suffering alcoholic.

The author has not been driven away from the Bible, God, or Jesus Christ. In fact, the need for all three was found to be great, and the way was open. Undeniably, there were and are times when the going is tough. A few AAs bridle at any mention of the Bible, God, or Jesus Christ. They load the meetings with their fatalism, fear, self-made descriptions of a "higher power," and talk of "spirituality versus religion." That's just the way it is. But it's not the way it is with most recovered and tolerant AAs in the author's own area. And, is it any different outside of A.A.? The critical thing in A.A. is its primary focus on the avoidance of drinking to prevent the devastating consequences found by most in their lives when they "hit bottom."

The author dived into A.A. He experienced removal of his obsession to drink. Later, with a clearer mind, he found new power and deliverance in his life as he studied and believed the Bible—sober! He also found special meaning for him in the Christian

---

[3] 2 Timothy 2:15.

[4] William L. Playfair, M.D. *The Useful Lie* (Illinois: Crossway Books, 1991), p. 94.

principles the early AAs borrowed, adopted, and adapted. He found new zest for researching and developing his own spritual growth through the Bible and a Bible fellowship.

The door was wide open to this when he completed his Eleventh Step. But the path began in his earliest A.A. days. At his second meeting, the author saw A.A.'s Twelve Steps on the wall of the meeting room. The phrase, "God as we understood Him," caught his attention. He knew there was room for him in Alcoholics Anonymous. And he badly needed room just about anywhere at the time, particularly in the kind of atmosphere where he would not be judged for his shortcomings but would be encouraged by the love, understanding, and service he found in A.A. The Steps pointed him back to the God of his understanding. The author has seen, from the pages of A.A.'s own history, the success that was achieved by likeminded believers in A.A.'s formative years in Akron between 1935 and 1939.

Bibliography

Publications by or about the Oxford Group & Oxford Group People

A Day in Pennsylvania Honoring Frank Nathan Daniel Buchman in Pennsburg and Allentown. Oregon: Grosvenor Books, 1992.

Allen, Geoffrey Francis. *He That Cometh*. New York: The Macmillan Company, 1933.

Austin, H. W. "Bunny". *Frank Buchman As I Knew Him*. London: Grosvenor Books, 1975.

Begbie, Harold. *Life Changers*. New York: G. P. Putnam's Sons, 1927.

———. *Souls In Action*. New York: Hodder & Stoughton, 1911.

———. *Twice-Born Men*. New York: Fleming H. Revell, 1909.

Belden, David C. *The Origins And Development Of The Oxford Group (Moral Re-Armament)*. D. Phil. Dissertation, Oxford University, 1976.

Bennett, John C. *Social Salvation*. New York: Charles Scribner's Sons, 1935, pp. 53-60.

Benson, Clarence Irving. *The Eight Points of the Oxford Group*. London: Humphrey Milford, Oxford University Press, 1936.

Braden, Charles Samuel. *These Also Believe*. New York: The Macmillan Company, 1949.

Brown, Philip M. *The Venture of Belief*. New York: Fleming H. Revell, 1935.

Buchman, Frank N. D. *Remaking The World*. London: Blandford Press, 1961.

Cantrill, Hadley. *The Psychology of Social Movements*. New York: John Wiley & Sons, Inc., 1941.

Clapp, Charles Jr. *The Big Bender*. New York: Harper & Row, 1938.

Clark, Walter Houston. *The Oxford Group: Its History and Significance*. New York: Bookman Associates, 1951.

Crothers, Susan. *Susan and God*. New York: Harper & Brothers, 1939.

Day, Sherwood Sunderland. *The Principles of the Group*. Oxford: University Press, n.d.

Eister, Allan W. *Drawing Room Conversion*. Durham: Duke University Press, 1950.

Ferguson, Charles W. *The Confusion of Tongues*. Garden City: Doubleday, Doran Company, Inc., 1940.

Foot, Stephen. *Life Began Yesterday*. New York: Harper & Brothers, 1935.

Forde, Eleanor Napier. *The Guidance of God*. Oxford: Printed at the University Press, 1930.

Grensted, L. W. *The Person of Christ*. New York: Harper & Brothers, 1933.

375

Grogan, William. *John Riffe of the Steelworkers*. New York: Coward—McCann, 1959.

Hamilton, Loudon. *MRA: How It All Began*. London: Moral Re-Armament, 1968.

Harris, Irving. *An Outline of the Life of Christ*. New York: The Oxford Group, 1935.

Harrison, Marjorie. *Saints Run Mad*. London: John Lane, Ltd., 1934.

Henson, Herbert Hensley. *The Group Movement*. London: Oxford University Press, 1933.

Holmes-Walker, Wilfrid. *New Enlistment* (no data available).

Howard, Peter. *Frank Buchman's Secret*. Garden City: New York: Doubleday & Company, Inc., 1961.

———. *That Man Frank Buchman.* London: Blandford Press, 1946.

———. *The World Rebuilt*. New York. Duell, Sloan & Pearce, 1951.

Hunter, T. Willard. *World Changing Through Life Changing*. Thesis, Newton Center, Mass: Andover-Newton Theological School, 1977.

———. *Uncommon Friends' Uncommon Friend*. A tribute to James Draper Newton, on the occasion of his eighty-fifth birthday. (Pamphlet, March 30, 1990).

———. *Press Release*. Buchman Events/Pennsyvania, October 19, 1991.

Jones, Olive M. *Inspired Children*. New York: Harper & Brothers, 1933.

———. *Inspired Youth*. New York: Harper & Brothers, 1938.

Kitchen, V. C. *I Was A Pagan*. New York: Harper & Brothers, 1934.

Lean, Garth. *Cast Out Your Nets*. London: Grosvenor, 1990.

———. *Good God, It Works*. London: Blandford Press, 1974.

———. and Martin, Morris. *New Leadership*. London: William Heinemann, Ltd., 1936.

———. *On The Tail of a Comet: The Life of Frank Buchman*. Colorado Springs: Helmers & Howard, 1988.

Leon, Philip. *The Philosophy of Courage or The Oxford Group Way*. New York: Oxford University Press, 1939.

Macintosh, Douglas C. *Personal Religion*. New York: Charles Scribner's Sons, 1942.

Macmillan, Ebenezer. *Seeking And Finding*. New York: Harper & Brothers, 1933.

Moyes, John S. *American Journey*. Sydney: Clarendon Publishing Co., n. d.

Murray, Robert H. *Group Movements Throughout The Ages*. New York: Harper & Brothers. 1935.

Newsweek, November 24, 1941.

Newton, James. *Uncommon Friends*. New York: Harcourt Brace, 1987.

Nichols, Beverley. *The Fool Hath Said*. Garden City: Doubleday, Doran & Company, 1936.

Raynor, Frank D. and Weatherhead, Leslie D. *The Finger of God*. London: Group Publications, Ltd., 1934.

Reynolds, Amelia S. *New Lives For Old*. New York. Fleming H. Revell, 1929.

Roots, John McCook. *An Apostle To Youth*. Oxford, The Oxford Group, 1928.

Rose, Cecil. *When Man Listens*. New York: Oxford University Press, 1937.

Rose, Howard J. *The Quiet Time*. New York: Oxford Group at 61 Gramercy Park, North, 1937.

Russell, Arthur J. *For Sinners Only*. London: Hodder & Stoughton, 1932.

———. *One Thing I Know*. New York: Harper & Brothers, 1933.

Sangster, W. E. *God Does Guide Us*. New York: The Abingdon Press, 1934.

Selbie, W. B. *Oxford And The Groups*. Oxford: Basie Blackwell, 1934.

Sherry, Frank H. and Mahlon H. Hellerich. *The Formative Years of Frank N. D. Buchman.* (Reprint of article at Frank Buchman home in Allentown, Pennsylvania).

Spencer, F. A. M., *The Meaning of the Groups.* London: Metheun & Co., Ltd., 1934.

Spoerri, Theophil. *Dynamic Out of Silence: Frank Buchman's Relevance Today.* Translated by John Morrison. London: Grosvenor Books, 1976.

Streeter, Burnett Hillman. *The God Who Speaks.* London: Macmillan & Co., Ltd., 1943.

The Bishop of Leicester, Chancellor R. J. Campbell and the Editor of the "Church of England Newspaper." *Stories of our Oxford House Party.*, July 17, 1931.

The Layman with a Notebook. *What Is The Oxford Group?* London: Oxford University Press, 1933.

Thornton-Duesbury, J. P. *Sharing.* The Oxford Group. n.d.

Time Magazine, November 24, 1941.

Twitchell, Kenaston. *Regeneration in the Ruhr.* Princeton: Princeton University Press, 1981.

Van Dusen, Henry P. "Apostle to the Twentieth Century: Frank N. D. Buchman." *Atlantic Monthly* 154 (July 1934): 1-16.

———. "The Oxford Group Movement." *Atlantic Monthly.* 154 (August 1934): 240-52.

Viney, Hallen. *How Do I Begin?* The Oxford Group, 61 Gramercy Park, New York., 1937.

Vrooman, Lee. *The Faith that Built America.* New York: Arrowhead Books, Inc., 1955.

Walter, Howard A. *Soul-Surgery: Some Thoughts On Incisive Personal Work.* 6th. ed. Oxford: at the University Press by John Johnson, 1940.

Weatherhead, Leslie D. *Discipleship.* London: Student Christian Movement Press, 1934.

———. *How Can I Find God?* London: Fleming H. Revell, 1934.

———. *Psychology And Life.* New York: Abingdon Press, 1935.

Williamson, Geoffrey. *Inside Buchmanism.* New York: Philosophical Library, Inc., 1955.

Winslow, Jack C. *Church in Action* (no data available to author).

———. *Vital Touch With God: How to Carry on Adequate Devotional Life.* The Evangel, 8 East 40th St., New York, n.d.

———. *When I Awake.* London: Hodder & Stoughton, 1938.

———. *Why I Believe In The Oxford Group.* London: Hodder & Stoughton, 1934.

Books by or about Oxford Group Mentors

Bushnell, Horace. *The New Life.* London: Strahan & Co., 1868.

Chapman, J. Wilbur. *Life and Work of Dwight L. Moody.* Philadelphia, 1900.

Cheney, Mary B. *Life and Letters of Horace Bushnell.* New York: Harper & Brothers, 1890.

Drummond, Henry. *Essays and Addresses.* New York: James Potts & Company, 1904.

———. *Natural Law in the Spiritual World.* Potts Edition.

———. *The Changed Life.* New York: James Potts & Company, 1891.

———. *The Greatest Thing in the World and other addresses.* London: Collins, 1953.

———. *The Ideal Life.* New York: Hodder & Stoughton, 1897.

——. *The New Evangelism*. New York: Hodder & Stoughton, 1899.

Findlay, James F., Jr. *Dwight L. Moody American Evangelist*. Chicago, University of Chicago Press, 1969.

Fitt, Emma Moody, *Day By Day With D. L. Moody*. Chicago: Moody Press, n.d.

Goodspeed, Edgar J. *The Wonderful Career of Moody and Sankey in Great Britain and America*. New York: Henry S. Goodspeed & Co., 1876.

Guldseth, Mark O. *Streams*. Alaska: Fritz Creek Studios, 1982.

Hopkins, C. Howard. *John R. Mott, A Biography*. Grand Rapids: William B. Erdmans Publishing Company, 1979.

James, William. *The Varieties of Religious Experience*. New York: First Vintage Books/The Library of America, 1990.

Meyer, F. B. *The Secret of Guidance*. New York: Fleming H. Revell, 1896.

Moody, Paul D. *My Father: An Intimate Portrait of Dwight Moody*. Boston: Little Brown, 1938.

Moody, William R. *The Life of D. L. Moody*. New York: Fleming H. Revell, 1900.

Pollock, J. C. *Moody: A Biographical Portrait of the Pacesetter in Modern Mass Evangelism*. New York: Macmillan, 1963.

Smith, George Adam. *The Life of Henry Drummond*. New York: McClure, Phillips & Co., 1901.

Speer, Robert E. *The Marks of a Man*. New York: Hodder & Stoughton, 1907.

——. *The Principles of Jesus*. New York: Fleming H. Revell Company, 1902.

Stewart, George, Jr. *Life of Henry B. Wright*. New York: Association Press, 1925.

Wright, Henry B. *The Will of God And a Man's Lifework*. New York: The Young Men's Christian Association Press, 1909.

Publications by or about Samuel Moor Shoemaker, Jr.

Shoemaker, Samuel Moor, Jr. . . . *And Thy Neighbor*. Waco, Texas: Word Books, 1967.

——. *A Young Man's View of the Ministry*. New York: Association Press, 1923.

——. *Beginning Your Ministry*. New York: Harper & Row Publishers, 1963.

——. *By the Power of God*. New York: Harper & Brothers, 1954.

——. *Calvary Church Yesterday and Today*. New York: Fleming H. Revell, 1936.

——. *Children of the Second Birth*. New York: Fleming H. Revell, 1927.

——. *Christ and This Crisis*. New York: Fleming H. Revell, 1943.

——. *Christ's Words from the Cross*. New York: Fleming H. Revell, 1933.

——. *Confident Faith*. New York: Fleming H. Revell, 1932.

——. *Extraordinary Living for Ordinary Men*. Michigan: Zondervan, 1965.

——. *Faith at Work*. A symposium edited by Samuel Moor Shoemaker. Hawthorne Books, 1958.

——. *Freedom and Faith*. New York: Fleming H. Revell, 1949.

——. *God and America*. New York: Book Stall, 61 Gramercy Park North, New York, n.d.

——. *God's Control*. New York: Fleming H. Revell, 1939.

———. *How To Become A Christian*. New York: Harper & Brothers, 1953.

———. *How To Find God*. Reprint From Faith At Work Magazine, n.d.

———. *How You Can Find Happiness*. New York: E. P. Dutton & Co., 1947.

———. *How You Can Help Other People*. New York: E. P. Dutton & Co., 1946.

———. *If I Be Lifted Up*. New York: Fleming H. Revell, 1931.

———. *Living Your Life Today*. New York: Fleming H. Revell, 1947.

———. *National Awakening*. New York: Harper & Brothers, 1936.

———. *One Boy's Influence*. New York: Association Press, 1925.

———. *Realizing Religion*. New York: Association Press, 1923.

———. *Religion That Works*. New York: Fleming H. Revell, 1928.

———. *Revive Thy Church*. New York: Harper & Brothers, 1948.

———. *Sam Shoemaker at His Best*. New York: Faith At Work, 1964.

———. *The Breadth and Narrowness of the Gospel*. New York: Fleming H. Revell, 1929.

———. *The Church Alive*. New York: E. P. Dutton & Co., Inc., 1951.

———. *The Church Can Save The World*. New York: Harper & Brothers, 1938.

———. *The Conversion of the Church*. New York: Fleming H. Revell, 1932.

———. *The Experiment of Faith*. New York: Harper & Brothers. 1957.

———. *The Gospel According To You*. New York: Fleming H. Revell, 1934.

———. *They're on the Way*. New York: E. P. Dutton, 1951.

———. "Those Twelve Steps As I Understand Them." *Best of the Grapevine: Volume II*. New York: The A.A. Grapevine, Inc., 1986.

———. *Twice-Born Ministers*. New York: Fleming H. Revell, 1929.

———. *Under New Management*. Grand Rapids: Zondervan Publishing House., 1966.

———. *What The Church Has to Learn from Alcoholics Anonymous*. Reprint of 1956 sermon. Available at A.A. Archives, New York.

———. *With The Holy Spirit and With Fire*. New York: Harper & Brothers, 1960.

Cuyler, John Potter, Jr. *Calvary Church In Action*. New York: Fleming H. Revell, 1934.

Harris, Irving. *The Breeze of the Spirit*. New York: The Seabury Press, 1978.

Knippel, Charles Taylor. *Samuel M. Shoemaker's Theological Influence on William G. Wilson's Twelve Step Spiritual Program of Recovery (Alcoholics Anonymous)*. Dissertation. St. Louis University, 1987.

Shoemaker, Helen Smith. *I Stand By The Door*. New York: Harper & Row, 1967.

Alcoholics Anonymous

Publications About

A Guide to the Twelve Steps of Alcoholics Anonymous. Akron: A.A. of Akron, n.d.

Alcoholics Anonymous. (multilith volume). New Jersey: Works Publishing Co., 1939.

Alcoholics Anonymous: An Interpretation of Our Twelve Steps. Washington, D.C.: "The Paragon" Creative Printers, 1944.

A Manual for Alcoholics Anonymous. Akron: A.A. of Akron, n.d.

B., Dick. *Anne Smith's Spiritual Workbook: An A.A.—Good Book Connection.* Corte Madera, CA: Good Book Publishing Company, 1992.

———. *Dr. Bob's Library: An A.A.—Good Book Connection.* Wheeling, WV: The Bishop of Books, 1992.

———. *The Oxford Group & Alcoholics Anonymous: An A.A.—Good Book Connection.* Seattle: Glen Abbey Books, 1992.

B., Jim. *Evolution of Alcoholics Anonymous.* New York: A.A. Archives.

B. Mel. *New Wine: The Spiritual Roots of the Twelve Step Miracle.* Minnesota: Hazelden, 1991.

Bishop, Charles, Jr. *The Washingtonians & Alcoholics Anonymous.* WV: The Bishop of Books, 1992.

———. and Pittman, Bill. *The Annotated Bibliography of Alcoholics Anonymous 1939-1989.* Wheeling W. Va.: The Bishop of Books, 1989.

Bufe, Charles. *Alcoholics Anonymous: Cult or Cure.* San Francisco: Sharp Press, 1991.

C., Stewart. *A Reference Guide To The Big Book of Alcoholics Anonymous.* Seattle: Recovery Press, 1986.

Central Bulletin, Volumes I-II. Cleveland: Central Committee, Oct. 1942-Sept. 1944.

Clapp, Charles, Jr. *Drinking's Not the Problem.* New York: Thomas Y. Crowell, 1949.

Cutten, C. B. *The Psychology of Alcoholism.* New York: Scribner's & Sons, 1907.

Conrad, Barnaby. *Time Is All We Have.* New York: Dell Publishing, 1986.

Darrah, Mary C. *Sister Ignatia: Angel of Alcoholics Anonymous.* Chicago: Loyola University Press, 1992.

Doyle, Paul Barton. *In Step With God.* Tennessee: New Directions, 1989.

E., Bob. *Handwritten note to Lois Wilson on pamphlet entitled "Four Absolutes."* (copy made available to the author at Founders Day Archives Room in Akron, Ohio, in June, 1991).

———. *Letter from Bob E. to Nell Wing.* Stepping Stones Archives.

Gray, Jerry. *The Third Strike.* Minnesota: Hazelden, 1949.

Hunter, Willard, with assistance from M. D. B. *A.A.'s Roots in the Oxford Group.* New York: A.A. Archives, 1988.

Knippel, Charles T. *Samuel M. Shoemaker's Theological Influence on William G. Wilson's Twelve Step Spiritual Program of Recovery.* Ph. D. diss. St Louis University, 1987.

Kurtz, Ernest. *AA The Story: A Revised Edition of "Not God: A History of Alcoholics Anonymous".* San Francisco: Harper/Hazelden, 1988.

———. *Not-God: A History of Alcoholics Anonymous.* Expanded Edition. Minnesota: Hazelden, 1991.

Morreim, Dennis C. *Changed Lives: The Story of Alcoholics Anonymous.* Minneapolis: Augsburg Fortress, 1991.

Pittman, Bill. *AA The Way It Began.* Seattle: Glen Abbey Books, 1988.

Poe, Stephen E. and Frances E. *A Concordance to Alcoholics Anonymous.* Nevada: Purple Salamander Press, 1990.

Playfair, William L., M.D. *The Useful Lie.* Illinois: Crossway Books, 1991.

Robertson, Nan. *Getting Better Inside Alcoholics Anonymous.* New York: William Morrow & Co., 1988.

Second Reader for Alcoholics Anonymous. Akron: A.A. of Akron, n.d.

Seiberling, John F. *Origins of Alcoholics Anonymous*. (A transcript of remarks by Henrietta B. Seiberling: transcript prepared by Congressman John F. Seiberling of a telephone conversation with his mother, Henrietta in the spring of 1971): Employee Assistance Quarterly. 1985; (1); pp. 8-12.

Sikorsky, Igor I., Jr. *AA's Godparents*. Minnesota: CompCare Publishers, 1990.

Smith, Bob and Sue Smith Windows. *Children of the Healer*. Illinois: Parkside Publishing Corporation, 1992.

Spiritual Milestones in Alcoholics Anonymous. Akron: A.A. of Akron, n.d.

Stafford, Tim. *The Hidden Gospel of the 12 Steps*. Christianity Today, July 22, 1991.

The Four Absolutes. Cleveland: Cleveland Central Committee of A.A., n. d.

Thomsen, Robert. *Bill W*. New York: Harper & Row, 1975.

Walker, Richmond. *For Drunks Only*. Minnesota: Hazelden, n.d.

———. *The 7 Points of Alcoholics Anonymous*. Seattle: Glen Abbey Books, 1989.

Wilson, Bill. *How The Big Book Was Put Together*. New York: A.A. Archives, Transcript of Bill Wilson Speech delivered in Fort Worth, Texas, 1954.

———. *Bill Wilson's Original Story*. Bedford Hills, New York: Stepping Stones Archives, n.d., a manuscript whose individual lines are numbered 1 to 1180.

———. *W. G. Wilson Recollections*. Bedford Hills, New York: Stepping Stones Archives, September 1, 1954 transcript of Bill's dictations to Ed B.

Wilson, Lois. *Lois Remembers*. New York: Al-Anon Family Group Headquarters, 1987.

Windows, Sue Smith. (daughter of AA's Co-Founder, Dr. Bob). Typewritten Memorandum entitled, *Henrietta and early Oxford Group Friends, by Sue Smith Windows*. Delivered to the author of this book by Sue Smith Windows at Akron, June, 1991.

Wing, Nell. *Grateful To Have Been There: My 42 Years with Bill and Lois, and the Evolution of Alcoholics Anonymous*. Illinois: Parkside Publishing Corporation, 1992.

Publications Approved by Alcoholics Anonymous

Alcoholics Anonymous. 3rd Edition. New York: Alcoholics Anonymous World Services, Inc., 1976.

Alcoholics Anonymous. 1st Edition. New Jersey: Works Publishing, 1939.

Alcoholics Anonymous Comes of Age. New York: Alcoholics Anonymous World Services, Inc., 1979,

As Bill Sees It: The A.A. Way of Life . . . selected writings of A.A.'s Co-Founder. New York: Alcoholics Anonymous World Services, Inc., 1967.

Best of the Grapevine. New York: The A.A. Grapevine, Inc., 1985.

Best of the Grapevine, Volume II. New York: The A.A. Grapevine, Inc., 1986.

Came To Believe. New York: Alcoholics Anonymous World Services, Inc., 1973.

Daily Reflections. New York: Alcoholics Anonymous World Services, Inc., 1991.

DR. BOB and the Good Oldtimers. New York: Alcoholics Anonymous World Services, Inc., 1980.

Pass It On. New York: Alcoholics Anonymous World Services, Inc., 1984.

The A.A. Grapevine: "RHS"—issue dedicated to the memory of the Co-Founder of Alcoholics Anonymous, DR. BOB. New York: A.A. Grapevine, Inc., 1951.

The A.A. Service Manual. New York: Alcoholics Anonymous World Services, Inc., 1990-1991.

The Co-Founders of Alcoholics Anonymous. New York: Alcoholics Anonymous World Services, Inc., 1972.

The Language of the Heart. Bill W.'s Grapevine Writings. New York: The A.A. Grapevine, Inc., 1988.

Twelve Steps And Twelve Traditions. New York: Alcoholics Anonymous World Services, Inc., 1953.

The Bible—Versions of and Books About

Authorized King James Version. New York: Thomas Nelson, 1984.

Bullinger, Ethelbert W. *A Critical Lexicon and Concordance to the English and Greek New Testament.* Michigan: Zondervan, 1981.

Burns, Kenneth Charles. *The Rhetoric of Christology.* San Francisco: San Francisco State University, May, 1991. An unpublished thesis for Master of Arts.

Harnack, Adolph. *The Expansion of Christianity in the First Three Centuries.* New York: G. P. Putnam's Sons, Volume I, 1904; Volume II, 1905.

Jukes, Andrew. *The Names of GOD in Holy Scripture.* Michigan: Kregel Publications, 1967.

Moffatt, James. *A New Translation of the Bible.* New York: Harper & Brothers, 1954.

New Bible Dictionary. 2nd Edition. Wheaton, Illinois: Tyndale House Publishers, 1987.

Revised Standard Version. New York: Thomas Nelson, 1952.

Serenity: A Companion For Twelve Step Recovery. Nashville: Thomas Nelson, 1990.

Strong, James. *The Exhaustive Concordance of The Bible.* Iowa: Riverside Book and Bible House, n.d.

The Abingdon Bible Commentary. New York: Abingdon Press, 1929.

The Companion Bible. Michigan: Zondervan Bible Publishers, 1964.

The Revised English Bible. Oxford: Oxford University Press, 1989.

Vine, W. E. *Vine's Expository Dictionary of Old and New Testament Words.* New York: Fleming H. Revell, 1981.

Young's Analytical Concordance To The Bible. New York: Thomas Nelson, 1982.

Zodhiates, Spiros. *The Hebrew-Greek Key Study Bible.* 6th ed. AMG Publishers, 1991.

Spiritual Literature-Non-Oxford Group

A Kempis, Thomas. *The Imitation of Christ.* Georgia: Mercer University Press, 1989.

Allen, James. *As A Man Thinketh.* New York: Peter Pauper Press, n.d.

———. *Heavenly Life.* New York: Grosset & Dunlap, n.d.

Barton, George A. *Jesus of Nazareth.* New York: The Macmillan Company, 1922.

Brother Lawrence. *The Practice of the Presence of God.* Pennsylvania: Whitaker House, 1982.

Carruthers, Donald W. *How to Find Reality in Your Morning Devotions*. Pennsylvania: State College, n.d.

Chambers, Oswald. *Studies in the Sermon on the Mount*. London: Simpkin, Marshall, Ltd., n.d.

Clark, Glenn. *Clear Horizons*. Vol 2. Minnesota: Macalester Park Publishing, 1941.

———. *Fishers of Men*. Boston: Little, Brown, 1928.

———. *God's Reach*. Minnesota: Macalester Park Publishing, 1951.

———. *How To Find Health Through Prayer*. New York: Harper & Brothers, 1940.

———. *I Will Lift Up Mine Eyes*. New York: Harper & Brothers, 1937.

———. *The Lord's Prayer and Other Talks on Prayer from The Camps Farthest Out*. Minnesota: Macalester Publishing Co., 1932.

———. *The Man Who Talks with Flowers*. Minnesota: Macalester Park Publishing, 1939.

———. *The Soul's Sincere Desire*. Boston: Little, Brown, 1925.

———. *Touchdowns for the Lord. The Story of "Dad" A. J. Elliott*. Minnesota: Macalester Park Publishing Co., 1947.

———. *Two or Three Gathered Together*. New York: Harper & Brothers, 1942.

Daily, Starr. *Recovery*. Minnesota: Macalester Park Publishing, 1948.

Eddy, Mary Baker. *Science and Health with Key to the Scriptures*. Boston: Published by the Trustees under the Will of Mary Baker G. Eddy, 1916.

Filmore, Charles. *Christian Healing*. Kansas City: Unity School of Christianity, 1936.

———, and Cora Filmore. *Teach Us To Pray*. Lee's Summit, Missouri: Unity School of Christianity, 1950.

Fosdick, Harry Emerson. *A Great Time To Be Alive*. New York: Harper & Brothers, 1944.

———. *As I See Religion*. New York: Grosset & Dunlap, 1932.

———. *On Being A Real Person*. New York: Harper & Brothers, 1943.

———. *The Man From Nazareth*. New York: Harper & Brothers, 1949.

———. *The Manhood of the Master*. London: Student Christian Association, 1924.

———. *The Meaning of Prayer*. New York: Association Press, 1915.

———. *The Meaning of Service*. London: Student Christian Movement, 1921.

Fox, Emmet. *Alter Your Life*. New York: Harper & Brothers, 1950.

———. *Find And Use Your Inner Power*. New York: Harper & Brothers, 1937.

———. *Power Through Constructive Thinking*. New York: Harper & Brothers, 1932.

———. *Sparks of Truth*. New York: Grosset & Dunlap, 1941.

———. *The Sermon on the Mount*. New York: Harper & Row, 1934.

———. Pamphlets: *Getting Results By Prayer* (1933); *The Great Adventure* (1937); *You Must Be Born Again* (1936).

Glover, T. R. *The Jesus of History*. New York: Association Press, 1930.

Gordon, S. D. *The Quiet Time*. London: Fleming, n.d.

Heard, Gerald. *A Preface to Prayer*. New York: Harper & Brothers, 1944.

Hickson, James Moore. *Heal The Sick*. London: Methuen & Co., 1925.

James, William. *The Varieties of Religious Experience*. New York: First Vintage Press/The Library of America Edition, 1990.

Jones, E. Stanley. *Abundant Living*. New York: Cokesbury Press, 1942.

———. *Along The Indian Road*. New York: Abingdon Press, 1939.

———. *Christ and Human Suffering*. New York: Abingdon Press, 1930.

————. *Christ at the Round Table.* New York: Abingdon Press, 1928.

————. *The Choice Before Us.* New York: Abingdon Press, 1937.

————. *The Christ of Every Road.* New York: Abingdon Press, 1930.

————. *The Christ of the American Road.* New York: Abingdon-Cokesbury Press, 1944.

————. *The Christ of the Indian Road.* New York: Abingdon Press, 1925.

————. *The Christ of the Mount.* New York: Abingdon Press, 1930.

————. *Victorious Living.* New York: Abingdon Press, 1936.

————. *Way To Power & Poise.* New York: Abingdon Press, 1949.

Jung, Dr. Carl G. *Modern Man in Search of a Soul.* New York: Harcourt Brace Jovanovich, 1933.

Kagawa, Toyohiko. *Love: The Law of Life.* Philadelphia: The John C. Winston Company, 1929.

Laubach, Frank. *Prayer (Mightiest Force in the World).* New York: Fleming H. Revell, 1946.

Layman, Charles M. *A Primer of Prayer.* Nashville: Tidings, 1949.

Lieb, Frederick G. *Sight Unseen.* New York: Harper & Brothers, 1939.

Ligon, Ernest M. *Psychology of a Christian Personality.* New York: Macmillan, 1935.

Link, Dr. Henry C. *The Rediscovery of Man.* New York: Macmillan, 1939.

Lupton, Dilworth. *Religion Says You Can.* Boston: The Beacon Press, 1938.

Moseley, J. Rufus. *Perfect Everything.* Minnesota: Macalester Publishing Co., 1949.

Oursler, Fulton. *Happy Grotto.* Declan and McMullen, 1948.

————. *The Greatest Story Ever Told.* New York: Doubleday, 1949.

Parker, William R. and St. Johns, Elaine. *Prayer Can Change Your Life.* New ed. New York: Prentice Hall, 1957.

Peale, Norman Vincent. *The Art of Living.* New York: Abingdon Press, 1937.

Rawson, F. L. *The Nature of True Prayer.* Chicago: The Marlowe Company, n.d.

Sheean, Vincent. *Lead Kindly Light.* New York: Random House, 1949.

Sheen, Fulton J. *Peace of Soul.* New York: McGraw Hill, 1949.

Sheldon, Charles M. *In His Steps.* Nashville, Broadman Press, 1935.

Silkey, Charles Whitney. *Jesus and Our Generation.* Chicago: University of Chicago Press, 1925.

Speer, Robert E.. *Studies of the Man Christ Jesus.* New York: Fleming H. Revell, 1896.

Stalker, Rev. James. *The Life of Jesus Christ.* New York: Fleming H. Revell, 1891.

The Confessions of St. Augustine. Translated by E. B. Pusey. A Cardinal Edition. New York: Pocket Books, 1952.

The Fathers of the Church. New York: CIMA Publishing, 1947.

Trine, Ralph Waldo. *In Tune with the Infinite.* New York: Thomas H. Crowell, 1897.

————. *The Man Who Knew.* New York: Bobbs Merrill, 1936.

Uspenskii, Peter D. *Tertium Organum.* New York: A.A. Knopf, 1922.

Weatherhead, Leslie D. *Discipleship.* New York: Abingdon Press, 1934.

————. *How Can I Find God?* New York: Fleming H. Revell, 1934.

————. *Psychology and Life.* New York: Abingdon Press, 1935.

Werber, Eva Bell. *Quiet Talks with the Master.* L.A.: De Vorss & Co., 1942.

Williams, R. Llewelen, *God's Great Plan, a Guide To the Bible.* Hoverhill Destiny Publishers, n.d.

Willitts, Ethel R. *Healing in Jesus Name.* Chicago: Ethel R. Willitts Evangelists, 1931.

Bible Devotionals

Chambers, Oswald. *My Utmost For His Highest*. London: Simpkin Marshall, Ltd., 1927.

Clark, Glenn, *I Will Lift Up Mine Eyes*. New York: Harper & Brothers, 1937.

Dunnington, Lewis L. *Handles of Power*. New York: Abingdon-Cokesbury Press, 1942.

Fosdick, Harry Emerson. *The Meaning of Prayer*. New York: Association Press, 1915.

Holm, Nora Smith. *The Runner's Bible*. New York: Houghton Mifflin Company, 1915.

Jones, E. Stanley. *Abundant Living*. New York: Abingdon-Cokesbury Press, 1942.

———. *Victorious Living*. New York: Abingdon Press, 1936.

Parham, A. Philip. *Letting God: Christian Meditations For Recovering Persons*. New York: Harper & Row, 1987.

The Upper Room: Daily Devotions for Family and Individual Use. Quarterly. 1st issue: April, May, June, 1935. Edited by Grover Carlton Emmons. Nashville: General Committee on Evangelism through the Department of Home Missions, Evangelism, Hospitals, Board of Missions, Methodist Episcopal Church, South.

The Two Listeners. *God Calling*. Edited by A. J. Russell. Australia: DAYSTAR, 1953.

Tileston, Mary W. *Daily Strength For Daily Needs*. Boston: Roberts Brothers, 1893.

Index

A

B

G

H

K

L

M

N

O

P

T

Inquiries, orders, and requests for
catalogs and discount schedules
should be addressed to:

Glen Abbey Books, Inc.
P.O. Box 31329
Seattle, Washington 98103

Toll-free 24-hour
Order and Information Line
1-800-782-2239
(All U.S.)